AN INTRODUCTION
TO INTERNATIONAL HEALTH

AN INTRODUCTION TO INTERNATIONAL HEALTH

Michael Seear

Canadian Scholars' Press Inc.
Toronto

An Introduction to International Health
Michael Seear

First published in 2007 by
Canadian Scholars' Press Inc.
180 Bloor Street West, Suite 801
Toronto, Ontario
M5S 2V6

www.cspi.org

Canadian Scholars' Press Inc. gratefully acknowledges financial support for our publishing activities from the Government of Canada through the Book Publishing Industry Development Program (BPIDP).

Library and Archives Canada Cataloguing in Publication

Seear, Michael, 1950-
    An introduction to international health / Michael Seear.

Includes bibliographical references and index.
ISBN 978-1-55130-327-7

    1. World health — Textbooks. 2. Public health — Developing countries — Textbooks. 3. Poverty — Developing countries — Textbooks. I. Title.

RA441.S43 2007   362.1   C2007-900597-7

Cover photo by Alain Robyns © European Commission Humanitarian Aid Office (ECHO), 2006. Reprinted by permission of ECHO.
Cover design: John Kicksee / KIX BY DESIGN
Interior design and layout: Brad Horning

11 12 13   5 4 3

Printed and bound in Canada by Marquis Book Printing Inc.

Canadä

This book is dedicated, with love and thanks,
to my wife Diana

In memoriam: Professor Don Hillman of Ottawa University,
whose lifetime of work and teaching in the field of international health
was an inspiration for everyone lucky enough to have known him.
For those who knew him, no words are necessary;
for those who didn't, no words are enough.

Table of Contents

A Note from the Publisher.. ix
List of Acronyms xi

PART I: WHAT IS INTERNATIONAL HEALTH?

Chapter 1: An Overview of International Health...3
Chapter 2: A History of Overseas Aid Initiatives 17

PART II: WHY IS POPULATION HEALTH SO POOR IN
DEVELOPING COUNTRIES?

Chapter 3: The Determinants of Population Health 35
Chapter 4: Poverty and Developing World Debt...51
Chapter 5: Malnutrition 73

PART III: WHAT IS THE EXTENT OF THE PROBLEM?

Chapter 6: Defining and Measuring Health...99
Chapter 7: Child and Adult Health Statistics for the Developing World....119

PART IV: WHAT CAN BE DONE ABOUT IT?

Chapter 8: Foreign Aid Projects, Large and Small 143
Chapter 9: Primary Health Care Strategies 165
Chapter 10: Basic Medical Care 189
Chapter 11: Poverty Alleviation and Debt Relief..213
Chapter 12: Human Rights Interventions 237

PART V: OTHER ASPECTS OF INTERNATIONAL HEALTH

Chapter 13: Natural and Humanitarian Disasters and Displaced Populations..........259
Chapter 14: Health of Indigenous Populations 283

PART VI: WORKING SAFELY AND EFFECTIVELY IN A
DEVELOPING COUNTRY

Chapter 15: Planning and Preparing for Safe, Effective Development Work.............307
Chapter 16: Managing a Sustainable Aid Partnership 329

Copyright Acknowledgments...347
Index 349

A Note from the Publisher

Thank you for selecting *An Introduction to International Health* by Michael Seear. The author and publisher have devoted considerable time and careful development (including meticulous peer reviews at proposal phase and first draft) to this book. We appreciate your recognition of this effort and accomplishment.

Teaching Features

The author has enhanced the book by adding pedagogy. Each chapter contains an opening quotation, a set of learning objectives, a thorough introduction, a concise summary, a detailed reference list, and recommended readings. The art program features engaging photographs and figures throughout.

List of Acronyms

ACT	Artemesin Combination Therapy
AIDS	Acquired Immune Deficiency Syndrome
APS	Aboriginal Peoples' Survey
BCG	Bacille Calmette-Guérin
BFHI	Baby-Friendly Hospital Initiative
BMI	Body Mass Index
BONGO	Business-Oriented International Non-Governmental Organization
BRAC	Bangladesh Rural Advancement Committee
CAP	Common Agricultural Policy
CDC	Centers for Disease Control
CEDR	Center for Effective Dispute Resolution
CERF	Central Emergency Response Fund
CIA	Central Intelligence Agency
CIDA	Canadian International Development Agency
CMR	Crude Mortality Rate
ComDT	Community-Directed Therapy
CRED	Center for Research on Epidemiology of Disasters
DAC	Development Assistance Committee
DALE	Disability-Adjusted Life Expectancy
DALY	Disability-Adjusted Life Years
DDA	Doha Development Agenda
DDT	Dichlorodiphenyltrichloroethane
DFID	Department for International Development
DFLE	Disability-Free Life Expectancy
DMP	Disaster Mitigation and Preparedness
DOT	Directly Observed Therapy
DOTS	Directly Observed Therapy using standardized Short course regimes
ECHO	European Commission's Humanitarian Aid Office
EHIPC	Enhanced Heavily Indebted Poor Countries
ENGO	Environmental Non-Governmental Organization
EPI	Expanded Program on Immunization
ERC	Emergency Relief Coordinator
FAC	Food Aid Convention
FACT	Field Assessment and Coordination Team
FAO	Food and Agriculture Organization
FAS	Fetal Alcohol Syndrome
FDI	Foreign Direct Investment

FEWS   USAID's Famine Early Warning System
FGM   Female Genital Mutilation
GAS   Group A streptococcus
GATT   General Agreement on Tariffs and Trade
GAVI   Global Alliance for Vaccines and Immunization
GDF   Global Drug Facility
GDP   Gross Domestic Product
G8   Group of Eight
GFAC   Global Food Aid Compact
GFATM   Global Fund to Fight Aids, TB, and Malaria
GIVS   Global Immunization Vision and Strategy
GNI   Gross National Income
GNP   Gross National Product
GOBI   Growth monitoring, Oral rehydration, Breast-feeding, Immunization
GOBI-FFF   Growth monitoring, Oral rehydration, Breast-feeding, Immunization–
                Female education, Family spacing, Food supplements for pregnant
                women
HAART   Highly Active Anti-Retroviral Therapy
HDI   Human Development Index
HELI   Health and Environmental Linkages Initiative
HIPC   Heavily Indebted Poor Countries
HIV   Human Immunodeficiency Virus
HPI   Human Poverty Index
HSA   Head Start Approach
IAG   Inter-Agency Group
IBFAN   International Baby Food Action Network
ICC   Inuit Circumpolar Conference
ICPD   International Conference on Population and Development
IDD   Iodine Deficiency Disorder
IDP   Internally Displaced Persons
IFF   International Financing Facility
IIT   Indian Institutes of Technology
ILO   International Labour Organization
IMCI   Integrated Management of Childhood Illnesses
IMF   International Monetary Fund
IMR   Infant Mortality Rate
iPAss   International Personnel Assessment
IPT   Intermittent Preventive Treatment
IRIN   Integrated Regional Information Network
ITK   Inuit Tapiriit Kanatami
MCA   Millennium Challenge Account
MCH   Maternal and Child Health
MDGs   Millennium Development Goals
MDRI   Multilateral Debt Relief Initiative

MGRS	Multi-centred Growth Reference Study
MMR	Maternal Mortality Ratio
MSF	Médecins Sans Frontières
NAMA	Non-Agricultural Market Access
NCHS	National Center for Health Statistics
NEPAD	New Partnership for Africa's Development
NGOs	Non-Governmental Organizations
OCHA	Office for the Coordination of Humanitarian Affairs
OCP	Onchocerciasis Control Program
ODA	Official Development Assistance
OECD	Organisation for Economic Co-operation and Development
OEEC	Organisation for European Economic Co-operation
OIHP	Office International d'Hygiene Publique
OPEC	Organization of the Petroleum Exporting Countries
ORS	Oral Rehydration Solution
PAHO	Pan American Health Organization
PEPFAR	President's Emergency Plan for AIDS Relief
PHC	Primary Health Care
PPP	Purchasing Power Parity
PRSPs	Poverty Reduction Strategy Papers
RAMOS	Reproductive Age Mortality Studies
RBM	Results-Based Monitoring
RCAP	Royal Commission on Aboriginal Peoples
REVES	Réseau Espérance de Vie en Santé
RINGO	Religious International Non-Governmental Organization
SAFE	Surgery, Antibiotic treatment, Facial cleanliness/handwashing, and Environmental changes
SAPs	Structural Adjustment Policies
SARS	Severe Acute Respiratory Syndrome
SMA	Simulated Milk Adapted
SMR	Standardized Mortality Ratio
SPHC	Selective Primary Health Care
STD	Sexually Transmitted Disease
TNC	Transnational Corporations
TRIPS	Trade-Related Intellectual Poverty Rights
U5MR	Under-Five Mortality Rate
UN	United Nations
UNCTAD	United Nations Conference on Trade and Development
UNDAC	United Nations Disaster Assessment and Coordination Team
UNDP	United Nations Development Programme
UNEP	United Nations Environment Programme
UNESCO	United Nations Educational, Scientific, and Cultural Organization
UNFPA	United Nations Population Fund
UNHCR	United Nations High Commissioner for Refugees

UNICEF	United Nations Children's Fund
UNISDR	UN International Strategy for Disaster Reduction
UNPFII	United Nations Permanent Forum on Indigenous Issues
US	United States
USAID	United States Agency for International Development
WGIP	Working Group on Indigenous Populations
WHO	World Health Organization
WTO	World Trade Organization

PART I

WHAT IS INTERNATIONAL HEALTH?

Chapter 1
**An Overview of
International Health**

Chapter 2
**A History of
Overseas Aid Initiatives**

An Overview of International Health

> There must be an ideal world,
> a sort of mathematician's paradise where
> everything happens as it does in textbooks.
> — Bertrand Russell

OBJECTIVES

After completing this chapter, you should be able to

- understand the scope of the subjects covered by the term "international health"
- understand the design and content of this book and how to get the most out of the material
- start to apply human faces and experiences to the abstract terms of poverty, malnutrition, and injustice

---

When the world's seven richest countries first decided to hold annual meetings, about 30 years ago, it is unlikely that the average person paid much attention. This is in marked contrast to the period leading up to the 2005 Group of Eight (G8) Conference at Gleneagles when it seemed as if the whole world was waiting for the latest word on debt relief. The health of developing populations (particularly the developing world debt) became a bandwagon that staggered under the weight of politicians, pop stars, and various other celebrities as they clambered aboard. When Tony Blair announced general agreement on the Multilateral Debt Relief Initiative, there was a very real sense of worldwide excitement. While the agreement may not quite live up to its billing, it cannot be denied that there is now widespread interest in the broad topic of international health.

This increased awareness of international issues has probably been fashioned by events that were large enough to reach news reports. A lot has happened over the last 20 or 30 years, but some of the issues that caught public attention included a steady increase in political freedom (South Africa, Eastern Europe), several widely reported famines (Ethiopia, Sudan), destructive civil wars (Rwanda, Bosnia), and natural disasters (Asian tsunami, Pakistani earthquake). The current level of interest was exemplified by the spontaneous public response to the Asian tsunami. So much money was given by private citizens that the Red Cross actually asked people to stop sending any more since they had enough!

Strangely enough, the increased demand for courses, books, and general information on the subject of international health falls well below the available supply. Although millions of people are directly and indirectly employed in the aid industry, there is no clearly defined preparatory educational path for entry into the field. In addition, international health is a broad subject that includes a very wide range of specialties. It is quite easy to be tucked away in a sub-specialist corner without having a good overview of the subject. Whether you are a pure researcher tied to a laboratory bench, a nursing student planning a career in development work, or a fieldworker in a large aid agency, this book aims to provide a detailed introduction to international health and its inevitable companion, the modern aid industry. I would like to wish a very warm welcome to anyone opening this book for the first time.

▮ THE SCOPE OF INTERNATIONAL HEALTH

Reading maketh a full man, conference a ready man, and writing an exact man.
—Sir Francis Bacon, 1561–1626

Introduction to International Health

The first question many people ask is, "What is international health?" Others will also want to know how it differs from global health and where tropical medicine, epidemiology, and public health all fit in. An all-inclusive definition of international health would be rather long, so it is perhaps more useful to define the subject using its broad basic aims. Taking that approach, international health can be defined as a subject that tries to find practical answers to the following questions:

1. Why is population health so poor in many developing countries?
2. What is the extent of the problem?
3. What can be done about it?

Before World War II, international health was largely the preserve of doctors and missionaries. As the industry has grown, ever increasing numbers of new specialists have been added to the list. Answering the first two questions above requires researchers, biostatisticians, and epidemiologists, but addressing the third one requires a small army. Health initiatives may include economic interventions (economists, business specialists, agronomists, small-scale bankers, etc.), medical initiatives (doctors, nurses, pharmacists, nutritionists, etc.), and human rights initiatives (politicians, rights activists, and constitutional lawyers). Increasingly, standards of project management are improving, which requires accountants, project managers, and the full range of support staff associated with any large company. Finally, a large part of many aid projects consists of trying to get people to change their behaviour; projects now also include psychologists, anthropologists, popular public figures, and even directors of soap operas.

A successful project certainly requires money and well-trained staff, but it must always be remembered that the most important people in the whole process are the target population. No matter how many talented specialists are included in the team, no initiative stands a chance unless local people are included (and listened to) at every stage of planning and implementation.

Contemporary Examples of International Health Problems

Figure 1.1: Global trends in life expectancy with time

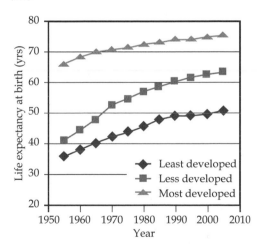

Source: United Nations Population Division (2004)

Forming an idea of the standards of population health in developing countries, based purely on available statistics, is difficult; the numbers are simply too large to comprehend. However, no matter how bad health indicators might be today, they are all a great deal better than they used to be. In the six decades since the end of World War II, life expectancy in many countries has increased by over 25 years

(Figure 1.1) and infant mortality rates have fallen sharply (Figure 1.2). The aid industry that grew steadily over the same period can probably claim some credit for these improvements (particularly due to immunizations and other public health interventions), but the final report on the achievements of foreign aid is a mixed one (Easterly, 2006) and will be discussed in detail later in the book.

Figure 1.2: Global trends in infant mortality with time

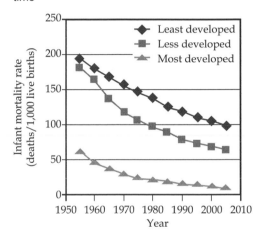

Source: United Nations Population Division (2004)

It must be remembered that global health statistics only represent averages based on studies in many very diverse countries. They are heavily weighted toward public health improvements in the largest countries. For example, when poverty and health statistics are broken down by region, East Asia (including China) and South Asia (including India), both show significant gains with time. However, other regions of the world, particularly Sub-Saharan Africa, have seen little or no improvement over many years (Figure 1.3).

Figure 1.3: Global trends of severe poverty with time

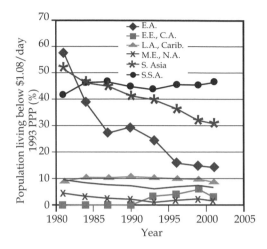

Source: Chen and Ravallion (2004)

E.A. (East Asia), E.E., C.A. (East Europe, Central Asia), L.A., Carib (Latin America, Caribbean), M.E., N.A. (Middle East, North Africa), S. Asia (South Asia), S.S.A (Sub-Saharan Africa)

The term "developing world" covers a broad spectrum of countries with widely varying health and social problems; there is certainly no simple list that applies to every developing country. Problems differ between countries and, as the HIV/AIDS epidemic has shown, new challenges also appear with time. The increasing prosperity of many countries over the last 20 years has produced a growing global middle class, bringing with it yet another set of health challenges. Diseases previously associated with a "Western" lifestyle, such as childhood obesity and smoking-related illness (particularly heart attacks and strokes), are increasing rapidly in many middle-income developing countries.

Of all the problems confronting developing countries, poverty and malnutrition stand out well above the crowd; both affect hundreds of millions of people around the world. In addition, wherever severe poverty and malnutrition are found, human rights abuses, inequity, and injustice will always be close behind. Some of the major problems confronting the developing world are as follows:

Poverty

A perfect example of an overwhelming statistic is the fact that over 2 billion people live below the World Bank poverty indicator of $2 per day (Chen & Ravallion, 2004). The two children shown in Figure 1.4, plus their parents and one other sibling, probably all exist each day on

Figure 1.4: These two children, plus another sibling and their parents, live with all their possessions on the pavement in New Delhi. (Courtesy of IDRC Photo Library; photographer Stephanie Colvey.)

less than the cost of a cup of coffee in Vancouver. As Figure 1.3 shows, there have been significant improvements in some parts of the world and the overall Millennium Development Goal for poverty (*UN Millennium Development Goals*, n.d.) will probably be met by 2015 but, again, these are averages and many parts of the world still do not share in this slowly increasing level of prosperity. Poverty traps populations within a vicious cycle of poor education, limited job opportunities, and chronic ill health. Wherever there is widespread poverty, there will inevitably be inequity and injustice as two of the principal contributory causes.

Malnutrition

The Food and Agriculture Organization estimates that over 800 million humans are malnourished, of which 200 million are children (Food and Agriculture Organization, 2005). Again, there have been slow improvements with time; large-scale famines are fortunately now much less common. Death from starvation has largely been replaced by the debilitating effects of chronic malnutrition, which saps the energy and the potential of huge numbers of the world's population. Through its effects on a child's immune response, malnutrition greatly increases the mortality from diseases such as gastroenteritis and measles.

Childhood Illnesses

The most recent statistical summary of childhood deaths, given in the 2005 World Health Report (World Health Organization, 2005), shows that 10.6 million children below the age of five years died from only a handful of conditions in 2003. This annual slaughter of children is made even worse by the fact that most of these children would have survived had they lived in a developed country. Over 2 million children died from respiratory infections, 1.7 million died from simple

Figure 1.5: Malnourished Karamoja children at a refugee camp in Northern Uganda. (Courtesy of IRINnews.org.)

Figure 1.6: Young child recovering from severe dehydration at a small hospital in the Democratic Republic of Congo. (Courtesy of ECHO Photo Library; photographer François Goemans.)

diarrhea, and 0.9 million died from malaria. Most of these cases are not only treatable but many are also completely avoidable with simple and affordable interventions. For example, roughly 400,000 children died from measles, a disease for which there is a 99 percent effective vaccine costing roughly $1 per child.

Pregnancy-Related Diseases

It is only within the last decade that serious attention has been paid to the health of women around the world; the poor quality of maternal health statistics reflects this history of neglect. The best available estimates suggest that well over 500,000 women die each year from pregnancy-related causes (World Health Organization, 2004); 99 percent of these occur in developing countries. Almost all of these deaths are completely avoidable with improved standards of care. For example, a quarter of the total simply bled to death. Although statistics are not accurately collected, it is widely believed that for every woman who dies, 10 to 20 times that number are left with disabling injuries such as bowel or bladder fistulas,

chronic infection, or permanent pain. This is one area of population health that has not improved with time. This statistic can only be improved by provision of better maternal health care.

Indigenous Health

From Canadian Inuit in the North to Australian Aboriginals in the South, there are roughly 300 million indigenous peoples around the world, forming at least 5,000 separate groups in over 70 countries (Alderete, 1999). Although their

Figure 1.8: Mayan children living in a Guatemalan camp for returned refugees. Their parents fled to Mexico in the 1980s to escape oppression by the Guatemalan army. The end of the war has brought greater safety for indigenous peoples, but they still suffer higher levels of poverty and ill health than the population averages. (Copyright Brian Atkinson; GlobalAware Image Database.)

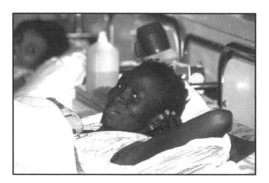

Figure 1.7: A young woman recovering from surgery for a urinary fistula following childbirth. She is in the Addis Ababa Fistula Hospital, which was started by Dr. Catherine Hamlin and Dr. Reginald Hamlin. (Courtesy of WHO Media Centre; photographer Pierre Virot.)

backgrounds are widely diverse, they frequently share a history of conquest and varying degrees of subsequent discrimination. As a result of this poor treatment, indigenous peoples share surprisingly common health problems that often include high rates of substance abuse, family violence, and suicide. Wherever records are available, indigenous health lags far behind the average levels of the majority population. For example, life expectancy is usually at least five to 10 years shorter. After a very long time, indigenous peoples are finally gaining an international voice, particularly in the area of self-determination.

War

From Bosnia to Guatemala and from Somalia to Sudan, modern war has changed. Fighting between countries has largely been replaced by internal wars marked by high levels of violence against civilian populations—usually further complicated by progressive economic and social collapse. This situation has given rise to the term "humanitarian disaster" (Burkle, 2006). Apart from the millions of people who have been killed over decades of war, there is also an incalculable cost for the survivors in terms of land mine injuries, the terrible legacy of child soldiers, confinement to a refugee camp, and the destruction of a country's entire social structure.

Natural Disasters

Natural catastrophes, such as earthquakes, hurricanes, and volcanoes, are not rare. The world has recently witnessed two of the most lethal disasters in history (Asian tsunami and Pakistani earthquake) and the most costly disaster in history (hurricane Katrina). As the world population grows, more and more people live in vulnerable areas of the world, so death rates from disasters climb steadily each decade (Guha-Sapir et al., 2004). Apart from the immediate loss of life, the cost for survivors is enormous in terms of property destruction and loss of livelihood. Although disasters cannot be

Figure 1.9: Some of the children who manage to escape, after being abducted by the Lord's Resistance Army in Northern Uganda, are cared for by the Gulu Support the Children Organization (GUSCO). These two children are being rehabilitated at the GUSCO camp in Gulu. (Courtesy of IRINnews.org, photographer Sven Torfinn.)

Figure 1.10: Earthquakes and volcanoes are not the only natural disasters; these children are running through a swarm of locusts attacking crops outside Dakar in Senegal. They are not as dramatic as an earthquake, but a large swarm can cause agricultural devastation. (Courtesy of IRINnews.org.)

prevented, their effects can be reduced by planning and preparation. The United Nations' recent International Strategy for Disaster Reduction is an attempt to improve the preparedness of developing world communities to face unexpected disasters.

Human Rights Abuses

Abuses of basic human rights are not confined to the developing world; if you search hard enough, they can be found, to some degree, in almost every country. However, the worst examples of abuse are found in developing countries, particularly those in the very poorest areas of the world. Examples include discrimination and oppression based on gender (female genital mutilation, exclusion of girls from school, etc.) or violence against particular ethnic and religious groups (Rwandan genocide, current humanitarian crisis in Darfur, and the collapse of former Yugoslavia). The full list is, unfortunately, a very long one. In the past, human rights have been looked on as a separate issue that stands on its own. However, this attitude has changed. It is now realized that peace and prosperity (and also successful aid projects) all depend on a fundamental foundation of benign governance that respects the rights of individuals (Annan, 2005). Beneficial changes in human rights are increasingly being included as a central feature of large-scale aid projects.

■ THE SCOPE OF THIS BOOK

Origins and Contents of the Book

This book grew out of the experience gained from teaching international health at the University of British Columbia, Canada. The original course was developed in response to numerous requests from students about working abroad. A major catalyst for that process was Dr. Kevin Chan's earlier guide to working overseas for University of Ottawa students. Professor John Gilbert kindly supported the course and gave it a home in his department.

Figure 1.11: A woman shelters from rain at the squalid al-Junaynah refugee camp in Western Darfur, Sudan. The camp inhabitants are fleeing brutal oppression by their own government. (Courtesy IRINnews. org, photographer Claire McEvoy.)

Well-informed undergraduates are a tough crowd to please. The research needed to answer their questions and survive numerous discussions of contentious issues has formed a firm foundation for the subsequent book. I'm very grateful to all of those students for that enforced discipline.

Several other people were also very helpful in the writing of this book. I'm particularly grateful to my employer, Children's and Women's Heath Center of British Columbia, for allowing me to take a sabbatical leave, during which most of the book was written. The following were also generous with their assistance: Dr. Kevin Chan (Chapter 15), Douglas Cubie (Chapters 12 and 13), and David Wilcox (Chapter 16). I am very grateful for their help.

As we have already seen, international health covers a wide range of subjects. It does not lend itself to a neat, linear narrative, so the chapters have been grouped into sections based on their relevance to the three main questions set at the beginning of this introduction: Why is population health so poor in developing countries? What is the extent of the problem? What can be done about it? The final section of the book is devoted to other aspects of international health such as refugees and disasters, Aboriginal health, and also how to plan overseas projects and work overseas effectively. Although the subject matter is often unavoidably medical in nature, it should be stressed that this is not a medical text and is written for a mixed audience; no previous medical training is necessary.

Enough information has been included within the text to allow a reader to gain a good grasp of the subject without the need for extra research. However, for those who are interested in further information on particular subjects, there are over 1,000 references and recommended books spread throughout the chapters. Tables and graphs are often used to illustrate points; references are added for the original data sources. Conventional notation is used for books (author, date, title, publisher) and scientific journals (authors, date, title, volume, pages):

- CDC. 2005. *Health information for international travel, 2005–2006.* Amsterdam: Elsevier Press.
- Jha, P., et al. 2006. "Low male-to-female sex ratio of children born in India: National survey of 1.1 million households." *Lancet, 367,* 211–218.

Other references will include Web sites for large organizations that are likely to remain unchanged:

- National Aboriginal Health Organization (NAHO) Web site at: www.naho.ca/english. Some reports, manuals, and booklets can be obtained by downloading them from the relevant Web sites.
- Lavizzari, L. 2001. *A guide for project management and evaluation: Managing for impact in rural development.* Can be downloaded from International Fund for Agricultural Development Web site at: www.ifad.org/evaluation/guide/.

Some other organizations (particularly the World Bank) have such long, multisyllable addresses that it is easier to give the Web site address and then find the title using their "search" function:

- Search First Nations and Inuit Health at Health Canada Web site at: www.hc-sc.gc.ca.

The modern aid industry has a reasonably long history; during that time, it has accumulated its own share of interesting characters. Under the heading "History Notes" (Box 1.1), each chapter includes a brief mention of someone who has made a major contribution to the field of international health. Finally, in the modern world, the rich are so rich and the poor are so poor that it is fairly simple to find incongruous examples of the differences in the lives lived by these two groups. In order to give some insight into the harsh reality of life in a developing country, examples are given in each chapter under the heading "A Moment of Zen" (Table 1.1). Although some of the

comparisons may seem surprising, they are all true; original information sources are provided.

Check Your Sources

> For my part, I consider that it will be found much better by all parties to leave the past to history, especially as I propose to write that history myself.
> —Winston Churchill, Speech to the House of Commons, 1948

Whether you prefer Churchill or the blunter style of Henry Ford (all history is more or less bunk), the message is the same—do not believe everything you read, particularly when it comes to complex social problems. Modern communications provide us with unprecedented access to endless sources of unedited information that must be used carefully. Unfortunately, when you ask the question, "Why are these people sick?" the answer is frequently some form of injustice. Trying to understand the roots of that injustice and simply getting to the truth of the story will present difficulties, particularly for those with a trusting nature. There is no substitute for detailed research followed by careful and thoughtful analysis. The point of this section is not to push a particular political agenda but simply to stress that easy access to unedited information carries with it the obligation to check those sources carefully.

The history of any conflict is usually written by the winners. It would be interesting to compare schoolbooks written during the apartheid regime in South Africa to those currently available. To an outsider it might even be difficult to imagine that they are describing the same events. A less extreme example might be found in the position of Native Indians in

---

Box 1.1: History notes

Amartya Sen (1933–)

Amartya Sen is an Indian economist whose work has had a profound effect on the broad subject of international health. His early work on the origins of famine highlighted what everyone knew but few had articulated. Superficially "simple" population health problems such as famine are far more complex than they initially seem. He showed that starvation is not due just to lack of food any more than poverty is due only to lack of money. At the root of most complex problems lies inequity. His later work, *Development as Freedom*, is also widely quoted. Based on a wide range of his early research, he further develops his arguments in favour of political and economic freedom.

Sen was born on a university campus established by the Indian philosopher and previous Nobel Prize winner, Rabindranath Tagore. He studied economics in India and England. After serving as master of Trinity College, Cambridge, he recently moved to Harvard University. He was awarded the Nobel Prize for Economics in 1998. Please follow the reference for more details (Nobel Foundation, 1998).

Table 1.1: A moment of Zen

Most common causes of either avoidable or treatable deaths in under-five year-olds during 2003:		1.8 million cosmetic surgical procedures performed in the United States, 2005. Top five operations:	
		Liposuction	324,000
		Nose reshaping	298,000
		Breast augmentation	291,000
		Eyelid surgery	231,000
		Tummy tuck	135,000
		8.5 million minimally invasive cosmetic procedures performed in the US, 2005. Top five operations:	
Neonatal causes	3.91 million		
Acute respiratory infection	2.03 million		
Diarrheal diseases	1.76 million	Botox injections	3.8 million
Malaria	853,000	Chemical peel	1.0 million
Measles	395,000	Microdermabrasion	838,000
HIV/AIDS	321,000	Laser hair removal	783,000
		Sclerotherapy	590,000
Total number of infectious and neonatal deaths of small children in 2003:		Total number of cosmetic procedures performed in the United States in 2005 (total estimated cost US $9,433,000,000):	
10.3 million		**10.3 million**	
Source: World Health Organization (2005)		Source: American Society of Plastic Surgeons (2005)	

the school texts of North American history; contemporary events are no different. Research into the events following the disintegration of Yugoslavia would also be strongly dependent on the source. Without getting involved with the issues, it is fair to say that Croatian Muslims, Albanian Macedonians, or Serbs from Kosovo would all have widely different interpretations of recent history. Equally, the prospect of writing a summary of recent events in the Middle East that was acceptable to all involved parties is difficult to imagine.

Examples of inequity and injustice are not difficult to find; any student of international health will constantly meet controversial topics. For example, anyone studying the health of poor labouring classes in India will soon discover the economic and social results of an ancient caste system that relegates Dalits or "untouchables" to a life of drudgery and abuse. This is a complex and inflammatory subject. The Indian government will point out that Dalits have a vote and their position in society is slowly improving. The Dalit class is less impressed by this opinion. Initiatives based on superficial research (particularly when combined with political or religious biases) are quite likely to make matters worse. Whether you are studying the suicide rate among Inuit teens or worsening health indicators of infants in Iraq, Sudan, North Korea, or southern Lebanon, the causes are complex (as are the solutions) and require serious study before leaping to conclusions.

■ SUMMARY

International health is, very broadly, the study of the health of populations living in low-income countries. Although poor levels of health are common in many developing countries, it is important not to concentrate solely on diseases and to remember that they are just the most visible result of underlying social disruption. The need to study both the diseases and their causes means that international health covers a very wide range of subjects. These vary from tropical medicine and primary health care at one end of the spectrum to epidemiology and economics at the other end, with a great many stops in between. The solutions to these problems are, of course, no less complex than their underlying causes.

Despite widespread improvements in health and prosperity over the last few decades, malnutrition, poverty, and all the ills that stem from them are still very common around the world. In fact, to the newcomer, the statistics can be quite overwhelming. At a time when citizens of industrialized countries are healthier than any time in history, hundreds of millions of people in the least developed countries still live lives of terrible deprivation. There is, of course, a natural human desire to assist people living under those conditions. Since the end of World War II, a complex mix of private, governmental, and international organizations has developed, with the overall aim of improving the health of populations in developing countries. Although this aid industry has certainly had its growing problems, there is a real sense that current developments such as the Debt Relief Initiative, the Millennium Development Goals, and several successful disease eradication efforts are all making a positive difference in the lives of people in the poorest countries of the world.

The modern aid industry is a multibillion-dollar organization that, directly and indirectly, employs many hundreds of thousands of people around the world. Although there are degree and post-graduate courses in international health in various large centres, there is a surprisingly limited amount of educational material considering the enormous demand for information on the subject. This book is designed to meet at least some of that demand by providing a broad overview of international health in as much detail as possible. Although the subject is unavoidably medical in nature, the book reflects the fact that a wide range of specialties is involved in the broad field of international health. It is not a medical textbook and is intended for readers with a wide range of past interests. I wish a very warm welcome to anyone who is approaching this subject for the first time and sincerely hope that this book will help you find your way through the complex but also fascinating subject of international health.

RESOURCES

References

Alderete, E. (1999). *The health of indigenous peoples*. Geneva: World Health Organization. Retrieved from www.who.int/hhr/activities/indigenous/en.

American Society of Plastic Surgeons. (n.d.). *Procedural statistics trends 1992–2005*. Retrieved from www.plasticsurgery.org/public_education/Statistical-Trends.cfm.

Annan, K. (2005). *In large freedom: Towards development, security, and human rights for all*. Retrieved from www.un.org/largerfreedom/contents.htm.

Burkle, F.M. (2006). "Complex humanitarian emergencies: A review of epidemiological and response models." *Journal of Postgraduate Medicine, 52*, 110–115.

Chen, S., & Ravallion, M. (2004). *How have the world's poorest fared since the early 1980s?* (World Bank Policy Research Group, working paper no. 3341). Retrieved from www.eldis.org/static/DOC15015.htm.

Easterly, W. (2006). *The white man's burden: Why the west's efforts to aid the rest have done so much ill and so little good*. New York: Penguin Press.

Food and Agriculture Organization. (2005). *The state of food insecurity in the world*. Retrieved from www.fao.org/sof/sofi/index_en.htm.

Guha-Sapir, D., et al. (2004). *Thirty years of natural disasters, 1974–2003: The numbers*. Louvain-la-Neuve: Presses Universitaires de Louvain. Retrieved from www.em-dat.net/documents/Publication/publication_2004_emdat.pdf.

Nobel Foundation. (1998). *Amartya Sen*. Retrieved from nobelprize.virtual.museum/nobel_prizes/economics/laureates/1998/sen-autobio.html.

UN Millennium Development Goals. (n.d.). Retrieved from www.un.org/millenniumgoals.

United Nations Population Division. (2004). *World population prospects: The 2004 revision population database*. Retrieved from esa.un.org/unpp/index.asp.

World Health Organization. (2004). *Maternal mortality in 2000: Estimates developed by WHO, UNICEF, UNFPA*. Geneva: Author. Retrieved from childinfo.org/areas/maternalmortality/maternal_mortality_in_2000.pdf.

World Health Organization. (2005). *World health report 2005: Statistical annex*. Retrieved from www.who.int/whr/2005.

Recommended Reading

Basch, P. (1999). *Textbook of international health* (2nd edition). Oxford: Oxford University Press.

Easterly, W. (2006). *The white man's burden: Why the west's efforts to aid the rest have done so much ill and so little good*. New York: Penguin Press.

Escobar, A. (1995). *Encountering development: The making and unmaking of the Third World*. Princeton: Princeton University Press.

Koop, C., Pearson, C., & Schwartz, M. (Eds.). (2001). *Critical issues in global health*. San Francisco: Jossey-Bass.

Mosse, D. (2005). *Cultivating development: An ethnography of aid policy and practice*. London: Pluto Press.

Rahnema, M., & Bawtree, V. (Eds.). (2005). *The post-development reader* (5th reprint). London: Zed Books.

Sachs, W. (Ed.). (2005). *The development dictionary* (11th reprint). London: Zed Books.

A History of
Overseas Aid Initiatives

> Peoples and governments have never
> learned anything from history,
> or acted on the principles deduced from it.
> —Hegel

OBJECTIVES
After completing this chapter, you should be able to

- understand the broad trends that have shaped the modern aid industry since its start after World War II
- understand the origins of the principal foreign aid institutions and organizations
- understand the long history of trial and error that lies behind the current large-scale foreign aid initiatives

---

At first glance, a history of the aid industry might seem to be a fairly dry subject. The newcomer could be forgiven for thinking that it has just been a long story of well-meaning governments giving money for worthwhile causes. Sadly, that is not even close to reality. If you want to understand the aid industry, you need to study it, "warts and all." Hegel's comments, above, certainly apply to the developing stages of the aid industry. From its start in the early post-war years, it rolled along, slowly gathering layer upon layer of government and private agencies. Uncoordinated, unanswerable to its constituents, and governed only by passing political and economic fads, it took a long time before the industry started learning from its mistakes.

The modern aid industry did not happen by accident. Its management framework and the philosophical and theoretical reasons behind current development initiatives have all changed significantly with time. The final structure has been fashioned by experiences gained from many years of trial and error, mistakes, and painfully learned lessons (painful to the poor, that is). The contemporary major debate over aid effectiveness is a broad response to that accumulated experience. In order to understand the modern aid industry and its ambitious plans for the next few decades, it is important to understand the details of the industry's history.

EARLY INTERNATIONAL HEALTH INITIATIVES

Without charity, I am nothing.
—Confucius, ca. 500 BC

If poverty could be cured by words, it would have been solved long ago. Since writing began, numberless pious platitudes have been written about charity and the poor. Confucius's comment above, taken from the *Analects*, certainly was not the first and there has been a lot more in the secular and religious literature since then. Laws protecting the poor were written by the cuneiform pen of Mesopotamia and the scratched quill of Elizabethan England three millennia later (Bloy, 2002; King, 1996;). Despite this, a great deal of history passed before humans reached the point where a group of prosperous countries could consider giving aid to less fortunate ones.

Some of the laws and practices introduced during the more benign periods of the Roman Empire could be considered as the earliest attempts at public health initiatives. The introduction of clean water (Rome's Trevi fountain is still fed by one of those early aqueducts), public baths, and toilets meant that ancient Rome could support a million people with

health standards no worse than Victorian London 19 centuries later.

The first recognizable aid project was conducted by the Spanish roughly 200 years ago. In response to the devastation caused by smallpox in the Spanish colonies, Charles IV sent Xavier De Balmis to spread the newly discovered vaccination process throughout Spanish holdings. In the absence of refrigeration, the vaccine was kept alive by sequential vaccination among a group of "volunteers" taken from La Coruna's Orphans Home. Leaving in 1803, the expedition vaccinated an estimated 100,000 people ranging from the Caribbean, South and Central America as far north as Texas, and subsequently in the Philippines, Macao, and Canton. They arrived back in Spain three years later (Aldrete, 2004). Whether this work was motivated by general altruism or just a pragmatic desire for healthier slaves is not recorded.

Box 2.1: History notes

Francisco Xavier de Balmis (1753–1819)

Born into a medical family, he first worked as a military surgeon in Spain's North African colonies. He later worked in Mexico as head of the Amor de Dios Hospital. He gained a reputation through his writing, particularly his translation of a French book on vaccination. When it was decided to spread the benefits of smallpox vaccination throughout the Spanish Empire, he was chosen as head of the project. In the absence of refrigeration, the vaccine was kept alive by sequential inoculation of 20 orphans taken along for the trip. The expedition left Spain in 1803, sailing for Venezuela, Mexico, and Cuba. He then sailed on to China, the Philippines, and finally home after over three years of travelling. Follow the reference for more information (Aldrete, 2004).

The United States has a long history of donating agricultural surpluses as food aid (Hanrahan, 2005). The first congressional grant for food aid was directed to Venezuela in 1812. Other large programs included food aid to Europe in 1919 and Russia in 1920. The program was formalized by Public Law 480 in 1954 (Food for Peace or pl480 program) and still continues to provide large volumes of food aid (Barrett & Maxwell, 2004, Fall).

The spread of steam-powered rail and sea transport during the 19th century also helped the spread of epidemics. Waves of infectious diseases spread through all the large cities, particularly the major ports. Smallpox, bubonic plague, yellow fever, and cholera were all commonplace illnesses (no different from the spread of SARS or avian influenza today) (Garrett, 1995). Responses to this new challenge were slow. After intermittent meetings in the late 19th century, the first international Sanitary Bureau was established in 1902 and included the United States and others from South America. This later grew into the Pan American Health Organization (PAHO).

The notion of a truly international health agency followed much the same course. The concept was first discussed at various international sanitary conferences from 1851 onwards, but it was not until 1907 that the Office International d'Hygiène Publique (OIHP) was first formed. Those early roots can be traced through the subsequent health section of the League of Nations and finally to the formation of the World Health Organization (WHO) in 1948.

The battle of Solferino between Austria and a joint French and Italian army in 1859 was the unlikely starting point for

Table 2.1: A moment of Zen

Net worth of the world's three richest people in 2004:	Annual GDP of the world's poorest countries:
William Gates: US $46.6 billion Warren Buffett: US $42.9 billion Karl Albrecht: US $23.0 billion	from #122, Georgia: US $5.091 billion to #184, Kiribati: US $0.062 billion
Total assets held by the three richest people in 2004:	Total annual GDP of the world's 62 poorest countries in 2004:
US $112.5 billion	**US $112.5 billion**

Source: "The world's richest people" (2004) Source: World Bank (2005)

the first international aid agency (the Red Cross). A travelling Swiss businessman, Henri Dunant, arrived in Solferino on the evening after the battle. He was horrified by the sight of wounded men simply left to die. He organized local women to nurse the wounded, paid for tents to be set up, and negotiated the release of Austrian doctors held by the French. The book he wrote describing the chaos was well received and helped him spread his ideas for improving the care of wounded soldiers. In 1863, the International Committee of the Red Cross was formed. The following year, the first Geneva convention was signed by 12 states. Its aim was to establish broad sets of accepted humanitarian behaviour during war (International Committee of the Red Cross, n.d.).

These slow steps toward today's international organizations needed to be supported by advances in the young sciences of epidemiology and tropical medicine. The need for well-trained doctors for the British Colonial service prompted the establishment of the first schools of tropical medicine—Liverpool in 1898 and London in the following year. Both have aged well and they remain acknowledged leaders in their field.

1940s AND 1950s: ORIGINS OF THE MODERN AID INDUSTRY

To understand the development of the aid industry, it is important to appreciate the major events of this period. The war had brought devastation to many countries, but it had also catalyzed unstoppable social movements; the times were certainly changing. Between about 1945 and 1990, the countries of the Eastern and Western blocs increasingly split apart—separated by an ideological and, in some places, physical barrier. In fact, it was the Soviet blockade of West Berlin that prompted one of the earliest large-scale aid initiatives. During 1948 and 1949, the United States, Britain, and France supplied the population of west Berlin entirely by air, shifting 2.3 million tons of food, coal, and other supplies (Griffin & Giangreco, 1988). This was also an early example of foreign aid and foreign policy becoming entangled.

Around the same time, a wave of nationalism swept the world from Africa to Asia. As the colonial masters shuffled out the back door, the two ideological blocs would spend the next few decades squabbling for influence over these newly independent states. Financial aid and military assistance were the tools used by both sides to gain political influence. In the process, money was wasted shamelessly on a succession of tyrants from Marcos

to Sese Seko (termed the "aidocracy" by Gelinas (1998), while the poor of those countries were viewed as little more than pawns in the great game.

President Truman's much quoted "4-point" inaugural speech in 1949 summed up the basic attitudes of the time (Bilger & Sowell, 1999):

- First, we will give unfaltering support to the United Nations and related agencies.
- Second, we will continue our programs for world recovery.
- Third, we will strengthen freedom-loving nations against the dangers of aggression.
- Fourth, we must embark on a bold new program for making the benefits of our scientific advances and industrial progress available for the improvement and growth of underdeveloped areas.

The modern aid industry is often dated to the Marshall Plan but it was, in fact, preceded by a larger aid project called the Lend-Lease Program, which began in 1941. Under that agreement, the United States provided food and military hardware to war allies, principally Great Britain, Russia, and China. By the end of the war, the United States had lent over $45 billion worth of supplies. In a forgotten lesson for the future, the allied countries were also allowed to repay the loans at below market interest rates.

Poor agricultural and industrial recovery following the war produced starvation and malnutrition in several European countries. The United States proposed a scheme for European reconstruction named after President Truman's then secretary of state,

George Marshall (Hogan & Galambos, 1989). The administration of the plan is worth noting because it has many lessons for the future of aid. Most importantly, it was a true joint venture with complete planning and administration of the money left in the hands of the European countries. America's role was largely to provide the cash. European countries formed the Organisation for European Economic Co-operation (OEEC) to run the project. This later grew to become the OECD and also formed the seeds of the future European common market.

Over a four-year period from 1947, over $13 billion worth of aid was distributed. The result was a rapid rebuilding of Europe and two decades of unbroken economic growth. Apart from being allowed to administer the projects themselves, it is also important to note that many European countries were given low interest rate loans (without added conditions) and were allowed to maintain their own protective trade barriers. Several were later granted outright debt forgiveness. Many of those countries are now major creditors and seem to have forgotten those early lessons! Much of the money was spent on American goods and contributed to the U.S. economic recovery. A strong Europe also helped limit the westward expansion of the new Soviet bloc.

This early successful program greatly influenced the planners of the time. Broadly speaking, aid was already separating into two camps (Tarp, 2000):

- *Aid directed toward economic growth:* examples include balance of payments assistance, agriculture and industrial investment, investment in infrastructure (ports, railways, power stations, roads, etc.) and, much later, poverty alleviation and debt relief.
- *Aid directed toward improved population health:* Examples include projects within the broad topic of health (from clean water and food to immunization and hospitals), but also education and later gender equity, human rights, democracy support, ecology, etc.

Around this time, the major international agencies that supported those development aims were also established. Following a meeting at Bretton Woods in 1944, the International Monetary Fund and World Bank were both established. They were initially intended to help rebuild larger Western countries and also stabilize international exchange rates. Both later concentrated more on economic development for poor countries. The General Agreement on Tariffs and Trade (GATT) was started at the same time (changed to World Trade Organization in 1994).

The United Nations was established in 1945 after an initial proposal by Roosevelt in 1942. It replaced the earlier short-lived League of Nations, but inherited some of its institutions such as the International Labour Organization. Numerous health-related UN bodies have subsequently been formed, including: Food and Agriculture Organization in 1945, UN International Children's Emergency Fund in 1946 (now UN Children's Fund since 1953, but it retains its original acronym), World Health Organization in 1948, and UN High Commissioner for Refugees in 1950 (originally UN Relief and Rehabilitation Administration).

Figure 2.1: The UN Relief and Rehabilitation Administration (UNRRA) was formed in the early days of the United Nations in order to support and repatriate European refugees. This 1946 picture shows a Sister of Charity distributing UNRRA food supplies to displaced children in Belgium. (Courtesy of the United Nations Photo library.)

Economic and health-related projects of the 1940s and 1950s were based on the optimistic feeling that technology and money could be used to eradicate poverty and ill health as they had in Europe. The "Big Push" was the order of the day. Economic programs were based on the theories attributed to Harrod and Domar. Growth was dependent on money—all you had to do was supply investment and infrastructure, and then growth would naturally follow (Easterly, 1997). Unfortunately, the practical lessons from the Marshall Plan were not heeded; the recipient countries were not included in the planning and implementation process so the expected growth did not appear. No matter how well intentioned projects might be, the imposition of roads, railways, and dams will produce no benefit without active involvement of the target population.

In the field of health, optimism seemed to be justified based on the discovery of antibiotics and other effective drugs. During the 1950s, top-down (vertical)

eradication programs were announced against a range of diseases (UNICEF, 1996a). Newly discovered penicillin worked well against yaws (a disfiguring chronic infection of skin and bones common in Africa and Asia). Over a million people were treated in Thailand alone. Other programs were started against malaria (based on chloroquine, proguanil, and DDT), tuberculosis (based on streptomycin, PAS, and isoniazid), leprosy (based on promin and dapsone), and trachoma (a chronic eye infection treated with newly developed antibiotic ointments).

Despite some successes, all these early eradication projects ultimately failed. They all foundered on the same shoals—the solid and immovable rocks of human nature and limited resources. Treating yaws is not too difficult. The response to treatment is quick and obvious, so people are prepared to co-operate. Unfortunately, most diseases are not so easily interrupted (certainly not tuberculosis, malaria, or HIV). Modern drugs are only one part of the eradication of most diseases. The full program must include education, changes in personal behaviour, and better living conditions. There are no quick fixes for the complexities of infectious diseases.

Modern HIV/AIDS researchers have had to relearn epidemiological lessons established decades ago (Henderson, 1999). Effective disease control requires coordinated programs aimed at multiple levels of intervention. The disease reservoir must be identified and treated, transmission must be interrupted (often at more than one level), and infectious contacts must be traced and treated. This all takes money, organization, and long-term changes in human behaviour. Of all these obstacles, the need to change human behaviour is probably the biggest.

So, the stage is set for the next phase of the industry's development. The early years following World War II saw the aid industry grow up from a tangled set of roots that included lessons derived from the reconstruction of post-war Europe, a desire for Cold War political advantage, a need for an economic return for all that money, and lastly, some measure of altruism (Hjertholm & White, 2000).

1960s AND 1970s: HOSPITALS, DAMS, BRIDGES, AND ROADS

To those peoples in the huts and villages of half the globe struggling to break the bonds of mass misery, we pledge our best efforts to help them help themselves.
—J.F. Kennedy, 1961

The start of the 1960s was declared the "first decade of development" by the United Nations and was ushered in by President Kennedy's "Alliance for Progress" and his much-quoted speech on development aid. The period began with growing enthusiasm for the "big plan" approach to development and also witnessed the continuing process of decolonization—17 newly independent African states were formed in 1960 alone. These young countries needed help with their early economic and social development, so aid was naturally directed toward them. More money available for more new countries could lead only to one thing—more bureaucrats. An endless succession of agencies was needed to feed this growing industry.

In 1960, the International Development Association was established within the World Bank to coordinate interest-free loans to poor countries. The European agency set up to administer the Marshall Plan aid was expanded in 1961 to become an international organization (Organisation for Economic Co-operation and Development). The following year, its Development Assistance Committee was established. In 1965, the U.N. Development Program was formed from two earlier bodies in order to help developing countries use aid more effectively. The following year, the UN Industrial Development Organization was formed specifically to help developing world industries. To add to the acronyms, individual countries started their own aid agencies around this time (USAID, Britain's DFID, Europe's ECHO, etc.). Finally, from Oxfam (1942) to the Jubilee 2000 Coalition (1996), non-governmental organizations were formed by the thousands.

Newly independent countries were not prepared to continue their colonial attitudes. Their collective voice slowly started to affect the aid debate, but their limited economic muscle made this a slow process. The non-aligned movement grew out of a conference at Bandung in 1955. It ultimately represented over 100 countries that wanted to enter the development debate, but were not prepared to align themselves with either of the great powers. Its main architects were Nehru, Nasser, and Tito. By the early 1960s, their combined voice persuaded the UN to call its first UN Conference on Trade and Development (UNCTAD) in 1964.

Despite regular four-year meetings, UNCTAD had little or no influence on international trade. The sense of frustration of non-aligned countries grew to such a level that in 1973, the UN called a meeting of the General Assembly to discuss development and international trade. The result was the declaration of a New International Economic Order that was accepted by the UN in 1974 (Johnson, 1978). It contained 18 clauses covering a range of issues from increased aid to trade liberalization that looks very similar to contemporary aid thinking currently celebrated as being brand new.

Thirty years later, it is hard to understand the high expectations surrounding the New Order — who remembers it now? Hopefully, the same fate does not lie in store for the Millennium Development Goals. The declaration was not legally binding and the developing bloc lacked significant influence to impose a serious development debate. Inevitably, the process degenerated into little more than rhetoric (labelled "the North-South debate" at the time). The oil-rich elites of the developing world had formed their own pressure group in 1960 (OPEC), but this influence was used sparingly.

However, not everything was wasted; the ghosts of UNCTAD and the New Order live on. They are easily seen today drifting through the failure of the Doha round of trade talks and the collapse of the WTO into various developing world pressure groups (see Chapter 11 for more details).

Apart from early benefits of the Green Revolution, the 1960s brought little help to the absolute poor — you have to own some land before you can benefit from agricultural advances. The initial enthusiasm for aid was also declining. In 1962, developed countries gave roughly 0.5 percent of their GDP in aid. The 1969 Pearson Commission on Aid used available mathematical models (plus a bit of guesswork) to arrive at the widely quoted recommendation that countries should give 0.7 percent of GDP as aid (Martens & Paul, 1998). By 1972, the DAC average was about 0.3 percent and it has fallen slightly since then (United States 0.16 percent in 2004) — see Chapter 8 for more details.

Health aid had few major successes in the 1960s. The push to import Western-style medical services was not successful, but no clear alternative was yet available. A multiagency report on the health of children in 1961 (Children of the Developing Countries) helped raise the profile of children's health needs and also of UNICEF. This ultimately led to UNICEF being awarded the Nobel Peace Prize in 1965 (UNICEF, 1996b). Just as early eradication efforts from the 1950s were being cancelled, the WHO decided to have one more try. The smallpox eradication program was announced in 1967 under the direction of Donald Henderson (Fenner et al., 1989). This remains one of the most striking examples of the successful use of foreign aid. Smallpox was declared eradicated from the world in 1978.

In a triumph of hope over experience, the United Nations introduced the second development decade with even more ambitious goals than they had declared for the first. The 1970s started with some signs that the poor would be included in the debate—the decade also included the famous Alma Ata Meeting on primary health care. Ultimately, these hopeful advances were overwhelmed by the steady economic decline induced by falling commodity markets and rising oil prices. Unfortunately, a specific emphasis on the needs of the poor was lost in this period of worsening economic news. In 1973, Robert McNamara, then president of the World Bank, made an influential speech encouraging aid donors and developing world governments to redesign their policies so as to meet the needs of the poorest 40 percent of the population and relieve their poverty directly (Loungani, 2003, December).Unfortunately, it would take another 20 years before this approach was adopted by World Bank economists (Bourguignon, 2004)!

Similar lessons were being learned in the field of health development. It was slowly becoming obvious that dialysis units and open-heart surgery were not contributing much to the fight against diseases of poverty. The donation of a modern urban hospital, packed with high-technology equipment, was not as useful as it might first have appeared. Apart from being out of reach of the rural poor, the cost of running such an institution could consume a significant portion of a small country's health budget (Morley et al., 1983).

Growing dissatisfaction with the poor results of health development made it obvious that change was necessary; the experience gained by a few developing

Figure 2.2: This early WHO photograph shows a Chinese barefoot doctor treating a production brigade worker with acupuncture needles. (Courtesy of the US National Library of Medicine.)

countries (particularly China's approach) attracted a great deal of attention. The "great leap forward" in 1958 had responded to rural health needs by developing local clinics staffed by medical orderlies, subsequently known as barefoot doctors. The reality was not as perfect as the political propaganda would suggest, but this basic needs approach did seem to offer an alternative model for development (Figure 2.2). The culmination was the Alma Ata Summit in 1978 and the subsequent Health for All Strategy that emerged from it (Perin & Attaran, 2003). Primary health care and services at the village level now supplanted the previous emphasis on shiny new hospitals (see Chapter 9 for details).

The end of these two decades of development saw health aid and economic aid moving in two very different directions. The health debate, with all its imperfections, did at least base its programs on what was best for the poor. Unfortunately, the organizers of economic aid responded to the debt crisis of the time by imposing conditional aid, the main aim of which was to make countries more prosperous so they could keep up with their debt obligations. It was expected that some of that prosperity would subsequently trickle down, but the poor were very much a secondary issue behind economic growth. It would be some time before common ground could be found between these two approaches.

1980s AND 1990s: STRUCTURAL ADJUSTMENTS, AID WITH CONDITIONS

The United Nations' optimistic call for a third development decade in 1980 was out of touch with reality. By the end of the 1980s, fieldworkers who had battled the effects of developing world debt, structural adjustment policies, deepening crisis in Sub-Saharan Africa, and the onset of HIV/AIDS epidemic labelled this the lost decade.

The failure of Mexico to meet its debt repayments in 1982 heralded the start of the developing world debt crisis. Full details of this period are given in Chapter 11. The solution of the day was based on ideologically based economic therapies (often called the Washington Consensus) that included privatization of state industries, trade liberalization,

and reduction in social spending on health, education, and food subsidies for the poor (Williamson, 2000). These economic interventions were collectively known as Structural Adjustment Policies (SAPs). By the end of the 1980s, it was already becoming clear that their effects were disastrous for the health of the poor (Cornia et al., 1987).

At the start of the second United Nations decade in 1972, the General Assembly had defined 24 countries as "least developed"; by 1991, this number had almost doubled to 47 countries. Despite 20 years of economic interventions, agreements, and binding resolutions, more countries than ever before were overwhelmed by debt. It was not until the 1990s that the World Bank and IMF responded to criticism of their policies by taking a new approach to poverty alleviation and debt relief. The Heavily Indebted Poor Countries Initiative (HIPC) in 1996, their second try in 1999 (enhanced HIPC), and recent initiatives aimed at absolute debt relief are the current results of that debate (Oxfam, 2005; World Bank, n.d.).

The Primary Health Care (PHC) era that started at Alma Ata and the subsequent Health for All Declaration meant that health aid began the decade with great optimism. Under the leadership of James Grant, UNICEF introduced targeted care for poor children in the form of the child survival revolution (UNICEF, 1996c). This involved a package of cost-effective therapies known by the acronym GOBI (Growth monitoring, Oral rehydration, Breast-feeding, and Immunization). Women's health later received more emphasis when Family spacing, Female education, and Food supplements during pregnancy were added (GOBI-FFF). In 1992, the program was expanded in a joint WHO/UNICEF initiative called the Integrated Management of Childhood Illnesses (IMCI). This treatment approach now forms the basis of child health policy in much of the developing world (World Bank, 1999).

Although real advances were made, particularly the expanded vaccine initiative, PHC did face significant problems. Financial considerations limited its implementation to a narrower focus than its initial originators intended (selective PHC) (Hall & Taylor, 2003). This gave an impression of inflexibility and limitation. What a rural subsistence farmer might want (care for his aching back) and what he gets with SPHC (breast-feeding advice, immunization for his children, and a lecture on safe sex) are not at all the same thing. Basically, people everywhere want the same thing—a well-equipped clinic run by well-trained staff who will meet their broad health needs. Immunizations and breast-feeding are measurably beneficial, but they do not match up to expectations in isolation.

The delivery of health services has, of course, continued to change since the PHC era, but it has not been replaced by a single philosophy. Current moves toward health sector reform are usually dated to an influential 1993 World Development Report and a subsequent World Health Report in 2000 (World Bank, 1993; World Health Organization, 2000). Changes obviously vary with region, but they include decentralization of health services, various forms of community financing, provision of a cost-effective package of services, and varying degrees of privatization (Berman, 1995). Primary health care slowly disappeared from view and is hardly mentioned in the current debate (see Chapter 9 for more details).

Table 2.2: Major events in the history of health aid

1803	De Balmis's international smallpox vaccination expedition
1848	General Report on the Sanitary Conditions of the Labouring Populations of Great Britain by Chadwick
1851	First International Sanitary Conference
1854	John Snow removes pump handle in London suburb during cholera outbreak
1863	International Committee of Red Cross forms
1898	First tropical medicine research centres—Liverpool and London
1902	Pan American Sanitary Bureau (becomes PAHO in 1949)
1919	League of Nations, International Health Section
1942	UN Relief and Rehabilitation Administration
1946	UNICEF formed
1948	WHO formed
1950s	Export of Western-style health care; first eradication campaigns (yaws, leprosy, TB, malaria)
1961	UNICEF report (Children of the Developing Countries)
1965	UNICEF awarded Nobel Peace Prize
1967	Smallpox eradication program starts
1978	Alma Ata meeting (start of PHC era)
1979	Smallpox eradicated
1980s	First case reports of HIV/AIDS; steady spread of HIV south through Africa; child survival revolution announced; UNICEF initiatives (GOBI, GOBI-FFF)
1987	Adjustment with a human face, UNICEF
1992	WHO/UNICEF introduce IMCI initiative
1993	WDR Report (*Investing in Health*) starts strong move toward health sector reform
1999	Roll Back Malaria Program
2000	Global Alliance for Vaccines and Immunizations
2002	GFATM (new approach to health funding)
2003	SARS epidemic

The 1993 report also marked a reunification of the two arms of development assistance since it emphasized the absolute need for economic growth combined with improved health; both are fundamental human needs. If they head in opposite directions, the only losers are the poor; it is now generally accepted that you cannot have one without the other. The classification of development initiatives into health aid and economic aid is obviously an oversimplification, but it does give some useful broad insights into the aid industry's history. Tables 2.2 and 2.3 summarize the major developments in these two areas since rich countries first started to assist poorer ones.

CURRENT APPROACHES: MILLENNIUM DEVELOPMENT GOALS

The more things change, the more they stay the same.
                                    — Alphonse Karr

At the beginning of each decade, the UN announced optimistic hopes for the first, second, third, and fourth development decades. Unfortunately, reality always lagged far behind those optimistic projections. However, the start of the new millennium does seem to have coincided with very real hopes that the future of the aid industry will be increasingly bright. There have been several promising developments, particularly an increasing emphasis upon the poor. It is also encouraging to see the two separate arms of the industry (economic aid and health projects) being merged into common projects with shared aims.

To some extent, the aid industry is just about back where it started in the 1940s and 1950s. The end of World War II has been replaced by the end of the Cold War. The "big plan" approach to

Table 2.3: Major events in the history of economic aid

1812	Food aid to Venezuela
1919	Food aid to post-war Europe
1920	Food aid to Russia
1929	British Colonial Development Act
1941	Lend-Lease Program
1945	United Nations formed; new UN agencies: FAO, UNHCR, EPTA
1947	Marshall Plan, OEEC forms
1948	Berlin airlift
1950s	Big projects (dams, roads, railway)
1950	Colombo Plan (British Commonwealth aid framework)
1954	US Public Law 480 (Food for Peace)
1955	Bandung meeting (start of non-aligned movement)
1960s	More agencies (UNIDO, UNDP, IDA); national aid agencies (USAID, DFID); start of NGO expansion; Green Revolution
1960	OPEC forms
1961	OECD forms and its development arm, DAC
1961	US Foreign Assistance Act (separates military and non-military aid)
1964	First UNCTAD meeting
1969	Pearson Commission (0.7 percent of GDP goal)
1972	McNamara reorganizes World Bank and emphasizes focus on the poor
1974	Declaration of New International Economic Order
1975	Lomé Convention (EU aid framework)
1980s	First structural adjustment loans; collapse of numerous developing economies; decade of increasing structural adjustment policies
1990s	Increasing criticism of IMF/WB economic policies; increasing emphasis on poverty relief and debt forgiveness; end of Cold War
1994	World Trade Organization forms
1996	HIPC initiative
1999	EHIPC initiative
2000	Millennium Development Goals
2001	Doha round of international trade talks
2003	Failed Cancun talks, G20 formed
2005	Hong Kong trade talks, tentative agreements
2005	Gleneagles G8; Multilateral Debt Relief Initiative

infrastructure projects of 40 or 50 years ago is now replaced or mirrored in some aspects of the Millennium Development Goals and can certainly be seen in Sachs' approach to development or the UNDP's new approach to solving everything (Kaul & Conceicao, 2006; Sachs, 2005). Early vertical eradication programs, once heavily criticized as remnants of colonialism, have been replaced by large initiatives targeted at specific diseases such as Roll Back Malaria (World Health Organization, n.d.). The term "vertical program" is no longer used in polite circles, but current projects against HIV/AIDS, tuberculosis, and malaria show their roots in those early eradication efforts of the 1950s and 1960s.

Following the UN General Assembly Meeting in 2000, 191 world leaders signed what has come to be called "Millennium Development Goals" or MDGs (*UN Millennium Development Goals*, n.d.). Of all the large-scale projects, this is the one that can claim to encapsulate the current thinking on development for the next 20 years. It can almost be viewed as a modern aid "constitution" because every new initiative is assessed by its ability to help meet one or more of the MDGs. A particularly promising step in this process is the introduction of measurable outcomes; the usual target date is 2015. The MDGs consist of eight broad goals:

1. Eradicate extreme poverty and hunger.
2. Achieve universal primary education.
3. Promote gender equality and empower women.
4. Reduce child mortality.
5. Improve maternal health.
6. Combat HIV/AIDS, malaria, and other diseases.
7. Ensure environmental sustainability.
8. Develop a global partnership for development.

It gets a bit more complicated because within these eight goals, there are 18 defined targets with 48 separate indicators to measure progress. For each target and indicator, a particular international body has been given the task of monitoring progress. For example, the first goal (eradicate extreme poverty and hunger) has two targets, each of which has separate monitored indicators of progress.

- *Target one:* Between 1990 and 2015, halve the proportion of people whose income is less than $1 per day.
  Indicators: The proportion of people living on less than $1 per day (monitoring body World Bank); poverty gap ratio (monitoring body World Bank); share of poorest quintile in national consumption (monitoring body World Bank).
- *Target two:* Between 1990 and 2015, halve the proportion of people who suffer from hunger.
  Indicators: Prevalence of underweight children under five years of age (monitoring body UNICEF-WHO); proportion of population below minimal level of dietary energy consumption (UN Food and Agriculture Organization).

Current research estimates that the annual cost of reaching these ambitious goals is US $40 billion to $60 billion per year. Clearly, a great deal of money and effort is required if these goals are to be reached.

■ SUMMARY

The modern global development industry is still relatively young; it mostly traces its roots to the reconstruction efforts in Europe following World War II. The framework of the industry and its broad ideas about the best ways to improve population health have all changed considerably since then. During that time, it has been fashioned by unavoidable external forces such as the Cold War, the end of colonialism, the 1980s economic crisis, and the HIV epidemic. Internally, the industry has been influenced by widely varying philosophies ranging from Washington's economic consensus to Alma Ata's theories on primary health care. The aid industry might now be approaching calmer maturity, but it certainly had a very difficult childhood!

Before embracing the orthodoxies of the day, it should be remembered that the aid industry has a long history of transient enthusiasms for new initiatives. Few people now remember the Global Initiative for Health for All by 2000 and fewer still can recall the announcement of the New International Economic Order. More importantly, who remembers past failures such as early disease eradication efforts, the structural adjustment era, or the use of aid for geopolitical advantage or economic gain? If these are just swept under the carpet or called unavoidable growing pains, future planners will not learn the available lessons. Whether we meet the Millennium Development Goals (MDGs) by 2015 or they just end up as a forgotten footnote to a future chapter depends on the ability of the development industry to appreciate the mistakes of the past and make suitable changes.

The widespread adoption of the MDGs is a very promising sign that the aid industry has learned some important lessons about the best way to do business. After passing through a period in the 1990s when the relevance of aid was seriously questioned, the industry's future is looking much brighter. Increasing volumes of foreign aid, combined with a fundamental focus on the needs of the poor and the use of published outcome measurements, all give very real hope that the wealth and influence of the richest countries can make a substantial contribution toward that most optimistic goal set over 25 years ago at Alma Ata—health for all.

RESOURCES

References

Aldrete, J. (2004). "The travels of Francisco Xavier de Balmis." *Southern Medical Journal, 97*, 375–378.

Barrett, C., & Maxwell, D. (2004, Fall). "PL480 food aid: We can do better." *American Agricultural Economics Association Magazine*, 53–57. Retrieved from www.choicesmagazine.org/2004-3/2004-3-12.pdf.

Berman, P. (1995). "Health sector reform: Making health development sustainable." *Health Policy, 32*, 13–28.

Bilger, D., & Sowell, R. (1999). *Point four program of technical assistance to developing nations.* Retrieved from www.trumanlibrary.org/hstpaper/point4.htm.

Bloy, M. (2002). *The 1601 Elizabethan Poor Law*. Retrieved from www.victorianweb.org/history/poorlaw/elizpl.html.

Bourguignon, F. (2004). *The poverty-growth-inequality triangle*. Retrieved from poverty2.forumone.com/library/view/15185.

Cornia, G., et al. (1987). *Adjustment with a human face*. Oxford: Oxford University Press.

Easterly, W. (1997). *The ghost of the financing gap: How the Harrod-Domar growth model still haunts development economics* (World Bank Development Research Group, paper 1807). Retrieved from www.eldis.org/static/DOC5720.htm.

Fenner, F., et al. (1989). *Smallpox and its eradication* (History of Public Health, no. 6). Geneva: World Health Organization. Retrieved from whqlibdoc.who.int/smallpox/9241561106.pdf.

Garrett, L. (1995). *The coming plague: Newly emerging diseases in a world out of balance*. London: Penguin.

Gelinas, J. (1998). *Freedom from debt: The re-appropriation of development through financial self-reliance*. London: Zed Books.

Griffin, R., & Giangreco, D. (1988). *Air bridge to Berlin: The Berlin crisis of 1948, its origins and aftermath*. Novato: Presidio Press.

Hall, J., & Taylor, R. (2003). "Health for all beyond 2000: The demise of the Alma Ata declaration and primary health care in developing countries." *Medical Journal of Australia, 178*, 17–20.

Hanrahan, C. (2005). *Agricultural export and food aid programs*. Retrieved from www.usembassy.it/pdf/other/IB98006.pdf.

Henderson, D. (1999). "Eradication: Lessons from the past." *Morbidity and Mortality Weekly Review, 48*, 16–22.

Hjertholm, P., & White, H. (2000). *Survey of foreign aid: History trends and allocation*. Institute of Economics, University of Copenhagen. Retrieved from www.econ.ku.dk/wpa/pink/2000/0004.pdf.

Hogan, M., & Galambos, L. (1989). *The Marshall Plan: America, Britain, and the reconstruction of Western Europe, 1947–1952*. Cambridge: Cambridge University Press.

International Committee of the Red Cross. (n.d.). *The Geneva Convention: The core of international humanitarian law*. Retrieved from www.icrc.org/Web/Eng/siteeng0.nsf/html/genevaconventions

Johnson, H. (1978). *The new international economic order* (University of Chicago selected paper 49). Retrieved from www.chicagogsb.edu/research/selectedpapers/sp49.pdf.

Kaul, I., & Conceicao, P. (2006). *The new public finance: Responding to global challenges*. Oxford: Oxford University Press.

King, L. (1996). *The code of Hammurabi*. Retrieved from www.yale.edu/lawweb/avalon/medieval/hammenu.htm.

Loungani, P. (2003, December). "Back to Basics: The global war on poverty." *Finance and Development*, 38–39. Retrieved from www.imf.org/external/pubs/ft/fandd/2003/12/pdf/basics.pdf.

Martens, J., & Paul, J. (1998). *The coffers are not empty: Financing for sustainable development and the role of the United Nations*. Retrieved from www.globalpolicy.org/socecon/ffd/paul.htm.

Morley, D., et al. (1983). *Practicing health for all*. Oxford: Oxford University Press.

Oxfam. (2005). *Beyond HIPC: Debt: Cancellation and the Millennium Development Goals* (Oxfam briefing paper 78). Retrieved from www.oxfam.org.uk/what_we_do/issues/debt_aid/downloads/bp78_hipc.pdf.

Perin, I., & Attaran, A. (2003). "Trading ideology for dialogue: An opportunity to fix international aid for health?" *Lancet, 361*, 1216–1219.

Sachs, J. (2005). *The end of poverty: Economic possibilities for our time*. New York: Penguin Press.

Tarp, F. (2000). *Foreign aid and development: Lessons learned and directions for the future*. London: Routledge.

UN Millennium Development Goals. (n.d.). Retrieved from www.un.org/millenniumgoals.

UNICEF. (1996a). *The 1950s: Era of the mass disease campaign.* Retrieved from www.unicef.org/ sowc96/1950s.htm.

UNICEF. (1996b). *The 1960s: Decade of development.* Retrieved from www.unicef.org/sowc96/1960s. htm.

UNICEF. (1996c). *The 1980s: Campaign for child survival.* Retrieved from www.unicef.org/sowc96/ 1980s.htm.

Williamson, J. (2000). "What should the World Bank think about the Washington consensus?" *World Bank Research Observer*, 15, no. 2. Retrieved from www.worldbank.org/research/ journals/wbro/obsaug00/pdf/(6)Williamson.pdf.

World Bank. (1993). *World development report 1993: Investing in health.* Retrieved from econ. worldbank.org/wdr.

World Bank. (1999). *IMCI information package.* Retrieved from www.who.int/child-adolescent-health/integr.htm.

World Bank. (2005). *World development indicators 2005.* Retrieved from www.worldbank.org/ data/wdi2005/.

World Bank. (n.d.). *The HIPC debt initiative.* Retrieved from www.worldbank.org/hipc/about/ hipcbr/hipcbr.htm.

World Health Organization. (2000). *World health report 2000: Health systems: Improving performance.* Retrieved from www.who.int/health-systems-performance/whr2000.htm.

World Health Organization. (n.d.). *The roll back malaria partnership.* Retrieved from www.rbm. who.int.

"The world's richest people." (2004). *Forbes.* Retrieved from www.forbes.com/2004/02/25/ bill04land.html.

Recommended Reading

Dijkstra, G. (2002). *Program aid and development: Beyond conditionality.* London: Routledge.

Kaul, I., & Conceicao, P. (2006). *The new public finance: Responding to global challenges.* Oxford: Oxford University Press.

Sogge, D. (2002). *Give and take: What's the matter with foreign aid?* London: Zed Books.

Tarp, F. (2000). *Foreign aid and development: Lessons learned and directions for the future.* London: Routledge.

Tisch, S., & Wallace, M. (1994). *Dilemmas of development assistance: The what, why and who of foreign aid.* Boulder: Westview Press.

PART II

WHY IS POPULATION HEALTH SO POOR IN DEVELOPING COUNTRIES?

Chapter 3
**The Determinants
of Population Health**

Chapter 4
**Poverty and
Developing World Debt**

Chapter 5
Malnutrition

The Determinants of Population Health

> Health is a state of compete physical, mental,
> and social wellbeing and not merely the
> absence of disease or infirmity.
> —Constitution of the World Health Organization, 1948

OBJECTIVES
After completing this chapter, you should be able to

- understand the principal requirements needed for a healthy life
- understand the relative contributions of the different basic needs to individual health
- understand the contribution of modern medical care to personal health
- appreciate some of the major determinants of health that appear once the basic needs have been met

---

When Chadwick first studied the effects of social class on mortality in Victorian England, he found that life expectancy at birth for the most privileged classes was 44 years and the infant mortality rate was above 100 per 1,000 live births. The poor of Dickensian London or Victor Hugo's Paris lived lives that were not essentially different from those lived in the shantytowns and *favelas* of today. Whatever it was that improved their health in the past probably has relevant application today. The health of the world's population has greatly improved since Chadwick's time, even among the poorest nations. During the 20th century, this trend accelerated. In the last 100 years, human life expectancy at birth has nearly doubled in some countries. The average American newborn in 1900 could expect to live 49 years. By 2000, that average baby could expect to live for 77 years.

This is the greatest improvement in human health in history, but it is neither widely appreciated nor fully understood.

Box 3.1: History notes

Sir Edwin Chadwick (1800–1890)

Chadwick was born in Manchester in 1800. While studying law, he earned extra money as a journalist writing review articles for London newspapers. His early work on poverty, sanitation, and the poor was widely read and this set the course for the rest of his long life. Although he never believed in the existence of bacteria, his work and studies led to major advances in the eradication of infectious diseases in urban areas. To his dying day, he (and his friend Florence Nightingale) believed that infections arose spontaneously among dirt. He made significant contributions to public health and Poor Law Reform, particularly with the establishment of official public health inspectors. His report, The Sanitary Condition of the Labouring Population, is widely considered to be the start of modern epidemiology and public health. Follow the link for more information (Porter & Porter, 1990).

The newcomer might assume that these improvements were most likely due to advances in medical care, but even a cursory examination shows this is not the explanation. Mortality rates from major killers such as tuberculosis in adults and measles in children fell steadily decades before specific therapies were discovered. Clearly, other mechanisms were involved.

There is a vast literature on the subject of health determinants. Although there is inevitable controversy, the major variables have been identified and health care is well down the list. Below a certain level of per capita income, health is governed by money and access to basic human needs. Strangely enough, once income rises above that level, health depends on a range of intangible factors such as social cohesion, income distribution, education, and social class. This is a fascinating subject that has great relevance for the design of modern aid projects.

INTRODUCTION TO THE BASIC REQUIREMENTS

Battles are only the terminal operations engaged in by those remnants of the armies which survived the camp epidemics.
— Zinsser, *Rats, Lice, and History*, 1934

The Egyptian civilization lasted roughly 3,000 years before it finally gave way to British rule—not bad when you consider that Canadian Federation is barely 150 years old. During all that time, the population survived without the benefits of anesthesia, antibiotics, or any knowledge of microbiology. Other early civilizations in Central America, the Indus and Yangtze River valleys, Rome, and Greece thrived for centuries even though their physicians had little more than primitive surgery and a handful of effective drugs (Cule & Porter, 2000).

It is likely that these early civilizations based their knowledge of population health on the experience gained from military campaigns. Once a large group of humans is crammed together with minimum attention to clean water and waste disposal, it soon becomes very obvious to an intelligent observer that some basic rules of hygiene are necessary. It is probable that more armies have been stopped by infection than by combat (Peterson, 1995).

Some armies took longer than others to sort these lessons out. As recently as the American Civil War, deaths among soldiers from infections such as typhoid, cholera, smallpox, and malaria (roughly 250,000) were nearly as high as those due to combat (roughly 350,000) (American civil war homepage, n.d.). Help arrived in the unlikely form of a society gardener called Frederick Law Olmsted (he was an early landscape architect and designed Central Park). While serving as head of the U.S. Sanitary Commission during the Civil War, Olmsted's Committee of Enquiry slowly forced the U.S. Army to improve living conditions and medical care for its soldiers (Frederick Law Olmsted, n.d.). The standards of hygiene in the British army (and the subsequent mortality) would have horrified any of the campaigning generals from ancient times. Long after Pacini's discovery of the bacterial cause of cholera (in fact, after his death from old age), the British army still persisted in the belief that a flannel body wrap was the best way to prevent cholera. The "cholera belt" was a standard part of army issue in the tropics until 1920 (Renbourn, 1957)!

Archeological evidence of existing Roman military camps shows clear evidence of their knowledge of the essentials of public health. Tents and cooking areas were placed well away from latrines and waste disposal. These ideas probably influenced early city design. Excavations at the middle-class holiday resort of Pompeii showed that all but the poorest houses had running water and central sewage disposal (*Soprintendenza archeologica di Pompei*, n.d.). Today, if you go to the slums of Dhaka in Bangladesh or Accra in Ghana, it would not take long before you work out why the inhabitants are unhealthy. There is clearly a minimum set of standards that must be in place before any sort of restful, healthy life is possible. Obviously these include clean water, shelter, food, and peace.

Table 3.1: A moment of Zen

Chance of a newborn Australian baby dying before its fifth birthday: six per 1,000	
For a Canadian baby: five per 1,000	
For a Swedish baby: three per 1,000	
Chance of an Angolan baby dying before its fifth birthday: 250 per 1,000	Chance of winning a prize in British Columbia's Scratch and Win Lottery:
One in four	**One in four**
Source: UNICEF (2006)	Source: British Columbia Lottery Corporation (n.d.)

As an exercise, it is well worth debating what basic features are required for a healthy society and then setting them in some sort of order. Ideas will vary, but the list given in the first column of Table 3.2 is the result of a debate among medical students and residents in Vancouver, British Columbia, Canada.

Whatever results your own debate produces, one point will be common to all; medical treatment, in the form of immunizations and obstetric care, does not appear until well down the list. It is important to remember that we are discussing population health rather than individual health. Anyone with a treatable emergency such as appendicitis or pneumonia will be very happy for access to good quality medical care. However, on a population basis, as we will discuss later in this chapter, medical care

Table 3.2: Basic requirements for a healthy life

Vancouver Medical Students	Clark and Quizilbash (2005)	Doyal and Gough (1991)	Maslow (1943)
• Peace • Easy access to clean water • Comfortable shelter • Adequate food supply • Employment with fair pay • Education for all • Stable judiciary/ police force • Immunization • Good-quality obstetric care • Democratic government structure • Free press and freedom of speech	• Housing or shelter • Food • Water • Work/jobs • Money/income • Clothes • Education and schools • Health/health care • Electricity/energy • Safety/security • Transport/car • Family and friends • Sanitation • Infrastructure • Leisure/leisure facilities	• Nutritional food and clean water • Protective housing • Safe work environment • Safe physical environment • Safe birth control and child-bearing • Appropriate health care • A secure childhood • Significant primary relationship • Physical security • Economic security • Appropriate education	• Basic physiological needs • Safety • Belonging and love • Esteem • Need to know and understand • Aesthetic needs • Self-actualization • Transcendence

does not have a big impact on population mortality rates, particularly when it is compared to the provision of the basic needs of food, shelter, water, and peace.

Over the last three or four decades, there has been a growing literature on the subject of population health (Evans, Barer, & Marmor, 1994; Raphael, 2004). It has become increasingly apparent that this is a very complicated topic. Some of the major determinants such as clean water, shelter, and food are quite obvious, but others are far less intuitive. For example, the health benefits of a free press or democracy are not immediately clear but, as the economist Amartya Sen (1983) pointed out in his famous study of famine, their benefits are measurable. His research prompted the famous statement that there has never been a famine in a functioning democracy or in a country with a free press. The health effects of these and other, even more intangible

determinants such as social cohesion are difficult to analyze, but their effects are very real (Lynch et al., 2001).

On first view, the basic needs for health are much the same as your grandmother's advice: Eat your greens, take some exercise, go to bed early, and do not misbehave. On a population basis, your grandmother's advice scales up to clean water, good nutrition, shelter, peace, and behaviour as a member of a social community rather than an individual.

The American psychologist, Abraham Maslow (1943), proposed a rather more complex list ranging from absolutely basic needs up to less definable requirements such as self-actualization and transcendence. Despite this, the base of his pyramid (commonly known as Maslow's hierarchy of needs) contains much the same essentials as those compiled by the Vancouver students. Similarly, the 11 basic needs summarized by Doyal and Gough

Figure 3.1: One of the most basic health requirements is a convenient supply of safe drinking water. This young Ethiopian woman has to collect her family's water from a public well and then carry it home on her back every day. (Photographer P. Virot; courtesy of WHO mediacentre.)

(1991) or the essentials of life defined by poor communities in South Africa (Clark & Quizilbash, 2005), all come to the same general conclusions — human societies have much the same basic hopes and dreams no matter where they live.

So far, we have defined the first few rungs of the ladder that populations must climb to reach a safe happy life; those steps include clean water, peace, food, shelter, fair employment, education, and a safe and stable community. This is, of course, all much neater and simpler in theory than in practice. In later sections, particularly Chapters 8 and 9, we'll examine the practical problems of implementation (not least of which is the money needed to pay for the initiatives). However, despite these practical difficulties, the widespread introduction of basic human needs is the best and most cost-effective way to spend aid money. Not surprisingly, many of the United Nations Millennium Development Goals are based on such initiatives (*UN Millennium Development Goals*).

THE EFFECT OF MONEY ON POPULATION HEALTH

I've been rich and I've been poor. Rich is better.

—Sophie Tucker

It would seem to be a logical assumption that the health of a population is reasonably correlated with its average income. As the regression line on the health-wealth curve shows (Figure 3.2), this holds true for low- and middle-income countries whose per capita GDPs fall below about US $5,000 (Wilkinson, 1996). These countries and

Figure 3.2: Life expectancy at birth plotted against Gross Domestic Product per capita for 108 countries

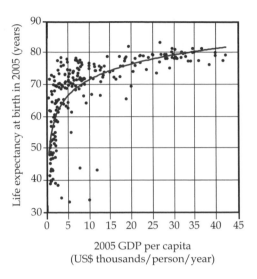

2005 GDP per capita
(US$ thousands/person/year)

Source: Central Intelligence Agency (2006)

Table 3.3: The effect of the HIV/AIDS epidemic on life expectancy in Southern Africa

Country	GDP Per Capita (US $1,000s)	Life Expectancy at Birth (years)
Ecuador	3,900	76.21
Jamaica	4,300	73.33
Sri Lanka	4,300	73.17
Namibia	7,800	43.93
South Africa	11,900	43.27
Botswana	10,100	33.87

Source: Central Intelligence Agency (2006)

their populations are the ones where well-planned health initiatives are likely to produce the greatest cost-effective benefits. The introduction of clean water, sanitation, or improved housing can all help to move people as quickly as possible up the steep part of the health-wealth curve.

Oddly enough, above the annual GDP per capita level of $5,000, the clear beneficial relationship between health and wealth breaks down. Some rich countries such as the United States, contain disadvantaged populations whose life expectancy can only be considered that of a Third World country. Other relatively poor areas of the world manage to maintain healthy populations despite low incomes. Table 3.3 shows the wide range of life expectancies found in countries with mid-range incomes. The adverse effects of the HIV/AIDS epidemic are particularly marked in the three southern African states. These mortality differences also exist within countries. There is a 20-year gap in life expectancy between Whites in the healthiest areas of the US and Blacks in the least healthy areas (Kaplan et al., 1996). This is equivalent to the difference in life expectancy between Japan and the worst parts of Bangladesh so there is clearly a great deal more to health than simply money (Diez Roux, 2001).

The relationship between health and wealth is fairly obvious and has been known about for a long time. Edwin Chadwick published his careful study of disease and mortality in Victorian London. When it was published in 1842, it shocked the Victorian middle classes. He showed clear health and mortality gradients between the five defined social classes, ranging from level one (the gentry) and level five (unskilled labourers). A typical quote from the book describes the poverty, overcrowding, filth, and disease common in London at that time:

Shepherd's Buildings consist of two rows of houses with a street seven yards wide between them; each row consists of what are styled back and front houses—that is, two houses placed back to back. There are no yards or out-conveniences; the privies are in the centre of each row, about a yard wide; over them there is part of a sleeping-room; there is no ventilation in the bed-rooms; each house contains two rooms, viz., a house place and sleeping room above; each room is about three yards wide and four long. In one of these houses there are nine persons belonging to one family, and the mother on the eve of her confinement.... (Edwin Chadwick, *Report into the Sanitary Conditions of the Labouring Population of Great Britain*, 1842)

Until about 1900, the relationship between life expectancy and per capita income in industrialized countries that Chadwick observed was no different from today's developing world. They both follow the same steep part of the curve shown in Figure 3.2. However, as countries grew richer, it became clear that there was a limit to that relationship; increasing wealth did not necessarily mean increasing health. By 1950, the curve had flattened off, demonstrating that above a certain level, further increases in income are not reflected in greatly increased life expectancies (Wilkinson, 1996). Remember that this is an average for many countries. As we shall see later, social gradients still exist within each of those countries no matter how high their average income.

The health transitions noted in developing countries have attracted considerable research since the analysis of methods used by successful countries clearly has relevance for the planning of health interventions in other high-mortality areas. For example, over the last 50 years, Tunisia has managed to

reduce its infant mortality from 150 per 1,000 down to 26.2 per 1,000, while life expectancy has increased by nearly 50 percent (50 years to 72 years) (Ben Hamida et al., 2005).

With time, the general shape of the curve has remained unchanged, although the inflection curve obviously moves to the right with increasing global prosperity. The causes behind the relationship between health and income for countries above the inflection point generate plenty of controversy, which will be covered later in this chapter. Analysis of the relationship for those countries below the inflection point is more straightforward. Slowly rising prosperity increasingly allows people to buy the basic necessities for health. As mentioned earlier, this includes access to clean water, efficient waste disposal, good nutrition for the family, comfortable shelter, and access to efficient medical care—all of which costs money. When this is combined with enlightened government health policies, the proportion of deaths due to infectious diseases falls and the numbers of children reaching their fifth birthday start to rise.

So far, a combination of money and basic needs implementation has helped our population move about halfway up the health-wealth curve. They are now about to bump their heads on the inflection point at the per capita income level around US $5,000. From here on, the story gets a lot more complicated.

THE EFFECT OF MEDICAL CARE ON POPULATION HEALTH

Medicine is a collection of uncertain prescriptions, the results of which, taken

collectively, are more fatal than useful to mankind. Water, air, and cleanliness are the chief articles in my pharmacopeia.
— Napoleon Bonaparte

No one who has received high-quality treatment in a modern hospital would argue that medical care is of no value. Although it may be a comforting service at a personal level, does the enormous expense and complexity of modern medicine make any measurable difference at a population level? We know that money and basic needs get a population moving up the health-wealth curve, but does the addition of medical care add any further significant benefits?

Modern medicine is a huge and ever-growing beast — over the last two decades, every developed country has had to deal with the problem of trying to control it but, until quite recently, research into outcomes and efficiency concentrated mainly on the financial costs of treatment. Illich's critical review of health care in 1976 helped start a more useful debate about whether those treatments actually achieved anything useful (Relman, 1988). Topics such as waiting lists, wide variations in use of procedures, and medical errors now attract serious attention (Roos, 1992), but it is still surprisingly difficult to tell how much value the industry actually produces for all that money.

In historical terms, medical advances did little to improve health during the first half of the 20th century; tuberculosis is a good example. As McKeown (1979) pointed out, the death rate from tuberculosis in all developed countries fell steadily decades before the discovery of effective drugs in the late 1940s and the introduction of tuberculosis vaccination in the 1950s. Population surveys using tuberculosis

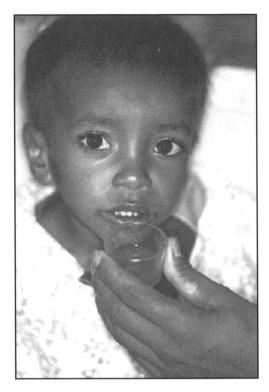

Figure 3.3: Although modern medical care is important in the control of many diseases, its value is limited unless it is combined with improvements in social conditions. The drug treatment this Ethiopian boy is receiving in St Peter's Tuberculosis hospital, Addis Ababa, will save his life, but it won't eradicate the disease from his community. That will require a coordinated approach combining TB treatment and testing with a range of social interventions such as better housing, nutrition, education, and employment. (Photographer Andy Crump; courtesy of Tropical Research Programme Image Library.)

skin tests in Britain during the 1940s and 1950s showed that most adults had still been exposed to the bacillus, but far fewer of them were contracting the disease. An increasingly healthy and prosperous population appeared to be able to resist TB, but what was the mechanism? Drug treatment was not the explanation since people weren't being treated; clearly other factors were involved. Medical care is certainly a major part of modern tuberculosis control programs but the eradication of this infection from a community requires a great deal more than effective drugs (Figure 3.3).

Acute rheumatic fever and rheumatic heart disease were the most common causes of death for Canadian children in 1900 (English, 1999). One hundred years later, the disease has almost disappeared even though the causative agent, group A streptococcus (GAS), can still be found in the throats of 5–10 percent of children after a 10-day course of antibiotics (Pichichero et al., 1999). Antibiotics did not cause the decline in rheumatic fever because the bacterial cause still exists. Decreasing bacterial virulence is also not an explanation because GAS remains a common cause of invasive bacterial disease at all ages (Davies et al., 1996); other mechanisms are obviously involved. Similarly, the death rate from whooping cough (pertussis) fell from 1,400 per million in 1860 to 100 per million in 1950 when effective vaccination was introduced. Over the same period, the death rate from measles fell from 1,200 per million down to 10 per million in the absence of any specific medical treatment.

People just seemed to get steadily stronger over the last century. There has to be a rational explanation, but just what is it? Now that infectious diseases are less important causes of mortality (at least until the HIV epidemic), it could be argued that medical treatment has a much greater part to play in the health of modern societies. Deaths from cancer, atherosclerosis, and other diseases of an aging population might not be governed by the same variables as infectious diseases

Figure 3.4: Longitudinal study of social class and mortality

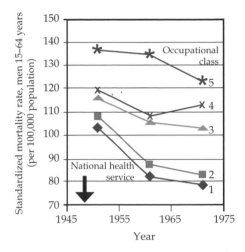

Changes in the adult male mortality rate, classified by occupational class, for the 20 years following the establishment of the National Health Service in Britain. Occupational class 1 (professional) to occupational class 5 (labourer).

Source: Black et al. (1982)

so all that money might finally be making a measurable change in modern life expectancy. However, the available data would argue against this.

The Black Report (Black, 1982) studied mortality rates in five defined socio-economic classes among the British population; complete data stretched back to 1911. Predictably, the data showed clear mortality differences between the social classes, but the important point revealed by the longitudinal study was that those mortality gradients remained constant with time (Figure 3.4). There was no change in the social class health gradient after the introduction of free health care for all with the introduction of the National Health Service (in fact, gradients worsened slightly). If medical care had a strong population health effect, then the poor's increased access to health care should have reduced the mortality gradient between classes, but it did not. The conclusion can only be that health care is probably not a major determinant of mortality rate.

Mackenbach et al. (1990) looked at studies of disease outcome in conditions that should be completely treatable with modern medical care (such as acute appendicitis). Even when medical care ought to have had the dominant effect, these studies showed that outcomes were more heavily influenced by socio-economic factors rather than medical treatment. In a review article that depended on well-informed estimates rather than measurements, Bunker et al. (1994) concluded that modern medicine (including screening tests, medical treatment, and immunization) explained only about 20 percent of the observed improvement in American life expectancy. Finally, there have been several doctors' strikes in various countries. Studies of mortality rates during these strikes are available, particularly for two strikes in Israel (Siegel-Itzkovitch, 2000; Steinherz, 1984). On both occasions, observed mortality rates actually improved during the strike, then worsened when the doctors started working again.

The average person living in a modern Canadian city probably does not think much about why he or she did not catch cholera, typhoid, or smallpox during the working day even though all those diseases were common in Canada in the early parts of the 20th century. The health of a population is largely determined by economic and social variables; medical care is in the difficult position of simply trying to tidy up the mess when something goes wrong. It cannot do much to improve population health, but it does stop it from getting worse.

A perfect example is given by the effect of contaminated water on population health in the prosperous town of Walkerton in Ontario, Canada. Widespread fecal contamination of the town's water supply made hundreds sick and seven died (Ali, 2004). Medical care certainly saved the lives of many infected individuals, but the provision of clean water would have avoided the problem altogether.

THE EFFECT OF SOCIAL INEQUALITY ON POPULATION HEALTH

So far, the combination of money and basic needs (plus a little help from medical care) has dragged our hypothetical population out of the Middle Ages. They are now well into the 20th century with a life expectancy around 60–70 years and per capita income of US $5,000 to $10,000. What are the variables that now determine whether they can slowly add more than a decade to this total and reach Japan, Sweden, and Australia up near the top of the list?

One thing is certain; the three variables we have examined so far are not the full story. For example, Americans and Portuguese have almost exactly the same life expectancy at birth (77.71 years versus 77.53 years), yet America's GDP per capita is over twice that of Portugal ($41,800 versus $18,400). Clearly, above a certain level, more money does not necessarily buy more health.

Similarly, most of the points on the flat part of the health-wealth curve represent wealthy OECD countries. They have all provided basic health needs for their populations for decades and, with the exception of the U.S., all have some form of national insurance to ensure easy access to health care for the poor. Despite this, life expectancy still varies greatly both within and between these countries. It is time to search for other variables influencing the health of wealthy populations.

Two early British studies helped to give some insight into the problem of health inequalities among wealthy countries. The Black Report (Black et al., 1982), released by the Thatcher government in 1980, confirmed what Chadwick had shown over 100 years earlier — there are large differences in mortality between different socio-economic classes in Britain. The report was controversial at the time because its observations and recommendations were well to the left of prevailing political opinion. The report is crammed with statistical data and is still well worth reading.

Figure 3.5 shows an example of the differences between child mortality rates

Figure 3.5: Three age-standardized childhood mortality rates plotted by social class

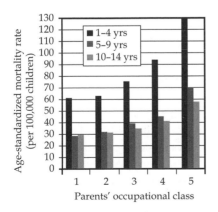

Occupational class 1 (professional) to occupational class 5 (labourer)

Source: Black et al. (1982)

for different social classes measured in Britain, but this finding is present in all countries. A significant socio-economic mortality gradient is a universal finding. It affects all age groups and is present in every country studied (Leon et al., 1992; Wilkins et al., 1990). One of the extraordinary findings is that this mortality difference persisted from the first data measurements in 1921 (Wilkinson, 1989). Even though the basic causes of mortality changed greatly over this time period (from tuberculosis to atherosclerosis), social class mortality gradients persisted. As mentioned earlier, there was also no change in the mortality gradient even after the introduction of free health care for all.

These points need emphasizing. When tuberculosis was common, it killed the poor more than the rich even though all levels of society were exposed to the bacillus. Later in the century, when cancer and atherosclerosis took tuberculosis's place, the rich still did far better than the poor. The only plausible explanation is that some factor associated closely with social hierarchies is bad for health. Even though this factor is expressed in terms of disease mortality, it seems to be independent of the type of disease and it also appears to be unaffected by medical care. No matter what type of disease is prevalent, its burden will always fall more heavily upon the poor.

It is not difficult to imagine that there is a mortality difference between the richest and the very poorest people in a given country. However, many subsequent studies have shown that mortality gradients exist within each of the broadly defined social classes. In fact, it looks as if human societies can be broken down into smaller and smaller levels, each with its own mortality gradient. Sergeants, on average, are not as healthy as majors, who in turn are not as healthy as generals. Poverty is not sufficient to explain these differences.

Marmot et al. (1978; 1991) limited the number of variables by studying mortality gradients within a single industry. They chose the British civil service where clearly defined occupational grades were used as an approximation of social class. They found that coronary heart disease mortality varied greatly between these civil service grades. Men in the lowest category had a three times higher mortality rate when compared to administrators in the highest grade. Differences in blood pressure, smoking rates, and cholesterol levels also differed significantly between the grades, but these explained only a small proportion of the observed difference in mortality rates. Clearly, other causes were operating.

Members of all these grades had sufficient money to meet basic needs so poverty was not an issue. Attention turned to the stress and lack of control associated with lower social position. Another well-known study in Alameda County, California, offered some clues (Berkman & Syme, 1979). The study showed that complex social interactions can have a significant effect on health. People without social ties had significantly higher mortality rates compared to those who had broad social interactions. There was also a significant gender difference. Marriage was more beneficial for men while contacts with friends, relatives, and membership in community groups was more important for women.

A joint study of Japanese men living in Japan, Hawaii, and California (Marmot et al., 1975) showed that as Japanese men lost their traditional contact with Japanese

society, there was an increasing mortality from coronary heart disease moving from Japan to California. This mortality gradient existed even after controlling for risk factors such as cholesterol, blood pressure, and smoking. In fact, although men in Japan smoked heavily, their rate of smoking-related diseases was relatively low. Something about traditional ties offers a health protection.

British civil servants are not the only primates with strict rules governing social behaviour. Studies of baboons, both in the wild and captivity, show that low-status animals suffer the greatest stress and mortality (Sapolsky, 1993). Captive Vervet monkeys examined after death have been shown to have multiple gastric ulcers, bite marks, and other injuries that probably all reflected their lower position in the local social hierarchy of the troop.

While it is clear that social and cultural environments have an impact upon health, human societies are so complex that it is difficult to identify the principal variables affecting population health. Concepts such as "social cohesion" or "social capital" are useful descriptive terms for the strength of cultural interactions, but they are difficult things to measure (Blane et al., 1996). More importantly, although they can be understood as determinants of health, they cannot be easily applied to a given society. Aid projects can provide clean water or immunizations, but how do you go about improving health variables such as social cohesion in any country, let alone a grindingly poor developing world population (Government of Canada, 2006)?

It is becoming increasingly apparent that the physiological effects of chronic social stress are major determinants of health in humans. The stress induced by the chronic deprivation of poverty is easy to understand, but it seems that even when someone has enough money, being at the bottom of the local pecking order is still enough to induce harmful physiological results.

Adverse effects on the immune system and the endocrine system have received particular attention as possible final common pathways linking stress to increased mortality (both in animals and humans) (Cohen et al., 1996), but it is, perhaps, the common feeling of lacking control over one's own destiny that starts the harmful stress response rolling. The final result is a mortality gradient that exists for almost every disease in every social category regardless of other personal risk behaviours.

Another source of stress that has attracted considerable research interest is the degree of income distribution within a country (Wilkinson, 1996). Being poor is bad enough, but being poor in a country where others are very rich appears to be a factor that exacerbates the effects of poverty on health. Rodgers (1979) was the first to show a relationship between life expectancy and income distribution. Numerous other studies have supported this original work both between countries and within countries (Kawachi et al., 1997). In a large study, Kaplan et al. (1996) also showed a clear relationship between income distribution and mortality within the 50 states of the United States.

As discussed earlier in this chapter, the major determinants of population health are clearly defined. Communities lacking access to water, peace, shelter, and food will obviously suffer from poor health. However, once these basic needs are met, there are still clear measurable differences among the health of outwardly similar populations. Clearly, there are other, less obvious factors determining health in more prosperous communities. Although the story is complex, a picture is slowly emerging. Inequalities in social position, lack of cultural and social cohesion, plus the added strain of unequal income distribution have all been shown to be correlated with life expectancy. It is at least a plausible explanation that the final common pathways linking these variables to health are the adverse physiological effects of stress.

■ SUMMARY

No matter what methods are used, the basic aim of any aid project is to improve the health of people living in poor regions. Clearly, before trying to improve population health, it is important to know which variables actually determine population health. This is not as obvious as it sounds — the aid industry has a history of following treatment trends that subsequently prove to have had little benefit (particularly for the rural poor). A clear understanding of health determinants prevents money from being wasted on initiatives that are unlikely to have widespread advantages.

For example, in the early years of the aid industry, too much emphasis was placed on curative medical treatment as the first response to widespread ill health. It took over 20 years before it was finally agreed at the 1978 Alma Ata meeting that far greater benefits could be gained for a given aid budget if the basic determinants of health are attended to first. Obviously, these include clean water, sanitation, housing, nutrition, and peace. Health care is surprisingly far down the list of cost-effective strategies.

Once the basic needs for existence are met, a wide range of less tangible factors appear. Humans are complex creatures; once their social conditions have improved beyond the level of bare survival, it is unlikely that the determinants of their health are going to be simple. Humans need to love and be loved. They need stable, peaceful societies and close social ties with family and friends. They need to feel they have control over their professional lives and, above all, they need to feel that there is a sense of equity and fairness within their society.

When these features are in place, a society can reach the final goal of population health — this is when mortality gradients no longer exist between social classes and the poorest in a country have the same mortality as the rich. When this happens, life expectancy for that country is probably as high as it is going to get. Some countries, such as Sweden, are close to this point, but it will be a long time before the majority of the world is anywhere near such a goal.

RESOURCES

References

Ali, S. (2004). "A socio-ecological autopsy of the E. coli 0157:H7 outbreak in Walkerton, Ontario, Canada." *Social Science and Medicine, 58*, 2601–2612.

American civil war homepage. (n.d.). Retrieved from sunsite.utk.edu/civil-war.

Ben Hamida, A., et al. (2005). "Health transition in Tunisia over the past 50 years." *East Mediterranean Health Journal, 11*, 181–181

Berkman, L., & Syme, L. (1979). "Social networks, host resistance and mortality: A nine-year follow-up study of Alameda County residents." *American Journal of Epidemiology, 109*, 186–204.

Black, D., et al. (1982). *Inequalities in health: The Black Report.* London: Penguin.

Blane, D., et al. (1996). *Health and social organization: Towards a health policy for the 21st century.* London: Routledge.

British Columbia Lottery Corporation. (n.d.). *Scratch and Win odds.* Retrieved from www.bclc.com/cm/scratchandwin/odds.htm.

Bunker, J., et al. (1994). "Improving health: Measuring effects of medical care." *Millbank Quarterly, 72*, 225–258.

Central Intelligence Agency. (2006). *The world factbook.* Retrieved from www.cia.gov/cia/publications/factbook/index.html

Clark, D., & Quizilbash, M. (2005). *Core poverty, basic capabilities and vagueness: An application to the South African context* (Global Poverty Research Group working paper no. 26). Retrieved from www.gprg.org/pubs/workingpapers/pdfs/gprg-wps-026.pdf.

Cohen, S., et al. (1996). "Health psychology: Psychological factors and physical disease from the perspective of human psycho-neuro-immunology." *Annual Review of Psychology, 47*, 113–142.

Cule, J., & Porter, R. (2000). *The timetable of medicine: An illustrated chronology of the history of medicine from pre-history to present times.* New York: Black Dog and Leventhal.

Davies, H., et al. (1996). "Invasive group A streptococcal infections in Ontario, Canada." *New England Journal of Medicine, 335*, 547–554.

Diez Roux, A. (2001). "Neighbourhood of residence and incidence of coronary heart disease." *New England Journal of Medicine, 345*, 99–106.

Doyal, L., & Gough, I. (1991). *A theory of human need.* London: MacMillan Press.

English, P. (1999). *Rheumatic fever in America and Britain: A biological, epidemiological, and medical history*. New Brunswick: Rutgers University Press.

Evans, R., Barer, M., & Marmor, T. (Eds.). (1994). *Why are some people healthy and others not?* New York: Aldine de Gruyter.

Frederick Law Olmsted, founder of landscape architecture. (n.d.). Retrieved from www.fredericklawolmsted.com.

Government of Canada. (2006). *Social capital as a public policy tool*. Retrieved from policyresearch.gc.ca/page.asp?pagenm=rp_sc_index.

Illich, I. (1976). *Limits to medicine: Medical nemesis, the expropriation of health*. London: Marion Boyers Publishers.

Kaplan, G., et al. (1996). "Income inequality and mortality in the United States." *British Medical Journal, 312*, 999–1003.

Kawachi, I., et al. (1997). "Social capital, income inequality and mortality." *American Journal of Public Health, 87*, 1491–1498.

Leon, D., et al. (1992). "Social class differences in infant mortality in Sweden: A comparison with England and Wales." *British Medical Journal, 305*, 687–691.

Lynch, J., et al. (2001). "Income inequality, the psychosocial environment and health: Comparisons of wealthy nations." *Lancet, 358*, 194–200.

Mackenbach, J., et al. (1990). "'Avoidable' mortality and health services: A review of aggregate data studies." *Journal of Epidemiology and Community Health, 44*, 106–111.

Marmot, M., et al. (1975). "Epidemiological studies of coronary heart disease and stroke in Japanese men living in Japan, Hawaii, and California." *American Journal of Epidemiology, 102*, 514–525.

Marmot, M., et al. (1978). "Employment grade and coronary heart disease in British civil servants." *Journal of Epidemiology and Community Health, 32*, 244–249.

Marmot, M., et al. (1991). "Health inequalities among British civil servants: The Whitehall II Study." *Lancet, 337*, 1387–1393.

Maslow, A. (1943). "A theory of human motivation." *Psychological Review, 50*, 370–396.

Mckeown, T. (1979). *The role of medicine: Dream, mirage, or nemesis?* Oxford: Basil Blackwell.

Peterson, R. (1995). "Insects, disease, and military history: The Napoleonic campaigns and historical perception." *American Entomologist, 41*, 147–160.

Pichichero, M., et al. (1999). "Incidence of streptococcal carriers in private pediatric practice." *Archives of Pediatric and Adolescent Medicine, 153*, 624–628.

Porter, D., & Porter, R. (1990). "The ghost of Edwin Chadwick." *British Medical Journal, 31*, 252.

Raphael, D. (Ed.). (2004). *Social determinants of health: Canadian perspectives*. Toronto: Canadian Scholars' Press.

Relman, A. (1988). "Assessment and accountability: The third revolution in medical care." *New England Journal of Medicine, 319*, 1220–1222.

Renbourn, E. (1957). "The history of the flannel binder and cholera belt." *Medical History, 1*, 211–225.

Rodgers, G. (1979). "Income and inequality as determinants of mortality: An international cross-section analysis." *Population Studies, 33*, 343–351.

Roos, N. (1992). "A close look at physicians' hospitalization style: The disturbing lack of logic in medical practice." *Health Services Research, 27*, 3861–3874.

Sapolsky, R. (1993). "Endocrinology alfresco: Psycho-endocrine studies of wild baboons." *Recent Progress in Hormone Research, 48*, 437–468.

Sen, A. (1983). *Poverty and famines: An essay on entitlement and deprivation*. Oxford: Oxford University Press.

Siegel-Itzkovitch, J. (2000). "Doctors' strike in Israel may be good for health." *British Medical Journal, 320*, 1561.

Soprintendenza archeologica di Pompei. (n.d.). Retrieved from www.pompeiisites.org.

Steinherz, R. (1984). "Death rates and the 1983 doctors' strike in Israel." *Lancet, 8368*, 107.

UN Millennium Development Goals. Retrieved from www.un.org/millenniumgoals.

UNICEF. (2006). *Child mortality statistical database*. Retrieved from www.childinfo.org/areas/childmortality/u5data.php

Wilkins, R., et al. (1990). "Changes in mortality by income in urban Canada from 1971 to 1986." *Statistics Canada Health Reports, 1*, 137–174.

Wilkinson, R. (1989). "Class mortality differentials, income distribution and trends in poverty 1921–1981." *Journal of Social Policy, 18*, 307–335.

Wilkinson, R. (1996). *Unhealthy societies: The afflictions of inequality*. London: Routledge.

Recommended Reading

Evans, R., Barer, N., & Marmor, T. (1994). *Why are some people healthy and others not?* New York: Aldine De Gruyter.

Farmer, P. (2001). *Infection and inequalities: The modern plagues*. Berkeley and Los Angeles: University of California Press.

Keating, D., & Hertzman, C. (Eds.). (1999). *Developmental health and the wealth of nations: Social, biological, and educational dynamics*. New York: The Guildford Press.

Marmot, M., & Wilkinson, R. (1999). *Social determinants of health*. Oxford: Oxford University Press.

McKeown, T. (1979). *The role of medicine: Dream, mirage, or nemesis?* Oxford: Basil Blackwell.

Raphael, D. (2004). *Social determinants of health: Canadian perspectives*. Toronto: Canadian Scholars' Press.

Sen, A. (1983). *Poverty and famines: An essay on entitlement and deprivation*. Oxford: Oxford University Press.

Wilkinson, R. (1996). *Unhealthy societies: The affliction of inequality*. London: Routledge.

Chapter 4

Poverty and Developing World Debt

It's the same the whole world over,
It's the poor wot get the blame
It's the rich wot get the pleasure,
Ain't it all a bloomin' shame?
—Anon

OBJECTIVES
Upon completion of this chapter, you should be able to

- appreciate the full range of the adverse effects that poverty imposes on a population
- understand the controversies surrounding the definition and measurement of poverty
- understand the unfair historical origins of the current developing world debt
- understand the magnitude of the debt and the adverse health effects that result from excessive debt repayments

Poverty and its inevitable companions, inequity and ill health, form a brutal trio that terrorizes the developing world. You will never find one of them without the other two being close by. Any study of international health must be based on a good understanding of poverty (and its big brother, developing world debt). Although debt and poverty can be analyzed separately, in practice, they are closely interrelated. The statistics regarding the extent and magnitude of poverty are staggering. At a time when people in developed countries live lives of great prosperity, as many as a billion people in developing regions live lives of absolute poverty, existing on less than US $1 each day. The enormous debt burden carried by many developing countries is not the only cause of this poverty, but it is a significant contributory factor. This chapter will concentrate upon the definition, measurement, and adverse effects of both poverty and the developing world's debt. Later sections, particularly chapters 8 and 11, will examine ways to reduce these common problems.

DEVELOPING WORLD POVERTY

Introduction to Poverty

> Poverty is the worst form of violence.
> —Mahatma Gandhi

The concept of providing universal prosperity for everyone (or at least the provision of some basic minimal standards) is a surprisingly recent one. Scientific and agricultural advances in the decades following World War II have led to unprecedented prosperity for a growing number of people. It is easy to forget that life for generations as recent as our grandparents was, in many cases, a great deal harder than standards we have today (Geremek, 1997).

When Queen Victoria took the throne in mid-19th-century England, the Industrial Revolution was a century old, but the benefits of steam power and agricultural innovation were very slow to come. Standards of waste disposal and clean water supply in Victorian London were little better than those in Rome 2,000 years previously. The richest maintained a health advantage secondary to improved nutrition and housing, but everyone was exposed to infectious diseases that are nowadays associated with only the poorest of developing countries. Tuberculosis remained the most common single cause of death until well into the 20th century. Water-borne diseases of poverty, such as cholera and typhoid, were a constant threat — in fact, Queen Victoria's husband died of typhoid he contracted while living in a palace!

The dreadful working conditions associated with the early factories (Blake's "dark satanic mills") produced a widespread underclass of working poor. Their lives are well documented in the works of Dickens, particularly the book *Oliver Twist*. These conditions were not confined to England but were widespread throughout the slowly developing countries of Europe and the squalid ghettos of America such as the Bowery and Hell's Kitchen in 19th-century New York. Clearly, there is nothing new about poverty. Ever since humans started to gather in cities, life for the majority of the agricultural based population was harsh:

> No arts; no letters; no society; and which is worse of all, continual fear and danger of violent death; and the life of man, solitary, poor, nasty, brutish, and short.
> —Thomas Hobbes, *Leviathan*, 1651

Progress in poverty eradication has been slow. Despite recent advances, huge numbers of people still live lives of wretched deprivation. Depending on who is counting, roughly 15–20 percent of the world's current population is below any conceivably acceptable minimum of daily life (Chen & Ravallion, 2004; Sala-i-Martin, 2002). From a percentage point of view, we have probably improved but, in terms of hard numbers, economic advances have still not trickled down to between 750 million and 1,000 million people.

As societies grew more sophisticated, it became clear that some support for the poor was necessary. These included

Established laws governing family
allowance and a national health service
date back to the first part of 20th
century when the social implications of
widespread poverty were slowly taken
more seriously. For example, during
World War I, the British government
was shocked to discover that significant
numbers of the country's young men were
so unhealthy from tuberculosis, chronic
malnutrition, and rheumatic fever that
they were not even fit enough to serve as
cannon fodder.

This raises the issue of the health risks of
poverty. The health effects of poverty begin
to operate from the moment of conception
and continue throughout the child's
life (Feuerstein, 1997). The intrauterine
environment of an undernourished mother
who may have conceived too young or too
often—combined with a crowded home
environment without clean water, a family
broken up by migrant labour or social
stress, a school without desks or qualified
teachers, a neighbourhood ruled by gangs
of violent youths, and an economy offering

Figure 4.1: Relationship between income and
educational level in five Latin American countries

workhouses, almshouses, care for
abandoned children, and the destitute
(Geremek, 1997). Distinction was made
between the worthy poor, who were
prepared to work for charity, and the
unworthy poor, who were not (and also
faced severe penalties). The first British
Poor Laws date back to Elizabeth I's reign
in the 16th century. They were prompted
by the results of a severe economic decline.
Those laws were slowly improved with
time and Britain serves as an example of
the beneficial impact of social legislation
on population health.

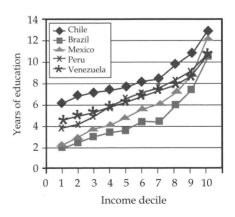

Source: Inter-American Development Bank (1999)

few poorly paid jobs—all limit the health and standard of living of children.

Whatever measure is used, the health of a poor society lags far behind that of a rich one. Even given the social advances in European countries, there is still, to this day, a marked difference in infant mortality rates between the poorest segments of society and the richest. In Scotland, the infant mortality rate in social class five is almost twice as high as that of social class one. In developing countries around the world, decreasing income is always closely related with poorer education (Figure 4.1) and increased child mortality (Figure 4.2). As discussed in Chapter 3, this relationship also holds for wealthy countries, but the differences are much less marked.

Ill health is poverty's first companion and the second is inequity; poverty rarely exists by itself. Low wages and lack of adequate land resources are usually associated with many other problems such as insecurity of employment, illiteracy, bad housing, large families, and exploitation (Sen, 1981). Poverty is

not an ennobling experience. Its effects on morale and expectations, combined with exhaustion from overwork and poor nutrition, imprison people within an endless cycle of hopelessness.

The connection between poverty and inequity greatly complicates the task facing those who wish to alleviate poverty. Until that underlying injustice is addressed, the chance of finding a long-term solution to the associated poverty is small. For example, attributing the health problems of Aboriginal Canadians living on the Labrador coast simply to lack of money, without considering the complex underlying social problems, would not be a firm foundation for a long-term solution. Whether you are a humanitarian who wants universal health and prosperity or a manufacturer who wants a bigger market for gadgets, it does not matter. Poverty eradication and all the benefits that stem from it must form the basis of your plan (Sachs, 2005).

Table 4.1: A moment of Zen

Figure 4.2: Relationship between income and child mortality in six developing countries

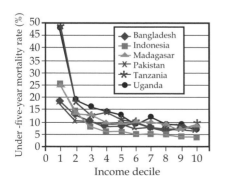

Source: Bonilla-Chacin & Hammer (1999)

Total 1999 European union agricultural subsidy for dairy cattle: US$17.3 billion per year (47.4 million per day)	~
Number of European union cattle in 1999: 22 million Average agricultural subsidy paid to a European farmer with a cow: **US $2 per day**	Average income in 1999 for 76 percent of all people living in Sub-Saharan Africa: **US $2 per day**
Source: Fowler (2002)	Source: Chen & Ravallion (2004)

Definitions of Poverty

The Western concept of poverty (having little or no money) is not sufficient to deal with the broader reality of poverty in developing countries. Lack of money is obviously a part of the picture, but poverty is also closely tied to social and cultural isolation, lack of education, marginalization, and absence of power. This does not mean that all poor people are vulnerable to ill health (any more than all vulnerable people are poor). If economically poor agricultural communities are given access to the basics of good health—such as schooling, immunization, clean water, and sanitation—then it is possible for them to lead a generally healthy life without access to a high income (Sen, 1999). This has clearly been demonstrated in many parts of the world, such as the Indian province of Kerala where population health measures are far better than per capita income figures would suggest (Michael & Singh, 2003).

The issue of poverty is too complex to resolve itself into a single descriptive phrase. The common definition, "Poverty is the state in which an individual or family has to spend more than 80 percent of their income on food," does not apply in many situations. How can the health and income of a hunter-gatherer Amerindian family from Venezuela be compared with those of an unemployed Inuit family living in the North of Canada? Clearly, before tackling the problem, it is necessary to understand there are different types of poverty that may require different solutions. In her 1997 book, *Poverty and Health*, Dr. Feuerstein recognizes several forms of poverty:

- *Economic poverty:* This is caused by low productivity and a poor resource base. It is reflected in low income, poor nutrition, and, inevitably, poor health. Typical examples include rural small holders dependent on adequate rainfall. The children have nothing to inherit and few opportunities, so they are caught in an unending cycle of poverty.

Figure 4.3: Unexpected disasters can produce sudden local poverty in affected areas. This Sri Lankan family survived the Boxing Day tsunami, but they lost their house and all their possessions. The father's fishing boat was destroyed so they also lost their family income. (Photographer Dr. W. Grut, Rose Charities.)

- *Instant and temporary poverty* (Figure 4.3): Sudden hazards such as earthquakes, drought, and war can cause instant poverty in an area. Some of these may be relatively short-lived. Conditions may improve following a permanent ceasefire or improved rains. In the same way, migration and population pressures may overwhelm an area that was previously reasonably prosperous, forming an "overcrowding" poverty.
- The *"new poor"*: Imposed national austerity measures or high inflation may precipitate poverty in significant percentage of a country by eroding income and savings.
- *Hidden poverty:* Examples include retirees living on small pensions who might have adequate shelter and food but lack sufficient extra income to heat their houses or seek health care.
- *Absolute poverty:* Such people are deprived of all the elements necessary to make an adequately healthy life. They lack access to safe water, shelter, or security and are more likely to remain in that condition despite improvements in society brought on by better market conditions.

The debate surrounding the definition and measurement of poverty is not simply sterile academic argument since the approach used to reduce poverty depends greatly on the definitions and explanations used to define that poverty. The World Bank, not surprisingly, has concentrated on a financial definition of poverty. It first defined the US $1 per day measurement in its 1990 *World Development Report* (Chen & Ravallion, 2004). This measurement has also been adopted as the scoring system for the Millennium Development Organization's goal of poverty attainment. Enthusiasts of "a dollar a day" analysis took the approach that emphasizng economic growth was the quickest way to reduce poverty. They implemented various economic recovery programs and structural adjustment policies that tended to concentrate on economic growth at the expense of the poor. The widely acknowledged failure of these structural adjustment programs was, in fact, one of the principal catalysts for debate in this area (SAP Review International Network, 2004).

The United Nations Development Programme (UNDP) took a very different attitude toward poverty assessment and alleviation. They adopted a much broader approach to poverty measurement based on the Nobel Prize-winning work of the Indian economist, Amartya Sen, and the leadership of the late Pakistani economist, Mahbub ul Haq. They developed a more comprehensive composite scoring system for classifying and measuring poverty based on variables such as health, education, gender equality, and political freedom. The best-known examples are the Human Development Index and Human Poverty Index. Results are published in the UNDP's annual *Human Development Report*.

This more inclusive approach to poverty has led to economic plans that actually consider the needs of the poor. Even the World Bank has been influenced by this movement. The World Bank and the International Monetary Fund prescribed economic interventions that no longer require the abolition of price supports on essential foods or steep reductions in spending on health and education. The World Bank's Enhanced Heavily Indebted Poor Countries initiative (EHIPC) is now based on "poverty reduction strategy papers (PRSPs)" that are developed by the target country. This process has to include that country's poor at every level of planning. The process is still relatively new, but early experience has been cautiously optimistic (Verheul & Rowson, 2001).

Measurement of Poverty

> We are not concerned with the very poor. They are unthinkable, and only to be approached by the statistician or the poet.
>
> — E.M. Forster, *Howard's End*, 1910

Seebohm Rowntree (1910) was the first to try and establish a baseline poverty level (called "poverty lines") by studying the cost of a minimum diet for a family of six for one week in the city of York. After adding a factor for shelter, clothing, fuel, and others, he arrived at a poverty line of 26 shillings per week for a family of six. At that time, 10 percent of the population fell below this line. There are, of course, many other ways to measure poverty. Each has its own methodological problems and errors. Simply put, there is no single measure (or definition) of poverty that reliably tracks the magnitude and extent of poverty around the world. The best approach is obviously to use different scores and measures in order to get a general idea of the progress of poverty reduction.

The commonly used measures of poverty are either based on a family's income or on an assessment of some of the services that money can buy (summarized in Table 4.2). Income is used for purchases such as food, education, and health

Table 4.2: Aspects of well-being and their associated poverty indicators

Variables	Income	Purchases	Results of Purchases	Final Sense of Well-Being	Inequality or Relative Poverty
Examples	• Wages • Crops • Welfare	• Food • Education • Fuel • Transport • Shelter • Clothes • Health care	• Nutrition levels • Health • Safe childbirth • Diplomas, degrees • Employment • Safety	Degree of: • Safety • Vulnerability • Powerlessness • Happiness • Optimism or hope	• Range from richest to poorest • Distribution of wealth
Poverty Indicators	• US $1/day • US $2/day • GDP/capita • Percentage of standardized national income	• Cost of basic needs analysis • Standard bag of groceries plus non-food essentials	• Composite scores of health, nutrition, longevity, and education • Human Development Index (HDI) and Human Poverty Index (HPI)	• Open-ended discussions and subjective reports • Gender Empowerment Measure (GEM)	• Lorenz Curve • Gini Index • Poverty Gap Index

care. Those purchases have results in terms of health, nutrition, education, and employment. The final outcome is hopefully healthy, educated children who become productive, happy adults. There are reasonable correlations between these variables, but they are far from perfect. For example, it is possible to have money and yet still be poor in some other aspect of your life such as nutrition, health, or happiness (Sen, 1999).

It is important to have an understanding of some of the common poverty indices because there are wide differences and considerable arguments between proponents of the various methods. Each of the measures has methodological problems, potential errors, and plenty of critics (Deaton, 2003). Sometimes, the criticism of various poverty measures can almost become an end in itself (Saith, 2005, October 22). There is a danger of forgetting that no matter what technique is used, vast numbers of people live lives of wretchedness on a daily basis.

The main measurement methods come under the following headings:

- *Income analysis (Sillers, 2002):* The US $1 per day measure, popularized by the World Bank, seems superficially simple but is based on some complex calculations that are open to considerable error. The basic income data is based on household surveys from a wide range of developed countries. Even this first step alone is open to criticism. Trying to compare different surveys done at different times in different countries is associated with many problems. The second step involves deriving a standard

currency so that the different incomes can be universally compared. Detailed price surveys around the world are analyzed in order to construct a purchasing power parity (PPP) dollar. This international dollar is intended to provide the same purchasing power within each country as a US dollar provides in the United States. It differs greatly from the official quoted exchange rate. Average per capita income in 2000 for India was $450. When placed in international PPP dollars, the average income rises to $2,340. To complicate matters further, the reference US dollar has changed recently from 1985 prices to 1993 prices so the measure is now US $1.08 per day. Critics of the technique exist on either side. Reddy and Pogge (2005) claim the method greatly underestimates the number of poor in the world because of a range of potential measurement errors. Sala-i-Martin (2002) and others claim it overestimates the number of poor in the world. Unfortunately, although this second group uses the US $1 per day terminology, they arrive at the calculation using different techniques — grounds for yet another disagreement! The US $1 per day measure is the most widely used poverty line despite its potential errors. Since it is also the official "scorecard" for the Millennium Development Goals, it will likely retain that position.
- *Consumption analysis (Deaton, 2003):* Household surveys of income have been shown to be less

Figure 4.4: These two boys, playing next to an open sewer, live in the Dharavi slum in the middle of Mumbai. They don't have many advantages, but, by any measure of poverty, they are better off than the ubiquitous pavement dwellers found throughout the city. (Photographer Stephanie Colvey; courtesy IDRC Photo Library.)

reliable than questions based on family consumption. The numbers appear to be more representative of a family's economic position over time. Inevitably, different countries have very different views on what constitutes a bare minimum when it comes to food and non-food essentials. Poverty lines based on these calculations are higher in richer countries because of greater expectations. Comparison between countries consequently can become difficult. The non-food component of the budget also varies between countries. Indonesia sets its poverty line assuming that families spend 80 percent of their income on food, while the United States assumes that it represents only a third of a poor household's expenditure. Significant variations also exist within a country. Bare minimum requirements vary significantly between rural and urban settings such that different rural and urban poverty lines may be set for a single country.

- *Multidimensional analysis (*United Nations Development Programme, *2005):* The UNDP in particular has concentrated on measuring compound indicators of poverty. The Human Development Index (HDI) consists of three components (education, average income, life expectancy at birth). The Human Poverty Index (HPI), although calculated slightly differently for developed and developing countries, is based on scores of longevity, educational achievement, and various measures of a decent standard of living, such as access to clean water.
- *Sense of well-being (*Salmen, 1995): Conventional measures of poverty are commonly based on the information obtained in household surveys. This more or less quantifiable information is used to provide various indices

of poverty. Some researchers have taken this process further to include more detailed questions about the lives of the poor. The results have given greater insight into the adverse effects of poverty. In particular, there is now a better understanding of the sense of vulnerability, fear, and powerlessness that are constant companions of the poor.

- *Relative poverty indicators* (Sillers, 2002): Absolute poverty measures such as US $1 per day can be used to calculate the population fraction or absolute numbers of people living below a minimum poverty line (Ravallion, 2003). More recently, there has been increased interest in measures of relative poverty (the distribution of income throughout a population from richest to poorest). The methods used are technical—distribution is often plotted using Lorenz lines and the degree of maldistribution is summarized in a single number, the Gini coefficient (United Nations Development Programme, 2003).

Magnitude and Trends of Poverty

In September 2000, the General Assembly of the United Nations agreed upon eight broad goals (UN Millennium Development Goals, n.d.) aimed at producing sustainable, social, and economic progress in the developing world. The first goal and its main target was to halve between 1990 and 2015, the proportion of people whose income is less than US $1 per day. An important feature of the MDGs is the fact that they have measurable and quantifiable end results. The end point chosen to measure poverty is the World Bank's US $1 per day measure. Using World Bank figures, the proportion of the world living on US $1 per day or less has fallen from 33 percent in 1981 (roughly 1.5 billion people at that time) to 18 percent in 2001 (roughly 1.1 billion people) (Chen & Ravallion, 2004). Using these same figures, 27.9 percent were living in poverty in 1990. Halving this rate gives a goal of 14 percent by 2015. As mentioned above, there are numerous debates concerning these figures. Some claim the poverty goal has already been reached (Bhalla, 2002; Sala-i-Martin, 2002) while others claim there has been no progress at all (Reddy & Pogge, 2005). No matter what the absolute numbers are, some comfort can be taken from the fact that most observers do at least agree on the fact that poverty is reducing (Figure 4.5).

Unfortunately, poverty is not reducing evenly in different regions. Expressed as an average for the whole world, it is probably safe to say that things are slowly

Figure 4.5: Relationship between income and child mortality in six developing countries

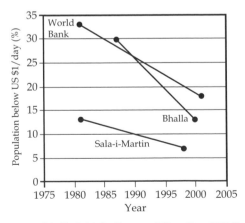

Source: Bhalla (2002); Chen and Ravallion (2004); Sala-i-Martin (2002)

improving but, on close observation, most of the progress has occurred in China and India. Studies of poverty in Africa, Latin America, and Central Asia show little or no gains over the past decade. Poverty has even increased in Sub-Saharan Africa (Chen & Ravallion, 2004) (Figure 4.6). Given the current improvements in total numbers, it is likely that the Millennium Development Goals on nutrition will be met by 2015. However, unless there are urgent changes, some areas will be left out of that significant achievement.

■ DEVELOPING WORLD DEBT

Introduction to Developing World Debt

The history of Third World debt is the history of a massive siphoning off by international finance of resources of the most deprived people. This process is designed to perpetuate itself, thanks to a diabolic mechanism whereby debt replicates itself on an ever greater scale, a

Figure 4.6: Progress in poverty reduction using the US $1 per day standard in different areas of the world over the last 25 years

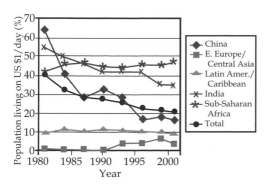

Source: Chen & Ravallion (2004)

cycle that can be broken only by canceling the debt.
—E.H. Guisse, UN Subcommittee on Human Rights

Debt is the worst poverty.
—Thomas Fuller, *Gnomologia,*1732

For almost 50 years, the poorest countries of the world have been consistently held back by the need to service an ever increasing financial debt owned by the richest countries in the world. At a time in world history of unprecedented prosperity, the foot dragging and failure of these wealthy countries to forgive the debt of the poorest nations is nothing less than an outrage (Millet & Toussaint, 2005).

The recent decision by G8 countries to forgive $40 billion of debt to the world's 18 poorest countries, combined with the doubling of aid to Africa, is certainly a good start, but much more needs to be done. Tony Blair and George Bush might be claiming credit for the developed world's change of heart toward debt, but it is quite likely that growing popular pressure from events such as the Live 8 Concert let them know that their voters were expecting changes (Live 8, n.d.).

Inevitably, popular stars such as Bono and Geldof have been criticized for using this event for personal gain. Whatever their motivations might be, most would agree that the enthusiastic support by millions of potential voters in the world's richest countries probably had a major influence on the G8 leaders. One thing is certain, popular stars understand popular culture. They have an enormous fan base and ready access to news media. The subsequent debate can become heated with hurriedly prepared facts recycled through newspapers, television, and radio. In the middle of all this, the details about debt relief can be elusive.

Origins of Developing World Debt

The Third World debt developed in three distinct stages. The first was the arbitrary imposition of debt onto newly independent countries by their previous colonial masters. The second was a decade of indiscriminate lending of vast amounts of money to poorly prepared dictatorships — money that was subsequently wasted and pillaged by corrupt governments with little or no benefits for their people. The third was a period of financial collapse secondary to rising interest rates and falling commodity prices. If recent developments become sustainable, then we hopefully now enter a fourth stage of debt forgiveness.

Phase One: Colonial Legacy (Third world debt, 2004)

> If a despotic power incurs a debt not for
> the needs or in the interest of the State
> but to strengthen its despotic regime …
> this debt is odious for the populations of
> all the State.
> — Alexander Sack, 1927

African countries did not ask to be colonized. The benefits of colonization were, at best, questionable so the ultimate imposition of debt by the departing colonizers should not automatically be accepted as being legal. A good example was Indonesia. After accumulating a debt caused by fighting Indonesian rebels for four years, the Dutch government left and then imposed that debt upon the very people they were fighting. In a similar way, the enforcement of apartheid in South Africa cost a great deal of money.

The government of the day had to raise money to pay for a large military machine. Its purpose was simply to enforce an evil system onto the mass of the country's population. It is difficult to see why the new South African government should pay the debts accumulated in their subjugation, which is rather like asking President Mandela to pay rent for his 25 years in jail!

There is plenty of historical precedent to justify refusal of unfair colonial loans. Ironically, the earliest example involved Britain and the United States. Following its war with Britain, the newly independent United States flatly refused to accept any imposed debt from its recent colonial master. Many other examples exist:

- *1867:* Mexico, under President Juarez, repudiated debts imposed by the departing Hapsburg Empire.
- *1898:* The US supported Cuba in its fight against the imposition of debts by Spain. This was the first application of the principal of "odious debt" since it was claimed that the debts were enforced by arms without consent of the people of Cuba.
- *1923:* Loans by the Royal Bank of Canada to President Tinoco of Costa Rica were deemed illegal since they were used to oppress the independence movement.
- *1925:* Newly independent Syria, Lebanon, and Iraq were deemed completely new countries and were not automatically responsible for any of the debt incurred by the Ottoman Empire.
- *1983:* The Vienna Convention on Succession of State Property

agreed that "debt of the predecessor state does not automatically pass to the newly independent state." Unfortunately, this convention has not been ratified by enough countries to carry sufficient legal weight.

• *Present day:* Division of Yugoslavia's debts among the new post-conflict republics is a topic of considerable current debate.

Succession to the liabilities of the colonial masters should be approached legally rather than financially since many feel that those original debts were illegal (Adams, 1991). By 1960, arbitrary impositions of colonial debt had already risen to $59 billion. The situation was worsened by the exorbitant 14 percent interest rate. Before these new countries had time to organize themselves, the debt burden rapidly grew out of control.

Phase Two: Indiscriminate Lending

The second cause of the debt mainly occurred during the decade of the 1970s. In this period, a rapid increase in oil prices produced huge profits for countries in the Middle East. This money was deposited with northern banks for investment. At that time, Europe was in a recession because of the effects of high energy costs, so banks looked to the developing world for their customers. It is just possible that some of the banks and consultants from the World Bank actually persuaded themselves they were doing a useful service. Borrowing cheap money seemed, at least on the surface, to be a good way of generating much needed development.

Unfortunately, it was an absolute disaster. It is easy to blame tyrants and corrupt officials, but it would be more sensible to blame the people who made the loans. Why was money given to people like Mobutu or Marcos? Even without the benefit of hindsight, it is obvious that money given to such people would be ultimately wasted and probably never repaid. Sometimes, money was lent simply out of greed. The 2004 book, *Confessions of an Economic Hit Man*, by John Perkins (Perkins, 2006) gives some insight into this area. Loan salesmen competed with each other to see who could give the largest loans to the biggest tyrants. Their approach was utterly callous; they were indifferent to the purposes that these loans were put. At other times, aid was used as a tool of foreign policy. The competition between East and West to extend their influence in the developing world meant that tyrannical regimes were supported with aid by the West simply because they were seen as the only feasible alternate to Soviet, Chinese, Cuban, or communist alternatives.

With this background, it is hardly surprising that much of the money was stolen for personal use or wasted on grandiose projects where failure was inevitable. There is no shortage of examples to choose:

• A huge proportion of the borrowed money — as high as 20 percent, according to the International Peace Research Institute in Stockholm (Hess, 1989) — was spent on arms. These arms allowed dictators to terrorize and murder their own people. Increased weapons sales, boosted profits for the major players in the arms industry (US, Britain, USSR, France, Germany), who also just happened to be major aid donors.

- The list of four-lane highways to nowhere or steel-and-glass presidential palaces is endless, but perhaps the greatest of all these fiascos is the Bataan nuclear power station. President Marcos of the Philippines was allowed to build a nuclear power station with international loans. Westinghouse (of Three Mile Island fame) was the chosen contractor. What could possibly go wrong? Charges of corruption are the least of the project's problems. Westinghouse admitted paying a friend of President Marcos a 5 percent commission in order to confirm selection. Westinghouse admits paying this $17.3 million simply as a "commission." No one knows how many millions more were looted by Marcos. Unfortunately, it gets worse. The project was eventually completed at a total of $2,200 million. It was built near Mount Pinatubo in a volcanic region. It was so close to a major geological fault line that it was considered unsafe to operate. The plant has never been used and it sits shiny and useless as a wonderful monument to the endless corruption of that decade of loans.
- Money wasted on useless projects is one problem; outright corruption and theft is another. Again, evidence is easy to find since the largest examples were so flagrant that they prompted major enquiries. Of the US $64 billion raised by Iraqi oil sales, an estimated US $10 billion was skimmed off by Saddam Hussein

(*Independent Inquiry into the Oil for Food Programme*, n.d.). Of the US and IMF loans given to bail out Russia's economy in the 1990s, US $10 billion found its way to various people, including Boris Yeltsin's daughter and the Russian Mafia! How much more sits in bank accounts of ex-dictators such as Baby Doc Duvalier?

- The prevailing morality of the Cold War allowed normal ethical considerations to be ignored. Loans were made for political and strategic reasons to a range of dictators and thugs, many of whom would have been jailed under the laws of the lending country; the final list is a long one. Loans were made to support Brazil's military dictatorship, Mobutu's tyranny over the Congo, and the corruption of Marcos in the Philippines. Private banks even lent money to apartheid South Africa in the face of global opposition to that regime.

The term "odious debt" can be applied to much of the money that was loaned to developing countries during the 1970s. This is a legal concept developed by Alexander Sack, a professor of international law (*Odious debts*, n.d.). He summarized it as follows:

If a despotic power incurs a debt not for the needs or in the interest of the State, but to strengthen its despotic regime, to repress the population that fights against it, etc., this debt is odious for the population of all the State. This debt is not an obligation for the nation; it is a regime's debt, a personal debt of the power that has incurred it, consequently it falls with the fall of this power.

In cases where the borrowed money was used against the people's interest, with the knowledge of creditors, the creditors can be said to have colluded in a hostile act against the people so the creditors should not legitimately expect to get their money back.

Phase Three: Financial Collapse

Unfortunately, around 1980, a number of events conspired to make a bad situation much worse. The era of Thatcher and Reagan coincided with rising interest rates and consequent increases in the size of debt repayments. In May 1981, the US prime rate peaked at 21.5 percent (Figure 4.7). Most of the loans were borrowed at variable rates, given at 1 percent above the US prime; such interest rates could be considered usurious. In addition, the rising oil price (Figure 4.8) that had

Figure 4.7: Prime US lending rate in the years leading up to the developing world financial crisis of the 1980s

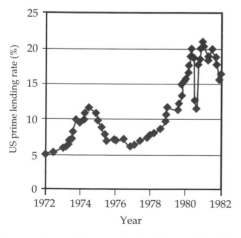

Source: Federal Reserve Bank of St. Louis (n.d.)

Figure 4.8: World oil price in 2004 US $ during the years leading up to the developing world financial crisis of the 1980s

Source: WTRG Economics (n.d.)

originally caused the decade of easy loans, now triggered a global recession with a sharp drop in the commodity prices that supported much of the exports of developing countries. The combination of falling commodity prices and rising interest rates meant that developing countries found themselves having to pay more with diminishing revenues.

Private banks in the North refused grants for new loans until previous ones had been repaid. The end of the Cold War and collapse of the Soviet state also had adverse effects. Financial support was reduced to many developing countries in the Soviet sphere. It was no longer pragmatic and necessary to support unjust tyrants against the threat of a communist "menace." Consequently, supplies of easy loans to a range of countries dried up (Patterson, 1997). The economies of developing countries were often shaped largely by one or two commodities, either mineral or agricultural. They did not have the flexibility to respond to the new economic demands, so failure of debt repayment became inevitable.

In August 1982, Mexico became the first country to threaten default on its debt repayments. Obviously, other countries were not far behind. Financial crises followed in Thailand, Russia, Brazil, Turkey, and Argentina to mention some of the major ones. For insight into this chaotic period, two books are essential reading: *Globalization and Its Discontents* (Stiglitz, 2002) and *The Chastening* (Blustein, 2003). The IMF and leading industrialized capitalist countries put up new loans and enabled the private banks to recover their initial outlay and avoid a series of international bank failures. Donor and multilateral institutions (particularly IMF and WB) used their financial leverage to impose financial adjustment policies upon the debtors. Those refusing to implement adjustments ran the risk of being cut off from any further credit. The subject of structural adjustment policies (SAPs) and subsequent developments will be discussed in detail later.

Magnitude of Developing World Debt

Under the influence of the factors noted above, the debt of the developing world rose steadily from $59 billion in 1960 to its current level around $2.5 trillion in 2004 (Figure 4.9)! The original loans have all been paid off, but thanks to the wonders of compound interest, the total keeps on rising. The principal international financial institutions involved with this extraordinary process are summarized in Table 4.3.

Until about 1990, the bulk of the debt was either in the form of official government loans (bilateral aid), loans from international financial institutions such as the IMF and the World Bank,

Figure 4.9: Developing world debt, by region, over the last decade

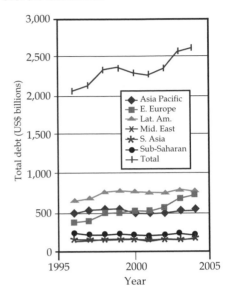

Source: International Finance Team (2005)

Table 4.3: International trade and the groups that run it

Bretton Woods Institutes
World Trade Organization (WTO/GATT)
International Monetary Fund (IMF)
World Bank
Group of Eight (G8)
Asia-Pacific Economic Cooperation (APEC)
Organisation for Economic Co-operation and
   Development (OECD)
Development Assistance Committee (DAC)
Paris Club
Non-Paris Club
London Club

Follow links in the References section for further information.

and long-term loans from large private banks. After the financial crisis of the late 1980s and early 1990s, the types of loan changed (Figure 4.10). Many developing countries could no longer get access to long-term bank loans so they substituted bond financing in place of bank credit. In order to finance trade, some are also able to obtain higher interest short-term loans. The mix of credit varies widely depending on the country. Private banks will extend credit to countries holding strategic assets such as gold or oil. Consequently, the debts of Venezuela and South Africa are weighted toward private lenders. However, many poor countries can obtain loans only from the IMF and the World Bank so these institutions hold the bulk of loans from the poorest countries. In 2003, the average division of the debt was:

- *Multilateral (international financial institutions):* $500 billion (20 percent)
- *Bilateral (countries or state guaranteed loans):* $500 billion (20 percent)

- *Private (large private banks):* $1,500 billion (60 percent)

As the debt grew, the debt repayments also rose. In 2003, developing countries transferred $370 billion to banking institutions in the richest countries. It is worth remembering that in that same year, those rich countries very generously gave $69 billion back in overseas aid. This paradox is not widely appreciated. As Figure 4.11 shows, despite all the "generosity" of rich countries, it should be remembered that the developing world gives five times more money to us than we give to them!

Because of many factors (including steadily falling commodity prices), it has become increasingly difficult for poor countries to pay even the minimum interest on their loans. Some have fallen so far behind that they will never be able to rid themselves of debt. As an example, Canada's external debt is roughly 10 percent of its GNP. In the most heavily

Figure 4.10: Principal types of developing world external debt over the last 35 years

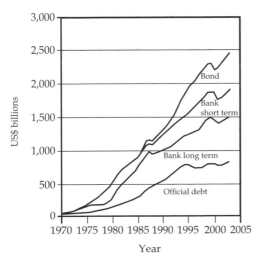

Source: International Finance Team (2005)

Figure 4.11: Total aid given to developing countries and total debt repayments received from developing countries over the last 25 years

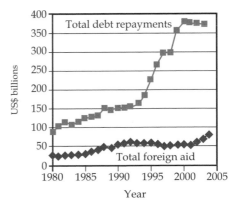

Source: Organisation for Economic Co-operation and Development (2004, n.d.)

indebted countries, the debt is 200–300 percent of the GNP. In such countries, debt payments consume 30–40 percent of the available budget. Typically, health spending for a developing country is 10 percent or less.

A complex picture finally boils down to this: In order for poor countries to pay the interest on what were frequently unjust loans, they have to divert funds away from the poorest segments of their societies. The result is a direct link between debt, increasing poverty, and unnecessary illness and death. Estimates vary, but the cumulative result of the debt has undoubtedly adversely affected the lives of millions upon millions of blameless children.

Developing World Debt Relief

It is important that the fundamental unfairness — even illegality — of the developing world debt is widely understood. This debt should certainly be forgiven not out of a sense of charity but simply because the debt had little to do with the people who are currently left with the bill. The first phase of the debt is probably illegal under the doctrine of non-succession of state debts. Many of the debts formed in the second phase should also be unenforceable under the principle of odious debt. In addition, the subsequent years of economic and social changes forced on developing countries by the IMF and the World Bank have clearly been shown to be harmful. The developing world debt and its contribution to an increasing spiral of poverty and misery is, to a large extent, the fault of the richest nations. Again, there is plenty of precedent to support the concept of low-interest loans and limited condition debt relief (Addison et al., 2004):

- Following World War II, the United States allowed Britain (a current G8 member) to repay loans at well below market rates in order to help the country recover from the effects of war.
- Britain's debt to the US following World War I was forgiven in the 1930s. Britain simply stopped paying! Jubilee estimates that the present value of that debt plus interest is US $14 billion.
- In 1953, European countries jointly agreed to grant Germany (a current G8 country) significant debt relief in order to help that country's struggling post-war economy. The process of international co-operation that resulted in that decision would serve as a useful model for a new approach to developing world debt.
- In 2000, major credit banks wiped out more than half of Russia's $31.8 billion debt. They also awarded a seven-year grace period free from repayment. This process did not include the lengthy six-year HIPC qualification process that is forced upon the poorest countries even though Russia had defaulted on previous payments. Russia is a member of the G8 group that helps to dictate the HIPC conditions.

The move to forgive some part of the enormous developing world debt (rather than simply rescheduling it on better terms) has been a very recent development. It is a long story that is fully covered in Chapter 11, but it can be briefly covered here. Not much more than 10 years ago, a feeling developed at many levels of society that developing world debt was a pressing problem that needed urgent attention. The first clear response was the introduction of the Heavily Indebted Poor Countries initiative (HIPC) by the World Bank in the mid-1990s. Although the first version was heavily criticized, it was at least a step in the right direction (World Bank, n.d.).

At a popular level, several large debt activist organizations formed, the best known of which was probably the United Kingdom Jubilee debt campaign (Jubilee Debt Campaign). In response to worldwide campaigns, plus support from several high-profile public figures, politicians in developed countries soon got the message. Debt relief found its way to the head of the Group of Eight (G8) annual agenda by 2000. This extraordinarily successful popular campaign reached its peak at the 2005 G8 meeting at Gleneagles when the leaders of the world's richest countries agreed to a substantial debt forgiveness strategy. This is not, by any means, the end of developing world indebtedness, but a valuable process has been started that will have benefits for the very poorest countries in the world.

■ SUMMARY

Along with malnutrition and social injustice, poverty is one of the major contributory factors to the widespread ill health found in developing countries. A detailed knowledge of all three is essential for any serious study of international health. No matter what measuring system is used, at a personal level, enormous numbers of people around the world live lives of absolute discomfort, eking out a precarious and uncomfortable existence on less than US $1 a day. Depending on the measurement methodology, 15–20 percent of the world's population lives without access to even the most basic essentials of a dignified and decent life.

In common with malnutrition, poverty is a subject that is commonly oversimplified. In practice, poverty is a complex issue with different presentations, different measurement techniques, and, of course, different solutions according to the underlying contributory causes. Comparing the degrees of poverty between a family of pavement dwellers in Calcutta and a rural indigenous family in Guatemala is a difficult challenge. Various measures of well-being have been devised that allow such comparisons to be made, ranging from the World Bank's US $1 per day calculation to complex composite measures of living standards. Although it is essential to have a unified measure of world poverty for monitoring and planning purposes, it is important to remember that all are open to significant measurement error.

At a national level, the debt accumulated by a great number of developing countries diverts limited resources away from essential services such as health and education, ultimately worsening life for the poorest in that country. Some countries are so heavily indebted that they have no possibility of ever paying off their debt. Recent moves toward debt cancellation for the most heavily indebted countries are long overdue, particularly when it is considered that much of that debt was imposed under very unfair conditions.

These are exciting times — there is a very real sense that progress is being made against world poverty. The recent significant move toward debt relief for the poorest countries, combined with measurable improvements in personal poverty levels, make it likely that the Millennium Development Goal for poverty will be met by 2015. However, it should still be remembered that average measures of global poverty are heavily influenced by

rapid improvements in China and India. There are still areas of the world where only very slow progress has been made against poverty — the problem is far from over.

RESOURCES

References

Adams, P. (1991). *Odious debts: Loose lending, corruption, and the Third World.* London: Earthscan.

Addison, T., et al. (2004). *Debt relief for poor countries.* New York: Palgrave MacMillan.

Asia-Pacific Economic Cooperation. (n.d.). Retrieved from www.apec.org.

Bhalla, S. (2002). *Imagine there's no country: Poverty inequality and growth in the era of globalization.* Washington: Institute for International Economics. Retrieved from poverty2.forumone.com/files/12978_Surjit_Bhalla_Two_Policy_Briefs.doc

Blustein, P. (2003). *The chastening: Inside the crisis that rocked the global financial system and humbled the IMF.* New York: Public Affairs.

Bonilla-Chacin, M., & Hammer, J. (1999). *Life and death among the poorest.* Washington: World Bank.

Bretton Woods Institutes. (n.d.). Retrieved from www.brettonwoodsproject.org.

Chen, S., & Ravallion, M. (2004). *How have the world's poorest fared since the early 1980s?* (World Bank Development Research Group working paper no. 3341). Retrieved from www.worldbank.org.

Deaton, A. (2003). *Measuring poverty in a growing world (or measuring growth in a poor world)* (National Bureau of Economic Research working paper no. 9822). Retrieved from www.nber.org/papers/w9822.

Federal Reserve Bank of St. Louis. (n.d.). *Economic data.* Retrieved from research.stlouisfed.org/fred2/.

Feuerstein, M. (1997). *Poverty and health: Reaping a richer harvest.* London: MacMillan.

Fowler, P., et al. (2002). *Milking the CAP: How Europe's dairy regime is devastating livelihoods in the developing world* (Oxfam briefing paper no. 34). Retrieved from www.oxfam.org/en/files/pp021210_Dairy.pdf

Geremek, B. (1997). *Poverty: A history.* Oxford: Basil Blackwell.

Group of Eight. (n.d.). Retrieved from www.g8.gc.ca.

Hess, P. (1989). "Force ratios, arms imports, and foreign aid receipts in the developing nations." *Journal of Peace Research, 26,* 399–412.

Independent Inquiry into the Oil for Food Programme. (n.d.) Retrieved from www.iic-offp.org.

Inter-American Development Bank. (1999). *Facing up to inequality in Latin America: Economic and social progress in Latin America 1998–1999.* Washington: Author.

International Finance Team. (2005). *Global development finance: Mobilizing finance and managing vulnerability.* Washington: World Bank.

Jubilee Debt Campaign. (n.d.). Retrieved from www.jubileedebtcampaign.org.uk.

Live 8. (n.d.). Retrieved from www.live8live.com.

Michael, E., & Singh, B. (2003). "Mixed signals from Kerala's improving health status." *Journal of the Royal Society of Health, 123,* 33–38.

Millet, D., & Toussaint, E. (2005). *Who owes who? Fifty questions about the world debt.* London: Zed Books.

O'Connor, J., & Robertson, E. (2003). *John Maynard Keynes, 1883–1946.* Retrieved from www-history.mcs.st-and.ac.uk/Mathematicians/Keynes.html.

Odious debts. (n.d.). Retrieved from www.odiousdebts.org.

Organisation for Economic Co-operation and Development. (2004). *External debt statistics 1998–2002*. Paris: Author.

Organisation for Economic Co-operation and Development. (n.d.). *Aid from DAC members*. Retrieved from www.oecd.org/dac/stats/dac.

Paris Club. (n.d.). Retrieved from www.clubdeparis.org.

Patterson, R. (1997). *Foreign aid after the cold war: The dynamics of multipolar economic competition*. Trenton: Africa World Press.

Perkins, J. (2004). *Confessions of an economic hit man*. San Francisco: Berrett-Koehler.

Ravallion, M. (2003). "The debate on globalization, poverty and inequality: Why measurement matters." *International Affairs, 79*, 739–754. Retrieved from www.chathamhouse.org.uk/pdf/int_affairs/inta_334.pdf.

Reddy, S., & Pogge, T. (2005). *How not to count the poor*. Retrieved from www.columbia.edu/~sr793/count.pdf.

Rowntree, B. (1910). *Poverty: A study of town life*. London: MacMillan.

Sachs, J. (2005). *The end of poverty: Economic possibilities for our time*. New York: Penguin Press.

Saith, A. (2005, October 22). "Poverty lines versus the poor: Method versus meaning." *Economic and Political Weekly*, 4601–4610. Retrieved from www.epw.org.in/showArticles.php?root=2005&leaf=10&filename=9272&filetype=pdf.

Sala-i-Martin, X. (2002). *The world distribution of income estimated from individual country distributions* (National Bureau of Economic Research working paper no. 8933). Retrieved from www.nber.org/papers/w8933.

Salmen, L. (1995). *Participatory poverty assessment: Incorporating poor people's perspectives into poverty assessment work* (World Bank Social Development Paper II). Washington: World Bank.

SAP Review International Network. (2004). *Structural adjustment: The SAPRI report. The policy roots of economic crisis, poverty, and inequality*. London: Zed Books.

Sen, A. (1981). *Poverty and famines: An essay on entitlement and deprivation*. Oxford: Clarendon Press.

Sen, A. (1999). *Development as freedom*. Oxford: Basil Blackwell.

Sillers, D. (2002). *National and international poverty lines: An overview*. Retrieved from www.povertyfrontiers.org/ev_en.php?ID=1075_201&ID2=DO_TOPIC.

Stiglitz, J. (2002). *Globalization and its discontents*. New York: W.W. Norton.

Third world debt: A continuing legacy of colonialism (South Centre Bulletin 85). (2004). Retrieved from www.southcentre.org/info/southbulletin/bulletin85/bulletin85.htm

UN Millennium Development Goals. (n.d.). Retrieved from www.un.org/millenniumgoals.

United Nations Development Programme. (2003). *Human development indicators*. Retrieved from hdr.undp.org/reports/global/2003/indicator/indic_126_1_1.html.

United Nations Development Programme. (2005). *Human development report 2005*. Retrieved from hdr.undp.org/reports/.

Verheul, E., & Rowson, M. (2001). "Poverty reduction strategy papers." *British Medical Journal, 323*, 120–121.

World Bank. (n.d.). *HIPC debt initiative*. Retrieved from www.worldbank.org/hipc/about/hipcbr/hipcbr.htm.

World Trade Organization. (n.d.). Retrieved from www.wto.org.

WTRG Economics. (n.d.). *Oil price history and analysis*. Retrieved from www.wtrg.com/prices.htm.

Recommended Reading
Bhalla, S. (2002). *Imagine there's no country: Poverty inequality and growth in the era of globalization*. Washington: Institute for International Economics.

Easterly, W. (2002). *The elusive quest for growth: Economists' adventures and misadventures in the tropics*. Cambridge: MIT Press.

Feuerstein, M. (1997). *Poverty and health: Reaping a richer harvest*. London: MacMillan.

Millet, D., & Toussaint, E. (2005). *Who owes who? Fifty questions about world debt*. London: Zed Books.

Perkins, J. (2004). *Confessions of an economic hit man*. San Francisco: Berrett-Koehler Inc.

Sachs, J. (2005). *The end of poverty: Economic possibilities for our time*. New York: Penguin Press.

Sen, A. (1981). *Poverty and famines: An essay on entitlement and deprivation*. Oxford: Clarendon Press.

Sen, A. (1999). *Development as freedom*. Oxford: Basil Blackwell.

Chapter 5

Malnutrition

The day that hunger is eradicated from the earth,
there will be the greatest spiritual explosion the world has ever known.
Humanity cannot imagine the joy that will burst into the world
on the day of that great revolution.
— Federico Garcia Lorca

OBJECTIVES
After completing this chapter, you should be able to

- understand the underlying causes, adverse effects, and prevalence of malnutrition in developing countries
- understand the different types of malnutrition ranging from micronutrient to macronutrient deficiencies
- understand the main methods used to measure and define malnutrition in population studies
- appreciate the common causes of inadequate food supply and understand the contribution of food aid to food security in developing countries

---

Malnutrition (and the more insidious effects of micronutrient deficiencies) blunt the development of affected children and also reduce their ability to survive serious infections such as measles and gastroenteritis. Along with poverty, malnutrition traps populations in a neverending cycle of ill health and poor productivity. Malnutrition is not simply due to lack of food any more than poverty is simply due to lack of money. Both are the end result of numerous interlocking social factors such as lack of education, social inequity, and chronic recurrent infections (Haddad & Ross, 2004). The effects of malnutrition are so widespread that estimating the mortality and morbidity directly attributable to malnutrition is very difficult.

As large famines have become less common, chronic moderate malnutrition has become much more important than acute severe starvation. Nowadays, malnutrition's main effect is to increase greatly the mortality from common childhood illnesses. Case mortality rates in measles, whooping cough, and bronchiolitis are many times higher among malnourished children. A detailed examination of malnutrition is essential for any understanding of population health.

INTRODUCTION TO MALNUTRITION

Basics of Malnutrition

If a choice must be made, free school meals are more important for the health of poor children than immunization programmes and both are more effective than hospital beds. (McKeown, 1980:1)

When you boil it right down, humans are basically mobile chemical factories. Using simple ingredients available at any supermarket, our cellular mechanisms are able to construct and maintain an organism of staggering complexity. The end results of all our efforts are carbon dioxide and water. Obviously, the fuel that keeps this process running is food (Gibney, Vorster, & Kok, 2002). Since every cell in the body requires nutritional support, it is not surprising that a shortage of food can produce disease in every organ of the body. The adverse effects of malnutrition are particularly important during rapid growth periods such as childhood and pregnancy.

After initial processing within the gut, food is absorbed into the bloodstream and lymphatic vessels before entering a huge variety of chemical pathways. Every

Table 5.1: A moment of Zen

Total US box office receipts for *Pirates of the Caribbean—the Curse of the Black Pearl*: **US $300 million**	Estimated annual human and economic costs of smallpox infection in 1967, the year the eradication program was announced: 1.5–2.0 million deaths/year US $1.0–1.5 billion/ year Total cost of smallpox eradication program, 1967–1979 (total, not annual): **US $300 million**
Source: Internet Movie Database (2006)	Source: Glynn & Glynn (2004)

organ has metabolic capacity, but the most important one is the liver. Larger molecules are slowly broken down in an oxidative process catalyzed by enzymes, which are often dependent on cofactors and minerals present in minute quantities in the diet. We capture the energy released during this chemical breakdown and use it to power our cellular processes. Small molecules are either stored for future use or used for immediate repair and growth. Apart from solid waste residues, our only final products are heat, carbon dioxide, and water.

Along with water and oxygen, our principal nutritional components are protein, carbohydrate, and fat (United States Department of Agriculture, 2006). These are the macronutrients on which the system principally depends. Under normal circumstances, our energy is largely derived from carbohydrates and, to a lesser extent, from fats. The body usually uses protein for building purposes, but it can turn protein into energy if required. A diet deficient in all three macronutrients is often referred to as protein-energy malnutrition. The body can compensate for some dietary deficiencies by manufacturing chemicals that it needs, but essential fats and amino acids cannot be made so they have to be present in the diet in varying amounts.

In addition to the macronutrients, a complete diet also contains dozens of micronutrients (United States Department of Agriculture, 2006). Most cannot be made, so they must be present in the diet. Micronutrients include essential vitamins such as thiamin, vitamin C, and folic acid, plus minerals such as iron, calcium, and iodine. Deficiencies of any one of these essential factors can result in serious disease even though the remainder of the diet is adequate. Examples include scurvy (vitamin C), anemia (iron), and hypothyroidism (iodine). Collectively, these are referred to as micronutrient deficiencies.

Causes of Malnutrition

> When I gave food to the poor, they called me a saint. When I asked why the poor were hungry, they called me a communist.
>
> — Dom Helde Camara

The newcomer to malnutrition might have the initial impression that malnutrition is simply a case of not having enough food. Although this is certainly part of the problem, it is nowhere near the full story. It is important not to oversimplify the problem of malnutrition because the underlying causes have to be understood fully before any practical sustainable treatment program can be implemented. Provision of food is obviously necessary for a starving population, but enabling that population to feed itself in a sustainable manner requires a complex program with multiple interventions based on a clear understanding of the local factors behind the malnutrition.

Obtaining adequate nutrition for adults is hard enough in a developing country, but the problem is considerably more complicated where children are concerned. Their total dependence upon caregivers means that an endless list of problems at the level of family and society can individually and collectively reduce the chances that a spoonful of food is ultimately going to be put in that child's mouth (Smith & Haddad, 1999). There are three broad groups of requirements that must be met before a population's children can have reliable nutrition (UNICEF, 1998):

- The first, of course, is adequate access to a reliable source of nutritious food (this is commonly referred to as household food security).
- There must be adequate care provided for children and women.
- There must be a safe and healthy society with adequate access to preventive care advice and basic health services.

Under each of these headings, there are numerous subheadings (Box 5.1). The possible range of complex interrelationships is almost endless. Each community will have its own set of contributory factors that underlines the

---

Box 5.1: Major determinants of a child's nutrition

Child:
- Recurrent illness (measles, gastroenteritis, whooping cough, TB, HIV)
- Chronic intestinal parasites

Mother/family/household:
- Lack of hygiene (food and water handling and storage)
- Poor child care (lack of stimulation, baby left in care of children)
- Inadequate support for mother (overwork, poor access to medical care, education, family planning, and child care advice)
- Family disruption (migrant labour, war, HIV, both parents working)
- Inadequate housing (access to clean water, sanitation, waste disposal)
- Inadequate food (lack of breast-feeding, poorly prepared infant formula feeds, poor-quality and irregular supply of food)

Society:
- Discrimination against women and girls (maldistribution of food within the household, unequal access to education and employment)
- Poor social support for the poor
- Violence, social chaos, war

---

absolute necessity for basing long-term intervention programs upon careful local research.

The following is only a short list of the possible variables that can ultimately affect the child's nutrition (Latham, 1997):

- *The child:* Chronic intestinal parasites and infections such as whooping cough, gastroenteritis, and measles can all contribute to a worsening spiral of malnutrition and an increased susceptibility to further infection. Recurrent attacks of gastroenteritis are a particularly

common precipitating cause of malnutrition in a child with marginal nutrition. Unfortunately, HIV infection and tuberculosis are both becoming increasingly common secondary factors.

- *The mother:* The combination of maternal poverty and lack of education leads to inadequate child-rearing practices. Two small meals a day given by an exhausted mother, with child care subsequently left in the hands of young siblings, is not a scenario that allows normal growth to occur. Lack of basic knowledge about breast-feeding, contraception, and nutritional requirements of children all contribute to the problem.

- *The family:* Traditional customs based on a stable extended family are not sufficient to meet the demands of life in an informal peri-urban settlement. Economic necessity that forces both parents to work or the loss of a father due to migrant labour, HIV, or war, places severe strains on disrupted family structures and inevitably results in poor care for the children.

- *The society:* Education for women, laws protecting children, and widespread provision of contraceptive and nutrition education often have low priorities in countries where money for social programs is limited. Traditional presence of gender inequity can also have profound effects on nutrition ranging from the maldistribution of food within the family all the way to limited access to employment and education.

The type of food in a child's diet can add extra complications. The use of high-volume, low-caloric density starch porridges can mean that the child may feel full even though he or she has still not obtained sufficient nutrition. The widespread dependence on a largely vegetarian diet can also be associated with nutritional problems. For example, high phytate levels in some cereal diets can inhibit absorption of calcium to the extent that it contributes to the development of rickets.

Prevalence of Malnutrition

Over the last three decades, the epidemiology of malnutrition has changed considerably. Famines and deaths due solely to starvation are, fortunately, becoming rare in most parts of the world. Nowadays, acute severe starvation has largely been replaced by the more insidious effects of chronic malnutrition (Pelletier et al., 1993). While death due to absolute starvation is now less common, affected children suffer from lifelong physical and developmental impairments that trap them within an endless cycle of poverty, ill health, and poor expectations.

No matter what criteria are used to define nutritional level, it is estimated that about 800 million humans suffer from some form of malnutrition (Food and Agriculture Organization, 2005). Children make up nearly a quarter of that total. At a time when Western countries are facing an epidemic of childhood obesity, many tens of millions of children in developing countries go to bed hungry every night (it should be added that obesity is an increasing problem in some middle-income developing countries). The numbers are too large to comprehend adequately, but 150–200 million children around the world suffer from chronic malnutrition (UNICEF, 2006).

- 150 million are underweight (low weight for their age).
- 67 million are wasted (low weight for their height).
- 175 million are stunted (low height for their age).

Many millions more suffer from micronutrient deficiencies such as vitamin A, iron, and iodine.

Over the last 10–15 years there have been improvements in rates of stunting (Figure 5.1) and underweight (Figure 5.2) in most areas of the world (see later in chapter for definitions), but huge numbers of children still have their ultimate potential limited by recurring

Figure 5.1: Recent trends in prevalence of stunting in different world regions

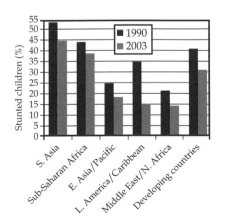

Source: UNICEF (2006)

Figure 5.2: Recent trends in prevalence of underweight children in different world regions

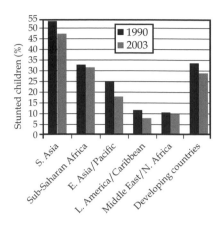

Source: UNICEF (2006)

cycles of illness and poor growth. A child who is moderately malnourished is five times more likely to die from infectious diseases than a well-nourished child, and the risk is twice as high for a severely malnourished child (Pelletier, 1994). The great majority of children who die from a combination of malnutrition and infection are either mildly or moderately undernourished (Pelletier et al., 1995) and often show no abnormal clinical signs other than their size. If height and weight are symmetrically reduced, they can look completely normal.

In many developing countries, a quarter to a third of all children have some degree of malnutrition (de Onis et al., 2000). When working in such countries, it is easy to become habituated to the sight of thin children and to forget the social and health costs associated with their poor diets. "All the kids here are skinny — what does it matter?" It matters a lot.

■ TYPES OF MALNUTRITION

Macronutrient, Protein-Energy Malnutrition (Ashworth et al., 2004)

When the intake of major nutrients (fat, carbohydrate, and protein) persistently falls 10–20 percent below minimal requirements, increasingly obvious changes occur. The final result depends on many other variables, including individual variations and associated infections; children and pregnant women are particularly vulnerable. Although every organ can be affected, the principal effects are covered under the following headings:

Growth (de Onis et al., 1993)

Without fuel, the body simply stops growing. The most obvious and easily measurable result of malnutrition is poor growth. The final result depends on the severity and extent of the malnutrition and also the age of onset. There are three common measurements used to assess growth: height for age, weight for age, and weight for height. Standardized charts allow a child's measurements to be compared to normal population values. The Body Mass Index (BMI) is harder to calculate so is used less commonly in surveys.

Children affected by relatively short-term malnutrition will have a weight that falls well below the mean for their age (underweight), but their height for age may be reasonably well preserved. Consequently, the child will also be well below normal on a chart of weight plotted against height (wasting). Chronic malnutrition reduces all aspects of growth. Weight and height for age will both be well below the mean for age (underweight and stunted), but their weight for height

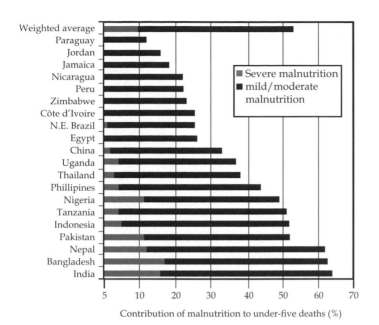

Figure 5.3: Estimated contribution of severe and moderate malnutrition to childhood deaths in 20 developing countries

Source: Pelletier et al. (1995)

may be fairly normal if both are reduced symmetrically.

The most extreme form of wasting and stunting results in two definable clinical conditions called marasmus (typically a very wasted, but symmetrically small child without edema) and kwashiorkor (typically a child with less growth failure, but obvious poor skin and edema). Although both are becoming increasingly uncommon, they still gain a disproportionate amount of attention in the malnutrition literature. Some even use the terms as if they were synonymous with malnutrition, which, of course, they are not. In practical terms, it is best to categorize degrees of malnutrition as mild, moderate, and severe and leave these two diagnoses for medical texts. Hopefully, nutritional advances will one day consign both of them to the history books.

Development (University of the West Indies, 1998)

Unfortunately, malnutrition can have a profound effect on neurological development and subsequent school performance. Early growth and organization of brain cells is dependent on adequate nutrition (before and after birth). Severe starvation at this age can have measurable and irreversible effects on subsequent brain development. Malnutrition in the early school years causes apathy, reduced activity, and lack of curiosity, which will inevitably reduce the child's ability to learn. Once again, the full picture depends on many other factors, particularly the effects of serious illness and associated iodine deficiency.

Immune Response (Keusch, 2003)

It has been known for a long time that severe malnutrition has profound adverse effects upon a child's immune system.

Relatively recent research has shown that mild and moderate malnutrition also pose significant risks to a child's health that are far greater than was previously appreciated. Such underweight or stunted children may, on first glance, look like rather skinny but otherwise fairly healthy youngsters. However, once they are stressed by infectious diseases, their mortality rate is greatly increased.

Of the approximately 10 million children a year who die from the major killers such as respiratory infections, diarrhea, malaria, and measles, it is estimated that the underlying effects of malnutrition were contributing causes to those deaths in 25–50 percent of the cases (Pelletier et al., 1995). Figure 5.3 shows the estimated contribution of malnutrition to child mortality in 20 developing countries. Note especially the low rate of severe malnutrition.

Micronutrient Malnutrition, Iron, Vitamin A, Iodine (Adamson, 2004)

Apart from the three major components of a normal diet, the body also requires dozens of other minerals and vitamins, often in very small amounts. Some of these chemicals are so commonly distributed that deficiency is almost unknown even among people suffering from poor nutrition. Others, such as iron, are often in marginal quantities even in a normal diet so deficiency can be found in any population around the world. It is possible to have micronutrient deficiencies even in the face of an apparently normal diet; consequently, micronutrient deficiency is often referred to as "the hidden hunger." Increasing effort is being put behind international efforts to eradicate micronutrient deficiencies, particularly in iodine, vitamin A, and iron.

Iodine Deficiency (International Council for the Control of Iodine Deficiency Disorders, n.d.)

Roughly a third of the world's population lives in areas where there is little or no iodine in the soil and consequently very little in the diet. Literally, hundreds of millions of people are at risk of iodine deficiency disorder (IDD), particularly in large parts of China. Iodine is an essential factor in thyroid hormone, which, in turn, is an essential factor needed for early brain development. Although some affected children suffer severe developmental delay, the problem is usually more subtle and manifests as poor school performance and lack of energy. Iodine deficiency is the single most common cause of preventable mental retardation and brain damage. For decades, many countries have legislated the addition of iodine either to table salt or cooking oil. Food fortification is effective and very cheap.

Vitamin A Deficiency (International Vitamin A Consultative Group, 2002)

Vitamin A is part of a large family of chemicals called carotenoids, which contribute to the colour of some foods such as carrots and mangos. Vitamin A is widely distributed in a normal diet, but large parts of the developing world are at high risk of deficiency, particularly their pediatric populations. Vitamin A is a cofactor in many important chemical reactions, consequently deficiency causes a wide range of abnormalities, including severe eye disease (xerophthalmia) that can ultimately lead to blindness and increased susceptibility to infections (particularly to measles and diarrheal diseases). It is estimated that 250,000–500,000 children become blind each year because of vitamin A deficiency. The majority of these children live lives of such deprivation that most die from the combined effects of malnutrition and further infections.

Administration of vitamin A at regular immunization visits has been shown to reduce all cause mortality by about 25 percent. The mortality rate for measles is almost halved with the addition of vitamin A, which is also beneficial for gastroenteritis. Since 1997, the WHO has advocated the routine administration of vitamin A at the same time as the child is vaccinated. Many countries now fortify foods such as maize, wheat, and sugar with vitamin A. Fortification is effective and also cheap.

Iron Deficiency (Olivares, 1999)

This is the most common micronutrient deficiency in the world, but appreciation of the adverse effects of iron deficiency in children has been a relatively recent development. Iodine and vitamin A fortification of foods were both widely introduced long before iron fortification was seriously discussed. Children born to iron-deficient mothers, whose breast milk is also low in iron, have only marginal stores at birth to deal with a period of rapid physical and neurological growth. It is estimated that at least half of the developing world's children between six months and two years of age are iron deficient during this critical development period. The worst affected are often found in countries where children are weaned onto a rice porridge low in iron.

Apart from its effect on children, severe iron deficiency anemia reduces the ability of adults to work and greatly increases the risk of childbirth for women. Fortifying infant foods with iron is practised widely in developing countries, but these foods are expensive and may not reach the worst-affected populations. Supplementation with iron-containing tablets and syrups is another approach, but delivering the supplements to the huge numbers of at-risk families is a problem (as is compliance with treatment). Recent research has developed the concept of fortification using a vitamin and mineral preparation (sprinkles) that can be easily added to the child's food (Schauer & Zlotkin, 2003). The problems of distribution and compliance still remain.

DEFINITION AND MEASUREMENT OF MALNUTRITION (use and interpretation of anthropometric indicators of nutritional status, 1986)

Measurement Systems: z-score, Waterlow, Wellcome, Gomez, BMI

Several methods of assessing malnutrition have been proposed, each with its own techniques, measurement errors, and cut-off definitions. Over the last 10 years, there has been a move toward standardization. Although most research is now based on the WHO recommended z-score methodology (Cogill, 2003), this is not universal in the literature so it is necessary to be familiar with the major measurement techniques shown in Table 5.2.

Small errors can make large differences in interpretation, particularly in small children. It is important to remember that any assessment of malnutrition must be based on simple, robust, and portable equipment that yields reproducible, statistically relevant results under what are often difficult conditions. The

Table 5.2: Available methods for assessing malnutrition

Method	Basic Measure	Expressed as	Mild	Moderate	Severe
Road to Health Growth Chart	Weight for age	Percent of median (percentiles also used)		<80% <3rd percentile	<60%
Gomez	Weight for age	Percent of median	75–90% (Grade I)	60–75% (Grade II)	<60% (Grade III)
Wellcome	Weight for age and presence of edema	Percent of median		60–80% no edema	<80% + edema (kwashiorkor); <60% no edema (marasmus)
Mid-upper Arm Circumference	Diameter of mid-upper arm	Centimetres		<12.5 cm	<11 cm
Triceps Skin-fold Thickness	Thickness of triceps skin-fold in millimetres	Percentiles	<3rd percentile for age		
Body Mass Index	Ratio of body weight to surface area	Percentiles	<3rd percentile for age		
Waterlow	Height for age and weight for height	Percent of median	Height for age <90% (stunting); weight for height <80% (wasting)		
WHO Reference	Height for age; weight for age; weight for height	Standard deviations from the median (Z)	−1Z	−2Z	−3Z

following methods are still used, or at least mentioned, in nutrition studies:

- *Road to health charts (de Onis & Yip, 1996):* Originally developed by Professor David Morley in Nigeria in 1970, successors are found in clinics all over the world, often with space to record immunizations. Charts vary so care is necessary before plotting a child and making conclusions.

The WHO's standard chart only has two lines on it: the upper represents the median weight for age for boys while the lower represents the third percentile for girls.

- *Gomez system (Gomez et al., 1956):* This was widely used in the 1960s and 1970s and still is used by some countries. Malnutrition is graded using weight for height measurements.

- *Wellcome classification (Wellcome Trust Working Party, 1970):* This system is falling out of use as severe malnutrition is becoming less common. It is based on weight for age and the presence of edema.
- *Upper arm circumference (Collins, 1996):* The diameter of the upper arm remains relatively constant between one and five years of age so this measurement can be used for rapid screening of large refugee populations, particularly when ages of children are unknown.
- *Skin-fold thickness (Frisancho, 1982):* It is strongly dependent on measurement technique. Small errors alter interpretation. It is occasionally used in long-term nutritional studies, but usually as a measure of obesity.
- *Body Mass Index (BMI) (Ferro-Luzzi et al., 1994):* Weight is expressed as ratio of surface area; calculation is needed. There is no cut-off value; BMI changes with age so newly published WHO tables are required (World Health Organization, 2006). It is more commonly used for obesity research.
- *Waterlow system (Waterlow et al., 1977):* Acute starvation (termed wasting) assessed using weight for height curves. Chronic starvation (termed stunting), assessed using height for age curves. Technique was adopted and developed by the WHO as its recommended method of nutrition assessment.
- *WHO Standard (Bern et al., 1997):* Addition of weight for age (underweight) to Waterlow; all are expressed as z-scores.

Reference Values, Percentiles, Percent of Median, z-Score

Since malnutrition is defined by comparing a child against standard values, the choice of those universal reference values is very important. Since the late 1970s, the WHO has used US growth charts developed by the National Center for Health Statistics (NCHS). They combined two sets of data: one for children under two years based largely on White Americans going back to 1929, and the other on older children from more recent and representative surveys of schoolchildren. Unfortunately, the two curves do not merge.

Validity of the NCHS reference data has been criticized for various reasons, including the age of the data, 24-month disjunction (i.e., the curves don't meet!), poor inclusion of breast-fed infants, narrow racial base, and unrepresentative incidence of obesity (de Onis, 1997). Apart from that, they are fine. The production of updated growth charts has necessarily been a slow process. The WHO multicentred growth reference study (MGRS) was proposed in 1994. After collecting growth data on several thousand children from widely different backgrounds, the updated charts were released in May 2006 (World Health Organization, 2006).

Once a reference has been chosen, the child's measurement must be expressed in relation to that standard. Inevitably, three different methods are used (Table 5.3) (Ge et al., 2001):

- *Percentiles:* The mid-position on any growth chart is referred to as the 50th percentile. It refers to the percentage of children who fall below this level. There is crowding of the lines at the tenth, fifth, and third percentiles so the technique

Table 5.3: Approximate relationship between the three methods used for defining a child's position on a growth chart

Malnutrition	Normal	Mild	Moderate	Severe	Very Severe
Z-Score	0	−1Z	−2Z	−3Z	−4Z
% of Median	100%	90%	80%	70%	60%
Percentile	50	15.8	2.28	0.13	<0.1

is of limited use for classification of underweight children.

- *Percent of the median:* The child's measured value is expressed as a percentage of the median reference value for his or her age—the most common method used in the past.
- *z-score:* The term "z" is shorthand for standard deviation. The child's deviation from the reference mean value is expressed in numbers of standard deviations. Interpretation of a z-score is independent of the child's age or gender and can also be manipulated statistically. It is the method of choice recommended by WHO.

This is not just statistical nitpicking—progress toward the Millennium Development Goal of halving malnutrition is monitored by nutritional surveys, which can be strongly skewed by careless measurements and choice of different methodology. For example, using NCHS/WHO reference tables, the median weight for a 22-month-old girl is 11.55 kg with a standard deviation of 1.22 kg. A girl of this age weighing 8.89 kg can be plotted three ways:

- *Percent of median:* Calculated by (8.89 / 11.55) × 100 = 77 percent. Classified as mild or grade I

malnutrition by Gomez, but as moderate malnutrition using Road to Health and Wellcome criteria. It is unclassified by Waterlow criteria since there are no weight for age norms.

- *Standard deviations below median (z-score):* Calculated by (11.55 − 8.89) / 1.22 = −2.18z. Classified as moderate malnutrition (underweight) using WHO's definition.

- *Percentiles:* Calculation: Below third percentile for age when plotted on standard weight for age NCHS/WHO growth chart. Interpretation is subjective.

FOOD SOURCES

Artificial (Non-breast) Feeding of Infants

Formula feeding is the longest lasting uncontrolled experiment lacking informed consent in the history of medicine.

—Frank Oski, MD, retired editor, *Journal of Pediatrics*

Babies have been successfully raised using formula feeds for many decades. In fact, the great majority of today's baby boomers (well over 50 percent) were fed solely on an infant formula. At first glance, it is difficult to imagine what could be wrong with infant formulas or the vast industry that makes them but, as usual, a closer look reveals a rather more complex story.

In the 18th century, parents who could afford it would often choose a wet nurse. In some cases, the baby was lodged with the nurse and taken back only when the child was weaned. In the 19th century, the practice of using animal milk grew in popularity (called "dry nursing"). Milk from cows, goats, mares, and donkeys was used; donkey milk was considered to be the best option (Apple, 1987). Although there was no knowledge of nutritional science, it was already obvious to 19th-century observers that children who were not breast-fed suffered a much higher mortality. Babies were fed by cup and spoon or with early versions of baby bottles. Until the discovery of the first rubber teat in 1845, nipples were made from soft leather or sponge.

Johann Simon published the first chemical analysis and comparison between cow and human milk in 1838, but this information was not used for development of artificial formulas until the 1860s. At that time, a German chemist, Von Liebig, and a Swiss inventor, Nestlé, both independently developed breast milk substitutes based on cow's milk, wheat, malt, and sugar. Despite its expense, this new approach to infant feeding spread rapidly around the world (Schuman, 2003).

By 1900, there were three available forms of infant feeding: breast milk, commercial breast milk substitutes, and numerous recipes and recommendations (formulas), all of which were based on condensed milk. This product was developed during the American Civil War when it was discovered that adding sugar to partially evaporated cow's milk extended its storage life. Cookbooks of the day usually included a recipe for evaporated milk formula. Typical additives included cow's milk, cod liver oil, orange juice, and sugar. By World War II, evaporated milk recipes had grown to become the most common form of infant nutrition.

The commercial baby food industry followed a similar course and introduced a variety of new formulas based on different fat sources. SMA (Simulated Milk Adapted) was introduced in 1919. Lactogen was introduced in 1920 and the research of a milk chemist and a Boston pediatrician resulted in a formula called Similac (similar to lactation) in 1924. By the time Mead Johnson introduced Enfamil in 1959, commercial milk had become the most common form of infant nutrition. This rise continued to replace breast-feeding as the norm. By the 1970s, only 25 percent of two- to three-month-old children in the US were breast-fed; this pattern was followed throughout most of the developed countries.

Legislation to establish minimum standards for infant formulas was surprisingly slow to arrive. It was not until the recognition of electrolyte abnormalities in some children fed commercial formulas that minimum legal standards for nutrients and testing were established in 1980. Formulas have continued to develop and a wide range of specialty products is now available, particularly for the complex nutritional requirements of pre-term infants.

A major factor behind the popularity of commercial formulas was aggressive marketing by the baby food industries. Apart from direct advertising, formula was also provided in hospital to new mothers, a practice that was supported by many pediatricians as a move toward "scientific motherhood." As the baby boom market decreased, the industry looked to developing countries for new markets where they could use much the same advertising practices (*International Baby Food Action Network*, n.d.).

So far so good. Current formula feeds are the result of many years of research and have a definite part to play in the nutrition of children in developed countries. However, the story is not so clear in developing countries where populations must raise small children without easy access to education, sanitation, or clean water. Under these circumstances, infant formulas may do far more harm than good. Apart from its socializing advantages, breast milk is sterile and nutritionally tailored for the baby. Its delivery is not complicated by malnutrition and infection resulting from incorrect mixing of the powder with dirty water by a mother who has not had any access to education.

As early as 1939, one of the pioneers of maternal and child health, Dr. Cicely Williams, was warning about the increased mortality associated with the replacement of breast-feeding by bottle-feeding in developing countries. Unfortunately, these warnings had no effect. The industry continued to depict healthy-looking babies in its advertisements, dressed salespeople as nurses (mother craft nurses), and provided free supplies of baby formula to maternity wards.

These promotion methods produced the same effect in the developing world as they had elsewhere. By the 1960s, it was clear that this trend was associated with greatly increased mortality among

---

Box 5.2: History notes

Dr. Cicely Williams (1893–1992)

Dr. Cicely Williams was born in Jamaica and was allowed to study medicine at Oxford because the war had left classes half empty. After graduating, she worked in the British Colonial Service. Her early studies of malnutrition in West Africa led her to identify and name kwashiorkor. When working in Malaysia, she was the first to criticize the infant food companies for their advertising practices. Her paper, "Milk and Murder," was influential and ultimately helped the slow process of re-establishing breast-feeding. She is widely considered the founder of the study of maternal and child health (MCH). During World War II, she narrowly survived imprisonment in a Japanese camp. After the war, she became the first head of MCH in the newly formed WHO. For more information, please follow the reference (Craddock, 1984).

---

bottled-fed children living in poverty. The term "commerciogenic malnutrition" was coined by Jelliffe (Jelliffe, 1972). He had already published a pamphlet, "Child Nutrition in Developing Countries," with the World Health Organization, which called attention to the dangers of bottle-feeding in poor populations.

The fight now began in earnest with publication, by War on Want in 1974, of a report on infant food promotion and its adverse effects called "The Baby Killer." Widespread interest in this campaign ultimately led to an international boycott of Nestlé products starting in 1977.

US Senate hearings in 1979 into the marketing of baby formula in developing countries and a subsequent joint WHO/UNICEF meeting on the same subject finally resulted in recommendations covering the international marketing of breast milk substitutes that was endorsed by the WHO in 1981 and reaffirmed through the "Innocenti Declaration" in 1990. The code places restrictions on advertising of baby formulas and requires that salespeople do not provide milk, Pablum, or promotional gifts in hospitals (*Infant Feeding Action Coalition, Canada*, n.d.). The code has no legal power, but it has been adopted into law by many developing nations. The promotion of infant formulas in these countries is now well controlled, but in countries without legislation, there is still plenty of evidence to suggest that the infant food industry does not fully comply with the WHO International Code (Aguayo et al., 2003). Regular reviews of the situation are published by the International Baby Food Action Network (IBFAN).

Breast-feeding, the Baby Friendly Initiative

It is almost as if breastfeeding takes the infant out of poverty for those first few months in order to give the child a fairer start in life and compensate for the injustice of the world into which it was born.

—James P. Grant, former executive director, UNICEF

The benefits of breast-feeding are so widely advertised that it is now easy to forget that only 30 years ago, there were real concerns that breast-feeding would almost die out as a cultural practice. Although breast-feeding has advantages both for the mother and child, it is important not to overstate the case; infants can grow and develop completely normally using properly prepared modern infant formulas. A mother who cannot breast-feed her child should not be made to feel that she has, in some way, failed her child. Breast-feeding is still the recommended form of infant feeding but, in a developed country, it is not a matter of life and death.

For a child born into poverty, the situation is very different. Exclusive breast-feeding in the first six months of

Figure 5.4: Young indigenous woman breast-feeding her baby in Darien Province, Panama. (Photographer Hector Barrios; courtesy IDRC Photo Library.)

life protects the child from a wide range of diseases, particularly malnutrition and gastroenteritis ("Effect of breastfeeding on infant and child mortality ...," 2000). The infant of an overworked mother who has to leave the baby with older children each day cannot be nourished adequately. Poverty forces the family to dilute the expensive feed to make it last longer. It is then mixed with contaminated water that cannot be sterilized because the family has no fuel.

Numerous studies have confirmed this observation. A Mexican study showed that bottle-fed babies living in poverty are six to 13 times more likely to die in the first two months of life compared to breast-fed babies, and four to six times more likely to die between three and five months (Palloni et al., 1994). UNICEF has estimated that the deaths of over a million children a year could be prevented with the exclusive breast-feeding of all children below the age of six months, which would reduce malnutrition and gastroenteritis.

Under these circumstances, it is vital that all new mothers are encouraged to breast-feed. Unfortunately, until relatively recently, hospitals did not encourage breast-feeding. In fact, practices such as mother and baby separation, rigid feeding regimes, and the convenience of formula food for staff all combined to reduce the emphasis on breast-feeding. Once widespread commercial formula advertising and provision of free milk in hospitals were added, it is easy to see why formula feed was steadily supplanting breast-feeding in many parts of the world; the fault is not entirely to be laid at the door of the baby food industry.

The first large attempt to repopularize breast-feeding was taken at a joint WHO/UNICEF meeting in 1989. The result was a pamphlet titled, *Protecting, Promoting, and Supporting Breastfeeding: The Special Role of Maternity Service* (World Health Organization, 1989). This contained several suggestions to improve the role of breast-feeding in maternity hospitals. The Baby Friendly Hospital Initiative (BFHI) that grew from this early report was launched as a joint UNICEF and WHO strategy in 1991.

The criteria for designation as a "baby-friendly hospital" include extra training for health care staff, the promotion of breast-feeding both before and after pregnancy, and support for breast-feeding by trained lactation consultants. The baby is roomed in with the mother to encourage breast-feeding on demand and the child is not given any commercial milk or pacifiers. The program also restricts use of free formula or other products provided by the formula companies. The concept has been very popular and has spread widely throughout the developed and developing world (*Baby-Friendly USA*, n.d.).

Taken together, the international code of marketing of breast milk substitutes plus the Baby Friendly Hospital Initiative have helped control the unregulated spread of formula foods and are slowly re-establishing breast-feeding as the nutrition of choice for young children.

Food Security

Starvation is characteristic of some people not having enough to eat. It is not the characteristic of there not being enough to eat. While the latter can be a cause of the former, it is but one of many possible causes. (Sen, 1983)

The Indian economist, Amartya Sen (1983), was the first to publish a serious study into the causes of famines. He examined four famines, but concentrated on the 1943 famine in Bengal. Up to that point, it was generally believed that famines were simply caused by intermittent crop failures in developing countries, an inevitable consequence of too many people and not enough food. Inevitably, some observers even blamed the victims themselves, either for having too many children or not working hard enough. However, Sen pointed out that the 1943 Bengal harvest was actually bigger than the 1941 harvest, which had not been a famine year. Clearly, there must have been many other factors involved.

The situation is no different from the great Irish Potato Famine of 1845. It is commonly believed that widespread crop failure and overpopulation resulted in the deaths of a million people and large-scale migration of the population to North America. On closer examination, it was not quite that simple (Woodham-Smith, 1992). The only crop affected by blight was the potato and the only people affected were the poor who relied on potatoes. Throughout the famine period, Ireland was a net exporter of grain to Europe and Britain. Similar to the later Bengal famine, there was no total shortage of food, just a shortage of potatoes and political will to redistribute the available grain surplus. Obviously, every famine has its own unique features. Whether you look at food shortage from a family or a national point of view, there is always a great deal more to starvation than lack of food (Peng, 1987).

One beneficial result of Sen's early work has been the development of famine early warning systems. These can give enough advance notice to allow time to mobilize increased food supplies to a high-risk area

---

Box 5.3: Common causes of poor food security

Poor food production:
- Poverty
- Crop failure, drought
- Lack of property rights, agricultural land, and pasture
- Lack of credit for seeds, fertilizers, or tools
- Lack of crop failure insurance

Poor food distribution:
- Poverty
- Corruption, hoarding, black market
- Lack of storage for surpluses
- Poor distribution infrastructure
- Absence of social safety net
- Religious or tribal discrimination
- Powerlessness of the poor
- War

(USAID's Famine Early Warning System, FEWS, is a good example). Some of the most common variables that can produce famine by interrupting production and distribution of food are given in Box 5.3. The term "food security" has evolved to describe the degree to which a population has access to food. Food security is said to exist when all people at all times have access to sufficient, safe, and nutritious food to meet their dietary needs plus an assured ability to acquire that food in an acceptable way (Cohen, 2005).

The majority of the world's poor people live in rural areas and depend on agriculture both for food and income. Unfortunately, many developing countries have neglected the rural sector, concentrating instead on urban areas and industrialization. Any attention paid to agriculture has been focused on cash crops for export rather than producing food for local consumption. Unfortunately, the aid industry has also given agriculture a low priority. Development funding directed specifically toward agriculture forms only a small percentage of overseas development assistance; this trend has only recently been changed (Food and Agriculture Organization, 2005). The FAO's own special program for food security was ratified at the world food summit only in 1996 and is still in the middle of changes following an external review in 2002 (Food and Agriculture Organization, 2006).

The direct and indirect benefits from agricultural improvement are numerous. Improved agricultural output raises nutritional levels and provides rural populations with income. Good farming practices also reduce ecological degradation and keep people "on the land." Failure of agricultural programs is a disaster for the health and prosperity of rural communities. The final result is migration of the rural poor into destitute shantytowns surrounding the major towns.

At the 1974 World Food Conference, delegates produced the declaration that "every man, woman, and child has the inalienable right to be free from hunger and malnutrition." The conference also predicted that this happy state would be achieved by 2000. Unfortunately, despite the gains of the Green Revolution, we are nowhere near achieving that goal. At the turn of the century, over 800 million people living in almost 90 nations are chronically malnourished. Delegates to the 1996 World Food Conference in Rome pragmatically accepted this failure of progress by setting a less ambitious goal of halving chronic malnutrition by the year 2015. This has subsequently been adopted as one of the first targets of the Millennium Development Goals set in 2000.

Figure 5.5: Trends in child malnutrition by region over the last 25 years

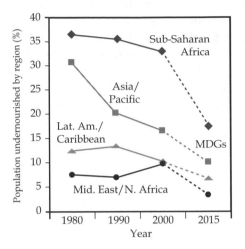

MDGs: Millennium Development Goals

Source: Food and Agriculture Organization (2005)

Insecurity of food supply has been around for a long time. In common with debt relief, it has attracted serious attention only in surprisingly recent times. As Figure 5.5 shows, there has been progress in reducing malnutrition, but much of those gains are based on progress in only two countries—India and China. Nutritional levels in many parts of the world will have to improve rapidly if the Millennium Development Goals on malnutrition are to be met by 2015.

Food Aid

Food aid was first provided to developing countries in the 1950s as a way for the United States and a few other countries (Canada, Japan, Australia, and European Union) to dispose of grain surpluses. Aid money was used to buy the grain and transport it to developing countries suffering production shortfall. It was initially seen as a benefit for farmers and poor alike but, as usual, it turned out to be a great more complicated than that. In humanitarian disasters, food aid has been of some value, but outside this narrow indication, it has generated enormous controversy and accusations that it produces more harm than good. The volume of food aid has fallen significantly since the 1960s and 1970s; the largest donors are the United States at around 50 percent, the European Union at 15 percent, and Canada at 5 percent.

Food aid has always attracted considerable criticism (Barrett, 2005). It is blamed for creating disincentives, depressing food prices, distorting markets, and delaying the need for policy reforms. Powerful vested interests, including agricultural producers, truckers, and shippers, all tend to slow the rate of change. In response to widespread criticism, the major food donors agreed upon a Food Aid Convention (FAC) in 1999, but the process lacked monitoring or enforcement. There is a strong move toward an effective

Global Food Aid Compact (GFAC) that will hopefully produce a more accountable and efficient food aid process.

Rather than being seen as altruism, some forms of food aid can be viewed as subsidized dumping of agricultural surpluses (Oxfam, 2005a). This has led to its inclusion in the current Doha round of international trade talks where it has been a topic of great irritation between the two sides. Finally, the donation of genetically modified crops has added further complexity, particularly following Zambia's much-publicized refusal of GM crop donations. Taken altogether, food aid is a very difficult issue.

It is important to remember that there are different types of food aid, each of which has its own advantages and disadvantages (Timmer, 2005):

- *Program food aid:* Food aid started in the 1950s with donations of agricultural surpluses from one government to another. The grains were usually sold in the recipient's

Figure 5.6: Donated cornmeal used in a supplementary feeding program for children in a refugee camp in the Democratic Republic of the Congo. (Photographer Francois Goemans; courtesy European Commission Humanitarian Organization Photo Library.)

local market and the money then used for other development activities. This "monetized" form of food aid has been heavily criticized, particularly since the proceeds of sales are usually tied to purchases from the donor country. Apart from depressing local food markets, the practice can also be viewed as subsidized dumping and an unfair means to open up new markets. Program food aid now forms only a small proportion of total donated food.

- *Project food aid:* Starting in the 1970s, food aid was used to support specific projects such as school feeding programs, payment in kind for development work projects, and food support for vulnerable women and children. Donations are distributed through NGOs, local government agencies, or the World Food Programme. Concerns about fostering dependency are minimized by targeting the donations to groups who have no other options. An obvious problem is the cost of shipping food. At least 50 percent of the aid grant is lost in shipping costs. It is more efficient to use the money to buy food locally or at least in neighbouring countries. The European Union has moved toward direct financing more quickly than the United States (Oxfam, 2005b).
- *Emergency food aid:* In the last 20 years, the distribution of free food to people suffering from natural disasters or political emergencies has become the major form of food aid. Even this seemingly simple process is open

to criticism. The response to the recent Asian tsunami is a good example. Although inland food production and markets recovered quickly in Sri Lanka, the World Food Program made only small purchases within the country. Even if these markets had failed, purchases would have been easier from India or Thailand. Inevitable delays in bulk transport also run the risk of flooding the local market with donated food at a time when the next harvest is due with inevitable results on the local economy. Again, direct donation of money would probably be more efficient in many cases.

■ SUMMARY

The broad topic of nutrition (both normal and abnormal) is an essential subject for anyone studying international health. Along with poverty and human rights, malnutrition lies at the root of the health problems affecting developing world populations. Despite its importance, a sophisticated understanding of severe malnutrition has been slow to develop. Prior to Amartya Sen's study of famine 20 years ago, it was generally thought that Malthus's early 19th-century theory was correct—malnutrition was an unavoidable feature of life in developing countries because there would always be too many people for the available food. The research stimulated by Sen's work subsequently showed that malnutrition is far more complex than that and is usually the result of numerous interrelated contributory factors.

Shortage of food is only one of many reasons behind malnutrition. For example, young children are totally dependent upon their parents who, in turn, are strongly influenced by their society. Consequently, numerous social problems ranging from civil war to lack of maternal education can all ultimately reduce a child's chances of obtaining adequate nutrition. Even if a local food shortage was originally due to drought and crop failure, the development of widespread starvation is ultimately a failure of distribution of food from the rest of the country. The persistent starvation in Darfur, Sudan, is mainly due to lack of political will, even though the original shortage of food was agricultural in nature.

Not surprisingly, the adverse effects of malnutrition are as complicated as its causes. With time, the epidemiology of malnutrition has changed. Although it is still possible to die from lack of food in some parts of the world, severe starvation is becoming increasingly uncommon. Nowadays, mild and moderate degrees of malnutrition are the principal problem. Apart from reducing the growth and development potential of entire generations of children, lesser degrees of malnutrition also reduce a child's immune function, which greatly increases the mortality from common diseases such as measles, pneumonia, and gastroenteritis. The more insidious effects of micronutrient deficiencies can also have severe clinical effects, even in children who might otherwise appear well nourished. Examples include scurvy, hypothyroidism, and anemia.

Over the last 10–15 years, measurable improvements have been made in worldwide levels of childhood malnutrition. However, these average figures are heavily influenced by improvements in India and China; there are still areas of the world where progress has been very slow. If the world is to meet the Millennium Development Goals on malnutrition, it is very important that nutrition initiatives are designed with a full appreciation of the problem's complexity. Many well-established interventions are available that have direct or indirect nutritional benefits. These include supplementary feeding programs, micronutrient fortification, maternal education, agricultural extension projects, and many others. Whatever approach is used, the project must be based on careful research so it can be tailored to meet the specific needs of the local population.

RESOURCES

References

Adamson, P. (2004). *Vitamin and mineral deficiency: A global program report.* Retrieved from www.micronutrient.org/reports/reports/Full_e.html.

Aguayo, V., et al. (2003). "Monitoring compliance with the International Code of Marketing of Breast Milk Substitutes in West Africa." *British Medical Journal, 326*, 127–133.

Apple, R. (1987). *Mothers and medicine: A social history of infant feeding, 1890–1950.* Madison: University of Wisconsin Press.

Ashworth, A., et al. (2004). "WHO guidelines for management of severe malnutrition in rural South African hospitals: Effect on case fatality and the influence of operational factors." *Lancet, 363*, 1110–1115.

Baby-Friendly USA. (n.d.). Retrieved from www.babyfriendlyusa.org.

Barrett, C. (2005). *Food aid after fifty years: Recasting its role.* London: Routledge.

Bern, C., et al. (1997). "Assessment of potential indicators for protein-energy malnutrition in the algorithm for integrated management of childhood illness." *Bulletin of the World Health Organization, 1* (Supp.), 87–96.

Cogill, B. (2003). *Anthropometric indicators measurement guide.* Food and Nutrition Technical Assistance Project. Retrieved from www.fantaproject.org/publications/anthropom.shtml.

Cohen, D. (2005). "Achieving food security in vulnerable populations." *British Medical Journal, 331,* 775–777.

Collins, S. (1996). "Using middle upper arm circumference to assess severe adult malnutrition during famine." *Journal of the American Medical Association, 276,* 391–395.

Craddock, C. (1984). *Retired except on demand: The life of Dr. Cicely Williams.* Oxford: Oxford University Press.

de Onis, M. (1997). "Time for a new growth reference." *Pediatrics, 100,* 8–9.

de Onis, M., & Yip, R. (1996). "The WHO growth chart: Historical considerations and current scientific issues." *Bibliotheca Nutritio et Dieta, 53,* 74–89.

de Onis, M., et al. (1993). "The worldwide magnitude of protein-energy malnutrition: An overview from the WHO Global Database on child growth." *Bulletin of the World Health Organization, 71,* 703–712.

de Onis, M., et al. (2000). "Is malnutrition declining? An analysis of changes in levels of child malnutrition since 1980." *Bulletin of the World Health Organization, 78,* 1222–1233.

"Effect of breastfeeding on infant and child mortality due to infectious diseases in less developed countries: A pooled analysis." (2000). *Lancet, 355,* 451–455.

Ferro-Luzzi, A., et al. (1994). "Body mass index defines the risk of seasonal energy stress in the third world." *European Journal of Clinical Nutrition, 48* (Supp. 3), 165–178.

Food and Agriculture Organization. (2005). *The state of food insecurity in the world.* Rome: Author. Retrieved from www.fao.org/sof/sofi/index_en.htm.

Food and Agriculture Organization. (2006). *Special Programme for Food Security.* Retrieved from www.fao.org/spfs.

Frisancho, A., et al. (1982). "Relative merits of old and new indices of body mass with reference to skin-fold thickness." *American Journal of Clinical Nutrition, 36,* 697–699.

Ge, K.-Y., et al. (2001). "Definition and measurement of child malnutrition." *Biomedical and Environmental Sciences, 14,* 283–291.

Gibney, M., Vorster, H., & Kok, F. (Eds.). (2002). *Introduction to human nutrition.* Ames: Iowa State University Press.

Glynn, I., & Glynn, J. (2004). *The life and death of smallpox.* Cambridge: Cambridge University Press.

Gomez, F., et al. (1956). "Mortality in second- and third-degree malnutrition." *Journal of Tropical Pediatrics, 2,* 7783–7788.

Haddad, L., & Ross, J. (2004). *5th report on the world nutrition situation.* Retrieved from www.unsystem.org/scn/Publications/AnnualMeeting/SCN31/SCN5Report.pdf.

Infant Feeding Action Coalition, Canada. (n.d.). Retrieved from www.infactcanada.ca.

International Baby Food Action Network. (n.d.). Retrieved from www.ibfan.org.

International Council for the Control of Iodine Deficiency Disorders. (n.d.). Retrieved from www.iccidd.org.

International Vitamin A Consultative Group. (2002). "Food fortification to reduce vitamin A deficiency." *Journal of Nutrition, 132* (Supp. 9), 2927–2933.

Internet Movie Database. (2006). *All-time USA box office.* Retrieved from www.imdb.com/boxoffice/alltimegross.

Jelliffe, D. (1972). "Commerciogenic malnutrition?" *Nutrition Review, 30,* 199–205.

Keusch, G. (2003). "The history of nutrition: Malnutrition, infection, and immunity." *Journal of Nutrition, 133* (Supp.), 336–340.

Latham, M. (1997). *Human nutrition in the developing world.* Rome: Food and Agriculture Organization. Retrieved from www.fao.org/DOCREP/W0073e/w0073e00.htm.

McKeown, T. (1980). *The role of medicine.* Princeton: Princeton University Press.

Olivares, M. (1999). "Anaemia and iron deficiency in children." *British Medical Bulletin, 55,* 534–543.

Oxfam. (2005a). *Food aid or hidden dumping?* (Oxfam briefing paper no. 71). Retrieved from www. oxfam.org/en/files/bp71_food_aid_240305.pdf.

Oxfam. (2005b). *Making the case for cash: Humanitarian food aid under scrutiny* (Oxfam briefing note). Retrieved from www.oxfam.org.uk/what_we_do/issues/conflict_disasters/downloads/ bn_cash.pdf.

Palloni, A., et al. (1994). "The effects of breastfeeding and the pace of childbearing on early childhood mortality in Mexico." *Pan American Health Organization Bulletin, 28,* 93–111.

Pelletier, D. (1994). "The relationship between child anthropometry and mortality in developing countries: Implication for policy, programs, and future research." *Journal of Nutrition, 124* (Suppl. 10), 2047–2081.

Pelletier, D., et al. (1993). "Epidemiological evidence for a potentiating effect of malnutrition on child mortality." *American Journal of Public Health, 83,* 1130–1133.

Pelletier, D., et al. (1995). "The effects of malnutrition on child mortality in developing countries." *Bulletin of the World Health Organization, 73,* 93–107.

Peng, X. (1987). "Demographic consequences of the great leap forward in China's provinces." *Population and Development Review, 13,* 639–670.

Schauer, C., & Zlotkin, S. (2003). "'Home fortification' with micronutrient sprinkles — a new approach for the prevention and treatment of nutritional anemia." *Journal of Pediatrics and Child Health, 8,* 87–90.

Schuman, A. (2003). "A concise history of infant formula." *Contemporary Pediatrics, 2,* 91–93.

Sen, A. (1983). *Poverty and famines: An essay on entitlements.* Oxford: Oxford University Press.

Smith, L., & Haddad, L. (1999). *Explaining child malnutrition in developing countries: A cross-country analysis.* Washington: International Food Policy Research Institute.

Timmer, C. (2005). *Food aid: Doing well by doing good* (Center for Global Development working paper). Retrieved from www.cgdev.org/content/publications/detail/5342.

UN Millennium Development Goals. (n.d.). Retrieved from www.un.org/millenniumgoals.

UNICEF. (1998). *The state of the world's children 1998: Focus on nutrition.* Retrieved from www. unicef.org/sowc98.

UNICEF. (2006). *Malnutrition.* Retrieved from www.childinfo.org/areas/malnutrition.

United States Agency for International Development. (n.d.) *Famine Early Warning System.* Retrieved from www.fews.net.

United States Department of Agriculture. (2006). *Food and Nutrition Information Center.* Retrieved from www.nal.usda.gov/fnic.

University of the West Indies. (1998) *Nutrition, health, and child development: Research advances and policy recommendations.* Washington: Pan American Health Organization.

"Use and interpretation of anthropometric indicators of nutritional status." (1986). *Bulletin of the World Health Organization, 64,* 929–941.

Waterlow, J., et al. (1977). "The presentation and use of height and weight data for comparing the nutritional status of groups of children under the age of 10 years." *Bulletin of the World Health Organization, 55,* 489–498.

Wellcome Trust Working Party. (1970). "Classification of infantile malnutrition." *Lancet, 2,* 302–303.

Woodham-Smith, C. (1992). *The great hunger: Ireland, 1845–1849.* London: Penguin.

World Health Organization. (1989). *Protecting, promoting and supporting breastfeeding.* Geneva: Author.

World Health Organization. (2006). *Global database on child growth and malnutrition.* Retrieved from www.who.int/nutgrowthdb/en.

Recommended Reading

Latham, M. (1997). *Human nutrition in the developing world*. Rome: Food and Agriculture Organization.

Leathers, H., & Foster, P. (2004). *The world food problem: Tackling the causes of under nutrition in the Third World*. Boulder: Lynne Rienner Publishers.

Savage-King, F., & Burgess, A. (2005). *Nutrition for developing countries*. Oxford: Oxford University Press.

Semba, R., & Bloem, M. (2001). *Nutrition and health in developing countries*. Totowa: Humana Press.

Sen, A. (1983). *Poverty and famines: An essay on entitlements*. Oxford: Oxford University Press.

PART III

WHAT IS THE EXTENT OF THE PROBLEM?

Chapter 6
Defining and Measuring Health

Chapter 7
Child and Adult Health Statistics for the Developing World

Chapter 6

Defining and Measuring Health

There are three kinds of lies: lies,
damned lies, and statistics.
—Probably Benjamin Disraeli,
but often attributed to
Samuel Clemens

OBJECTIVES
After completing this chapter, you should be able to

* understand the importance of defining and measuring health
* appreciate the difference between extent of disease and burden of disease
* know the definitions of the commonly used health variables
* understand how data is collected and the errors involved

Ill health and poverty are intimately related. They run as two intertwined strands throughout the subject of international health; you will never find one without the other. Neither can be understood until they can be measured so several agencies spend a great deal of time and money trying to collect accurate data. There is, of course, some overlap, but the World Bank tends to concentrate on poverty research while the World Health Organization, UN Population Division, and UNICEF collect vast amounts of information about population health. As we saw in Chapter 4, the measurement

of poverty is a contentious subject, open to a great deal of criticism and potential error. The measurement of ill health is, if anything, even worse because there is not even a fully agreed-upon definition of health to act as a reference point. Quite apart from straightforward measurement error, the conclusions of health or poverty studies can both be significantly altered simply by changing the basic definitions of the study variables. Whether you are using US $1 per day figures to assess poverty or disability-adjusted life years to assess health, it is very important to have a good working knowledge of the definitions and potential problems associated with their derivation. This chapter will concentrate on the techniques used to measure population health.

INTRODUCTION TO HEALTH MEASUREMENT

History of Health Measurement

> Not everything that counts can be counted and not everything that can be counted, counts.
> —Sign in Einstein's Princeton office

As far as it is possible to tell, the only measure of health recorded through most of human history was a simple head count. For many centuries, various administrations kept some record of the population depending on whether they wanted to tax them or recruit them to the army. King David of Israel ordered a census over 3,000 years ago: "… Go number Israel from Beersheba even to Dan; and bring the number of them to me, that I may know it (1 Chronicles 21:2)." At least 2,000 years earlier than David, the Babylonians had been keeping population tax records pressed into squares of mud. As far as governments were concerned, you were either dead or alive. Ill health and early death were probably so much a part of daily life that no one even thought to quantify it.

Census taking was an established part of Roman and Greek city administration; the first known census of the Roman Empire occurred in 28 BC (it was 4,603,000) (*Roman census figures*, n.d.). As a good example of the problems generated by statistics, no one knows if this referred only to males or whether women, children, and slaves were included. Accurate interpretation of raw numbers always requires an understanding of the methodology used. Although plenty of observers described the effects of plague as it swept through 14th- and 15th-century Europe (particularly the Arab historian and philosopher Ibn-Khaldun), it was still some time before anyone studied the broad causes of death.

As early as 1523, the earl of Essex ordered that parish clerks should submit a record of deaths each week to act as an early warning against a plague epidemic. Data collection was only intermittent until Charles II put it on a more formal basis in the mid-17th century (Greenberg, 1997). These "Bills of Mortality" were published for the public to read; with steady improvements, they were continued until the middle of the 19th century. The table of diagnoses from 300 years ago (Box 6.1), again, demonstrates the need for clear standard definitions in medical research.

For unknown reasons, a wealthy London shop owner, John Graunt, became interested in the accumulated information held within these bills. His book, *Observations on the Bills of Mortality* (published in 1662), is widely accepted as the first attempt to measure population health (Rothman, 1996). Consequently,

---

Box 6.1: Common diagnoses used in early "Bills of Mortality"

- Chrisoms (death before baptism)
- Headmouldshot (inflamed brain)
- Planet struck (paralyzed)
- Rising of the lights (lung disease)
- Imposthume (abscess)
- Purples (spotted fever)
- Loosness (dysentery)

Source: Slought Museum (n.d.)

Box 6.2: History notes

John Graunt (1620–1674)

John Graunt was born in London into a middle-class 17th-century family. He received a basic education and was then apprenticed in his family shop. His business grew and he became quite a wealthy man. He mixed with the well-known people of his day, including Samuel Pepys.

  Charles II had earlier introduced a system of weekly death registration (Bills of Mortality), which were intended to act as an early warning system of plague outbreaks. For unknown reasons, Graunt made a detailed study of these documents and published his findings, "Observations on the Bills of Mortality," in 1662. This is generally accepted as the earliest study of population health in the English language. Despite his low social status as a merchant, he was elected as a Fellow to the newly formed Royal Society, but it took a bit of pushing from the King. Follow the reference for more details (Rothman, 1996).

Graunt is variously described as one of the earliest demographers and epidemiologists. This work and similar studies by William Petty and Edmund Halley (1693) (of comet fame) gained wide recognition, not so much because of an interest in improving the lives of the poor but because life insurance had just been introduced; the earliest insurers wanted actuarial data to predict how long people might live at different ages.

Over the next two centuries, progress in the measurement of population health was very slow. Although gifted observers like John Snow and Ignaz Semmelweis were able to make valuable advances based on their own clinical observations

(Daniels, 1998; *John Snow Society*, n.d.), it took a long time before population health was measured in a meaningful way. The absence of hard data meant that, even in the mid-19th century, doctors still believed infection was spread by dirty air and that most diseases were the result of imbalanced humours. Apart from the invention of anaesthesia, there had been little improvement since Hippocrates.

It was not until the 1860s that William Farr of the British General Registry Office applied statistical techniques to the observations of Snow and others to prove that infected water was the cause of disease (Bingham et al., 2004). The subsequent move by European cities to build sewage treatment plants was the first large-scale benefit to result from the new study of health measurement. Later, Ross and McKendrick placed the study of disease on a formal mathematical basis and provided powerful epidemiological tools to examine the causes of disease, which were put to good use in 1950 by Doll and Hill, who finally proved that smoking is bad for you.

During the 1960s and 1970s, large-scale aid projects needed to measure the end points of their interventions. Most of the current tools for measuring burden of disease were developed around this time (Figure 6.1). In 1990, these new tools were used in a joint project between Harvard University, WHO, and the World Bank during their first study of global health (World Health Organization, n.d.-b). However, there is still great room for improvement in the standards of health measurement. Even today, despite the obvious need for accurate data, less than a third of the world's countries collect detailed population health information.

Why Measure Health?

Information is vital to the advance of any science. Without carefully collected data, treatments can be based only on the unreliable foundation of personal bias. One of the greatest doctors of the 19th century, Rudolph Virchow, made himself very unpopular by disagreeing with the humoral basis of disease, but even he did not believe in the germ theory of disease. Some of the principal reasons for measuring health are listed below:

- *Surveillance of major diseases:* The first Bills of Mortality were intended to act as an early warning of plague epidemics. The 2003 epidemic of Severe Acute Respiratory Syndrome (SARS) and concerns about the spread of avian influenza show that regular surveillance is still very important (Centers for Disease Control and Prevention, n.d.). The World Health Organization's Epidemic and Pandemic Alert and Response section has the responsibility

for coordinating a number of disease surveillance initiatives (World Health Organization, n.d.-a). These include networks for surveillance of influenza, cholera, yellow fever, and plague.

- *Project monitoring and evaluation:* Population health measurement is a vital part of outcome assessment in any large-scale health initiative, particularly disease eradication programs; the necessary techniques were refined during the smallpox eradication program. The Millennium Development Goals include several defined and measured health outcomes that require careful monitoring of maternal and child health diseases; WHO, UNICEF, and UNAIDS are the main agencies responsible (*UN Millennium Development Goals*, n.d.). Targeted programs against tuberculosis, HIV/AIDS, polio, leprosy, and malaria all also need accurate data-monitoring progress.

Figure 6.1: Modern epidemiological monitoring techniques were developed in the 1960s and 1970s during the smallpox eradication program. This 1975 photograph shows one of the many thousands of volunteer smallpox officers crossing a bamboo bridge to visit a remote village in Bangladesh. (Photographer Dr. S. Foster; courtesy of the Public Health Image Library.)

- *Health planning:* In the past, diseases that killed most people were assumed to be the greatest public health threats so they attracted the bulk of health spending. However, once the broader burden of disease was measured, unexpected conditions such as accidents and mental illness became more obvious public health threats. This information can significantly affect decisions made about the distribution of available health money. Health measurement is also necessary to guide cost containment measures and the reorganization of existing health systems ("Measuring the efficiency of health systems," 2001).
- *Population health surveillance:* States have a responsibility to monitor the health of their population; in Canada, this is the responsibility of Statistics Canada. Basic measurements include registration of birth, death, and marriage status plus derived variables such as infant and maternal mortality rates. Most developed countries also have some form of disease control and surveillance structure that can investigate newly identified health problems. Snow's early identification of cholera or James Lind's study of scurvy have their modern counterparts in the early identification of HIV/AIDS in California by the US Centers for Disease Control during the 1980s ("Pneumocystis pneumonia—Los Angeles," 1981).

MEASURING THE AMOUNT OF DISEASE

Basic Definitions

If you want to inspire confidence, give plenty of statistics. It does not matter that they should be accurate, or even intelligible, as long there is enough of them.

— Lewis Carroll

In epidemiological studies, it is often easier to identify and count diseases (numerator) than it is to count the total number of people at risk (denominator). This makes it difficult to determine accurate values for a wide range of indicators. Inaccuracies due to poorly defined denominators can significantly affect the conclusions of a health study. A few basic definitions are necessary for this chapter; further epidemiological information can be found in several good texts (Norman & Streiner, 2003).

- *Rates:* A rate indicates the number of times an event happens in a particular population over a given time span. Its calculation requires a defined period of time, a defined population, and the number of defined events. For example, a birth rate requires the number of live births (in a year) and the total population to turn it into a rate. Errors and uncertainties will affect both the numerator and denominator. When rates are calculated for particular sections of a community such as infants, newborns, or under fives, they are referred to as specific rates.

- *Incidence:* Incidence measures the number of new cases of a given disease that develop in a specific time (usually a year). If 12 people catch tuberculosis each year in a population of 1,000, then the incidence is 1.2 percent. For very small numbers, the incidence is sometimes expressed per 100,000 people. Incidence represents your risk of catching a disease. If you move into that community and live like the average person, then your risk of catching tuberculosis that year is 1.2 percent.

- *Prevalence:* The prevalence is a measure of how much disease there is in a population at a given point in time and is used to guide provision of health services. Prevalence is calculated by dividing the number of people with the disease at any particular time point by the population at risk. Diseases of low incidence, such as cystic fibrosis, may have a high prevalence on the hospital ward simply because some will require frequent long-term admissions. Consequently, the need for health services for cystic fibrosis is higher than its simple calculated incidence would suggest.

Vital Statistics

Most countries at least pay lip service to the concept of collecting a basic package of health information on its citizens. The need for extensive infrastructure and a large budget means that this collection is often incomplete and, in many developing countries, is almost non-existent. These so-called vital statistics usually include registration of birth, death, marriage status, migration, and population.

- *Population count:* The foundation of all health measurements is the size of the population at risk—every rate requires a denominator based on accurate population information. Examples include numbers of pregnant women or children under five years. This data is obtained by regular national census, often performed about every decade. In between census years, a fair estimate of the population and its subdivisions can be gained from regular analysis of the demographic data contained in the vital statistics. Table 6.1 shows a greatly simplified summary of the United Kingdom's population in 2003. Subdivision into age groups allows calculation of specific indicators such as age-specific mortality rates.

- *Mortality registration:* Once the information gained from accurate death registration is added to the basic population data, a wide range of health indicators can be calculated. The simplest is a crude mortality rate (number of deaths in a given time divided by the total population in that period) but, as mentioned above, a wide range of specific rates can also be calculated (maternal mortality rate, infant mortality rate, etc.). Mortality rates are also used to calculate two other commonly quoted variables: Standardized Mortality Ratio (SMR) and also Life Expectancy at Birth. It is estimated that 70 percent of deaths worldwide are not certified (Sibai, 2004); data often relies on

Table 6.1: Population statistics for United Kingdom, 2003

Age Group (years)	Population (1,000s)	% in Age Group (%)	Deaths (1,000s)	Age-Specific Mortality Rate (deaths per 1,000)
0–4	2,848.2	5.7	3,682	1.3
5–14	6,299.8	12.6	725	0.1
15–24	6,304.0	12.67	2,634	0.4
25–44	14,485.7	29.1	14,001	1.0
45–64	11,971.3	24.0	62,755	5.2
65–74	4,158.6	8.3	87,714	21.1
75+	3,788.3	7.6	331,898	87.6
Totals	49,855.9	100	503,409	10.1

Source: UK Office of National Statistics (2003)

retrospective questions from the family (verbal autopsy), which has obvious implications for the accuracy of health surveys (Snow et al., 1992).

- *Birth registration:* In many countries, a child is denied even the most basic registration of its existence at birth. Many children die of early neonatal causes before they are even registered. They are mourned by their family, but not even known to the state. UNICEF estimates that 30 percent of all births worldwide are unregistered, ranging from 22 percent in East Asia and the Pacific to 70 percent in Sub-Saharan Africa (UNICEF, 2006a). Apart from introducing errors into health estimates, lack of a birth certificate can adversely affect a child throughout life. In some countries, a birth certificate is required for attendance at school, treatment in clinic, immunization, obtaining credit, opening a bank account, or getting a passport. In some cases, there may be deliberate lack of birth registration intended to minimize the size of a particular ethnic minority such as Roma in Central and Eastern Europe.

System for Monitoring Health

It has always been important to monitor population health, but the establishment of the Millennium Development Goals in 2000 brought the need for accurate health monitoring into focus. The MDGs set specific targets for a range of improvements in education, status of women, the environment, poverty, and, of course, health. Four of the goals require the measurement of specific health outcomes. When the goals were established, it was well understood that monitoring information would often be incomplete and much of the data would require mathematical modelling rather than hard measurement. The MDGs have acted as a catalyst for much-needed improvements in the gathering and measurement of health information — rather late in the day.

Two initiatives have been introduced that aim to improve the overall quality of the information available:

- *Global Monitoring Report (World Bank, 2005a):* Beginning in early 2004, the World Bank and IMF committed joint staff and funds toward an annual review of progress toward the Millennium Development Goals. The first *Global Monitoring Report* appeared in 2004. Its aim is to monitor

the policies and actions of both developed and developing countries toward achieving the accepted targets.

- *Health Metrics Network (World Health Organization, n.d.-e):* A large alliance of countries, international partners, plus the Bill and Melinda Gates Foundation, came together in 2005 to form the Health Metrics Network. It is an initiative of the World Health Organization. The aim is to create a harmonized framework for the collection of health information that can then be shared on a global basis. The network also intends to provide technical and financial support for the establishment of these networks. Since a large part of the world does not even collect details of birth and death, this is a very ambitious undertaking, but also one that is long overdue.

Table 6.2: A moment of Zen

	Annual number of births (1,000s):	
	Austria	75
	Canada	328
	Czech Republic	91
	Denmark	63
	Finland	55
	France	744
	Germany	687
	Hungary	95
	Ireland	63
	Italy	531
	Japan	1,167
	Netherlands	190
	New Zealand	55
	Norway	55
	Poland	365
Total number of children below the age of five who die every year in the developing world from completely treatable and avoidable diseases:	Singapore	40
	South Korea	467
	Spain	447
	Sweden	95
	United Kingdom	663
	United States	4,134
	Total annual births (2004) in 21 developed countries:	
10,600,000	**10,600,000**	
Source: UNICEF (2006d)	Source: World Health Organization (2006b)	

Measurement Error

Humanum est errare; perseverare diabolicum: To err is human; to repeat errors is particularly dumb.
— Lucius Annaeus Seneca

In many developing countries, neither births, deaths, nor population are routinely recorded. Consequently, a calculated rate that depends on death registration for the numerator and accurate population information for the denominator is likely to suffer from a few errors. Research has shown wide variations between government health statistics and the results of independent surveillance studies (Arudo et al., 2003). In some cases, the final numbers are little more than informed guesses. This is not a criticism of the agencies that spend a great deal of time and effort on collecting data; it is simply the reality facing data gatherers. Before basing a decision upon published health data, it is vital that some thought is given to the accuracy of that data.

Cooper et al. (1998) expressed the point clearly in their paper on measurement error in the global burden of disease study: "The statistics which appear in national ministries and international agencies are mainly guestimates formed from models, extrapolations, and common sense, constrained largely by the need to avoid deviating too far from previous estimates." It must be remembered that the data in the *Global Burden of Disease Report* represents the best efforts given the current standards of health collection. The WHO data-gathering agencies try, as far as possible, to base their estimates on more than one source of information in order to improve accuracy, but the results should still be considered as the best available data rather than a reference gold standard.

A recent study by the World Health Organization showed that death registration was complete for only 64 out of 115 countries (Mathers et al., 2005). Coverage ranged from close to 100 percent in Europe to less than 10 percent in Sub-Saharan Africa. Only 23 countries had data that was considered more than 90 percent complete and where ill-defined causes of death accounted for less than 10 percent of the total. It should be remembered that even when deaths are properly registered, the process is still not a completely reliable source of information (Lu et al., 2000). Use of imprecise terms such as "heart failure" conveys little to the medical researcher. Similarly, compound causes of death are very difficult to classify properly. For example, a malnourished, unimmunized child who catches measles and dies from the subsequent pneumonia may be classified under several headings. Researchers have only recently begun to look at contributory causes of death (Pelletier et al., 1995).

Apart from errors involved in the raw mortality rates, the broader field of health

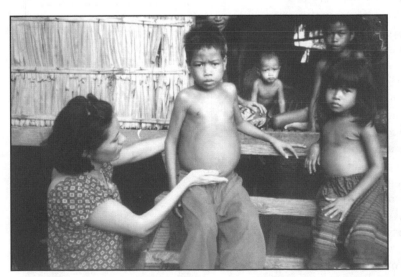

Figure 6.2: Despite researchers' best efforts, the collection of basic health data is unavoidably complicated by the limited resources and difficult patient access in many rural areas. The photograph shows a schistosomiasis survey worker in a remote Cambodian village. (Courtesy Dr. W. Grut, Rose Charities.)

measurement includes many other derived variables, each of which has its own particular errors. For example, poverty-associated inequalities in health are a popular topic of research. Unfortunately, different researchers rely on different means of measuring economic status. It has been clearly shown that varying the choice of economic measure will influence the final conclusion of the study of health and equality (Houweling et al., 2003). These effects can be so large that published differences in health and inequality between countries may be more of an artifact than a reality.

▌MEASURING THE BURDEN OF DISEASE

Let not your conception of disease come from words heard in the lecture room or read from a book. See, and then reason and compare and control. But see first.
— William Osler

Measurements of mortality are relatively easy to compile, but they are very crude indicators of the overall effects of disease, both on the individual and on society. If a person dies, those potential years of lost life, production, and earnings have a profound effect that is not captured by a simple mortality statistic. Even if someone survives a disease, he or she may be left with disability for varying periods. That again is not adequately assessed if patients are simply classified as dead or alive.

For over 30 years, increasingly sophisticated measurement tools have been devised to provide information both on the frequency of disease but also on the burden of disease carried by those who bear some form of disability. This

requires a large amount of extra effort compared to simple mortality calculations, but the results have profound effects on the debate concerning health care. Once burden of disease is measured, a range of unexpected diseases (particularly mental illness and accidents) become much more obvious causes of potential lost life. This has important implications for the allocation of health care budgets.

Two broad classes of measurement have emerged over time: health expectancy and health gaps; Figure 6.3 expresses these concepts graphically. Curve 1 represents a mythical population that lives in perfect health for 80 years and then suddenly dies. Curve 2 is a life expectancy curve for an average country. The difference between the two (area "C") is the health "gap" or lives lost due to various premature diseases. Curve 3 represents the life expectancy curve for complete health. Area "A" is that population's expectancy of a disease-free life, while area "B"

Figure 6.3: Idealized life expectancy curves

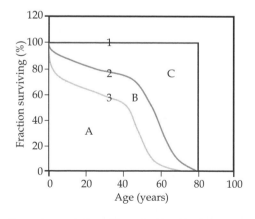

Curve 1: population with perfect health, then sudden death at 80; Curve 2:
typical life-expectancy curve for an average population; Curve 3: life-expectancy curve for perfect health.

represents the further life lived with some degree of limitation.

The concept of years of potential life lost was used in the early 1980s by the Ghana Health Assessment Team (1981) in order to improve their ability to measure the results of health spending in that country. Their shift from mortality data to burden of disease assessment produced unexpected results. They found that diseases with the highest health burden were not being targeted; money was principally going to a high-cost referral hospital that contributed very little to the health of the rural population. Based on these results, the government placed greater emphasis on community-based health care strategies that provided many times greater savings in life-years per dollar spent.

Subsequent research has produced a wide range of population health measures designed to integrate both mortality and morbidity into a single number. The best-known examples include the Disability-Adjusted Life Expectancy (DALE), published for 190 countries by the World Health Organization in 1999 (Mathers et al., 2001), and the Disability-Adjusted Life Years (DALY), used as a basis for the 1990 and 2000 Global Burden of Disease studies (World Health Organization, n.d.-d).

Measuring Health Expectancies

The conventional calculation of life expectancy considers people either as alive and healthy or dead. Obviously, this is unrealistic; every population includes people who are alive and yet limited in some degree by a persistent health disability. In order to measure the total life expectancy and the life expectancy in good health, it is necessary to weight different disabilities with regard to their

severity, duration, and age of onset. Several indices have been developed for this purpose, including the Disability-Free Life Expectancy (DFLE) and Disability-Adjusted Life Expectancy (DALE) (Murray & Lopez, 1997b).

Early estimates of Disability Free Life Expectancy, developed by Sullivan (1971), were dichotomous — that is, all disabilities were considered equal. An international research network, Réseau Espérance de Vie en Santé (REVES), was established in 1989 with the objective of using this tool to assess and compare the health of populations. The more recently developed DALE (Murray & Lopez, 1997b) adjusts for differences between disabilities based on self-reported health status and subjective allocation of weighted disease scores. Since personal opinions about degree of disability differ between cultures, care is

Figure 6.4: Trends in total, and health-adjusted life expectancies over 20 years for the United Kingdom

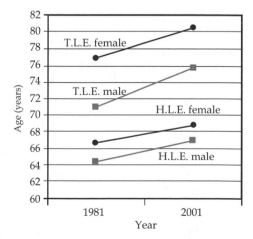

H.L.E.: healthy life expectancy; T.L.E.: total life expectancy

Source: Parliamentary Office of Science and Technology (2006)

required when adjusted life expectancies are compared between populations.

As shown in Figure 6.3, no matter what method is used to define good health, the result is two life expectancy curves: a disability-free life expectancy (curve 3) and a higher number representing total life expectancy (curve 2). Obviously, the difference between the two is the increasing burden of disability as the population ages. Figure 6.4 shows how total and health-adjusted life expectancies have changed in the United Kingdom over the last 20 years. The slopes of the total life expectancy and the healthy life expectancy lines are similar. This suggests that the observed increase in lifespan is not just an extension of ill health but is a real improvement in healthy life. The gender difference between healthy life expectancy is much smaller than it is for total life expectancy.

Revised data by Mathers et al. (2001) calculated for 191 countries produced

Table 6.3: Disability-adjusted life expectancy for the top five and bottom five countries measured in 1999

Rank	Country	Disability-Adjusted Life Expectancy (years)
1	Japan	74.5
2	Australia	73.2
3	France	73.1
4	Sweden	73.0
5	Spain	72.8
187	Botswana	32.3
188	Zambia	30.3
189	Malawi	29.4
190	Niger	29.1
191	Sierra Leone	25.9

Source: Mathers et al. (2001)

some interesting findings. Compared to developed countries, life in Sub-Saharan Africa is significantly shorter and the time lived with disability is twice as long. Table 6.3 lists average healthy life expectancy for the top five and bottom five countries in the survey. The difference between the best and the worst is startling. People in Japan or Australia can expect to have 50 years more healthy life than the average person living in Sierra Leone!

Measuring Health Gaps

On two occasions, I have been asked, "Pray Mr. Babbage, if you put into the machine wrong figures, will the right answers come out?" I am not able rightly to apprehend the kind of confusion of ideas that could provoke such a question.

— Charles Babbage, inventor of the first programmable calculating machine, 1791–1871

The Disability-Adjusted Life Year (DALY) has been adopted by the World Bank and WHO as the standard method for measuring total disease burden so it is important to have some idea about its calculation. The equations look impressive when written out in full and can give a misleading impression of scientific precision. However, the old computing adage should always be remembered: If you feed those equations bad basic data, you'll get garbage out no matter how complex the calculations might appear. By the time incomplete raw data have been manipulated and weighted, the final result can be open to several questions.

Summing up the full range of diseases in a single number is an ambitious undertaking. How can the death of a malnourished nine-month-old be compared to an HIV-positive 25-year-old woman who is well controlled on treatment? The DALY is one of a number of "summary health measures" designed to answer this question by estimating the total burden of disease (Gold et al., 2002). The final result is expressed in units of years of life lost. The method is based on measuring two components of ill health: years lost due to premature death (YLL) and years lost to disability (YLD) (Mathers et al., 2003):

$$DALY = YLL + YLD$$

A wide range of data is needed to feed this seemingly simple equation, including mortality statistics (numbers and causes of death) and disability statistics (age of onset and average duration of disability, plus average distribution of disability severity). Apart from the poor standard of data collection in many countries, the use of subjective weighting for age and disease is also a source of criticism (Anand & Hanson, 1997).

- Years lost from premature death (YLL). The basic calculation is simple:

$$YLL = \text{expected years of life} - \text{age at death}$$

It is assumed that men live an average of 80 years and women live 82.5 years. This is the only gender inequity allowed in DALY calculations. Unfortunately, it gets more complex once age at death is weighted by its "value" (Arnessan & Nord, 1999). The extremes of age are counted less than early adulthood and the final figure is also discounted at 3 percent per year. Once the weights and discounts are applied, an infant death corresponds to 33 DALYs.

- Years lost to disability (YLD). Again, the basic equation is simple:

$$YLD = \text{duration of disability} \times \text{disability weight}$$

Complications occur with the choice of disability adjustment. Disability score varies from zero (perfect health) to one (dead); blindness is scored at 0.6 and loss of a limb is 0.3. For example, a five-year-old girl who loses a leg to cancer is expected to live a further 77.5 years with her disability. Once this is adjusted by disability weight, non-uniform age adjustment, and annual discount, it results in 10.5 YLDs.

A previously healthy young man who suffers paraplegia at 20 years and dies of a heart attack at 60 years has lost years of life due to disability and also to premature death. The final DALY takes into account both those separate factors. Table 6.4 gives an example of these calculations taken from the first Global Burden of Disease study (Lopez, 2005) by listing the most common causes of years lost to premature death (YLL), years lost to disability (YLD), and total disease burden (DALY).

Table 6.4: World's leading causes of premature mortality, disability, and disease burden measured in the 1990 Global Burden of Disease study

	Mortality (YLL)		Disability (YLD)		Total Disease Burden (DALY)	
Rank	Disease	% Total YLL	Disease	% Total YLD	Disease burden	% Total DALY
1	Pneumonia	12.0	Depression	10.7	Pneumonia	8.2
2	Diarrheal disease	10.4	Iron-deficiency anemia	4.7	Diarrheal disease	7.2
3	Perinatal conditions	9.1	Falls	4.6	Perinatal conditions	6.7
4	Ischemic heart disease	4.6	Alcohol abuse	3.4	Depression	3.7
5	Measles	4.0	COPD	3.1	Ischemic heart disease	3.4
6	Tuberculosis	3.8	Bipolar disease	3.0	Cerebrovascular disease	2.8
7	Cerebrovascular disease	3.6	Congenital anomalies	2.8	Tuberculosis	2.8
8	Malaria	3.0	Osteoarthritis	2.8	Measles	2.7
9	Road traffic accidents	2.9	Schizophrenia	2.6	Road traffic accidents	2.5
10	Congenital anomalies	2.2	Obsessive-compulsive disorders	2.2	Congenital anomalies	2.4

Source: Lopez (2005)

▌SOURCES OF POPULATION HEALTH INFORMATION

To study the phenomena of disease without books is to sail an uncharted sea, while to study books without patients is not to go to sea at all.

— William Osler

It has become very clear over the last 10–15 years that mortality statistics offer only a very restricted view of population health. In order to gain a deeper understanding of the complex variables underlying population health, it is necessary to find information on growth, nutrition, education, immunization, and many others. For those who plan large-scale health interventions, it is necessary to have access to much broader information, including economic data, population statistics, and even measured deficiencies of the existing health system. Although there are many sources of information, the following section gives information on the largest useful databases for health information concerning children and adults.

Child Health Data

Basic Mortality Rates

The most commonly used indicators of child mortality are: Infant Mortality Rate (IMR) (number of infant deaths in a year divided by the number of live births in the same year) and the Under Five Mortality Rate (U5MR) (number of children who die before their fifth birthday among a cohort of children born in a year). In many parts of the world, 5 percent of live births are dead by one month of age, 10 percent by one year (IMR, 100 per 1,000 live births), and 15 percent by five years (U5MR, 150 per 1,000 live births).

Both IMR and U5MR have been chosen as indicators for the Millennium Development Goals Project, so updated information is available at the Millennium Development Goal Indicator Database. Both are also included in UNICEF's annual *State of the World's Children Report* (UNICEF, 2006d) and the WHO's annual *World Health Report* (World Health Organization, 2006b).

Causes of Mortality

Although burden-of-disease measures, such as the DALY, are increasingly replacing simple mortality data in adults, this methodology can be questioned for very small children. Trying to calculate the years of life lost in a six-month-old child who dies from a combination of malnutrition and dehydration requires the use of a number of adjustment factors. Consequently, most observers still use mortality figures to assess the major diseases of children. The best source for updated information is the statistical annex of the annual *World Health Report* (World Health Organization, 2006b). In its most recent report, there were 10.6 million deaths of children under five. The most common causes were neonatal, acute respiratory infections, and diarrheal diseases.

Child Growth

As discussed in Chapter 5, the principal measures of child growth are underweight, stunting, and wasting. The prevalence of underweight children below five years of age is a Millennium Development Goal indicator; updated information for this variable can be found on the MDG Indicators Database (*UN Millennium Development Goals*, n.d.). A larger and more organized source of information is the Child Nutrition Database found at the UNICEF Web site (UNICEF, 2006b). The WHO also maintains a small Database on Child Growth and Malnutrition (World Health Organization, 2006a).

Nutrition

The United Nations Food and Agricultural Organization is the principal source of nutritional statistics. The statistical database at its main Web site (Food and Agriculture Organization, n.d.) deals with global data ranging from forestry to fish production. However, the organization also produces an annual summary of nutrition called the "State of Food Insecurity" (Food and Agriculture Organization, 2005), which is an excellent source for information on food supply and prevalence of malnutrition.

Education

The vital place of education in overall population health and development is reflected in the fact that five of the MDG targets involve measures of education. These include gender ratio of school enrolment and proportion of children starting grade one who finish grade five. Updated information is available at the MDG Indicators Database. However, most education-monitoring research is done by the UN Educational, Scientific, and Cultural Organization (UNESCO). MDG indicators plus a host of other educational data can be found at the UNESCO Institute for Statistics (n.d.).

Immunization

Immunization statistics collected from a range of organizations are summarized on a regular basis by WHO and UNICEF. The latest immunization summary (UNICEF, 2006c) is now available and provides a wide range of immunization data per country for the six major child vaccines (pertussis, tetanus, measles, polio, diphtheria, BCG).

Adult Health Data

General Mortality Statistics

There has been a move away from mortality statistics toward the use of summary measures of health such as the DALY. This concept was first introduced on a large scale during the 1990 Global Burden of Disease study. The GBD study generated enormous amount of information, which was gradually published in the years following the initial study. Summaries can be found at the Global Burden of Disease 1990 Web site (World Health Organization, n.d.-b). Many other research articles analyzing various aspects of the original data are also available in the medical literature (Murray & Lopez, 1997a). The second Global Burden of Disease Study was carried out in 2000. Again, the latest summaries can be found at the GBD 2002 Web site (World Health Organization, n.d.-c), the medical literature (Mathers et al., 2003), and also WHO's publication, *World Health Statistics 2005*.

Maternal Mortality and Morbidity

Improvements in maternal health are important Millennium Development Goals. Two of the indicators include Maternal Mortality Ratio (number of maternal deaths in a year per 100,000 live births) and the proportion of births attended by skilled health personnel. Updated information can be found at the MDG Indicators Database. The primary data are held on UNICEF's Maternal Health Database (UNICEF, n.d.). The usual problems of incomplete birth and death registration complicate the collection of accurate data. The average world figure for maternal mortality ratio is 400, but it is over 800 in Sub-Saharan Africa. Lifetime risk of maternal death varies from one in 2,800 in developed countries to less than one in 20 in parts of Sub-Saharan Africa. The UNICEF Maternal Health Database also includes information on female morbidity, particularly statistics on female genital mutilation, antenatal care, contraceptive use, and fertility.

Population Statistics

Population numbers are a vital part of health measurement so there are plenty of sources of current information. The UN Population Information Network is a good starting point (United Nations Population Division, n.d.).

Contraception

Condom use is a Millennium Development Goal in terms of combatting HIV/AIDS. Clearly, information on the broader subject of contraception use is also of importance. The UN publication, *World Contraceptive Use 2003*, can be downloaded from the UN Population Division Web site (United Nations Populations Division, 2005a). Current information on contraceptive use and fertility rate is also available at the UNICEF Maternal Health Database (UNICEF, n.d.).

Clean Water and Sanitation Access

Target 10 of the Millennium Development Goals is to halve the proportion of people without sustainable access to safe drinking water and sanitation. Statistics on the availability of sanitation are available at the Demographic and Social Statistics section of the UN Statistics Database (United Nations Statistics Division, 2005). The WHO also devotes an entire Web site to the topic of water sanitation and health (World Health Organization, n.d.-f).

Other Useful Sources

The UN Common Database (United Nations Statistics Division, 2006) has a seemingly endless list of information grouped under 29 major headings (United Nations Statistics Division, 2006). You can study everything from cement production to fertility rates. If you are looking for obscure information, this is a good place to start.

The World Bank's (2005b) annual publication, *World Development Indicators*, summarizes a wide range of development indicators. The 2005 version includes 800 indicators in 83 tables; so again, this is a good place to start if you are looking for obscure numbers.

The CIA's (2006) World Factbook Web site provides easily digestible information for foreign travellers. Apart from giving details of just about every country in the world, it also gives some data on the major demographic indicators such as mortality, population, and economic indicators. It is an excellent first source for those travelling to exotic places.

Finally, the United Nations World Population database (United Nations Population Division, 2005b) and the World Bank Health, Nutrition and Statistics (HNP) database (World Bank, n.d.), both offer convenient collections of health data on a wide range of topics.

■ SUMMARY

Twenty years ago, developing world health research was dominated by studies of child mortality. It was generally thought that infectious diseases were the main health problem while the dreadful annual mortality of women during childbirth received very little attention. Time has changed all those attitudes. An emphasis on children is obviously important, but a healthy society requires healthy adults and research now reflects that view. For a variety of reasons — particularly the need to monitor large-scale projects such as the Millennium Development Goals and the demands of cost effective health planning — it has been necessary to introduce better measures of population health over the last two decades to meet these new demands.

Health research has moved away from simple mortality data and has increasingly adopted more sophisticated measures of the social burden that diseases produce. In addition to the shorter-term pain and suffering caused by disease or death, significant health problems also impose a longer-term burden both on the affected individual and also the broader society. Using a variety of techniques, it is now possible to estimate the "cost" of different diseases in terms of years of life lost. It should always be remembered that although these newer measurement techniques offer a greater insight into population health, they do bring their own problems, including the increased expense of complex data gathering plus increased chances of measurement and calculation error.

Despite these problems, newer measurement techniques such as Disability-Adjusted Life Expectancy

(DALE) and Disability-Adjusted Life Years (DALY) now have an established place in the measurement of population health. The principal insight gained from their use has been an understanding that non-lethal diseases, such as mental ill health and traffic accidents, actually produce a greater burden of disease for society than the more intuitively obvious common causes of mortality. Apart from being useful in the monitoring of large-scale health projects, these newer measurement tools also allow health planners to target their limited budgets toward those diseases that cause the greatest burden in their local population.

RESOURCES

References

Anand, S., & Hanson, K. (1997). "Disability-adjusted life years: A critical review." *Journal of Health Economics, 16*, 685–702.

Arnessan, A., & Nord, E. (1999). "The value of DALY life: Problems with ethics and validity of disability-adjusted life years." *British Medical Journal, 319*, 1423–1425.

Arudo, J., et al. (2003). "Comparison of government statistics and demographic surveillance to monitor mortality in children less than five years old in rural Western Kenya." *American Journal of Tropical Medicine and Hygiene, 68*, 30–37.

Bingham, P., et al. (2004). "John Snow, William Farr, and the 1849 outbreak of cholera that affected London." *Public Health, 118*, 387–394.

Centers for Disease Control and Prevention. (n.d.). *Severe Acute Respiratory Syndrome.* Retrieved from www.cdc.gov/ncidod/sars.

Central Intelligence Agency. (2006). "Guide to rank order pages." In *The world factbook.* Retrieved from www.cia.gov/cia/publications/factbook/docs/rankorderguide.html.

childinfo.org/areas/birthregistration/countrydata.php.

Cooper, R., et al. (1998). "Disease burden in Sub-Saharan Africa: What should we conclude in the absence of data?" *Lancet, 351*, 208–210.

Daniels, I. (1998). "Historical perspectives on health. Semmelweis: A lesson to relearn?" *Journal of the Royal Society of Health, 118*, 367–370.

Doll, R., & Hill, B. (1950). "Smoking and carcinoma of the lung: A preliminary report." *British Medical Journal, 2*, 739–748.

Food and Agriculture Organization. (2005). *The state of food insecurity in the world 2005.* Retrieved from www.fao.org/sof/sofi.

Food and Agriculture Organization. (n.d.). *FAO Statistics.* Retrieved from www.fao.org/waicent/portal/statistics_en.asp.

Ghana Health Assessment Team. (1981). "A quantitative method of assessing the health impact of different diseases in less developed countries." *International Journal of Epidemiology, 10*, 1075–1089.

Gold, M., et al. (2002). "HALYS and QALYS and DALYS, oh my: Similarities and differences in summary measures of population health." *Annual Review of Public Health, 23*, 115–134.

Greenberg, S. (1997). "The 'Dreadful Visitation': Public health and public awareness in 17th-century London." *Bulletin of the Medical Library Association, 85*, 391–401.

Halley, E. (1693). *An estimate of the degrees of mortality of mankind, drawn from curious tables of the births and funerals at the City of Breslaw.* Retrieved from www.pierre-marteau.com/editions/1693-mortality/halley-text.html.

Houweling, T., et al. (2003). "Measuring health inequality among children in developing countries: Does the choice of indicator matter?" *International Journal for Equity in Health, 2*, 8–20.

John Snow Society. (n.d.). Retrieved from www.johnsnowsociety.org.

Lopez, A. (2005). "The evolution of the Global Burden of Disease framework for disease, injury and risk factor quantification: Developing the evidence base for national, regional, and global public health action." *Globalization and Health, 1,* 5–13.

Lu, T., et al. (2000). "Accuracy of cause-of-death coding in Taiwan: Types of miscoding and effects on mortality statistics." *International Journal of Epidemiology, 29,* 336–343.

Mathers, C., et al. (2001). "Healthy life expectancies in 191 countries—1999." *Lancet, 357,* 1685–1691.

Mathers, C., et al. (2003). *Global burden of disease in 2002: Data sources, methods, and results* (Health Policy discussion paper no. 54). Retrieved from www.who.int/healthinfo/paper54.pdf.

Mathers, C., et al. (2005). "Counting the dead and what they died from: An assessment of the global cause of death data." *Bulletin of the World Health Organization, 83,* 171–177.

"Measuring the efficiency of health systems." (2001). *British Medical Journal, 323,* 295–296.

Murray, C., & Lopez, A. (1997a). "Mortality by cause for eight regions of the world: Global Burden of Disease Study." *Lancet, 349,* 1269–1276.

Murray, C., & Lopez, A. (1997b). "Regional patterns of disability-free life expectancy and disability-adjusted life expectancy: Global Burden of Disease Study." *Lancet, 349,* 1347–1352.

Norman, G., & Streiner, D. (2003). *PDQ Statistics.* Hamilton: B.C. Decker.

Parliamentary Office of Science and Technology. (2006). *Healthy life expectancy* (POSTnote no. 257). Retrieved from www.parliament.uk/parliamentary_offices/post/pubs2006.cfm.

Pelletier, D., et al. (1995). "The effects of malnutrition on child mortality in developing countries." *Bulletin of the World Health Organization, 73,* 443–448.

"Pneumocystis pneumonia—Los Angeles." (1981.) *Morbidity and Mortality Weekly Report, 30,* 250–252.

Roman census figures. (n.d.) Retrieved from www.csun.edu/~hcfll004/romancensus.html.

Rothman, K. (1996). "Lessons from John Graunt." *Lancet, 347,* 37–39.

Sibai, A. (2004). "Mortality certification and cause of death reporting in developing countries." *Bulletin of the World Health Organization, 82,* 83.

Slought Museum. (n.d.). *Bills of Mortality, London.* Retrieved from slought.org/content/410265/.

Snow, R., et al. (1992). "Childhood deaths in Africa: Uses and limitations of verbal autopsies." *Lancet, 340,* 351–355.

Sullivan, D. (1971). "A single index of mortality and morbidity." *HSMHA Health Report, 86,* 347–354.

UK Office of National Statistics. (2003). *Review of the registrar general on deaths in England and Wales* (Series DH1, no. 36). Retrieved from www.statistics.gov.uk.

UN Millennium Development Goals. (n.d.). Retrieved from www.un.org/millenniumgoals.

UNESCO Institute for Statistics. (n.d.). *Statistical tables.* Retrieved from www.uis.unesco.org/ev.php?URL_ID=5275&URL_DO=DO_TOPIC&URL_SECTION=201.

UNICEF. (2006a). *Birth registration: Statistical tables.* Retrieved from www.childinfo.org/areas/birthregistration.

UNICEF. (2006b). *Malnutrition.* Retrieved from www.childinfo.org/areas/malnutrition/.

UNICEF. (2006c). *Immunization summary 2006.* Retrieved from www.unicef.org/publications/index_31046.html.

UNICEF. (2006d). *State of the world's children 2006: Statistics.* Retrieved from www.unicef.org/sowc06/statistics/statistics.php.

UNICEF. (n.d.). *Maternal health.* Retrieved from www.childinfo.org/eddb/maternal.htm.

United Nations Population Division. (2005a). *World contraceptive use 2005.* Retrieved from www.un.org/esa/population/publications/contraceptive2005/WCU2005.htm.

United Nations Population Division. (2005b) *World population prospects.* Retrieved from esa.un.org/unpp.

United Nations Population Division. (n.d.). *United Nations population information network: Data.* Retrieved from www.un.org/popin/data.html.

United Nations Statistics Division. (2005). *Demographic and social statistics: Social indicators.* Retrieved from unstats.un.org/unsd/demographic/products/socind/default.htm.

United Nations Statistics Division. (2006). *United Nations common database.* Retrieved from unstats. un.org/unsd/cdb.

World Bank. (2005a). *Global Monitoring Report 2005.* Retrieved from www.worldbank.int.

World Bank. (2005b). *World development indicators 2005.* Retrieved from www.worldbank.org.

World Bank. (n.d.). *Health, nutrition and population.* Retrieved from www.worldbank.org/hnpstats.

World Health Organization. (2005). *World Health Statistics 2005.* Retrieved from www.who.int/healthinfo/statistics/en/.

World Health Organization. (2006a). *Global database on child growth and malnutrition.* Retrieved from www.who.int/nutgrowthdb/database/en/.

World Health Organization. (2006b) *World health report 2005: Statistical annex.* Retrieved from www.who.int/whr/2005/annex/en/index.html.

World Health Organization. (n.d.-a). *Epidemic and pandemic alert and response.* Retrieved from www.who.int/csr.

World Health Organization. (n.d.-b). *Global burden of disease 1990.* Retrieved from www.who.int/healthinfo/bod1990study.

World Health Organization. (n.d.-c). *Global burden of disease 2002.* Retrieved from www.who.int/healthinfo/bodabout.

World Health Organization. (n.d.-d). *Global burden of disease project.* Retrieved from www.who.int/healthinfo/bodproject.

World Health Organization. (n.d.-e). *Health metrics network.* Retrieved from www.who.int/healthmetrics.

World Health Organization. (n.d.-f). *Water sanitation and health.* Retrieved from www.who.int/water_sanitation_health.

Recommended Reading

Merson, M., Black, R., & Mills, A. (2005). *International public health: Diseases, programs, systems, and policies.* Sudbury: Jones and Bartlett.

Murray, C., et al. (Eds.). (2005). *Summary measures of population health: Concepts, ethics, measurement, and application.* Geneva: World Health Organization.

Norman, G., & Streiner, D. (2003). *PDQ statistics.* Hamilton: B.C. Decker.

Streiner, D., & Norman, G. (1998). *PDQ epidemiology.* Hamilton: B.C. Decker.

World Health Organization. (2005). *Preventing chronic diseases: A vital investment.* Geneva: World Health Organization.

World Health Organization. (2005). *World Health Statistics 2005.* Retrieved from www.who.int/healthinfo/statistics/en/.

Chapter 7

Child and Adult Health Statistics for the Developing World

Medicine, to produce health,
has to examine disease;
and music, to create harmony,
must investigate discord.
— Plutarch

OBJECTIVES
After completing this chapter, you should be able to

- understand the magnitude of avoidable child mortality in developing countries
- appreciate the central role of the mother in the safe growth and development of children
- understand the major causes of adult morbidity and mortality in the developing world and their trends with time
- understand the magnitude and underlying causes of maternal mortality

Over the last two or three decades, population health research has provided an increasingly sophisticated understanding of ill health in developing countries. Health assessment tools and the focus of health research have had to change to accommodate these improvements in our understanding of the complexity of disease. More recently, the need to monitor the Millennium Development Goals has added further emphasis to the need for accurate population health data.

However, it should always be remembered that the newer measurement methods rely on complex calculations that are open to sampling error, measurement error, and problems of inaccurate data sources.

Chapter 6 examined the difficulties of measuring disease accurately. In this chapter, we will examine the results of that research in order to answer the questions: What is the magnitude of morbidity and mortality in different regions of the world and what are the major underlying causes of that ill health? This is not a sterile academic topic—high-quality health data is an absolutely essential foundation for good health care. When combined with modern methods of risk analysis, it allows planners to adjust their programs to meet local requirements in the most cost-effective way. Because of the unique problems associated with pregnancy-related diseases, maternal mortality will be reviewed as a separate adult category.

ADULT HEALTH IN THE DEVELOPING WORLD

Common Causes of Mortality

Twenty-five years ago, the world's leading experts in cardiovascular diseases warned of an impending epidemic of heart disease in developing countries. This warning was largely ignored.
—Gro Brundtland

Much of the information about adult mortality in the developing world is based either on registration of births and deaths or information collected during population surveys. Although many parts of the developing world are now producing more reliable data, the results should always be viewed as a best estimate rather than a gold standard, particularly where data from Sub-Saharan African countries are concerned. It should also be remembered that the term "developing world" is simply a term of convenience referring to a large number of individual states. Average values calculated for such a heterogeneous collection of countries are just that—averages. They provide some information on broad trends, but individual variations may be very large.

Table 7.1: A moment of Zen

	Following strikes in early 2005, the Vietnamese government raised the minimum wage in cities to US $55 per month.
Average monthly salary paid to Michael Jordan to endorse Nike running shoes:	Average monthly salary paid to 36,364 minimum-wage workers to make Nike running shoes:
US $2.0 million	**US $2.0 million**
Source: Goldman & Blakeley (2006)	Source: IPS News Agency

There will always be differences between individual states and also between different communities within those countries.

Although times and their diseases have changed, the original 1990 Global Burden of Disease Study still has great value as a source of research data. Study surveys, reviews, and basic statistical data can be found on the WHO Web site (World Health Organization, n.d.-c). The WHO also maintains a separate site for the 2000 study results (World Health Organization, n.d.-d). The review article by Mathers and Loncar is the most current update (Mathers & Loncar, 2005). It also includes tabulated data by country and region plus projections for 2030.

Mortality in 1990

Fifty million people died in 1990, 12.7 million of whom were children below the age of five. The great burden of this mortality fell on developing countries; 98 percent of all childhood deaths and 83 percent of deaths in people 15–59 years occurred in developing countries (World

Box 7.1: History notes

Lillian Wald (1867–1940)

As with Virchow, it is difficult to imagine how someone managed to achieve so much in one lifetime. Wald was born to a wealthy middle-class American family and studied to be a nurse. She rebelled against strict hospital practice and took further training to join the newly formed visiting nurses who worked in the poorest areas of New York. She later coined the term "public health nurse" and, as an educator and administrator, helped them to become a respected professional organization. Based on her experiences of the squalor of the Lower East Side, she devoted the rest of her life to improving the conditions of the poor. The centre she started for the poor (the Henry Street Project) is still running today (as is the Public Health Nursing Organization). Her advocacy led to school nurses, school meals, the Women's Trade Union League, and respect for the rights of immigrants. Not surprisingly, she was also instrumental in the New York State women's suffrage movement. It is impossible to list all the health initiatives started by this dynamo. After her funeral, the US president, New York governor, and New York mayor each talked about her life's work to a packed Carnegie Hall audience. For more information, visit the Jewish Women's Archive at www.jwa.org.

Table 7.2: Leading causes of death in 1990

Rank	Developed Countries	Developing Countries
1	Ischemic heart disease	Pneumonia
2	Cerebrovascular disease	Ischemic heart disease
3	Lung cancer	Cerebrovascular disease
4	Pneumonia	Diarrheal diseases
5	Chronic obstructive lung disease	Perinatal diseases
6	Colon cancer	Tuberculosis
7	Stomach cancer	Chronic obstructive lung disease
8	Road traffic accidents	Measles
9	Suicide	Malaria
10	Diabetes mellitus	Road traffic accidents

Source: Murray & Lopez (1996)

Apart from pneumonia at number four, the dominant causes of mortality were atherosclerotic vascular disease and cancer. In contrast, five of the leading causes of mortality in developing countries (pneumonia, diarrheal diseases, tuberculosis, measles, and malaria) were infectious. However, the effect of a growing middle class is shown by the presence of atherosclerotic vascular diseases at second and third positions on the table, even in developing countries (Gaziano, 2005). The HIV/AIDS epidemic had not yet reached the "top 10."

Mortality in 2002

The most recently updated and analyzed global burden of disease reports that 57

Health Organization, n.d.-c). At the time of the first global study, the world was more clearly split between developed and developing countries. There was, of course, a global middle class formed from developing countries with relatively low mortality rates, but their growth had not yet had a big impact on mortality rate statistics.

As Table 7.2 shows, by 1990, developed countries had almost eradicated infectious diseases as a major cause of mortality.

million people died in 2002, 10.6 million of whom were children under five years of age (Mathers & Loncar, 2005). The great bulk of these child deaths still occurred in developing countries, but there has been a shift in distribution of deaths in the 15–59 year group. The increasing development of China, Brazil, and other low-mortality areas of the developing world (Friedman & Wyman, 2005) has effectively formed a global middle class that has greatly altered the distribution of mortality. The 2002 data is displayed in Table 7.3 under three headings: developed countries, developing countries (low mortality), and developing countries (high mortality).

The common causes of mortality for developed countries in 2002 did not change significantly compared to 1990. The so-called diseases of affluence, or lifestyle, have firmly established themselves as the major causes of mortality in prosperous countries. Progress against these will require significant alterations in population behaviour as we will discuss later. The major change in high-mortality developing countries is the appearance of HIV/AIDS at number two on the list (World Health Organization, 2005a). Other infectious diseases also remain major causes of mortality (diarrheal diseases, malaria, tuberculosis, pneumonia, and measles). However, even in these countries, atherosclerosis is becoming increasingly common.

Among low-mortality developing

Table 7.3: Leading causes of death in 2002

Rank	Developed Countries	% Total	Developing, Low Mortality	% Total	Developing, High Mortality	% Total
1	Ischemic heart disease	22.8	Cerebrovascular disease	13.8	Pneumonia	10.0
2	Cerebrovascular disease	13.3	Ischemic heart disease	9.7	HIV/AIDS	9.6
3	Lung cancer	4.5	Chronic obstructive lung disease	9.5	Ischemic heart disease	9.3
4	Pneumonia	3.3	Pneumonia	3.7	Perinatal diseases	6.6
5	Chronic obstructive lung disease	3.2	Perinatal diseases	3.6	Diarrheal diseases	5.5
6	Colon cancer	2.6	Tuberculosis	3.3	Cerebrovascular disease	5.3
7	Diabetes mellitus	1.8	Stomach cancer	3.1	Malaria	4.4
8	Suicide	1.8	Road traffic accidents	3.0	Tuberculosis	3.6
9	Hypertensive heart disease	1.7	Lung cancer	2.8	Chronic obstructive lung disease	2.8
10	Stomach cancer	1.6	Hypertensive heart disease	2.7	Measles	2.5

Source: Mathers & Loncar (2005)

Figure 7.1: Smoking rates are falling in most industrialized countries, but they are rising rapidly in the developing world. The WHO estimates that tobacco-related diseases kill 5 million people every year; this is expected to double by 2025. The photograph shows a man smoking while fishing in the Ouro Preto River in Brazil. (Photographer Denis Marchand, with permission of IDRC Photo Library.)

countries, the more dubious benefits of increasing prosperity are clearly visible in the fact that cerebrovascular disease, ischemic heart disease, and chronic obstructive lung disease hold the top three spots; all are closely linked, epidemiologically, to behavioural factors such as smoking (Ezzati et al., 2005), sedentary lifestyle, and excess nutrition. However, infectious diseases still retain their hold with tuberculosis and pneumonia on the list, along with perinatal diseases.

Causes of Morbidity and Total Burden of Disease

> Health is my expected heaven.
> —John Keats

As discussed in the last chapter, the total burden of disease is calculated by adding the years lost to disability (YLD) to the years of life lost from early mortality

(YLL). A high under-five-year mortality will skew the results because of the large number of years lost due to a child's death. Non-lethal disabling conditions do not cause as many years of lost life, but the additive effect of common disabling diseases does have a significant impact upon the final list of significant causes of disease burden (Feachem, 1995).

Morbidity and Burden of Disease in 1990

The most surprising finding of the first 1990 study of morbidity was the heavy burden caused by neuropsychiatric disorders (Chisholm et al., 2005). As Table 7.4 shows, four of the top 10 causes of years lost to disability in 1990 were psychiatric diseases (obsessive compulsive disorder, schizophrenia, bipolar disorder, and depression). It should be remembered that this was the first attempt at assessing global disability. As time passed, data collection improved and the range of diseases included in the definition of

Table 7.4: Leading causes of morbidity and total disease burden in 1990

Rank	Years Lost to Disability	% Total YLD	Total Burden of Disease	% Total DALY
1	Depression	10.7	Pneumonia	8.2
2	Iron-deficiency anemia	4.7	Diarrheal disease	7.2
3	Falls	4.6	Perinatal diseases	6.7
4	Alcohol abuse	3.4	Depression	3.7
5	Chronic obstructive lung disease	3.1	Ischemic heart disease	3.4
6	Bipolar disorder	3.0	Cerebrovascular disease	2.8
7	Congenital anomalies	2.8	Tuberculosis	2.8
8	Osteoarthritis	2.8	Measles	2.7
9	Schizophrenia	2.6	Road traffic accidents	2.5
10	Obsessive compulsive disorder	2.2	Congenital anomalies	2.4

Source: Lopez (2005)

disabilities increased as experience was gained.

As mentioned above, almost a quarter of the deaths in 1990 occurred in children less than five years of age. This enormous burden of potential years lost to avoidable diseases dominates the list of disease burden. Pneumonia, diarrheal diseases, perinatal conditions, and measles all reflect the high rate of childhood disease in the developing world. The HIV/AIDS epidemic had not yet grown sufficiently to enter the top 10 list.

Morbidity and Burden of Disease in 2002

Direct comparisons between the leading causes of years lost due to disability between 1990 and 2002 should be made with caution because of the changes and improvements made to measurement techniques with time. Table 7.5 shows that depression remains the most common cause of morbidity, although the burden is considerably higher among females (World Health Organization, n.d.-e). Alcohol and drug use disorders are nearly

six times higher among males compared to females and make up at least a quarter of male neuropsychiatric diseases (United Nations Office for Drug Control, 2000).

The table also lists global estimates of total disease burden. HIV/AIDS is a major contributor to years of life lost due to disability in high-mortality developing regions, but its effect is much smaller in low-mortality regions of the world. When the distribution of disease burden is examined, more than 80 percent of years lost from disability occur in developing countries. Developing world populations not only face shorter lives but they also have less healthy lives compared to those in developed countries.

Although deaths in under-five-year-old children formed a smaller percentage of total deaths in 2002, the list of major disease burdens is still dominated by perinatal conditions, pneumonia, and diarrheal diseases. The most obvious change in the 2002 list is the appearance of HIV/AIDS at number two as a cause of mortality and number three as a cause

Table 7.5: Leading causes of morbidity by gender and total disease burden in 2002

Rank	Years Lost to Disability, Male	% Total YLD	Years Lost to Disability, Female	% Total YLD	Total Burden of Disease (YLL + YLD)	% Total DALY
1	Depression	9.6	Depression	13.9	Perinatal disease	6.5
2	Alcohol abuse	5.8	Pregnancy-related diseases	6.4	Pneumonia	5.8
3	Hearing loss	4.8	Cataracts	4.9	HIV/AIDS	5.8
4	Cataracts	4.5	Hearing loss	4.4	Depression	4.5
5	Schizophrenia	2.8	Osteoarthritis	3.1	Diarrheal disease	4.1
6	Perinatal disease	2.8	Vision loss	2.7	Ischemic heart disease	3.9
7	Bipolar disorder	2.5	Schizophrenia	2.7	Cerebrovascular disease	3.3
8	Asthma	2.3	Perinatal disease	2.6	Malaria	3.0
9	Vision loss	2.3	Bipolar disorder	2.4	Road traffic accidents	2.6
10	Cerebrovascular disease	2.2	Migraine	1.9	Tuberculosis	2.4

Source: Mathers & Loncar (2005)

of total disease burden (World Health Organization, 2005a).

Practical Solutions

The devil has put a penalty on all things we enjoy in life. Either we suffer in health or we suffer in soul or we get fat.

— Albert Einstein

Vast amounts of money are spent on health care, even by developing countries; the continuing high level of mortality from avoidable and treatable diseases suggests there is room for improvement in its distribution. As the *World Development Report* pointed out in 1993, "For the world as a whole in 1990, public and private expenditure on health services was about US $1,700 billion or 8 percent of total world product. High-income countries spent almost 90 percent of this amount, for an average of US $1,500 per person. Developing countries spent about US $170 billion or 4 percent of their GNP, for an average of $41 per person" (World Bank, 1993). Budget increases are slow, so there is clearly a need to use the available financial resources in the most cost-effective manner possible.

Whatever motivations might have guided developing world health expenditure in the past (status quo, inherited colonial practices, bias toward urban areas and those with money, etc.), those decisions were not often based on scientific research. Despite the emphasis on primary health care introduced at Alma Ata in 1978, many developing countries still spend a disproportionate amount of their health budgets on expensive urban hospitals that do little for the health of their rural populations (Cueto, 2004; World Health Organization, 2000). Dating from the original work by the Ghana Health Assessment Team in 1981, a more results-based approach to decision making has slowly crept into the budget allocation process in developing countries. This is reflected in the establishment of a Commission on Macroeconomics and Health, under the chairmanship of Jeffrey Sachs in 2000 (World Health Organization, n.d.-b). Although the potential errors associated with the DALY methodology should always be considered, the technique does provide health planners with a tool to identify major health problems and measure the effectiveness of any interventions (Anand & Hanson, 1997).

With time, techniques developed in the business world, such as risk assessment and cost-effectiveness analysis, are now finding their way into the area of public health. The World Health Organization has moved with the times and devotes parts of its main Web site to both these topics. Apart from the use of overly contrived acronyms, they are useful sources of information. Both the WHO-STEPS Web site (STEP-wise approach to risk factor Surveillance) and the WHO-CHOICE Web site (CHOosing Interventions that are Cost Effective) contain introductory manuals that can be downloaded, plus relevant research articles (Tan-Torres et al., 2003; World Health Organization, 2003, n.d.-a, n.d.-f).

The introduction of results-based decision making is long overdue. One of the major obstacles to the widespread acceptance of primary health care, following Alma Ata, was the great difficulty in demonstrating and quantifying any potential benefits (Magnussen et al., 2004).

If modern health assessment tools had been available in 1978, it is possible that heated debate about the topic might have generated more illumination and a bit less warmth.

Risk Assessment

The first attempt at identifying risk factors on a global basis was published in the *World Development Report 1993* (World Bank, 1993). Table 7.6 gives the most recently updated mortality risk factor analysis by development level and gender. As expected, the major risks in high-mortality developing countries are underweight (contributing to at least 50 percent of childhood deaths) (World Bank, 2006), micronutrient deficiencies, unsafe sex, and poor sanitation. Even in these countries, some of the risk factors of affluence such as tobacco, cholesterol level, and overweight are starting to become obvious. This trend is taken to its extreme in developed countries where blood pressure, cholesterol level, overweight, tobacco, and alcohol are the dominant risk factors. Infectious risks and unsafe sex are still important factors in low-mortality developing countries, but the risks from blood pressure, cholesterol, and tobacco show they are doing their best to catch up with the affluent lifestyle.

Cost-Effective Interventions

Since health budgets in developing countries are limited, it is necessary to plan health interventions to achieve the greatest benefits for least cost. Once risk factors have been identified, then it is possible to base cost-effective interventions on that information. At the time of the *World Development Report 1993*, the World Bank used this approach to identify a suggested basic package of treatments aimed at addressing the major risk factors found in

Table 7.6: Attributable mortality by risk factor, gender, and development

	Developing Countries, High Mortality		Developing Countries, Low Mortality		Developed Countries	
	Male	Female	Male	Female	Male	Female
Deaths (millions)	13.8	12.7	8.6	7.4	6.9	6.6
	% Total	% Total	% Total	% Total	% Total	% Total
Risk factors:						
Underweight	12.6	13.4	1.8	1.9	0.1	0.1
Iron deficiency	2.2	3.0	0.8	1.0	0.1	0.2
Vitamin A deficiency	2.3	3.3	0.2	0.4	<0.1	<0.1
Zinc deficiency	2.8	3.0	0.2	0.2	<0.1	<0.1
Blood pressure	7.4	7.5	12.7	15.1	20.1	23.9
Cholesterol	5.0	5.7	5.1	5.6	14.5	17.6
Overweight	1.1	2.0	4.2	5.6	9.6	11.5
Low fruit and vegetable intake	3.6	3.5	5.0	4.8	7.6	7.4
Low physical activity	2.3	2.3	2.8	3.2	6.0	6.7
Unsafe sex	9.3	10.9	0.8	1.3	0.2	0.6
Tobacco	7.5	1.5	12.2	2.9	26.3	9.3
Alcohol	2.6	0.6	8.5	1.6	8.0	<0.1
Illicit drugs	0.5	0.1	0.6	0.1	0.6	0.3
Poor sanitation/water	5.8	5.9	1.1	1.1	0.2	0.2
Pollution, urban	0.9	0.8	2.5	2.9	1.1	1.2
Pollution, indoors	3.6	4.3	1.9	5.4	0.1	0.2
Lead exposure	0.4	0.3	0.5	0.3	0.7	0.4

Source: World Health Organization (2002)

the global study of disease. The per capita cost for each of these interventions is listed inTable 7.7.

The so-called $12 basic package attracted criticism at the time (Pearson, 2000). The average health spending by developing countries in 1993 was roughly US $4–$5 per capita; it was felt that more than doubling this budget was hopelessly unrealistic. Rather than being taken too literally, the package is better used as a reminder that cost-effective analysis can lead to more equitable distribution of available health budgets. There are several examples of similar approaches. The early UNICEF Child Survival Revolution was designed around a package of four services (growth monitoring, oral rehydration, breast-feeding, and immunization) and the subsequent Integrated Management of Childhood Illness Program followed much the same philosophy (Gurry, 1990; Lambrechts, 1999). More recently, the Millennium Development Goals were

Table 7.7: 1993 World Development Report Basic Package of Health Interventions

Intervention	Per Capita Cost (1990) in US $
Extended immunization program	$ 0.5
School health (education plus deworming)	$ 0.3
Public health education (safe sex, tobacco, nutrition)	$ 1.4
Tobacco and alcohol control	$ 0.3
AIDS-prevention program	$ 1.7
Short-course chemotherapy for tuberculosis	$ 0.6
Management of sick children (pneumonia, dehydration)	$ 1.6
Prenatal and delivery care	$ 3.8
Family planning	$ 0.9
Treatment of sexually transmitted diseases	$ 0.2
Basic medical care (minor trauma and infections)	$ 0.7
Total	$12.0

Source: World Bank (1993)

designed to meet major health problems identified by cost-effective analysis.

CHILD HEALTH IN THE DEVELOPING WORLD

The child was diseased at birth, stricken with a hereditary ill that only the most vital men shake off. I mean poverty; the most deadly and prevalent of all diseases.

—Eugene O'Neill

Before starting this section, it is important to address the widespread misconception that treating sick children in developing countries is a pointless exercise: "High child mortality is just nature's way of keeping the population down." This notion is completely false. In developing areas of the world, children represent a form of security that will provide support to the parents when they are too old to earn a living. Consequently, families will continue to have children until they can be sure that at least a few will survive to adulthood. Once families are confident that their children stand a good chance of living, fertility rates start to drop.

The American demographer, W.S. Thompson (1929), described a four-stage process (demographic or fertility transition) that is followed by most countries as they emerge from poverty. It is characterized by large families during periods of poor health care, followed by a steady fall in family size once living standards and health care start to improve (see "Family Planning," Chapter 9, for more details). There is no unified fertility theory that explains this observation to everyone's satisfaction (there are several that raise furious debate) (Hirschman, 1994).

This trend does not depend on access to contraception. Birth rates in Ireland and Italy both fell during a period when contraception was illegal in those countries. Figure 7.2 shows that contraception use increases sharply once the under-five mortality falls below about 50 per 1,000 live births. Roughly speaking, families will take contraceptive advice once there is a perception that 95 percent of their newborns will survive to their fifth birthday. This may seem paradoxical, but in order to control population growth, it is necessary to improve the

Figure 7.2: Contraceptive use and under-five mortality rate

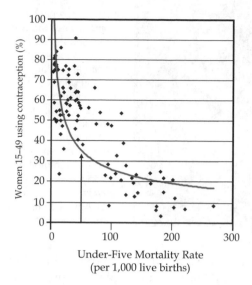

Sources: UNICEF (2006a, 2006c)

survival of children. Economic and social development, plus education for women, are ultimately the best contraceptives.

Common Causes of Mortality

> Time and fever burn away beauty from thoughtful children and the grave proves the child ephemeral.
> —W.H. Auden, *Lay your sleeping head*

Before interpreting statistical results, it is important to appreciate their potential measurement errors. The denominator for many child mortality death rates is the number of live-born children in a year. In developed countries, there is much debate surrounding this seemingly obvious definition. Countries that define a live-born child as one with any slight movement will have a higher denominator (and lower infant mortality rate) compared

to those using a more rigid definition of life (such as "fully sustained breathing"). Countries can move up and down the IMR league table simply by changing statistical definitions. In the developing world, much larger potential errors are caused by the fact that births (whether alive or dead) are often not registered at all (UNICEF, 2005b).

Child deaths have been monitored since the 1950s, but there was no clearly organized methodology and data distribution system until surprisingly recently. The 1990 World Summit for Children in New York generated an ambitious plan of action for child health, which acted as a catalyst for broad improvements in monitoring. The UN Population Division and UNICEF started the large task of organizing the available data from 1960 onwards (Hill et al., 2000). They also placed great emphasis on

Figure 7.3: Trends in child mortality rates

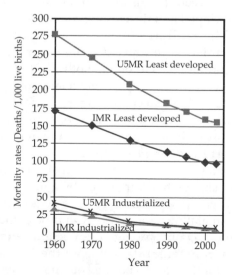

IMR: infant mortality rate; U5MR: under-five mortality rate

Source: UNICEF (2006a)

Figure 7.4: The bond between a mother and child is so close that, from a health point of view, the two are inseparable. A mother's levels of health and education are the principal determinants of her child's chance of reaching his or her fifth birthday. The photograph shows a Guatemalan mother getting to know her new infant. (Courtesy Pan American Health Organization photo gallery.)

making the results available to researchers through publications and the UNICEF Web site (UNICEF, 2006a). Although considerable practical problems still exist, the annual publication of child mortality data by UNICEF is a huge improvement on previous methods. Figure 7.3 shows the most recent trends in child mortality for developed and developing countries.

The pediatric psychologist, D.W. Winnicott, summed up the complete reliance of a child on its mother with his famous saying, "There is no such thing as an individual child." Figure 7.5 shows that there is almost a linear relationship between infant mortality and maternal mortality for 173 countries. Clearly, whatever harms a mother will also harm her child. Child care given by a healthy, educated woman, who has access to postnatal care and advice, can protect the infant against a range of infectious and environmental dangers. As the *World Health Report 2005* pointed out, no serious advances in child mortality can be made until equivalent attention is paid to female health, particularly education, gender

equality, and pregnancy-related medical care (World Health Organization, 2005c).

The *World Health Report 2005* revealed that nearly 10.6 million children below the age of five years died in 2003. We can measure the numbers, causes, and

Figure 7.5: Infant and maternal mortalities plotted for 173 countries

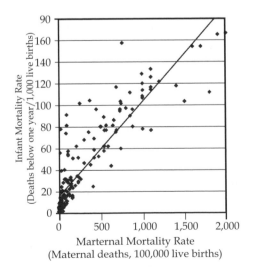

Sources: UNICEF (2006a, 2006c)

even estimate the tens of millions of potential years of life lost, but how do we measure the accumulated grief produced by these tragedies? Some will believe that developing world families are hardened to the death of children — the loss of one from eight is much easier to bear than the loss of one from two. This is not true. Perhaps a new measure of sadness is required; a grief-adjusted life year. Maybe this would help to put a human face on these otherwise unimaginable numbers.

Table 7.8 lists the most common causes of childhood death up to five years of age. The largest single cause of death within this age range is due to diseases within the first four weeks of life (neonatal deaths). Improvements in vaccination coverage, increasing emphasis on sanitation, and use of oral rehydration solution have greatly reduced deaths from diarrhea and measles. Pneumonia is now the most common infectious cause of death, but HIV/AIDS is firmly established on the list

Table 7.9: Leading causes of neonatal death (first four weeks of life)

Disease	Deaths (1,000s)
Severe infection	1,016
Pre-term birth	1,083
Birth asphyxia	894
Congenital anomalies	294
Neonatal tetanus	257
Diarrheal disease	108
Others	258
Total	3,910

Source: World Health Organization (2005c)

and will probably overtake measles in the near future (UNICEF, 2005a).

Table 7.9 gives the most common causes of death for those children who die within the first four weeks of life. While the under-five mortality reflects average health standards of a society averaged over a period of years, the neonatal mortality is more an indicator of pregnancy and early health care standards. Causes of neonatal death are split fairly evenly between infectious diseases and the complications of pregnancy and delivery (asphyxia and prematurity).

Since 98 percent of all child deaths occur in developing countries, it is fair to assume that if all those sick children had been treated in a developed country, the majority (over 90 percent) would have survived. Whatever the exact figure might be, most of those deaths were avoidable or treatable; either way, millions upon millions of children die unnecessarily every year. Effective treatments exist for pneumonia, malaria, diarrhea, and neonatal infections. Reliable vaccines have almost abolished polio and can do the

Table 7.8: Leading causes of death in children under five years

Cause	Deaths (1,000s)
Neonatal (first month)	3,910
Acute respiratory infections	2,027
Diarrheal diseases	1,762
Malaria	853
Measles	395
HIV/AIDS	321
Injuries	
• Unintentional	291
• Intentional	14
Others	1,023
Total	10,596

Source: World Health Organization (2005c)

same for measles and neonatal tetanus. HIV transmission from mother to child can be efficiently inhibited by the use of anti-retroviral therapy and the neonatal causes of death can also be significantly reduced by the presence of well-trained attendants during pregnancy and delivery. The problem of child mortality is not due to lack of treatment options—it is due to lack of political will.

Practical Solutions

The 1978 Alma Ata Meeting was the first time that widespread pediatric primary health care therapies were discussed. The impetus produced by this meeting led to the WHO/UNICEF child survival revolution announced in 1980. There is much more on this topic in Chapter 9 but, briefly, UNICEF concentrated on a package of four primary health care initiatives summed up by the acronym GOBI (Growth monitoring, Oral rehydration therapy, Breast-feeding, and Immunization). Later on, three extra letters were added to make it GOBI-FFF (Female education, Family spacing, and Food supplements for pregnant women) (Kuhn et al. 1990).

There is no doubt that these early initiatives have had a measurable impact on child survival. Oral rehydration therapy alone is thought to save as many as a million children each year (Baqui & Ahmed, 2006). The expanded immunization program has halved deaths from measles and tetanus and almost eradicated polio (*Global Polio Eradication Initiative*, n.d.). These improvements are reflected in the steady decline in childhood mortality each year, as shown in Figure 7.3. Unfortunately, UNICEF's child survival "revolution" lost impetus in the 1990s, probably because of competing

Figure 7.6: Recent trends in prevalence of underweight children

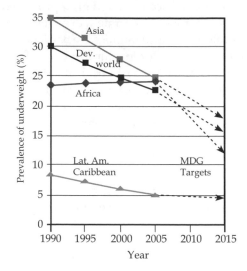

Lat. Am.: Latin America; Dev. world: Developing world; MDG: Millennium Development Goals

Source: de Onis et al. (2004)

demands for financial resources in the broader health field and lack of sufficient commitment by developed countries.

For every childhood death, there are many times that number suffering from disabling but non-lethal illness. Measuring trends in something as diverse as childhood morbidity is difficult; one approach is to use measures of growth and nutrition as surrogate indicators of general health. Using underweight (low weight for age, Figure 7.6) and stunting (low height for age, Figure 7.7) as mixed indicators of acute and chronic malnutrition, there have been significant improvements in both over the last 15 years (de Onis et al., 2004).

One of the major Millennium Development Goals is to reduce under-five mortality by 75 percent before 2015 (*UN Millennium Development Goals*, n.d.).

Figure 7.7: Recent trends in prevalence of stunted children

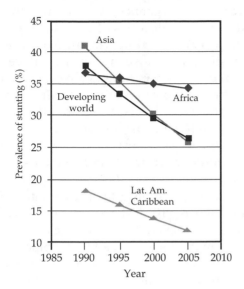

Source: de Onis et al. (2004)

Many parts of the developing world are on track to meet this optimistic target. However, in some areas, particularly Sub-Saharan Africa, progress has stalled for a variety reasons, not least of which is the increasingly severe HIV/AIDS epidemic. Another MDG child health target is to halve the prevalence of underweight children by 2015. Again, as Figure 7.6 shows, most regions are likely to meet this target except for Sub-Saharan Africa where underweight prevalence has actually increased recently.

A recent meeting in Bellagio (Bhutta, 2004) of senior researchers from several institutions has also highlighted the fact that a large proportion of child deaths can be avoided with simple interventions. The group published their findings and called for a second Child Survival Revolution (Black et al., 2003). They emphasized the need for combined interventions aimed at improving pregnancy-related care, together with basic pediatric preventive care. This topic is discussed in greater detail in chapters 9 and 10.

MATERNAL HEALTH IN THE DEVELOPING WORLD

Common Causes of Mortality

There is a crying need for an international agency for women. Every stitch of evidence we have, right across the entire spectrum of gender inequality suggests the urgent need for a multilateral agency. The great dreams of the international conferences in Vienna, Cairo, and Beijing have never come to pass. It matters not the issue: whether it's levels of sexual violence, or HIV/AIDS, or maternal mortality, or armed conflict, or economic empowerment, or parliamentary representation, women are in terrible trouble. And things are getting no better.

—Stephen Lewis addressing a high-level panel on UN reform, 2006

If resolutions could sort out maternal deaths, the problem would have been solved long ago. Since the Inter-Agency Group (IAG) held their first international conference on safe motherhood in 1987 (*Safe Motherhood Inter-Agency Group*, n.d.), there have been many more meetings and good intentions, including the International Conference on Population and Development in 1994, the Fourth World Conference on Women in 1995 (plus their regular follow-up evaluations), and the Millennium Development Goals in 2000. The pattern of rather more talk than action is demonstrated byTable 7.10.

Table 7.10: Percentage of births attended by skilled personnel

Region	1990	2003	Births in 2003 (millions)
Sub-Saharan Africa	40	41	26.9
South Asia	27	38	37.1
East Asia, Pacific	45	76	31.6
Latin America, Caribbean	74	86	11.6
Total developing world	41	57	120.0

Source: UNICEF (2006b)

It shows that the fraction of births assisted by a skilled attendant in Sub-Saharan Africa was 40 percent in 1990. After more than a decade of paperwork, it was 41 percent in 2003 (UNICEF, 2006b).

It must be remembered that pregnancy-related ill health is only one of many examples where the lives of women receive insufficient attention. It doesn't matter what aspect of a woman's life in the developing world is examined — the effects of war, economic indicators, levels of personal violence, human rights, access to education, or HIV/AIDS — women always do worse than men. As Stephen Lewis has pointed out, there is an urgent need to improve the historical second-class status of women that exists in many parts of the world. He has suggested the establishment of a new international agency that will basically have the same mandate for women that UNICEF currently has for children.

Maternal mortality is defined as the death of a woman while pregnant or within 42 days of termination of that pregnancy (this has recently been increased to one year after pregnancy). Deaths are either direct (complications of pregnancy and delivery) or indirect (death from pre-existing disease such as heart failure). Three separate indicators are calculated using the basic mortality data: maternal mortality ratio (maternal deaths per 100,000 live births), maternal mortality rate (maternal deaths per 100,000 women of reproductive age), and lifetime risk of pregnancy-associated death.

Making accurate estimates of maternal mortality is difficult. It requires knowledge of a range of variables, including accurate information about deaths of women at reproductive age, the cause of death, and whether or not the woman was pregnant or had been recently pregnant (World Health Organization, 2006). Unfortunately, only a few developing countries register births and deaths, fewer still record cause of death, and hardly any note pregnancy status on the death certificate. In the absence of accurate registration data, various approaches are used to obtain accurate mortality estimates. These include direct household surveys, the sisterhood method (information is obtained by interviewing family members about survival of their adult sisters), and Reproductive Age Mortality Studies (RAMOS) — research is concentrated only on deaths of women of reproductive age.

In response to the need for better information, the WHO, UNICEF, and UNFPA co-operated in 1990 to improve standards of data collection and dissemination. They subsequently published updated summaries of maternal mortality statistics in 1995 and 2000 (World Health Organization, 2004). The UNICEF Web site also publishes annual

Table 7.11: Magnitude of maternal mortality in the developing world

Region	Maternal Mortality Ratio (per 100,000 births) in 2000	Number of Maternal Deaths in 2000	Lifetime Risk of Maternal Death in 2000	Maternal Mortality Ratio (per 100,000 births) in 1995	Number of Maternal Deaths in 1995
Africa	830	251,000	1 in 20	1,000	272,000
Northern Africa	130	4,600	1 in 210	200	7,200
Sub-Saharan Africa	920	247,000	1 in 16	1,100	265,000
Asia	330	253,000	1 in 94	280	217,000
Eastern Asia	55	11,000	1 in 840	55	13,000
Southcentral Asia	520	207,000	1 in 46	410	158,000
Southeastern Asia	210	25,000	1 in 140	300	35,000
Western Asia	190	9,800	1 in 120	230	11,000
Latin America Caribbean	190	22,000	1 in 160	190	22,000
Oceania	240	530	1 in 83	260	560
Developing world	440	527,000	1 in 61	440	512,000

Source: World Health Organization (2004)

statistics (UNICEF, 2006c). Table 7.11 gives the broad world figures for maternal mortality ratio, number of deaths, and a woman's lifetime risk of maternal death for year 2000. Numbers are also given for 1995 for comparison.

There are inevitable similarities between maternal deaths and childhood deaths. The vast majority of both are either treatable and/or avoidable. Table 7.12 shows that in one in four cases, the woman simply bled to death. This is a completely treatable condition—most of these women would have lived if they had delivered in a developed country. Not surprisingly, most deaths occurred in developing countries,

principally in Sub-Saharan Africa and India (World Health Organization, 2004). Less than 1 percent of maternal deaths occur in developed countries. If women do not die in developed countries, then there is no good reason why they should be dying anywhere else. Women and children differ in one important respect— childhood mortality is decreasing after two decades of interventions, but progress in maternal mortality has been very slow, with no measurable change in maternal mortality ratio between 1995 and 2000. Despite a lot of fine words, women's health still appears to have a scandalously low priority (Oxfam, 2004).

Table 7.12: Common causes of maternal mortality

Causes	Fraction
Direct causes:	
Bleeding	25%
Infection	13%
Eclampsia	12%
Obstructed labour	8%
Abortion	
complications	13%
Other direct causes	8%
Indirect causes:	20%
Malaria	
Anemia	
Malnutrition	
HIV/AIDS	
Heart disease	

Source: World Health Organization (2004)

It should always be remembered that for every woman who dies, there are millions more who suffer chronic disabling complications of pregnancy. It has been estimated that of the nearly 120 million women who give birth each year, roughly 50 percent experience some form of complication during pregnancy (Ashford, 2002). Ten to 15 percent of these women subsequently develop chronic disabilities such as severe anemia, incontinence, fistulae from uterus to bladder or colon, depression, chronic pain, and infertility. As another example of the low priority placed on women's health, there is little accurate information about this huge burden of disease. The WHO Department of Reproductive Health and Research has only recently started to formalize the collection of data concerning maternal morbidity (Gulmezoglu et al., 2004). Clearly, better data concerning the broad subject of reproductive health is an urgent priority.

Practical Solutions

The statistics concerning poorly managed pregnancy and delivery are staggering. As we have discussed above, each year, over half a million women die during pregnancy. Complications of delivery leave millions more women with disabilities and contribute to the deaths of nearly 4 million newborns. What makes it worse is that most of this mortality and morbidity is completely avoidable.

Although primary health care has produced great improvements in the health of children, it has had less effect on maternal mortality. Sanitation and immunizations are fine for a population, but they do not scratch the surface of pregnancy-associated diseases. Pregnancy and delivery are associated with sudden and unpredictable complications that can only be treated by having rapid access to trained attendants and basic medical care (World Health Organization, 2005b). Numerous studies have shown that the major determinants of outcome in pregnancy are access to competent antenatal care and delivery by a trained attendant. This is reflected in the Millennium Development Goals, which include two maternal targets. The first is a 75 percent reduction in maternal mortality rate by 2015 and the second is to increase the number of pregnancies attended by competent personnel. In reality, the two are not separable; reducing maternal mortality requires the presence of a trained attendant; you don't get one without the other.

History provides plenty of support for the need for midwives. Sweden adopted a national policy favouring the presence of a midwife for all births in the 19th century. By 1900, the maternal mortality ratio in Sweden had fallen to 230 per 100,000 live births (Högberg, 2004). In contrast, the United States focused on hospital delivery by doctors and paid little attention to midwives. The maternal mortality ratio in the United States was still 700 per 100,000 live births in 1930 and did not fall until increasing emphasis was placed on the need for trained birth attendants.

Obviously, the presence of a midwife needs to be backed up by access to a wide range of services. Even routine obstetric procedures such as Caesarean section or blood transfusion will require relatively expensive staff and equipment. Table 7.7 provides some idea of these costs (US dollars) in 1990. The total cost of immunization and school health programs is US $0.80 per capita compared to US $3.80 per capita for comprehensive obstetric care. However, it is worth it. Whether looked at from the point of view of child health, maternal health, or the general standard of living in a community, serious investment in maternal health is highly cost effective and long, long overdue (Adam, 2005). Medical treatments will be covered in more detail in Chapter 10, but briefly, a comprehensive intervention plan aimed at reducing neonatal maternal death would consist broadly of the following (World Health Organization, 2005b):

- *Prenatal care:* During pregnancy, women should have access to regular monitoring (including testing for HIV and syphilis), intermittent preventive treatment for malaria, supplementation of micronutrients (particularly iron, vitamin A, and calcium), and macronutrient supplementation for the poorest women.
- *Care during delivery:* Every delivery should be attended by

a trained midwife with access to higher level care when necessary, including safe transportation. Minimum facilities in the referral center should include safe blood transfusion, drugs for treatment of basic complications (infections, hypertension, and seizures), and access to Caesarean section. There should also be basic resuscitation equipment for treating unstable children (suction, incubator, oxygen). For HIV-positive women, there should be a national protocol for labour management, backed by regular supplies of anti-retroviral drugs.
- *Postnatal care:* The new mother and child should have access to breast-feeding advice, post-delivery medical care, family-planning advice, and follow-up for her child (such as immunizations and breast-feeding advice).

It is a lot of work, but it is worth it (Adam, 2005)!

■ SUMMARY

The 1990 Global Burden of Disease Study had a profound effect on the subsequent measurement of population health. Simple mortality data has increasingly been replaced by broader measures of the total burden of ill health imposed by common diseases. Morbidity measurements became just as important as mortality measurements once it was shown that non-communicable diseases (mental ill health, road traffic accidents, tobacco-related diseases) caused a greater disease burden than HIV, tuberculosis, and malaria combined. The growing emphasis on health promotion and disease prevention has also stimulated research into the risk factors behind the major diseases. Finally, a much-needed emphasis is now being placed on maternal mortality and the risks associated with pregnancy.

In the past, the health industry has sometimes had a history of investing in expensive treatments without first checking to see if they are the most efficient way of improving population health. A good example was the early assumption that exporting Western-style medical care to developing countries was the best way to improve their widespread health problems. It took 20 years and an international meeting at Alma Ata before it became widely accepted that those expensive urban hospitals had actually done very little to improve the lives or health of the developing world's rural majority.

The best way (in fact, the only way) to avoid these problems is to base any health initiative on the best available epidemiological health research. The planning methods, first pioneered by the Ghana Health Assessment Team 25 years ago, are increasingly being adopted by the developing world health industry. The Ghanaian team's response to a limited health budget was to support initiatives that had the best predictable benefits for the lowest costs. They were the first to adopt the business techniques of risk analysis and cost-benefit analysis, which allowed them to modify their own plans so they could meet the most important needs of their local population.

Accurate health information has immediate applications in terms of population health initiatives. Knowledge of trends in morbidity and mortality, combined with an understanding of the underlying behavioural causes, allows health projects to be planned in the most effective manner possible. This is an essential topic for anyone who plans to work in the field of developing world health care.

RESOURCES

References

Adam, T. (2005). "Cost-effectiveness analysis of strategies for maternal and neonatal health in developing countries." *British Medical Journal, 331,* 1107–1114.

Anand, S., & Hanson, K. (1997). "Disability-adjusted life years: A critical review." *Journal of Health Economics, 16,* 685–702.

Ashford, L. (2002). *Hidden suffering: Disabilities from pregnancy and childbirth in less developed countries.* Washington: Population Reference Bureau. Retrieved from www.prb.org/pdf/HiddenSufferingEng.pdf.

Baqui, A., & Ahmed, T. (2006). "Diarrhea and malnutrition in children." *British Medical Journal, 332,* 378–382.

Bhutta, Z. (2004). "Beyond Bellagio: Addressing the challenge of sustainable child health in developing countries." *Archives of Disease in Children, 89,* 483–487.

Black, R., et al. (2003). "Where and why are 10 million children dying each year?" *Lancet, 361,* 2226–2234.

Chisholm, D., et al. (2005). "Cost effectiveness of clinical interventions for reducing the global burden of bipolar disorder." *British Journal of Psychiatry, 187,* 559–567.

Cueto, M. (2004). "The origins of primary health care and selective primary health care." *American Journal of Public Health, 94,* 1864–1874.

de Onis, M., et al. (2004). "Methodology for estimating regional and global trends of child malnutrition." *International Journal of Epidemiology, 33*, 1–11.

Ezzati, M., et al. (2005). "Role of smoking in global and regional cardiovascular mortality." *Circulation, 112*, 456–458.

Feachem, R. (1995). *The health of adults in the developing world: A summary*. Washington: World Bank.

Friedman, T., & Wyman, O. (2005). *The world is flat: A brief history of the twenty-first century*. New York: Farrar, Straus, and Giroux.

Gaziano, T. (2005). "Cardiovascular disease in the developing world and its cost-effective management." *Circulation, 112*, 3547–3553.

Ghana Health Assessment Team (1981). "A quantitative method of assessing the health impact of different diseases in less developed countries." *International Journal of Epidemiology, 10*, 1075–1089.

Global Polio Eradication Initiative. (n.d.). Retrieved from www.polioeradication.org.

Goldman, L., & Blakeley, K. (2006). "The celebrity 100." *Forbes.com*. Retrieved from www.forbes.com/lists/2006/06/12/06celebrities_money-power-celebrities-list_land.html.

Gulmezoglu, A., et al. (2004). "WHO systematic review of maternal mortality and morbidity: Methodological issues and challenges." *BMC Medical Research Methodology, 4*, 16–24. Retrieved from www.pubmedcentral.nih.gov/picrender.fcgi?artid=481067&blobtype=pdf.

Gurry, D. (1990). "Child health in the third world." *Medical Journal of Australia, 153*, 635–637.

Hill, K., et al. (2000). *Trends in child mortality in the developing world, 1960–1996*. Retrieved from www.childinfo.org/areas/childmortality/methodology.php.

Hirschman, C. (1994). "Why fertility changes?" *Annual Review of Sociology, 20*, 203–233.

Högberg, U. (2004). "The decline in maternal mortality in Sweden: The role of community midwifery." *American Public Health Association, 94*, 1312–1320.

Kuhn, L., et al. (1990). "Village health workers and GOBI-FFF: An evaluation of a rural program." *South African Medical Journal, 77*, 471–475.

Lambrechts, T. (1999). "Integrated management of childhood illness: A summary of first experience." *Bulletin of the World Health Organization, 77*, 582–594.

Lopez, A. (2005). "The evolution of the Global Burden of Disease framework for disease injury and risk factor quantification: Developing the evidence base for national, regional, and global public health action." *Globalization and Health, 1*, 5–12.

Magnussen, L., et al. (2004). "Comprehensive versus selective primary health care: Lessons for global health policy." *Health Affairs, 23*, 167–176.

Mathers, C., & Loncar, D. (2005). *Updated projections of global mortality and burden of disease, 2000–2030: Data sources, methods, and results*. Retrieved from www.who.int/healthinfo/bodestimates/en.

Murray, C., & Lopez, A. (Eds.). (1996). *The global burden of disease: A comprehensive assessment of mortality and disability from diseases, injuries, and risk factors in 1990 and projected to 2020*. Cambridge: Harvard University Press.

Oxfam. (2004). *The cost of childbirth: How women are paying the price for broken promises on aid* (Oxfam briefing paper, no. 52). Retrieved from www.oxfam.org.uk/what_we_do/issues/debt_aid/downloads/bp52_childbirth.pdf.

Pearson, M. (2000). *DALYs and essential packages* (Department for International Development briefing paper). Retrieved from www.dfidhealthrc.org.

Safe Motherhood Inter-Agency Group. (n.d.). Retrieved from www.safemotherhood.org/about/.

Tan-Torres, T., et al. (2003). *Making choices in health: WHO guide to cost effectiveness analysis*. Geneva: World Health Organization.

Thompson, W. (1929). "Population." *American Journal of Sociology, 34*, 959–975.

UN Millennium Development Goals. (n.d.). Retrieved from www.un.org/millenniumgoals.

UNICEF. (2005a). *A call to action: Children, the missing face of AIDS.* Retrieved from www.unicef. org/publications.

UNICEF. (2005b). *The "rights" start to life: A statistical analysis of birth registration.* Retrieved from www.unicef.org/publications.

UNICEF. (2006a). *Child mortality.* Retrieved from www.childinfo.org/areas/childmortality.

UNICEF. (2006b). *Delivery care.* Retrieved from www.childinfo.org/areas/deliverycare.

UNICEF. (2006c). *Maternal mortality.* Retrieved from www.childinfo.org/areas/ maternalmortality.

United Nations Office for Drug Control. (2000). *World Drug Report 2000.* Oxford: Oxford University Press.

World Bank. (1993). *World development report 1993: Investing in health.* Retrieved from www. worldbank.org.

World Bank. (2006). *Repositioning nutrition as central to development: A strategy for large-scale action.* Washington: World Bank. Retrieved from www.worldbank.org/.

World Health Organization. (2000). *World health report 2000: Health systems: Improving performance.* Retrieved from www.who.int/whr/2000/.

World Health Organization. (2002). *World health report 2002: Reducing risks, promoting health life.* Retrieved from www.who.int/whr/2002.

World Health Organization. (2003). *WHO STEPS Surveillance Manual.* Retrieved from www.who. int/chp/steps/manual/en/.

World Health Organization. (2004). *Maternal mortality in 2000: Estimates developed by WHO, UNICEF, UNFPA.* Retrieved from www.childinfo.org/areas/maternalmortality.

World Health Organization. (2005a). *AIDS Epidemic Update 2005.* Retrieved from www.who. int/hiv/epiupdates/en/.

World Health Organization. (2005b). *Pregnancy, childbirth, postpartum, and newborn care: A guide for essential practice.* Retrieved from www.who.int/reproductive-health/publications/pcpnc/.

World Health Organization. (2005c). *World health report 2005: Make every mother and child count.* Retrieved from www.who.int/whr/2005/en.

World Health Organization. (2006). *Reproductive health indicators: Guidelines for their generation, interpretation, and analysis for global monitoring.* Retrieved from /www.who.int/reproductive-health/publications/rh_indicators/index.html.

World Health Organization. (n.d.-a). *CHOosing Interventions that are Cost Effective.* Retrieved from www.who.int/choice.

World Health Organization. (n.d.-b). *Commission on Macroeconomics and Health.* Retrieved from www.who.int/macrohealth.

World Health Organization. (n.d.-c). *Global burden of disease 1990.* Retrieved from www.who. int/healthinfo/bod1990study.

World Health Organization. (n.d.-d). *Global burden of disease project.* Retrieved from www.who. int/healthinfo/bodproject.

World Health Organization. (n.d.-e). *Mental health.* Retrieved from www.who.int/mental_health/ en.

World Health Organization. (n.d.-f). *STEP-wise Approach to Risk Factor Surveillance.* Retrieved from www.who.int/chp/steps.

Recommended Reading

Bale, J., et al. (2004). *Improving birth outcomes, meeting the challenges in the developing world.* Washington: National Academic Press.

Seear, M. (2000). *Manual of tropic pediatrics.* Cambridge: Cambridge University Press.

Tan-Torres, T., et al. (2003). *Making choices in health: WHO guide to cost effectiveness analysis.* Geneva: World Health Organization.

World Health Organization. (2005). *Pregnancy, childbirth, postpartum, and newborn care (PCPNC): A guide for essential practice.* Geneva: World Health Organization.

PART IV

WHAT CAN BE DONE ABOUT IT?

Chapter 8
Foreign Aid Projects, Large and Small

Chapter 9
Primary Health Care Strategies

Chapter 10
Basic Medical Care

Chapter 11
Poverty Alleviation and Debt Relief

Chapter 12
Human Rights Interventions

Foreign Aid Projects, Large and Small

No one would remember the Good Samaritan
if he'd only had good intentions.
He had money as well.
— Margaret Thatcher

> **OBJECTIVES**
> After completing this chapter, you should be able to
>
> - understand the major sources of development financing and how much is given
> - appreciate the potential benefits of aid and some of its major successes but also understand the long list of failures and some of the major problems that caused them
> - understand the wide range of opinions behind the current debate on aid effectiveness and the changes in aid initiatives that have been caused by that debate

As we discussed in Chapter 2, the modern aid industry traces its roots to the US-funded Marshall Plan, which contributed greatly to the reconstruction of Europe after World War II. Since then, the industry has grown steadily until it now consumes many tens of billions of dollars each year and employs unknown numbers of administrators, bureaucrats, short- and long-term fieldworkers, and countless other volunteers and fundraisers. In this chapter, we will take a closer look at what has been achieved by all this effort.

During these five or six decades, well over a trillion dollars have been spent on projects that range from the sublime to the ridiculous. There have been some identifiable successes, but equally, there have been some spectacular failures. Balancing the ledger is not easy. For every successful eradication project (smallpox, polio, and leprosy), there are plenty of tyrants supported by Cold War directed aid to be put in the minus column. For every child who was fed as a result of aid-funded agricultural advances, there is another who went to bed hungry because of the restrictions imposed on the poor during the structural-adjustment era.

Depending on where you place your emphasis, aid can be made to seem absolutely essential or a complete waste of time; as usual, it all depends on who is doing the counting. Even two of the world's best development economists cannot agree upon whether aid is of any value or not — see Easterly versus Sachs in the pages of the *Washington Post* (Easterly, 2005, March 13). Anyone who wishes to work within the current aid industry framework should understand both the mistakes of the past and the origins of the optimistic plans for the future. Aid can achieve great things, but there is room for huge improvements in areas such as coordination, planning, and sustainable funding. If the industry does not rise to the challenges set by the Millennium Development Goals, it risks becoming increasingly irrelevant over the coming years.

WHAT IS AID AND WHY DO WE DO IT?

It won't change the world
It won't improve relations among men

It will not shorten the age of exploit-
    ation
But a few men have a bed for the night
For a night the wind is kept from them
The snow meant for them falls on the
    roadway.
—Bertolt Brecht, "A Bed for the Night"

As usual, the definitions, agencies, and acronyms can get a bit confusing. Development aid (also called overseas development assistance, international aid, overseas aid, or foreign aid) is generally used to describe the various forms of financial aid given by governments. These may range from low-interest rate loans to straightforward donations. Usually, at least 25 percent of the aid should be a true donation to qualify for the term "aid." Financial aid should be distinguished from technical assistance (donation of a particular expertise rather than money), military assistance (specialist training and military hardware given to allies), and humanitarian assistance (short-term aid designed to relieve suffering from a disaster).

Money is administered and distributed by aid agencies. These range from large government organizations (US Agency for International Development, Department

Table 8.1: A moment of Zen

Cumulative total of financial aid given by OECD countries since 1950 (principally intended to reduce poverty and debt): US $1.0 trillion	Number of stars in the average galaxy: 100 billion	
	Total number of stars in 25 galaxies:	Total value of developing world debt in 2003:
Cumulative total of financial aid expressed in 2003 dollars: **US $2.5 trillion**	**2.5 trillion**	**US $2.5 trillion**
Source: Organisation for Economic Co-operation and Development (n.d.)	Source: Feynman (1998)	Source: *Joint External Debt Hub* (n.d.)

for International Development in United Kingdom, and European Community Humanitarian Office) down to thousands of private organizations working at various distances from government. Some depend largely on government grants while others are fully supported by voluntary donations.

The term "NGO" is commonly used to describe the private agencies. It was originally an official designation by the United Nations, but numbers are now far too large for the UN to monitor (*Non-governmental organizations research guide*, n.d.). The acronyms take on a life of their own, such as BONGO (Business-Oriented International NGO), RINGO (Religious International NGO), ENGO (Environmental NGO), and so on. Red Cross sits in a category of its own since it has an international mandate to support the Geneva Convention.

Since about 1990, the main justification for giving aid has been poverty reduction. While much of aid is devoted toward this worthwhile aim, it is by no means the full story. It would be naïve to believe that the donation of such large sums of money is motivated purely by altruism (Dunning, 2004). A billion here and a billion there can buy a lot of influence, particularly among countries that desperately need that money. It is usually not difficult to find some degree of political advantage or commercial self-interest behind the allocation of aid by different countries (Olofsgard & Boschini, 2002). Political motives did not end with the Cold War but were simply replaced by others, including the war against drugs and, more recently, the war against international terrorism (Taylor, 2005). Commercial advantages include aid "tied" to products from the donor country and expansion of markets for its exporters (Chatterjee & Turnovsky, 2004).

The principal recipients of American aid are currently Israel, Egypt, Afghanistan, and Iraq. While some of these countries are very poor, there are certainly other considerations behind the distribution of this aid. Other donors particularly favour ex-colonies. Examples include Portugal (Angola and Mozambique), France (Côte d'Ivoire and Cameroon), and Belgium (Democratic Republic of Congo).

While the history of aid was covered in detail in Chapter 2, it is worth reviewing the main trends. Very broadly speaking, leaving aside emergency assistance, aid projects fall into two main groups — those targeted directly at economic growth and/or poverty reduction (budget support and investment in infrastructure, industry, and agriculture) and those aimed mainly at improved health (principally investment

---

Box 8.1: History notes

Florence Nightingale (1820–1910)

Florence Nightingale is often portrayed as a caricature of a starched Victorian nurse. In reality, she was a major scientist who made significant contributions to a variety of disciplines, including nursing, public health, hospital planning, and mathematics. She was an excellent mathematician (she invented pie charts) and was the first woman elected to the Royal Statistical Society. At a time when women from her privileged background were expected to stay at home, she left for Germany to take nursing training. She wrote over 200 books and articles during her life; one of those books, Notes on Nursing, is still in print. Go to the reference to learn more (Florence Nightingale Museum, n.d.).

in health, but includes social changes, environment, education, and governance). Initially, both shared common general goals, but during the 1980s and 1990s, they diverged and followed very different philosophical paths. Relatively recently, large-scale initiatives, particularly the Millennium Development Goals, have brought them back together.

The dominant economic theory guiding the early aid industry was based on the work of economists Harrod and Domar (Easterly, 1999). Since poor countries clearly lacked enough capital for expansion, they proposed that the donation of external funds would help these countries to build infrastructure, invest in new industry, and subsequently grow. This accumulationist theory sounded plausible and had worked in post-war Europe, but it did not work in most developing countries (Easterly, 2002). It should be added that not all economists agreed with this theory, most notably Peter Bauer (Bauer & Yarney, 1957). By the late 1970s, this approach had left the developing world littered with expensive white elephants — dams, railways, and high-technology hospitals with little evidence of the promised growth.

After the Alma Ata meeting in 1978, with its emphasis on primary health care (PHC) for the poor, health aid moved away from technological solutions and more toward the provision of basic essentials for a healthy life. Earlier enthusiasm for top-down disease-eradication programs and expensive hospitals was replaced by an emphasis on such things as sanitation, immunization, clean water, and more appropriate medical care. The early enthusiasm for PHC was such that optimists talked of "health for all by 2000." This was a wonderful dream, but

Utopianism never survives pragmatic reality. Despite lengthy arguments over the interpretation and implementation of PHC, preventive strategies subsequently led to some of the most easily identifiable successes of aid (Hall & Taylor, 2003), particularly widespread immunization.

At about the same time, the increasing failure of developing countries to meet debt payments (starting with Mexico in 1982) induced an equally sharp change of direction for economic aid. In an attempt to make poor countries better at paying debts, financial aid was tied to enforced economic restructuring that usually included reduced spending on social programs. This so-called structural adjustment era did not lead to increased economic growth and the associated cutbacks on social spending were certainly harmful to the poor (Botchwey, Collier, et al., 1998). By the mid-1990s, it was clear another philosophical shift was going to be necessary.

The newest change in aid can be dated to the Heavily Indebted Poor Countries Initiative in 1997 and the Millennium Development Goals in 2000 so we are still very early in the process. Health aid has returned to large-scale-focused disease programs such as Roll Back Malaria, but has retained its primary health care roots. Economic aid now includes programs focused on the poor and even includes the poor in the project design process. Perhaps the biggest change has been an increasing emphasis on outcome measurement (particularly within the MDGs) — a promising sign that the industry is finally maturing and taking responsibility for its actions (Rogerson et al., 2004).

▍WHERE DOES THE MONEY COME FROM?

Sources of Income for Developing Countries

Financial aid for poor countries is derived from five broad sources: (1) government assistance or overseas development assistance (ODA), (2) foreign direct investment by private banks and corporations (FDI), (3) non-governmental organizations (NGOs) supported by a combination of voluntary giving, and (4) government support, and, finally, (5) remittances sent home by foreign workers.

Official Development Assistance (ODA)
(Hjertholm & White, 2000)

These are grants or loans from one country to another (also called "bilateral aid"). The principal stated aim is usually economic development or poverty relief, although, as discussed earlier, there are often other considerations behind aid allocation. The expenses of technical co-operation are included in aid, but grants for military purposes are not included. As Figure 8.1 shows, aid volumes decreased during the 1990s, secondary to reduced funding following the end of the Cold War and a growing feeling of cynicism about the overall effects of aid. Several international initiatives around 2000 have re-energized attitudes toward the world's poor; this is reflected in the recent increased flows. Hopefully, this is not a temporary enthusiasm.

Foreign Direct Investment (FDI) (United Nations Conference on Trade and Development, n.d.)

Non-governmental foreign investments in developing countries are several

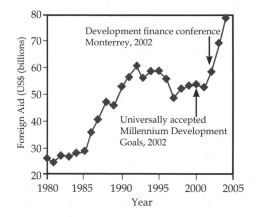

Figure 8.1: Annual development aid given by OECD countries over the last 25 years

Source: Organisation for Economic Co-operation and Development (n.d.)

times larger than total ODA assistance. Subsidiaries of transnational corporations (TNC) contribute the great proportion of FDI. The domestic advantage from such investment is not easy to determine. For example, importation of goods by the company, management fees, profit repatriation, and interest charged on loans can all limit the economic gain that a host economy might sustain. Obviously, the results will largely depend on the conditions of the host economy and its degree of sophistication in being able to regulate foreign investment (Loungani & Razin, 2001).

United Nations' figures estimate that in 2004, 42 percent of the global $644 billion investment money went to countries with developing world status. FDI has been rising at such a rate that some have predicted that it would eclipse the value of ODA. This is unlikely to occur because of the volatility of FDI. Basically, foreign investment goes where there is a reasonable likelihood of making money. Although $20 billion was invested in Africa during 2004, the money principally flowed to areas of oil and mining research. FDI is certainly an important part of the growth of more advanced developing countries but, for the highly indebted group that cannot attract foreign investment, ODA remains the principal source of outside funding.

Non-governmental Organizations and Voluntary Giving (Adelman, 2003)

As the response to the Asian tsunami and hurricane Katrina showed, the generosity of individual citizens of developed countries appears to be considerably higher than that of their governments. The network of NGOs, religious ministries, charitable donations, and business donations is too diverse for accurate estimates, but US figures give some idea of the magnitude of private charity:

- Aid by private US foundations ($1.5 billion/year)
- Aid by US businesses ($2.8 billion/year)
- American NGOs ($6.6 billion/year in grants)
- Religious overseas ministries ($3.4 billion/year)
- US college scholarships, foreign students ($1.3 billion/year)

Private charity may be roughly of the same magnitude as governmental ODA. Traditionally, NGOs have concentrated on raising funds from their own countries. Advertisements for World Vision and Oxfam are good examples. More recently, there has been a move for some international NGOs to start raising funds from the population of the host developing country. This follows a trend among many

organizations to decentralize their decision making to missions and community-based organizations within the target country. There is also an apparent growing social responsibility among some of the major names in the business community. The Soros Foundation, the Turner Foundation, and particularly the Bill and Melinda Gates Foundation all contribute huge amounts of private money for aid work. Warren Buffett's donation of US $31 billion from his personal fortune to the Gates Foundation in June 2006 has made that organization a very influential aid agency.

At present, NGOs are not seen as a direct alternative to ODA particularly since many of them do get some slice of the ODA pie, either as direct grants or at least some form of tax relief. This situation may change in time if the long-term public perception of government-to-government aid becomes more cynical. NGOs might attract more funding if they are seen as a less bureaucratic, more flexible alternative.

Remittance Income (Chami et al., 2005)

Remittance income is money sent home by family members who are working overseas. In some countries, remittance income forms a substantial proportion of a country's source of finance. Guyana in South America and Bangladesh are typical examples. A 2002 study estimated remittance income averaged $81 billion per year throughout the 1990s. The World Bank estimated remittance income in 2004 at $122 billion. Although there is controversy about whether remittance money has a significant effect on a country's development, it is widely accepted that remittance income is probably second only to FDI as a source of funds for developing countries. The total is often not included in aid calculations because some economists feel that remittance income in large quantities can actually have a negative effect on a country's growth.

Official ODA: Who Gives What?

> Each economically advanced country will progressively increase its official development assistance ... to reach a minimum net amount of 0.7 percent of its GDP by the middle of the decade.
> — UN Resolution 2626, October 1970

Thirty-five years have passed since the United Nations Assembly adopted the first Resolution concerning ODA spending in which it set the well-known donation target of 0.7 percent of a country's GDP. Although aid volumes have increased over this period, the average ratio of donor countries' ODA to GDP has actually decreased (Figure 8.2) and remains well below the target of 0.7 percent. The term "gross national income" (GNI) is now more commonly used than "gross domestic product" (GDP). GNI is GDP minus international taxes plus the receipts of international companies. After a period of a few lean years, the subject of aid is back on the agenda.

The end of the Cold War meant that the US and Russia cut back some of their strategic aid support; consequently, during the 1990s, aid totals fell significantly (Dunning, 2004). Several events contributed to the recent increased emphasis upon aid. These include an influential report by an international panel of finance leaders (Zedillo et al., 2001), and a growing public awareness of the

Figure 8.2: Average fraction of Gross National Income donated by OECD countries over the last 25 years

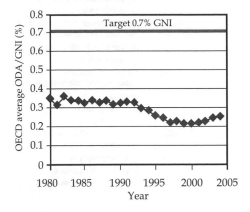

Source: Organisation for Economic Co-operation and Development (n.d.)

importance of helping the world's poor. The United Nations responded by holding an international conference on financing development at Monterrey in Mexico during 2002 (*Report of the international conference on financing for development*, 2002). The conference endorsed the 0.7 percent target and urged countries to increase their spending in order to support the Millennium Development Goals announced in 2000. The initial response has been promising.

As noted above, there are several sources of development money, but it is the official ODA that gets all the attention. The Organisation for Economic Co-operation and Development (OECD) is a group formed by the world's 30 richest countries. Its roots lie within the origins of the modern aid industry. It grew out of the Organization for European Economic Co-operation (OEEC), which was set up to administer the money given to Europe by the Marshall Plan in 1947. Many of

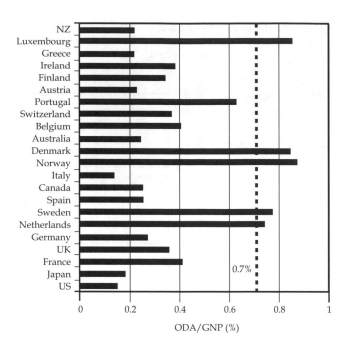

Figure 8.3: Aid as a percentage of Gross National Income for OECD countries in 2004

Source: Organisation for Economic Co-operation and Development (n.d.)

the member countries have, in the recent past, received aid and have also asked for debt forgiveness, but you would never have guessed it based on their current development policies.

The group's Development Assistance Committee (DAC) consists of 22 of those countries that, together, donate the majority of ODA. Several non-DAC countries also give aid (several Arab countries, South Korea, Taiwan, Cuba, and Brazil), but statistical details are much harder to find. Only five DAC countries currently exceed the target of 0.7 percent ODA/GNI (Figure 8.3). The average for all 22 countries is below 0.3 percent. In terms of dollars, the United States is the largest single donor with US $18.9 billion in 2004 (Figure 8.4). The picture is very different when aid is expressed as a percentage of a country's economic output. Under these circumstances, the US was nearly at the bottom at 0.16 percent in 2004.

Phantom Aid: Inflating the Figures!

Quite apart from criticism aimed at the quantity of aid given by the DAC members, there is also extensive criticism of the quality of that aid. A recent report by the charity Action Aid, released in England in 2003 (Action Aid International, 2003), claimed that a large portion of international aid never reaches the intended target for a variety of reasons that include:

- *Tied Aid (Organisation for Economic Co-operation and Development, 2001):* Aid that is tied to purchases from the donor country is an inefficient form of development assistance. Instead of creating new business opportunities in the recipient country, the benefits remain principally with the donor's economy. Ultimately, the imported services and goods end up being more expensive than

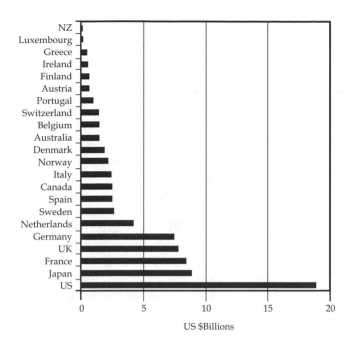

Figure 8.4: Overseas development aid given by OECD countries in 2004

Source: Organisation for Economic Co-operation and Development (n.d.)

if the trouble had been taken to help the host country become a manufacturer, not an importer.

- *Overpriced technical assistants (Hirvonen, 2005):* Anyone who has ever worked in a developing country will be familiar with the sight of three sweaty White people and a local driver rushing around in a white four-wheel drive Toyota with a flag. Where do they go? What do they do? Nobody knows, but it all costs lots of money. Technical assistants are necessary, but they do not need to charge salaries and overheads that are often much higher than the local average income. (They should also be well-qualified professionals, but that is a story for another chapter.)

- Other problems include aid that is not targeted to poor countries, funds earmarked for debt relief double counted as aid, and aid wasted on excessive administration and transaction costs.

Action Aid's first estimate was that 60 percent of all aid is "phantom aid." Subsequent criticism of the methodology by the DAC (Carey, 2005) has caused them to readjust their figures, but it is safe to assume that a good portion of claimed assistance never reaches the intended recipients.

DIFFICULTIES CONFRONTING AID PROJECTS OF ANY SIZE

Does Aid Achieve Anything Useful?

Well, we are in for another bumpy ride! This section will address the issue of whether all the money and effort poured into aid is justified by the end results. There are, of course, strong opinions on each side of the debate (Sachs, 2005; Vasquez, 2001). They tend to choose examples that illustrate their particular point and ignore the ones they do not like. Once one considers the range of variables induced by different funding sources and the widely varying scope and scale of different project designs and then finally add the unique complexities of different countries, it is hardly surprising that sometimes aid can be shown to work (Clemens et al., 2004) and sometimes (rather more often) there is not much benefit to be found (Hansen & Tarp, 1999; Tsikata, 1998).

Examining the outcomes of a single large aid project will illustrate some of these points. In 1960, the Kariba Dam and power station project was completed at a gorge on the Zambezi River between what were then Northern and Southern Rhodesia. The project was largely funded by the World Bank and, at that time, the dam was one of the biggest in the world. Money was given and a dam was built; clearly on that level, it was a successful aid project (World Commission on Dams, 2000).

However, if you scratch the surface, the conclusions are not quite so simple. The 100 people who were killed building the dam are not usually discussed and neither are the 57,000 Batonga who were forcibly displaced from their traditional home. Their displacement was poorly planned and was often associated with violence. To this day, the displaced Batongas live in absolute rural poverty — well documented by Dr. Sekai Nzenza-Shand (1997). They certainly did not benefit from this project — neither did the thousands of animals who were stranded and drowned. The much-publicized animal rescue

operation (Operation Noah) meant that the animals gained far more attention than the Batongas.

On the other side, the Zambian copper industry gained a source of cheap electricity — surely that was a clear benefit? Unfortunately, drought during the 1990s meant that the turbines did not turn so the old coal-powered station had to be restarted. Environmentally, the huge lake increased the spread of malaria and schistosomiasis. Conversely, the hydroelectricity was certainly ecologically friendlier than the old coal-powered station. The lake provides a modest kapenta fishing industry, but the water was only of limited value for agricultural development because of the absence of irrigation pumping equipment. When everything is balanced out, was this project a success or a failure? By picking the facts that fit your biases, it can be made into an ecological disaster or an economic triumph. Now multiply this by the total number of aid projects and then decide if aid is of any value!

Before reviewing some of the rather gloomy literature on aid effectiveness, it is best to start by reminding ourselves that, under certain circumstances, aid can be of great value. Just because it can be shown that aid has frequently been administered and directed very badly does not mean that aid is a waste of time; the baby should not be thrown out with the bath water. The response to the poor outcome of badly administered aid should not be the cancellation of all aid; the response should be to administer aid properly (Sachs, 2005).

So, let us start with some of the good news. Under a variety of headings, carefully targeted aid has produced identifiable and measurable benefits:

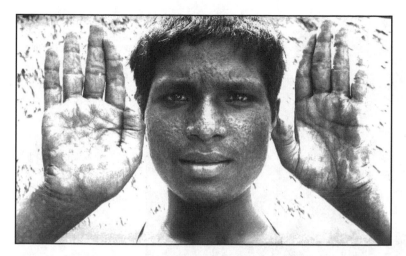

Figure 8.5: Thanks to the aid-funded smallpox eradication program, this picture will hopefully never be seen again. Until its eradication, smallpox had killed countless millions of people. In 1967 alone (the year the eradication program was announced), the WHO estimated that 15 million people contracted the disease and 2 million died. In this 1975 photograph, a young Bangladeshi man shows the characteristic palmar scars from earlier smallpox infection. (Photographer Dr. S. Foster; courtesy the Public Health Image Library.)

- *Health:* The World Health Organization's program against smallpox was the first time that a major disease had been eradicated (Henderson, 1999) (the Severe Acute Respiratory Syndrome, SARS, can possibly be added to that short list). There are other less well-known but still highly successful programs against polio (now eradicated from the Western Hemisphere) (*Global Polio Eradication Initiative*, n.d.), leprosy, river blindness (Onchocerciasis) (*Carter Center River Blindness (Onchocerciasis) Program*, n.d.), guinea worm (Dracunculiasis), and elephantiasis (Filariasis) (*Global Alliance to Eliminate Lymphatic Filariasis*, n.d.).
- *Agriculture:* Aid money and technical assistance led to the agricultural advances collectively known as the Green Revolution. Millions of people were lifted out of hunger across India and South Asia as a direct result of this funding.
- *Technology:* Expert technical assistance helped the Indian government establish its world famous Indian Institutes of Technology (IITs). These are now well recognized as centres of excellence.
- *Disaster relief:* Although the responses to the Asian tsunami and Pakistani earthquake were inevitably chaotic, there is no doubt they contributed to saving lives and accelerated the rebuilding process. Both responses were a long way from perfect, but the circumstances and working conditions were very difficult. In the short term, many people have

Figure 8.6: Survivors of the Asian tsunami living in a temporary camp on the east coast of Sri Lanka. Until their lives can return to normal, their daily needs for water, food, and shelter, plus the rebuilding of their villages and livelihood, all depend heavily on overseas aid. (Photographer Dr. W. Grut; courtesy Rose Charities.)

been saved with acute aid. In the long term, aid has also helped affected countries rebuild and recover more quickly.

- *Social change:* US aid tied to profound land ownership reform formed the basis of Taiwan's rapid post-war growth. Aid supported the struggling move toward democracy in South Africa and has also supported election monitoring in countries around the world.

Unfortunately, it is not difficult to find many examples of aid that have been less successful. Again, it is important to remember that this is not a criticism of aid in general, but is a comment on the way that aid has been practised for the past 50 or 60 years.

Another approach to the question of aid effectiveness is to try to find a correlation between donated money and some form of measurable economic benefit. Since one

of the main stated aims of aid has always been economic growth, the obvious starting point is to plot growth of GDP against financial aid. In the absence of good governance, the results are not promising whether one looks at a continent or small individual countries (Burnside & Dollar, 2004; Doucouliagos & Paldam, 2005). For example, the countries of Sub-Saharan Africa received US $400 billion in aid between 1970 and 2000. Aid expressed as a percentage of those countries' gross national income grew continuously from 5 percent up to a maximum of about 18 percent. Throughout this period, economic growth actually fell so that many of these countries are poorer now than they were in 1970 (Erixon, 2005).

On a smaller scale, the Solomon Islands in the Pacific have received aid for many years, particularly from Australia. Despite this assistance, the country's government and economy deteriorated steadily to such an extent that Australia was finally forced to send troops to keep peace in the nation

(Brown, 2005). A similar picture applies to Papua New Guinea. The causes behind the poor performance of these countries are obviously complex and are not necessarily directly due to aid but, at the very least, aid certainly did not help reverse the underlying problems.

The fundamental economic theories behind the aid and growth equation attributed to Harrod and Domar have been clearly disproved (Easterly, 1999). Numerous empirical studies have shown little or no correlation between aid and growth across a wide range of variables (Boone, 1996; Doucouliagos & Paldam, 2005). There are, of course, dissenting views. Clemens et al. (2004) found a positive relationship between growth and aid once projects aimed at political and humanitarian goals where removed, since these could not be expected to produce positive short-term growth. Other studies have shown little or no correlation between aid and growth when examining types of aid, types of donor, characteristics of recipient countries, and various time periods (Rajan & Subramanian, 2005). If there is a relationship between these two variables, it certainly is not a strong one.

About the only feature that most papers agree upon is that aid sometimes can be shown to work in countries with good policy environments. "Good" in this context refers to countries demonstrating benign governance, budget restraints, control on inflation, and a degree of openness in international trade (Burnside & Dollar, 2004; Tsikata, 1998). The response has been that aid money is steadily moving away from "difficult partnership" countries toward those viewed as being better governed (Beynon, 2003).

This has produced a growing dilemma that can only get worse. The countries that attract aid because of their history of good governance probably are not greatly in need of it. Conversely, the countries most in need are increasingly excluded because aid (certainly as currently structured) clearly does not work in an environment of corrupt or inept leadership (Dollar & Levin, 2005). In fact, under those circumstances, aid can make matters worse by supporting evil regimes. As many as a quarter of the world's population lives in such countries — they certainly need help, but how can it be introduced (Department for International Development, 2005)?

After all this, what is the answer to the initial question, "Does aid achieve anything?" Obviously, the only answer can be, "It all depends...." To stand any chance of success, aid needs to be based on careful research and a deep understanding of the involved community. For too long, aid decisions have been based on ideological trends in political and economic thought. The modern industry must be built on a solid, evidence-based foundation (Killick, 2004). It needs to be targeted, sustainable, and supported by knowledgeable, hard-working people over a long period of time. Finally, measurable end points must be in place. These lessons were available, for those who wanted to look, as early as the Marshall Plan. There are some hopeful signs that they are finally being learned and applied in the field, but there is still a long way to go before the industry becomes a coordinated, professional body that answers to its constituents (Riddell et al., 2000).

Common Problems and Some Practical Solutions

Aid projects both large and small fail for a wide variety of reasons. Misguided economic theories are only one small part of the problem. Anyone who has travelled extensively will know that the working environment in many developing countries is not easy. A little project that seemed simple when discussed in Vancouver, Canada, can become wildly impractical when the team steps off the bus in Afghanistan (What were we thinking?). These problems do not all have instant solutions, but understanding the range of obstacles confronting the average project will at least help with the planning process.

Larger-scale problems with aid include outright corruption, misguided spending on projects unlikely to benefit the poor, the creation of a dependent mindset in the recipients, interrupted flows of aid with lack of sustainability, lack of inclusion of local people in the solution to their own problems, and adverse effects upon a weak economy by the sudden influx of large amounts of money. This last problem is often called "Dutch disease" after the adverse effects on the Dutch economy following the discovery of extensive gas deposits. Rather than helping Holland's economy, the sudden wealth increased the strength of its currency and reduced the competitiveness of its manufactured goods. The final result of "easy money" pouring into an unprepared economy was harmful (Nkusu, 2004).

The responses to some of these problems are basically those encouraged by Jeffrey Sachs (2005). For aid to be effective, it must be based on clear research, planned with the full involvement of local people, be targeted on specific pro-poor projects, and monitored efficiently; funding must be sustainable; and, finally, outcomes must be measured. These are not difficult concepts, but it has certainly taken the aid industry a long time to start considering them (Riddell et al., 2000).

At the practical level of implementation, every team faces a predictable set of obstacles common to anyone who has travelled extensively. These include:

- *Working environment:* Shortages of water, electricity, and waste disposal.
- *Living environment:* Often hot and humid climate, crowded and noisy workplaces, and the added difficulties of a new language and culture.
- *Potential dangers*: These depend on the country, but include infectious diseases, violence, and, most common of all, motor vehicle accidents.
- *Organizational difficulties:* Complex bureaucracy, commissions to be paid, and the endless reports and paperwork that the granting agency demands.
- *Equipment and supplies:* Shortages and import restrictions on technical equipment plus difficulties of cost and maintenance.

Again, these problems cannot be avoided, but they can certainly be managed with adequate planning (Rose & Keystone, 2006). Chapter 16 is entirely devoted to the important topic of travel preparation and the ways to work safely and effectively in a developing country. Briefly, they can be summarized quite easily: Make careful plans based on a detailed understanding of the country before you go, and include local people at every step of the process. While that may seem too obvious to need stating, this writer's experience suggests that these lessons are well worth repeating. Before becoming involved in an aid project, please read Chapter 16 carefully.

IMPROVING AID EFFECTIVENESS: THE FUTURE OF THE AID INDUSTRY

In many respects, the new century represents a watershed for the aid industry. There is a strong feeling that changes are necessary, but just what should those changes include? Opinions obviously differ widely. At one extreme is the Cato Institute's 2005 *Handbook for Congress*, which recommends that the debts of heavily indebted countries should be forgiven as long as they agree not to receive any further foreign aid. The government should then abolish the US Development Agency and end all government-to-government aid programs because there is no scientific evidence supporting their effectiveness.

A less extreme view holds that aid will simply become increasingly irrelevant. As we discussed above, more advanced developing countries will gradually lose their need for aid as foreign direct investment take over while the worst-run countries lack the institutional capacity to gain any benefit from aid (Brown, 2005). As time passes, attention will increasingly focus on these fragile or difficult partnership countries. The most pessimistic views predict that poor return on invested aid will gradually lead to these countries being abandoned to their fate.

At the other end of the spectrum are the supporters of huge multinational initiatives backed by steadily increasing flows of aid money. Examples include the ambitious Millennium Development Goals or proposals such as the "big push"

popularized by Jeffrey Sachs (2005) and the more recent UNDP plan along similar lines (Kaul & Conceicao, 2006). Somewhere in the middle is the pragmatic approach that we should try our best to learn from past experience and use that knowledge to keep chipping away at the problem with tools that actually work. Easterly (2005, March 13) has termed this "piecemeal reform."

Whatever direction is ultimately taken, there are many encouraging signs that the aid industry accepts the need for major reforms aimed at improving aid effectiveness. Recent initiatives have included the International Conference on Financing for Development at Monterrey in 2002, the DAC Working Party on Aid Effectiveness in 2003 (*DAC working party*, n.d.), and the High Level Forum on Harmonization of Aid in Rome 2003 and in Paris 2005 (*Aid Harmonization & Alignment*, n.d.).

The end result of these and similar meetings has been the development of a general consensus on what makes an effective aid system. Because of its importance in establishing the basic framework of aid for the next two decades, these general guiding principles have been referred to as the Monterrey Consensus (Rogerson et al., 2004). They broadly consist of the following approaches:

- Aid should be a compact (Rogerson et al., 2004) — a serious undertaking between two committed and equal parties, each of which has obligations. Developing countries have a responsibility to practise good governance and to establish their own development priorities. Donors undertake to support those "homegrown" priorities with technical assistance and more predictable and sustainable aid flows. The donor community also undertakes major policy changes, most notably openness in international trade.

- The Millennium Development Goals will serve as the principal guides for development priorities, at least over the next decade. These clearly established (and almost universally agreed-upon) cross-country targets also serve as measurable indicators of progress that will increase accountability for donors and recipients.
- Poverty Reduction Strategy Papers (*World Bank PovertyNet*, n.d.) will form the basis of defining a developing country's development priorities. Development aims will be established by a broad consultation process (that includes the poor) within the recipient country. The process will be supported, but not directed, by major donors. Early experience with PRSPs has been cautiously optimistic. Clearly, balancing the priorities of the developing countries against those of the donor agencies will not be easy. In view of the history of invasive imposed projects attempted in the past, tact will be required.
- A new approach to aid conditionality (Department for International Development, 2004): There has been a long history of conditions attached to aid, ranging from fairly benign changes through to major imposed economic restructuring. Harsh

experience has shown that conditionality does not work. In countries that do not have adequate institutions in place, aid (with or without conditions) appears to have little or no benefit. However, conditionality cannot be easily removed. The growing awareness of poor aid outcomes means that taxpayers demand some accountability for the donated money. This implies some form of performance evaluation of the recipient country, which, inevitably, leads to the problem of what to do if a country fails to meet any of those obligations. The most likely response over the next decade will be increasing use of performance-based aid allocation accompanied by a shift of support toward relatively well-governed developing countries. The problem of how to support poorly governed states in crisis is unresolved and remains a major dilemma facing the aid community (Department for International Development, 2005; Dollar & Levin, 2005). Another approach is to apply a set of clearly defined accreditation criteria to any country that applies for aid. Those that pass this first test will subsequently be offered aid without further conditions attached. This is the approach used by the new US Millennium Challenge Account.

The new century has seen the establishment of a few agencies who have broken with patterns of the past and are built on the general guidelines just outlined. Does the PRSP process represent a new era in planning for poor and will we meet the Millennium Development Goals? So far it is too early to tell, but one important point is that the involved agencies are at least monitoring outcomes and publishing their results. This alone is a big improvement over the past. The following are examples of newly developed agencies that follow the general Monterrey approaches to aid:

- *US Millennium Challenge Account (MCA) (Millennium Challenge Corporation, n.d.):* The promised increment in aid pledged by the United States at the 2002 Monterrey Meeting was used to establish a new funding mechanism called the Millennium Challenge Account. Available funds were intended to rise to US $5 billion by 2006. A developing country is considered eligible for funding only if it meets a series of rating indicators of good governance and development potential. The requirements are stringent but, once a country has met the test, they have access to funding that they can apply flexibly without additional conditions. Unfortunately, delays in congressional authorization have slowed the introduction so the fund started on a smaller scale with funds of US $1 billion. The MCA is intended to minimize bureaucracy and has no representation in developing countries where it works through the staff of USAID.
- *Global Fund to Fight AIDS, TB and Malaria (GFATM) (Global Fund to fight AIDS, Tuberculosis and Malaria, n.d.):* The global fund was launched in January 2002 following a call for a new method of aid funding by Kofi Annan. It was authorized earlier at the G8 Summit in Genoa in 2001. It is intended that financial support from G8 countries and private donors, particularly the pharmaceutical agencies, will provide support funds in excess of the money already given as ODA; it is not intended to be yet another slice of the existing ODA pie. Since its launch, it has attracted $2.2 billion of funding and in the first two rounds of grants it has dispersed $1.5 billion in grants to 160 programs in 85 countries. Inevitably, there have been budget shortfalls. The fund was optimistically aiming at $10 billion annually, but funding is currently far behind that target. In keeping with the new consensus behind aid, the fund offers technical assistance, high-quality scientific review and, for those projects that pass these steps, it provides condition-free financing. Responsibility for developing the initial proposal lies with the various interest groups within a developing country. The overall guiding principle for the fund is that its assistance cannot replace or reduce other sources of funding that already exist to fight these three diseases. The fund is purely a financing and support mechanism; it is not an implementation program. Although there has been no time

for a long-term comprehensive evaluation, the fund has achieved an extraordinary amount in its short existence (Poore, 2004).

- *The International Financing Facility Proposal (IFF) (Department for International Development and HM Treasury, 2003):* The aim of the IFF is to accelerate the availability of funding for Millennium Development Goal projects. At Monterrey, countries pledged a steady increase in aid (roughly $16 billion per year in total) from 2006 onwards. The IFF is an optimistic attempt to make some of that long-term funding available rapidly by raising money in the bond market with the understanding that those bonds will be paid back some time in the future by the promised increases in aid. This shows a touching faith in the international promises made by politicians but, if it works, it will hopefully help accelerate the MDG process. The IFF is a proposal of the British government that is currently proceeding through a broad consultative process. If it does get off the ground, estimates are that it would provide up to an additional $50 billion a year in short-term financial assistance between now and 2015. Clearly, there are a large number of details still to be sorted out, not least of which is how the money is dispersed.
- *The New Partnership for Africa's Development (NEPAD) (New Partnership for Africa's Development, n.d.):* The NEPAD strategy was developed at the Summit Meeting

of the Organization of African Unity in July 2001. The primary objectives are much the same as previous initiatives that include poverty eradication, sustainable growth and development, and acceleration of gender equality. The strength of NEPAD is that it emphasizes Africa's solutions for African problems. The direction will be under the heads of states of the African union. At present, NEPAD acts more as an advocacy role but, in future, it will attract funds to support its own projects.

■ SUMMARY

There are two components to a successful overseas development program. Firstly, there must be a sustainable supply of adequate funding and, secondly, that money must be spent wisely. The history of the international aid community shows there has been room for improvement in both of these areas. The range of variables confronting aid evaluation researchers is so great that even the optimists find it difficult to show convincing evidence of long-term economic benefit among the major aid recipients.

Although total aid donations have increased over the last three or four decades, all but a handful of countries still fall well below the 1970 U.N. resolution that countries should give 0.7 percent of their gross domestic product in aid. There have also been concerns that aid has too often been used to gain political or economic advantage for the donor rather than being aimed purely at the welfare of the poorest. Similarly, although development financing has supported some highly successful international projects over the years, there is also a widespread impression that standards of project planning and management could be significantly improved.

Fortunately, the new millennium appears to have coincided with a greatly energized aid industry. In response to falling overseas aid donations in the early 1990s, the richest countries have responded with commitments to increase annual donations on a steady basis. In 2006, total overseas aid exceeded US $100 billion for the first time ever. However, there is still a long way to go before the majority of rich countries still give more than half of the 0.7 percent of GDP target. The universally ratified Millennium Development Goals have also set new standards in terms of project organization, management and, above all, outcome measurement. These are exciting times in the field of international aid. With the combined increases in funding and a greater commitment to professional project planning and management, it is possible that the majority of the ambitious millennium goals will actually be met by 2015.

RESOURCES

References

Action Aid International. (2003). *Real aid: An agenda for making aid work*. Retrieved from www.actionaid.org.uk/_content/documents/real_aid.pdf.

Adelman, C. (2003). "The privatization of foreign aid: Reassessing national largesse." *Foreign Affairs, 82,*82-85.

Aid Harmonization & Alignment. (n.d.). Retrieved from www.aidharmonization.org.

Bauer, P., & Yarney, B. (1957). *The economics of underdeveloped countries*. Chicago: University of Chicago Press.

Beynon, J. (2003). *Poverty efficient aid allocations – Collier/Dollar revisited* (ODI Economics and Statistics Unit working paper). Retrieved from www.odi.org.uk/esau/publications/working_papers/esau_wp2.pdf.

Boone, P. (1996). "Politics and the effectiveness of foreign aid." *European Economic Review, 40,* 289–329.

Botchwey, K., Collier, P., et al. (1998). *Report by a group of independent experts: External evaluation of the Extended Structural Adjustment Facility*. Washington: International Monetary Fund. Retrieved from www.imf.org/external/pubs/ft/extev/esaf2.pdf.

Brown, O. (2005). *Aiding and abetting: Dilemmas of foreign aid and political instability in the Melanesian Pacific*. Winnipeg: International Institute for Sustainable Development. Retrieved from www.iisd.org/pdf/2005/security_aiding_or_abetting.pdf.

Burnside, C., & Dollar, D. (2004). *Aid, policies and growth: Revisiting the evidence* (World Bank working paper 3251). Retrieved from www.worldbank.org by searching "Aid, policies and growth."

Carey, R. (2005). "Real or phantom aid?" *DAC News*. Retrieved from www.oecd.org.

Carter Center River Blindness (Onchocerciasis) Program. (n.d.). Retrieved from www.cartercenter.org/healthprograms/program2.htm.

Cato Institute. (2005). *Cato handbooks for Congress: Policy recommendations for the 108th Congress*. Retrieved from www.cato.org/pubs/handbook/handbook108.html.

Chami, R., et al. (2005). "Are immigrant remittance flows a source of capital for development?" *IMF Staff Papers, 52, no. 1.* Retrievable from www.imf.org/External/Pubs/FT/staffp/2005/01/pdf/chami.pdf.

Chatterjee, S., & Turnovsky, S. (2004). *Tied versus untied foreign aid: Consequences for a growing economy*. Unpublished manuscript. Retrieved from www.repec.org/sce2004/up.26251.1074819500.pdf.

Clemens, M., et al. (2004). *Counting chickens when they hatch: The short-term effect of aid on growth* (Centre for Global Development working paper 44). Retrieved from www.cgdev.org/content/publications/detail/2744.

DAC working party on aid effectiveness. (n.d.). Retrieved from www.oecd.org/dac/effectiveness.

Department for International Development. (2004). *Partnership for poverty reduction: Changing aid "conditionality"*. Retrieved from www.dfid.gov.uk/pubs/files/conditionalitychange.pdf.

Department for International Development. (2005). *Why we need to work more effectively in fragile states*. Retrieved from www.dfid.gov.uk/pubs/files/fragilestates-paper.pdf.

Department for International Development and HM Treasury. (2003). *International finance facility*. Retrieved from www.concordeurope.org/download.cfm?media=pdfUK&id=626.

Dollar, D., & Levin, V. (2005). *The forgotten states: Aid volumes and volatility in difficult partnership countries (1992–2002)*. OECD Development Assistance Committee. Retrieved from www.oecd.org/dataoecd/32/44/34687926.pdf.

Doucouliagos, H., & Paldam, M. (2005). *Aid effectiveness on growth: A meta study*. University of Aarhus, Institute of Economics. Retrieved from ftp://ftp.econ.au.dk/afn/wp/05/wp05_13.pdf.

Dunning, T. (2004). "Conditioning the effects of aid: Cold War politics, donor credibility, democracy in Africa." *International Organization, 58*, 409–423.

Easterly, W. (1999). "The ghost of the financing gap: Testing the growth model used in the international financial institutions." *Journal of Development Economics, 60*, 423–438.

Easterly, W. (2002). *The elusive quest for growth: Economists' adventures and misadventures in the tropics*. Cambridge: MIT Press.

Easterly, W. (2005, March 13). "A modest proposal." *Washington Post*, BW03. Retrieved from www.washingtonpost.com/wp-dyn/articles/A25562-2005Mar10.html.

Erixon, F. (2005). *Aid and development: Will it work this time?* Retrieved from www.policynetwork.net/uploaded/pdf/Aid_&_Development_final.pdf.

Feynman, R. (1998). *Six not so easy pieces*. New York: Perseus Books.

Florence Nightingale Museum. (n.d.). Retrieved from www.florence-nightingale.co.uk.

Global Alliance to Eliminate Lymphatic Filariasis. (n.d.). Retrieved from www.filariasis.org.

Global Fund to fight AIDS, Tuberculosis, and Malaria. (n.d.). Retrieved from www.theglobalfund.org.

Global Polio Eradication Initiative. (n.d.). Retrieved from www.polioeradication.org.

Hall, J., & Taylor, R. (2003). "Health for all beyond 2000: The demise of the Alma Ata Declaration and primary health care in developing countries." *Medical Journal of Australia, 178*, 17–20.

Hansen, H., & Tarp, F. (1999). *Aid effectiveness disputed*. Development Economics Research Group, University of Copenhagen. Retrieved from www.econ.ku.dk/derg/papers/Aid_Effectiveness_Disputed.pdf.

Henderson, D. (1999). "Eradication: Lessons from the past." *Morbidity and Mortality Weekly Report, 48* (Supp. 1), 16–22.

Hirvonen, P. (2005). "Stingy Samaritans: Why recent increases in development aid fail to help the poor." *Global Policy Forum*. Retrieved from www.globalpolicy.org/socecon/develop/oda/2005/08stingysamaritans.pdf.

Hjertholm, P., & White, H. (2000). *Survey of foreign aid: History, trends, and allocations* (University of Copenhagen discussion paper). Retrieved from www.econ.ku.dk/wpa/pink/2000/0004.pdf.

Joint External Debt Hub. (n.d.). Retrieved from www.jedh.org.

Kaul, I., & Conceicao, P. (2006). *The new public finance: Responding to global challenges*. Oxford: Oxford University Press. Retrieved from www.undp.org/newsroom/20060128-npf.shtml.

Killick, T. (2004). "Politics, evidence, and the new aid agenda." *Developmental Policy Review, 22,* 29–53.

Loungani, P., & Razin, A. (2001). "How beneficial is foreign direct investment for developing countries?" *Finance and Development, 38, no. 2.* Retrieved from www.imf.org/external/pubs/ft/fandd/2001/06/loungani.htm.

Millennium Challenge Corporation. (n.d.). Retrieved from www.mcc.gov.

New Partnership for Africa's Development. (n.d.). Retrieved from www.nepad.org.

Nkusu, M. (2004). *Aid and the Dutch disease in low-income countries: Informed diagnoses for prudent prognoses* (IMF working paper 49). Retrieved from www.imf.org/external/pubs/ft/wp/2004/wp0449.pdf.

Non-governmental organizations research guide. (n.d.). Retrieved from docs.lib.duke.edu/igo/guides/ngo.

Nzenza-Shand, S. (1997). *Songs to an African sunset.* Melbourne: Lonely Planet.

Olofsgard, A., & Boschini, A. (2002). *Foreign aid: An instrument for fighting poverty or communism?* Unpublished manuscript. Retrieved from people.su.se/~bosch/foreign_aid.pdf.

Organisation for Economic Co-operation and Development. (2001). *Untying aid to the least developed countries.* Retrieved from www.oecd.org/dataoecd/16/24/2002959.pdf.

Organisation for Economic Co-operation and Development. (n.d.). *Aid from DAC members.* Retrieved from www.oecd.org/dac/stats/dac.

Poore, P. (2004). "The Global Fund to fight AIDS, Tuberculosis, and Malaria (GFATM)." *Health Policy and Planning, 19,* 52–56.

Rajan, R., & Subramanian, A. (2005). *What undermines aid's impact on growth?* (IMF working paper 126). Retrieved from www.imf.org/external/pubs/ft/wp/2005/wp05126.pdf.

Report of the international conference on financing for development. (2002). New York: United Nations. Retrieved from www.un.org/esa/ffd/ffdconf/.

Riddell, R., et al. (2000). "The quality of aid: Toward an agenda for more effective international development cooperation." *Christian Aid.* Retrieved from www.christian-aid.org.uk/indepth/0004qual/quality1.htm.

Rogerson, A., et al. (2004). *The international aid system 2005–2010: Forces for and against change* (Overseas Development Institute working paper 235). Retrieved from www.odi.org.uk/publications/web_papers/aid_system_rogerson.pdf.

Rose, S., & Keystone, J. (2006). *International travel health guide.* Amsterdam: Mosby Elsevier.

Sachs, J. (2005). *The end of poverty: Economic possibilities for our time.* London: Penguin Press.

Taylor, S. (2005). "When wars collide: The war on drugs and the global war on terror." *Strategic Insights, 4, no. 6.* Retrieved from www.ccc.nps.navy.mil/si/2005/Jun/taylorJun05.asp.

Tsikata, T. (1998). *Aid effectiveness: A survey of the recent empirical literature.* Washington: International Monetary Fund, Policy Development and Review Department. Retrieved from www.imf.org/external/pubs/ft/ppaa/ppaa9801.pdf.

United Nations Conference on Trade and Development. (n.d.). *Foreign direct investment.* Retrieved from www.unctad.org/fdi.

Vasquez, I. (1998). "Official assistance, economic freedom, and policy change: Is foreign aid like champagne?" *Cato Journal, 18,* 275–286.

World Bank PovertyNet. (n.d.). Retrieved from www.worldbank.org/poverty/strategies/index.htm.

World Commission on Dams. (2000). *Case study: Kariba dam-Zambezi River basin.* Cape Town: Author. Retrieved from www.dams.org/docs/kbase/studies/cszzmain.pdf.

Zedillo, E., et al. (2001). *Financing for development.* New York: United Nations. Retrieved from www.un.org/reports/financing/recommendations.htm.

Recommended Reading

de Waal, A. (1998). *Famine crimes: Politics and the disaster relief industry in Africa*. Bloomington: Indiana University Press.

Erixon, F. (in press). *Quid pro quo: Aid, Bretton Woods, and bankruptcy*.

Hancock, G. (1989). *Lords of poverty: The power, prestige, and corruption of the international aid business*. New York: Atlantic Monthly Press.

Knack, S. (2003). *Democracy, governance, and growth (economics, cognition, and society)*. Ann Arbor: University of Michigan Press.

Maren, M. (1997). *The road to hell: The ravaging effects of foreign aid and international charity*. New York: Free Press.

Rieff, D. (2002). *A bed for the night: Humanitarianism in crisis*. New York: Simon and Schuster.

Terry, F. (2002). *Condemned to repeat: The paradox of humanitarian action*. Ithaca: Cornell University Press.

Chapter 9

Primary
Health Care Strategies

Primary health care is essential health care based on practical,
scientifically sound and socially acceptable methods and technology,
made universally accessible to individuals and families
in the community through their full participation
and at a cost that the community and the country
can afford to maintain at every stage of their
development in the spirit of self-determination.
— WHO/UNICEF, Alma Ata, 1978

OBJECTIVES
After completing this chapter, you should be able to

- understand the importance of preventive medicine and health
  promotion strategies in the maintenance of population health
- appreciate the practical problems associated with implementing
  primary health care initiatives
- understand the evolution of primary health care strategies and
  their contribution to current maternal and child care initiatives
- understand the organization and funding of developing world
  health services

Primary Health Care (PHC) is a bit like love; nobody can describe it accurately, but everyone seems to know when they have it. Health Canada's (n.d.) definition (PHC describes all services that play a part in health, such as income, housing, education, and environment) is too inclusive to be of much value; basically, PHC includes just about everything. The bureaucratic definition from WHO/ UNICEF at the top of the page is not much better. In its narrowest definition, PHC is the provision of competent medical treatment for the common diseases in a community and represents the first point of contact between the population and health care services. In this form it is also called "primary medical care" (*Primary Health Care Research and Information Service*, n.d.).

However, the broader concept of comprehensive PHC, developed at Alma Ata, is based on a much deeper understanding of the socio-economic roots underlying ill health. Rather than concentrating simply on medical treatments, PHC is extended to include the promotion of health based on the philosophy of equity, appropriate technology, and community involvement. Of particular importance is the central inclusion of people in planning solutions to their own problems. Emphasis is also placed on making sure that any therapies are universally acceptable, affordable, and technically appropriate. Of all the health care systems around the world, Cuba and, to a great extent, Canada remain closest to the philosophical ideals of the original Alma Ata Declaration.

Anyone studying international health will soon get used to a steady stream of acronyms; PHC will be one of the most common. In practice, PHC is used to describe everything from an overall philosophy of national health care down to the distribution of a couple packets of oral rehydration solution. For newcomers to the aid industry, it is very important to have a good idea about what does (and does not) constitute PHC. For over 25 years, PHC has acted as a fundamental guiding principle for much of the health planning for developing countries. Consequently, this chapter will look carefully at the early development of the principles of PHC and their subsequent implementation around the world.

DEVELOPMENT OF PRIMARY HEALTH CARE

Some argue that primary health care was an experiment that failed; others contend that it was never truly tested.
— Lesley Magnussen

The benefits of basic medical care and sanitation were not discovered at Alma

Table 9.1: A moment of Zen

Al-Ilm educational project, in the Tharparkar region of Pakistan, estimates the following costs to educate 25 children for a year: Cost of thatched building: 10,000 Rupees	
Monthly costs (teacher's salary, books and supplies): 3,500 Rupees	Average cost of cosmetic botulinum toxin solution: Can $16 per unit
Total annual cost to teach 25 children, including building the classroom, teaching supplies, and teacher's salary: 52,000 Rupees	Average number of units needed to treat a man's face (rapidly growing customer base): 60 units
Can $1 is about 52 Rupees	Total cost to remove wrinkles from a man's face for three months plus sales tax:
Can $1,000	**Can $1,000**

Source: Al-Khidmat Welfare Society (n.d.)

Ata. Many centuries earlier, Roman military surgeons cleaned open wounds with acetum, boiled surgical instruments, built ventilated hospitals with under-floor heating, and even isolated patients with fevers (Kennedy, 2004). From Augustus's time, military doctors were well paid and some probably lived in homes with sewage disposal and running water. It is a mystery why it took the rest of Europe so long to relearn these lessons after Rome fell in the 5th century. It was not until the mid-19th century that Virchow, Florence Nightingale, and Chadwick introduced the notion of public health to Europe, particularly the need for cleanliness, good housing, and nutrition (Rosen, 1993).

On the other side of the Atlantic, Lemuel Shattuck was making similar discoveries in America. Shattuck had already made significant contributions to the organization of public schooling before moving to Boston to work as a publisher. After persuading the Massachusetts legislature to introduce registration of births and deaths, he was subsequently appointed as head of a committee to study the sanitary conditions in the State of Massachusetts. The subsequent report (Shattuck, Banks, & Abbot, 1850) was an extraordinary document that was 100 years ahead of its time. The committee's recommendations included the promotion of child health, improvements in housing, introduction of community health workers, and emphasis on community participation through the establishment of sanitary associations.

Unfortunately, public health tends to have an image problem; it is just not very exciting. Anyone who has tried to teach the benefits of sewage treatment plants to medical students will understand this point. For a range of reasons, including the power of the medical establishment and the public perception of a need for medicine, curative medicine always seems to overshadow preventive medicine (Seear, 2004). This was certainly the case when newly independent countries started running their own health care systems in the 1950s and 1960s. They inherited Western colonial services, which emphasized high-technology, urban-based curative care—famously described by Professor Morley as "disease palaces."

As discussed in Chapter 2, the public health programs of the day concentrated on vertical eradication programs, most noticeably against smallpox, yaws, and malaria. These programs were usually not integrated within the health services of the individual countries or even with each other; each usually had its own budget and staff. Although progress was made against a few individual diseases (most notably smallpox, but also yaws and tuberculosis), it was clear to many that this was an inefficient way to address the health needs of a population. Some of the principal problems were:

- Relatively high-technology, urban-based hospitals with sub-specialty services consumed disproportionate amounts of the national health budget.
- These large hospitals were usually concentrated in major cities and contributed little to the health of rural population.
- The overall philosophy of imposed care rather than inclusive prevention strategies excluded the population from contributing to their own health.

By 1970, it was clear to many countries that curative medicine had significant limitations, particularly for their rural populations. Several countries responded by introducing various forms of village health centres, often staffed by nurse clinicians or medical orderlies. In 1975, a joint WHO-UNICEF report (Djukanovich & Mach, 1975) was produced, which examined successful primary health care systems in a variety of countries, including Cuba, China, Tanzania, and Venezuela. Again, their conclusion was that "Western" medical systems were not adequate to meet the health of developing world populations. The Chinese experience with "barefoot doctors" was particularly influential at the time (Sidel, 1972).

The literature of the day also reflected the growing realization that reorganization of developing world health services was long overdue. The influential 1974 report by Health Canada, known as the Lalonde Report (Lalonde, 1974), was the first acknowledgement by an industrialized country that medical care was only a small contributor to population health (far behind lifestyle effects and environmental influences). The report identified four variables that affected health and emphasized that governments should take a far broader approach toward improving population health. Ivan Illich's popular book, *Medical Nemesis* (1975), went further in asserting that medical care was not only almost irrelevant to health but, in areas where it consumed a large portion of the budget, it was even detrimental to population health.

The level of interest was so high that an international conference was called to discuss primary health care in 1978 (Cueto, 2004).

Alma Ata Declaration

An acceptable level of health for all people of the world by the year 2000 can be obtained through a fuller and better use of world's resources, a considerable part of which is now spent on armaments and military conflicts.

— Alma Ata Declaration, 1978

Tension between the major communist powers at the time led to disagreement about the site of the meeting. It was ultimately held in Alma Ata, the capital

Figure 9.1: In 1978, representatives from 134 countries and 67 international organizations met to discuss health care in the developing world. The photograph shows delegates in the Lenin convention centre at Alma Ata. Although the conference's ambitious dream of health for all by 2000 was not met, the decisions and resolutions confirmed at the meeting had a profound effect upon subsequent health policy around the world. (Courtesy Pan American Health Organization photo gallery.)

of Kazakhstan, after the Soviet Union agreed to cover the meeting expenses. Although the Chinese had been major proponents of the meeting, they ultimately refused to attend. The meeting was the biggest single-issue international forum that had ever been held. It was attended by 134 governments and 67 international organizations (Cueto, 2004). After years of preceding preparatory discussions, delegates were well prepared for the topics. There was a definite feeling that this was going to be a landmark occasion. Not surprisingly, the resolutions were accepted unanimously. This consensus was subsequently confirmed at a meeting of the World Health Assembly the following year.

The eight elements constituting primary health care, plus the basic philosophical principles of the meeting, are summarized in boxes 9.1 and 9.2. Basically, Alma Ata was no less than an attempt to refashion the health systems of developing countries. It should be added that this methodology (particularly the emphasis on community involvement and disease prevention) is equally applicable to developed countries; this became increasingly obvious once the HIV/AIDS epidemic started to spread.

The director general of the WHO, Halfdan Mahler, was a leading proponent of PHC. During a speech in 1976, he first introduced the concept that comprehensive introduction of preventive health methods could conceivably lead to widespread improvements in world health by the end of the century. This optimistic goal caught

---

Box 9.1: The basic principles of Primary Health Care

Equity:
- Equal access for all people irrespective of income.

Community participation:
- There must be meaningful involvement of the community in the planning, implementation, and maintenance of health services.

Intersectoral coordination:
- PHC extends beyond provision of health care and requires coordinated action by all sectors involved in the population health, including agriculture, education, housing, and industry.

Appropriate technology:
- In keeping with the principle of self-reliance, the technology associated with health care should be scientifically sound, adapted to local needs, robust, and easily maintained.

Box 9.2: The eight elements of Primary Health Care

Education:
- Health promotion and education given in local language.

Nutrition:
- Promotion of breast-feeding as the norm for all babies plus nutrition supplements for high-risk children.

Sanitation:
- Universal access to clean drinking water and safe waste disposal.

Maternal and child health:
- Maternal and child care to include antenatal care, under-five clinics, and family planning.

Immunization:
- Universal access to WHO-recommended vaccination schedule.

Disease control:
- Prevention and control of endemic diseases backed by local epidemiological research.

Medical care:
- Appropriate treatment of common diseases and injuries.

Essential drugs:
- Reliable supplies of cheap and appropriate drugs tailored to local requirements.

the imagination and was subsequently termed "Health for All by 2000." After Alma Ata, PHC was adopted as the means to achieve this end (World Health Organization, 1981).

It is not an exaggeration to say that there was a very real sense of euphoria following the meeting. The idea of health for all captured the spirit of the time; a brave new world seemed possible where poverty and avoidable ill health could be eradicated through widespread application of the principles of PHC. In many ways, it was similar to the current debate surrounding the "big push" approach advocated by Sachs (2005). Inevitably, pragmatic reality soon started to lower those initial idealistic expectations.

After Alma Ata: Selective versus Comprehensive PHC

> There is nothing more difficult to take in hand, more perilous to conduct, or more uncertain in its success, than to take the lead in the introduction of a new order of things, because the innovator has for enemies all those who have done well under the old conditions and lukewarm defenders in those who may do well under the new.
>
> — Machiavelli

Even the greatest proponents of PHC would have to admit that the complete reorganization of the world's health services was a rather ambitious aim! Apart from the need for huge investments in money and work, real political will is needed to overcome opposition from vested interests, particularly the medical establishment, the pharmaceutical industry, and the status quo of the aid industry represented particularly by the

World Bank's opinion (Hall & Taylor, 2003).

Less than a year after Alma Ata, two researchers from the Rockefeller Foundation published a paper that analyzed the principal causes of death among the world's children (Walsh & Warren, 1979). They suggested that it would be more realistic if proven elements of PHC could be directed toward the principal lethal diseases. They were not critical of Alma Ata's approach (now termed "comprehensive" PHC), but their pragmatic recommendation of selective therapies became influential in the implementation of Alma Ata's original plan.

The Rockefeller Foundation subsequently held a meeting of major organizations at Bellagio, which included Robert McNamara, the head of the World Bank, and James Grant, the future director of UNICEF. The meeting adopted the notion of selective PHC, initially proposed by Walsh and Warren. The selective PHC pragmatists and the comprehensive PHC idealists subsequently feuded for the next decade (Magnussen et al., 2004). With a few exceptions, most countries settled for some form of watered-down PHC, so it could be said that the pragmatists won. Whether the children of the developing world won or lost is still a matter of debate (Sanders, 2004).

UNICEF, under the leadership of Grant, embraced selective PHC. For no clear reason, they selected four of the elements of PHC (Growth monitoring, Oral rehydration, Breast-feeding, and Immunization). The so-called "child survival revolution" was based on this GOBI strategy. Belated realization that women were important for the health of children led to the addition of three

"Fs" to the strategy (Female education, Family spacing, and Food supplements for pregnant women). This focused approach can be traced to the later joint WHO-UNICEF initiative called the Integrated Management of Childhood Illnesses, which will be covered in Chapter 10. In practice, even GOBI-FFF did not achieve widespread adoption (Kuhn et al., 1990). Limitations of money and political will meant that many countries simply concentrated on immunization and oral rehydration. Although these two therapies have probably saved millions of children's lives, their use is still far away from the original ideals of comprehensive PHC.

With all of its problems, PHC has been around for over 20 years, so it is useful to examine what has been achieved. In terms of providing the basic elements of PHC, Figure 9.2 shows that there have been slow improvements in the provision of PHC basics such as clean water, breast-feeding, and sanitation. Obviously, the biggest

winner after Alma Ata was immunization. The PHC initiative acted as a catalyst for immunization services as we shall see later in this chapter. Other aspects of PHC, such as provision of skilled birth attendants and breast-feeding, are also improving, but they still have a long way to go.

In terms of the clinical results of PHC, it is difficult to interpret the available research. While it is true that infant and under-five mortality rates have fallen significantly since 1980 (Figure 9.3), it is not clear how much of that drop was due to PHC interventions. There are many studies of village health, but methodological problems usually mean that there is no control group (Afari et al., 1995). A large study by the British Medical Research Council in Gambia (Hill et al., 2000) examined mortality rates over a 15-year period between villages with and without PHC services (community health

Figure 9.2: Provision of the basic elements of PHC in developing countries over 25 years

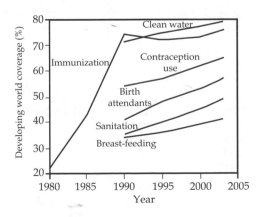

Source: Bangaarts & Johansson (2002); Joint Monitoring Programme for Water Supply and Sanitation (n.d.); UNICEF (2006c, 2006d, 2006e)

Figure 9.3: Diarrheal, measles, and total under-five death rates over the last 25 years

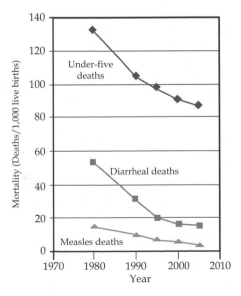

Source: Hill et al. (1997); UNICEF (2006b); World Health Organization (n.d.-a)

nurse, a village health worker, and trained traditional birth attendants). Basic clinic services and a vaccination program were accessible to both villages. Figure 9.4 shows that infant mortality rates fell steadily, in both PHC and non-PHC villages, over the course of the study. Although the child death rates were usually lower in the PHC group, by the end of the study they were almost identical. It is important to remember that control groups often get better on their own.

A few countries such as China, Cuba, Sri Lanka, and Kerala State in India followed the principles of comprehensive PHC; all have much better population health indices than might be predicted from their per capita income. Cuba's socialized health care system provides free basic services for all citizens and places emphasis on preventive medicine and public participation in health care. Table 9.2 shows that Cuba's child mortality rates and life expectancy are comparable with those of much richer countries and are very much better than other countries with similar per capita incomes.

Unfortunately, the high ideals of the Alma Ata meeting have not been met. Ironically, the Millennium Summit (organized to discuss the poor state of

Figure 9.4: Infant (IMR) and child (CMR) mortality rates, in PHC and non-PHC villages, over 15 years

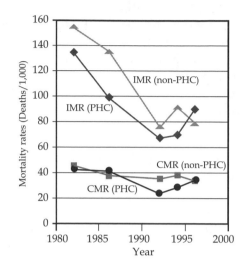

PHC: primary health care; IMR: infant mortality rate; CMR: child mortality rate

Source: Hill et al. (2000)

world health) was held in the very year that Alma Ata had predicted there would be universal health for all. In retrospect, most countries exchanged a poorly funded imitation of Western medicine for a poorly funded imitation of PHC. The fact that neither system worked very well is not

Table 9.2: Comparative health indicators for Cuba, India, and the US

	Infant Mortality Rate Per 1,000 Live Births	Under-Five Mortality Rate Per 1,000 Live Births	Maternal Mortality Ratio Per 100,000 Live Births	Life Expectancy at Birth Years	GDP/Capita
Cuba	6	8	33	77.23	3,300
India	63	87	540	64.35	3,400
US	7	8	17	77.71	41,800

Source: Central Intelligence Agency (2006); UNICEF (2006b)

a criticism of either Western medicine or PHC; it simply represents the inevitable results of underfunding and poor health service organization.

CLINICAL ELEMENTS OF PRIMARY HEALTH CARE

The basic components of PHC, outlined at Alma Ata, are widely used in overseas health initiatives. Anyone working overseas will soon meet programs designed around one or more of these basic elements, so it is important to have some detailed background information on each of them.

Immunization

> I should not fail to write to some of our doctors very particularly about it, if I knew any one of them that I thought had virtue enough to destroy such a considerable branch of their revenue, for the good of mankind.
> —Letter by Lady Mary Montagu, 1689–1762, describing the benefits of smallpox vaccination in Turkey

Immunization has been one of the undeniable success stories of the aid industry. Polio has been eradicated from the Western hemisphere and may well be eliminated completely within the next decade (*Global Polio Eradication Initiative*, n.d.). Measles-related deaths are falling rapidly (*Joint Measles Initiative*, n.d.) and whooping cough, neonatal tetanus, childhood tetanus, and diphtheria are now all rare diseases in large parts of the developing world (Davey, 2003). Huge problems still exist in terms of sustainable funding and increasing coverage, but immunization remains the most cost-

effective form of development aid.

Although immunization is cost effective, that does not mean it is cheap. Figures from 10 years ago estimated the cost of fully immunizing a child ranged from US $10–$25 depending on the country (Brenzel et al., 1994). When these expenses are scaled up to 90 percent coverage in all developing countries, the final bill is significant and considerably more than developing countries can afford. Immunization programs continue to rely heavily on external funding.

The original Expanded Program on Immunization (EPI) grew out of the success of the smallpox eradication

Figure 9.5: These children, photographed in a village near the Mekong River, are certainly not rich, but with a combination of preventive health strategies and access to an affordable package of essential medical treatments, they should be able to live healthy lives. (Photographer Dr. W. Grut; courtesy Rose Charities.)

program and predated Alma Ata by four years (Henderson, 1989). At the time, reliable vaccines were available for six diseases (diphtheria, pertussis, tetanus, measles, polio, and tuberculosis). Passive protection of newborns against tetanus was also achieved by including tetanus immunization for pregnant women as part of routine antenatal care. The current joint WHO-UNICEF plan for the future of vaccinations is summarized in the Global Immunization Vision and Strategy (GIVS) (World Health Organization, 2005a). Extensive information is also available on WHO's Immunization, Vaccines, and Biological Web site (World Health Organization, n.d.-c).

The potential benefits of immunization have made it attractive to a wide range of donors. The launch of the Global Alliance for Vaccines and Immunization (GAVI) in 2000 is a good example (*Global Alliance for Vaccines and Immunizations*, n.d.). This is a joint public-private partnership that includes UNICEF, WHO, the Bill and Melinda Gates Foundation, World Bank, plus others. Apart from providing funds to purchase vaccines and support the cost of immunization programs, the fund also supports other initiatives in the area of vaccines.

To add further confusion, there are also individual initiatives against specific vaccine preventable diseases such as measles and polio. The Joint Measles Initiative (*Joint Measles Initiative*, n.d.) between the American Red Cross and a number of other agencies, started in 2001, has already been able to show a significant drop in measles-related deaths. The Global Polio Eradication Initiative (*Global Polio Eradication Initiative*, n.d.) was first proposed by the World Health Assembly in 1988. At the time, the polio

virus was endemic in 125 countries and it was estimated that 1,000 children were paralyzed every single day. By 2003, only six countries in the world still had endemic polio and fewer than 800 children were paralyzed during the entire year.

Breast-feeding

Formula feeding is the longest lasting uncontrolled experiment lacking informed consent in the history of medicine.
— Frank Oski

For many reasons, exclusive breast-feeding is by far the best and safest nutritional source for babies in the developing world. Apart from the obvious advantages of bonding and nutrition, breast-feeding protects the infant from a range of infectious dangers, particularly gastroenteritis. It has clearly been shown that the mortality of bottle-fed children living in poverty is several times higher than that of exclusively breast-fed infants. The topic of breast-feeding is covered in detail in Chapter 5.

Concerns about declining breast-feeding rates in the developing world led to the Innocenti Declaration on the promotion and support of breast-feeding (UNICEF, n.d.-c) and the development of the Baby-Friendly Hospital Initiative in 1991 (UNICEF, n.d.-a). Despite these initiatives and serious attempts to curb unfair marketing practices by some baby formula companies, rates of exclusive breast-feeding in developing countries have remained low. In 2003, the WHO and UNICEF recognized this problem by initiating a renewed global strategy for infant and young child feeding (World Health Organization, 2003), which aims to revitalize efforts to promote adequate feeding of young children under developing world conditions.

Oral Rehydration Therapy

The discovery that sodium transport and glucose transport are coupled in the small intestine so that glucose accelerates absorption of solute and water was potentially the most important medical advance this century.

— *Lancet*, editorial

The claim made by the *Lancet* editor above ("Water with sugar and salt," 1978) may be an underestimate. In terms of numbers of children saved, the discovery of oral rehydration solution is one of the greatest medical advances of all time. Despite significant progress over the past decade, diarrheal diseases still kill nearly 2 million children every year (O'Ryan et al., 2005). Most of these deaths occur in children less than two years of age; almost all of whom lived in a developing country. Millions more survivors are chronically weakened by recurrent episodes of gastroenteritis that limit their growth and development potential.

Fifty years ago, the main focus of diarrheal research was cholera. Huge epidemics still affected large areas of the world with high case fatality rates. At the time, medical opinion viewed oral rehydration as a treatment of last resort—much less useful than intravenous rehydration. In the 1950s, various concoctions of carrot soup (Selander, 1950) and dehydrated bananas (Fries et al., 1950) were suggested, but conventional management involved administration of intravenous fluids. Apart from the fact that oral rehydration ultimately proved to be a better treatment, the equipment and

personnel needed for intravenous therapy made it too expensive and cumbersome to be of value when treating hundreds of patients at a time.

Children were also invariably fasted for many days because of the belief that the intestinal lining was unable to absorb anything. Intravenous therapy was based on early studies of water and electrolyte losses by Darrow (1949). By 1960, researchers had discovered that sugar and sodium are transported across the gut by a common mechanism, both in rats (Curran, 1960) and later in humans (Philips, 1964). Young researchers from the National Institute of Health, working at the Cholera Research Laboratory in Dacca, built on this research and introduced the first formal studies of oral rehydration therapy in cholera by the mid-1960s (Hirschhorn et al., 1968). Similar work was achieved by researchers at the Johns Hopkins Center for Medical Research.

The Indo-Pakistan War of the period and the resulting social chaos provided ample opportunity to test this newly developed therapy against the full range of diarrheal diseases (Ruxin, 1994). Published results rapidly gained attention. By 1979, UNICEF was distributing small sachets of ORS crystals worldwide. Although there are many reasons for the fall in diarrheal deaths since then, treatment with ORS has certainly been a large part of that progress. In 1980, 4.6 million children died of diarrhea. By 2003, this had more than halved (O'Ryan et al., 2005). UNICEF has continued to distribute ORS, but also encourages local production and home preparation.

With time, the use of ORS has changed slightly with greater emphasis being placed on uninterrupted feeding. Prior to this, it had been recommended that food should be withheld, but it was found that this contributed to weight loss during the disease episode. There has also been considerable debate concerning the optimum levels of sugar and particularly sodium in the ORS mix. However, the fundamental basis of treatment is unchanged (Victoria et al., 2000). Unless the child is unconscious, the majority of children can be managed through the episode with careful nursing and oral therapy.

It should always be remembered that provision of ORS is in no way a cure for the underlying social disruption that produced the diarrhea in the first place. The provision of ORS is a valuable therapeutic tool, but it can be defined as PHC only when it is part of a larger coordinated strategy aimed at all levels of the problem, including sanitation, clean water initiatives, education, and provision of ORS when necessary. This issue is discussed at length in Werner et al.'s book, *Questioning the Solution* (1997).

Water and Sanitation

> We shall not finally defeat AIDS, tuberculosis, malaria, or any of the other infectious diseases that plague the developing world until we have also won the battle for safe drinking water, sanitation, and basic health care.
> —UN Secretary General Kofi Annan

As mentioned above, it took a surprisingly long time for observers to work out that poor sanitation was at the root of widespread ill health. After discovering the causes of the problem, there was then another lengthy delay before anyone chose to do anything about it. Although clean water and sanitation

attract a lot of research attention, it should always be remembered that they do not occur in isolation. They are simply a small part of a much larger problem of environmental chaos that exists throughout much of the developing world. No significant improvement in diseases of poverty can be made without a comprehensive multisectoral approach that addresses all levels of the problem. Handing out bottled water in a slum does not constitute primary health care.

Sanitation is an enormous subject; it could easily fill a book on its own. However, the major points are covered under the following headings:

Drinking Water

Clean water is a fundamental requirement for a decent life. As Box 9.3 shows, there has been some progress since Alma Ata. Over 75 percent of the world now has access to safe drinking water, but that still leaves over a billion people who drink filthy water on a daily basis. The spread of many infectious diseases is directly associated with dirty water, including bacteria (*E. coli, Salmonella*), viruses (hepatitis A, rotavirus), helminths (*Schistosomiasis*, guinea worm), and protozoa (*Giardia, amebiasis*) (Checkley et al., 2004). Mosquitoes also depend on infected water for their larval stage. The importance of clean water is reflected in Millennium Development Goal target number 10, which aims to cut in half, by 2015, the proportion of people without sustainable access to safe drinking water and basic sanitation (*UN Millennium Development Goals*, n.d.).

The United Nations has reflected this consensus by declaring 2005 to 2015 the international decade for action on clean water (UN-Water, 2005). The WHO

Water, Sanitation, and Health Web site also provides information on the broader aspects of water safety, ranging from drinking water, waste-water treatment, and water-borne infectious diseases (World Health Organization, n.d.-d). The WHO and UNICEF maintain a joint monitoring program for water supply and sanitation that provides updated estimates of drinking water and sanitation coverage based on household surveys (Joint Monitoring Programme for Water Supply and Sanitation, 2000).

Population growth has produced severe shortages of water in many parts of the world. Water's increasing scarcity has made it an increasingly valuable commodity; naturally, private sector companies have grown to service this need. The dominant companies are Thames Water, Vivendi, and Suez. Battle lines are drawn between those who believe clean water should be free and those who feel it should be paid for like any other service. The problem first became apparent in Bolivia when Bechtel obtained water rights for an area that included the town of Cochabamba (Olivera & Lewis, 2004). Local activists organized widespread demonstrations that forced the government to reverse the privatization. Predictably, the poor are no better off than before since they have simply swapped privatized fees for local corruption.

Personal Hygiene

It must always be remembered that simply providing clean water is not sufficient on its own to make a significant impact on disease. Where populations have not had access to education, it is important to combine the provision of water with education on its use. This includes safe storage methods, care of

pumps and wells, and personal hygiene. Apart from diarrheal diseases, lack of clean water is closely associated with a general lack of health, including skin and eye infections (particularly trachoma). Worldwide, 1.4 million people are blind due to trachoma (Resnikoff et al., 2004)—a completely avoidable disease! The global alliance for the elimination of trachoma by the year 2020 relies on the SAFE strategy: Surgery, Antibiotic treatment, Facial cleanliness/handwashing, and Environmental changes (Emerson et al., 2006). Of all of these, regular cleanliness based on a good supply of clean water is the most important preventive factor.

Sanitation and Housing

Good-quality housing and sanitation are both essential requirements for a healthy population. Poor living conditions produce ill health through a number of mechanisms. Overcrowded, squalid huts provide breeding places for a number of disease vectors, including mosquitoes, fleas, and ticks. The mosquito is the worst of these vectors, spreading malaria, yellow fever, dengue, and filariasis. Poor handwashing, inadequate waste disposal, and absence of food and water storage inevitably lead to childhood diarrheal diseases. Poor air quality, particularly indoor smoke from cooking with wood or coal, predisposes children to a high rate of respiratory diseases; respiratory infections now kill more children than diarrheal diseases each year (2.2 million versus 1.7 million).

Finally, no restful or decent family life is possible when living under such circumstances. The 2000 Global Burden of Disease Study clearly showed that mental illness (particularly depression) is the most common cause of years lost to disability in the developing world (Stein & Gureje, 2004). The daily grind of living under unbearable survival conditions is behind much of this morbidity. Poor living conditions are also closely associated with substance abuse, family violence, and child abuse; all are widespread (and often unacknowledged) problems in overcrowded settlements (Poznyak et al., 2005).

Polluted and overcrowded peri-urban slums are death traps for children. The World Health Organization estimates that 291,000 children were killed in 2003 from unintentional accidents such as traffic accidents, drowning, and poisoning; a further 14,000 were murdered (World Health Organization, 2005b). High levels of air pollution, open piles of household waste, low or absent standards for industrial waste disposal, chaotic traffic, and a host of other dangers lie in wait for careless children (Creel, 2002). The Global Burden of Disease Study estimated that 35 percent of the total burden of disease worldwide is due to environmental hazards (Kjellstrom, 1999). The WHO and United Nations Environment Program (UNEP) run a joint program called the Health and Environmental Linkages Initiative (HELI) (World Health Organization, n.d.-b). The project helps developing countries to address environmental problems through pilot projects and the development of measurement tools that can support urban planning decisions.

Although it takes many years to improve general living conditions in urban areas, disease control must work on a shorter time scale. One technique that can bring faster results is control aimed at the major disease-carrying biting insects. Vector control is no substitute for adequate standards of urban planning, but it does offer well-tested methods of interrupting some common diseases while longer-term urban solutions slowly develop (Townson et al., 2005). Vector-control techniques include treated bed nets (malaria), indoor residual spraying (Chagas disease), insect traps and screens (Trypanosomiasis), and large-scale spraying (Onchocerciasis).

Family Planning

> Population increases in a geometric ratio, while the means of subsistence increases in an arithmetic ratio.
> —Thomas Malthus, 1766-1834

Any attempt to control family size must inevitably clash with a wide range of ingrained taboos, social rules, laws, and cultural traditions. It is a complex and contentious topic that does not resolve itself into the simplistic provision of contraceptives. Even a cursory Internet search will turn up some very strange views. Some of these opinions will seem less paranoid if it is remembered that family planning programs often consist of rich White people telling poor non-White people to have fewer children. Given the colonial past, this often well-intentioned policy can be viewed in a number of ways by those previously colonized. Conspiracy theories abound. Once political and religious views are added to the mix, the rhetoric can become heated. The situation can be defused, to some extent, by placing less emphasis on contraception as the only means of controlling population growth. It also helps to steer clear of the topic of abortion.

Over the last 50 years, population growth rates have slowed almost everywhere in the world. Developing countries now appear to be following a trend that began

Figure 9.6: The demographic trend: As prosperity slowly rises, a country's death rate usually falls faster than its birth rate. Population rises until a new equilibrium is reached. In a few industrialized countries, a fifth stage has been reached where birth rates fall below death rates so that population starts to fall.

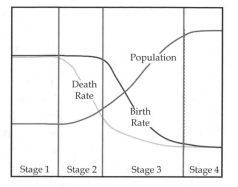

in Europe around the time of the Industrial Revolution. The model for the steady drop in fertility rate that appears to accompany improved prosperity was first devised by Thompson in 1929. The four stages are shown graphically in Figure 9.6. Prior to the Industrial Revolution, population remained low and relatively stable because of high birth and death rates. As living standards began to improve, death rates fell steadily, probably due to improvements in food supply and public health. What is not so obvious is that fertility rates also started to drop sharply about a decade later. During this period, the population increased since death rates fell faster and earlier than birth rates. Once birth and death rates stabilized at stable low levels, the population levelled off. In a few countries, such as Japan and Italy, there appears to be a fifth stage during which the birth rate falls so far that the population gradually decreases with time.

It is not likely that contraception had a major impact on this decline since rapid decreases in fertility were observed in Italy and Ireland during periods when contraception was illegal. As Figure 9.7 shows, lifetime fertility starts to drop sharply once the under-five mortality rate falls below about 50 per 1,000 live births (less than 5 percent). Table 7.7 in Chapter 7 shows a similar finding. These figures would suggest that contraception use is not widely considered until there is a general perception in society that children stand a 95 percent chance of surviving to adulthood.

Clearly, a full explanation of the drop in fertility rate is complicated. Improvements in female education change women's attitudes to the obligations of child-bearing. Once a society starts to value women, they become increasingly influential in making family-planning decisions. While

Figure 9.7: Lifetime fertility and under-five mortality (2000–2005) plotted for 168 countries

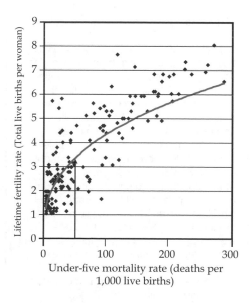

Sources: UNICEF (2006b, n.d.-b)

contraception is part of the picture, it is probably no more important than the influence of television or films on changes in generally accepted values. The success of educational "soap operas," developed by Miguel Sabido in Mexico, has shown that significant changes in personal beliefs can be effected by television (Population Media Center, 2003).

Family-planning programs such as the International Planned Parenthood Foundation and the United Nations Family Planning Association have worked for decades to supply women in developing countries with contraceptives and family-planning advice. This task is not easy in conservative societies, particularly when the topic of safe abortion is raised. In most developing countries, induced abortion is restricted by law. The WHO estimates that 30 million abortions are performed each year in the developing world, 20 million

of which are unsafe (Mondigo & Indriso, 1998). An estimated 70,000 women die each year as a result of unsafe abortion and many more survive with permanent injuries.

Most developing countries now have national family-planning programs, but they are usually limited to contraception and sterilization. Sexuality and fertility involve the most complex of human relations; simplistic approaches, built solely on contraception, are unlikely to have lasting effects (Bangaarts, Johansson, 2002). At a societal level, women must be able to achieve levels of social status and education that allow them to manage their own health and sexual decisions. They must also be provided with family-planning services that cover the full range of reproductive health problems, including infertility management, treatment for

Box 9.3: History notes

Miguel Sabido

Miguel Sabido was working for a Mexican television company when he had the idea of using "soap operas" to spread health information. The first series dealt with family planning. Its success led to others that addressed HIV/AIDS, family violence, and alcohol abuse. Education given through a medium that was accessible to much of the population rapidly caught on. The Sabido method is now termed "educational entertainment" and is widely used as a public health tool around the world. In Tanzania, the radio soap opera, "Twende no Wakati" ("Let's be modern"), was credited with having a significant effect on contraceptive use. It became one of the most popular programs in the country. Follow the reference for more information (Population Media Center, 2003).

Figure 9.8: Female literacy rate and teenage pregnancy rate (2000–2004) plotted for 160 countries

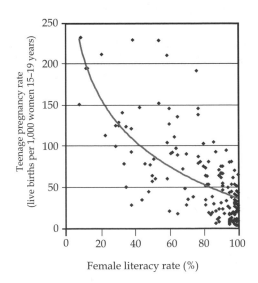

Sources: UNICEF (2006a, n.d.-b)

sexually transmitted diseases, and domestic violence.

Equally complex problems include the provision of sex education for children in school. This is essential to prepare them for safe sexual relations as adults, particularly in a world altered by the HIV epidemic. As shown in Figure 9.8, there is a close relationship between teenage pregnancy rate and female literacy rate. Prevention of adolescent pregnancy and reduction of sexually transmitted diseases will require social acceptance of sex education and contraceptive services for teenagers. This is a huge challenge, both for conservative cultures and for conservative funding agencies.

THE ORGANIZATION OF HEALTH CARE SERVICES IN DEVELOPING COUNTRIES

Over the last 60 years, a number of theoretical and political trends have influenced the delivery of health services in developing countries. Until the Alma Ata Meeting in 1978, the predominant system was based on a curative Western model. After Alma Ata, the emphasis shifted from cure to prevention under the PHC model. Although the PHC era has never been officially declared closed, it has been obvious over the last 15 years that serious attempts at reorganizing health care systems are long overdue. This more recent trend is usually dated to the 1993 World Development Report (*Investing in Health*) (World Bank, 1993), which summarized the need for extensive changes, both in the services provided and in the administration and funding methods used to pay for those services.

The World Health Organization's Report in 2000 (*Health Systems: Improving Performance*) took these recommendations further. The emphasis on cost efficiency and outcome measurement reflected the changing attitudes of the times. The Western and PHC models have both slowly given way to a newer, more results-based approach (at least in theory). The current trend is, perhaps, best called the "business model."

In order to understand a health system, it is necessary to answer three broad questions: (1) What services should be provided? (2) How is it all paid for? (3) How is the system organized? Obviously, this is a subject that would fill several books, but broad comments can be made under the following headings.

What Services Should Be Provided?

The 1993 World Development Report followed the philosophy of selective PHC first proposed a decade earlier (Walsh & Warren, 1979). The report emphasized that limited budgets should be spent in the most cost-effective way and proposed two standard packages of health care aimed at getting the maximum benefit from a limited budget. These consisted of a public health package (expanded program on immunization, school health, micronutrient supplementation, tobacco, alcohol, and HIV/AIDS control programs) and a medical services package (tuberculosis treatment, reproductive health care, family planning, basic management for sick children, and treatment of sexually transmitted diseases). At the time, it was estimated that widespread implementation of these basic services would reduce mortality and morbidity in children by 20–30 percent and among adults by 10–20 percent. The emphasis of the Millennium Development Goals on cost-effective, achievable targets follows a similar philosophy.

Health services inevitably expand to

fill the available health budget, so some form of health rationing will always be necessary, both for rich and poor countries. The development of tools to measure risk factors and assess treatment outcomes now allows health planners to design cost-effective initiatives aimed at the diseases and risks that carry the greatest burden of illness in their country. For the foreseeable future, this is likely to be the dominant model of service delivery in developing countries.

Funding Developing World Health Services

Health services are funded by a variety of mechanisms around the world, including tax-based funding (Canada, United Kingdom), mandatory health insurance (Germany, Japan, Costa Rica), voluntary private health insurance (United States, South Africa), community-based funding (Bamako Initiative, Thailand), direct out-of-pocket payments (much of the developing world), and overseas government or NGO funding (often against targeted initiatives).

In rural areas of the developing world, income is so low that the tax base is not sufficient to support government health services. Similarly, private insurance is still in its infancy in low-income developing countries. Even in the relatively prosperous Caribbean, it is estimated that only 12 percent of families are covered by health insurance and only three of 19 states offer some form of insurance (Barret & Lalta, (2004). In practice, the poor must choose between underfunded, poorly supplied government clinics or they must pay money to private practitioners or private pharmacists, or rely upon the services of traditional healers (ranging from Nganga of Zimbabwe to Ayurvedic in India).

In response to the severe cutbacks in health spending that occurred in the 1980s, a number of countries introduced user fee systems; the Bamako Initiative was the best known (Soucat et al., 1997). This was a pragmatic attempt to fund the implementation of PHC during an era of economic recession brought on by structural adjustment policies. Raising money is not, of course, the only problem with funding. Once the money has been obtained, it has to be used equitably and efficiently. User fees, if used wisely, can occasionally be shown to have benefits, but they also have the inevitable result of reducing health care utilization by the poor (Uzochukwu & Onwujekwe, 2004), who cannot afford even the smallest fees. Increasing the costs associated with illness can force the poorest families to choose between food and medicine. In many cases, the money raised is so small that by the time it has been collected and passed through several administrative hands, the final result is not worth all the effort.

There is considerable pressure to remove user fees, but it must be ensured that other forms of funding take their place, otherwise services will deteriorate even further (Gilson & McIntyre, 2005). This should be possible since African governments pledged to allocate at least 15 percent of their annual budgets to improve their health sectors at the Abuja Conference in 2000. It has been estimated that removal of user fees in Sub-Saharan Africa could prevent over 200,000 child deaths annually by giving affordable medical access to the poorest in the region (Jamas et al., 2005). However, this assumes that policy makers substitute sufficient alternative financing.

For the future, higher-income developing countries will probably move toward a mixed model of tax-based, government-funded services along with private care funded out of pocket and by health insurance. Low-income areas of the world will continue to rely upon government-funded clinic systems and a variety of targeted health initiatives often externally funded by donors. Such programs are increasingly being integrated into existing health services. User fees for the poorest people will hopefully be largely removed. It is also hoped that the resulting funding gap will be replaced by increased government spending.

Organization of Health Services in the Developing World

There is considerable support available for countries going through the process of health sector reform. The World Bank provides assistance through its Flagship Program on Health Sector Reform and Sustainable Financing (World Bank, n.d.). A joint Pan American Health Organization and USAID initiative supports a similar program called the Latin America and Caribbean Regional Health Sector Reform Initiative (n.d.). Services offered include rational pharmaceutical choices, management and leadership training, and quality-assurance techniques.

The common theme of modern health care reorganization is decentralization. There is a strong move to shift decision making out to the peripheral municipalities. This does not mean that governments have no part to play, but it changes their role to that of funding provider and general overall guide for the country's health services. While decentralization of funding has been shown to be beneficial for maternal and child health in Bolivia (Partnerships for Health Reform, 2000) or immunization services in Zambia (Blas & Limbambala, 2001), it is, as usual, not altogether simple. A large World Bank

study of the effects of decentralization on childhood immunization showed that decentralization improved immunization rates in low-income countries but reduced coverage rates in middle-income countries (Khaleghian, 2004).

Decentralization requires competent management. For example, patients follow the available services so decentralization produces a heavier patient load in peripheral clinics; this requires increased staff and training. Government funding must be sufficient to meet these peripheral needs for personnel and supply costs and the associated bureaucracy must be streamlined so that payments are provided on time (Partnerships for Health Reform, 2000). Continuing government oversight is necessary to ensure that projects are not hijacked by local elites and also that patients are not double charged for services that have already been paid for by the government. Despite its potential problems, the trend for the future organization of government health care in developing countries will probably be increasing decentralization.

SUMMARY

■ During the 1970s, there was an increasing recognition that the aid industry, as it was organized at the time, did not seem to be making any real headway against the poor standards of population health in developing populations. At meetings in 1975 and 1976, the World Health Assembly made a commitment to reverse this trend. The Assembly believed that development assistance and modern scientific advances should be able to provide a minimal standard of dignified living for every person in the world by the turn of the century. The slogan for this movement subsequently became "Health for all by the year 2000." The problem, of course, was implementation — how was this noble aim to be achieved?

A number of developing countries, particularly China, India, and some from Latin America, had already accumulated years of experience in tackling their own health problems with very limited financial resources. Their experience suggested that preventive health initiatives were considerably more cost effective than those based solely upon curative medicine. Each country differed, but a general consensus was reached about the most valuable elements of preventive care. These included an emphasis on breast-feeding, improved sanitation and clean water, access to basic medical care, immunizations, fertility-control information, and (most revolutionary of all) the inclusion of the poor in the debate.

Under the energetic leadership of WHO's Director General Halfden Mahler, the principles of what came to be called Primary Health Care (PHC) gained worldwide acceptance. The final result was an international meeting at Alma Ata in 1978, by the end of which there was universal support for the ambitious goal of health for all by 2000 based on worldwide implementation of the principles of primary health care. Inevitably, the dream of changing the world's medical system was easier in theory than practice. However, despite problems of implementation and years of divisive argument between the comprehensive and selective PHC camps, a great deal of good was still achieved. Worldwide programs on water and sanitation, immunization, breast-feeding, and distribution of oral rehydration therapy have all had a huge impact on the health of developing world populations.

More recent experience (particularly with the HIV/AIDS epidemic) has shown that effective initiatives must be aimed at multiple layers of a problem. Treatment and prevention are not antagonistic but are simply part of a continuum, all parts of which need to be included. It has taken over 25 years, but the recent Millennium Development Goals and the enhanced Heavily Indebted Poor Countries initiative both show how preventive social strategies can be combined with scientific advances to produce multilayer approaches to the problems of ill health and poverty.

RESOURCES

References

Afari, E., et al. (1995). "Impact of primary health care on child morbidity and mortality in rural Ghana: The Gomoa experience." *Central African Journal of Medicine, 41*, 148–153.

Al-Khidmat Welfare Society. (n.d.). Retrieved from www.alkhidmat.org.pk.

Bangaarts, J., & Johansson, E. (2002). "Future trends in contraceptive prevalence and method mix in the developing world." *Studies in Family Planning, 33*, 24–36.

Barret, R., & Lalta, S. (2004). *Jamaican National Health Fund: A critical management tool that encourages efficiency in health services* (Inter-American Development Bank technical paper, soc 138). Retrieved from www.iadb.org/sds/doc/SOCHealthFinancingJamaicaIDBDOCS381262.pdf.

Blas, E., & Limbambala, M. (2001). "User payment, decentralization, and health service utilization in Zambia." *Health Policy and Planning, 16*, 19–28.

Brenzel, L., et al. (1994). "Immunization programs and their costs." *Social Science and Medicine, 39,* 527–536.

Central Intelligence Agency. (2006). *The world factbook.* Retrieved from www.cia.gov/cia/publications/factbook.

Checkley, W., et al. (2004). "Effect of water and sanitation on childhood health in a poor Peruvian peri-urban community." *Lancet, 363,* 112–118.

Creel, L. (2002).*Children's environmental health: Risks and remedies* (Population Reference Bureau briefing paper). Retrieved from www.prb.org/pdf/ChildrensEnvironHlth_Eng.pdf.

Cueto, M. (2004). "The origins of primary health care and selective primary health care." *American Journal of Public Health, 94,* 1864–1874.

Curran, P. (1960). "Sodium, chloride, and water transport by rat ileum in vitro." *Journal of General Physiology, 43,* 1137–1148.

Darrow, D. (1949). "Disturbances of water and electrolytes in infantile diarrhea." *Journal of Pediatrics, 3,* 129–156.

Davey, S. (2003). *State of the world's vaccines and immunization.* Geneva: World Health Organization. Retrieved from www.who.int/vaccines/en/sowvi2002text.shtml.

Djukanovich, V., & Mach, E. (Eds.). (1975). *Alternative approaches to meeting basic health needs of populations in developing countries: A joint UNICEF/WHO study.* Geneva: World Health Organization.

Emerson, P., et al. (2006). *Implementing the SAFE strategy for trachoma control.* Retrieved from www.cartercenter.org/documents/2302.pdf.

Fries, J., et al. (1950). "Dehydrated banana in the dietetic management of diarrheas of infancy." *Journal of Pediatrics, 37,* 367–372.

Gilson, L., & McIntyre, D. (2005). "Removing user fees for primary care in Africa: The need for careful action." *British Medical Journal, 331,* 762–765.

Global Alliance for Vaccines and Immunizations. (n.d.). Retrieved from www.vaccinealliance.org.

Global Polio Eradication Initiative. (n.d.). Retrieved from www.polioeradication.org.

Hall, J., & Taylor, R. (2003). "Health for all beyond 2000: The demise of the Alma Ata Declaration and primary health care in developing countries." *Medical Journal of Australia, 178,* 17–20.

Health Canada. (n.d.). *About primary health care.* Retrieved from www.hc-sc.gc.ca/hcs-sss/prim/about-apropos/index_e.html.

Henderson, R. (1989). "World Health Organization's Expanded Program on Immunization: Progress and evaluation report." *Annals of the New York Academy of Sciences, 569,* 45–68.

Hill, A., et al. (2000). "Decline in mortality in children in rural Gambia: The influence of village-level primary health care." *Tropical Medicine and International Health, 5,* 107–118.

Hill, K., et al. (1997). *The recent evolution of child mortality in the developing world.* Retrieved from www.basics.org/publications/pubs/papers/hill.pdf.

Hirschhorn, N., et al. (1968). "Decrease in net stool output in cholera during intestinal perfusion with glucose-containing solutions." *New England Journal of Medicine, 279,* 176–181.

Illich, I. (1975). *Medical nemesis: The expropriation of health.* London: Calder and Boyars.

Jamas, C., et al. (2005). "Impact on child mortality of removing user fees: Simulation model." *British Medical Journal, 331,* 747–749.

Joint Measles Initiative. (n.d.). Retrieved from www.measlesinitiative.org.

Joint Monitoring Programme for Water Supply and Sanitation. (2000). *Global water supply and sanitation assessment 2000.* Retrieved from www.wssinfo.org/pdf/GWSSA_2000_report.pdf.

Joint Monitoring Programme for Water Supply and Sanitation. (n.d.). *Water data.* Retrieved from www.wssinfo.org/en/21_wat_intro.html.

Kennedy, M. (2004). *A brief history of disease, science, and medicine.* Mission Viejo: Asklepiad Press.

Khaleghian, P. (2004). "Decentralization and public services: The case of immunization." *Social Science and Medicine, 59,* 163–183.

Kjellstrom, T. (1999). "How much global ill health is attributable to environmental factors?" *Epidemiology, 10*, 573–584.

Kuhn, L., et al. (1990). "Village health workers and GOBI-FFF: An evaluation of a rural program." *South African Medical Journal, 77*, 471–475.

Lalonde, M. (1974). *A new perspective on the health of Canadians: A working document.* Ottawa: Government of Canada. Retrieved from www.hc-sc.gc.ca/hcs-sss/com/lalonde/index_e.html.

Latin American and Caribbean Regional Health Sector Reform (LACHSR) initiative. (n.d.). Retrieved from www.lachsr.org.

Magnussen, L., et al. (2004). "Comprehensive versus selective primary health care: Lessons for global health policy." *Health Affairs, 23*, 167–176.

Mondigo, A., & Indriso, C. (1998). *Abortion in the developing world.* London: Zed Books.

O'Ryan, M., et al. (2005). "A millennium update on pediatric diarrheal illness in the developing world." *Seminars in Pediatric Infectious Disease, 16*, 125–136.

Olivera, O., & Lewis, T. (2004). *Cochabamba! Water war in Bolivia.* Cambridge: South End Press.

Partnerships for Health Reform. (2000). *Reducing maternal and child mortality in Bolivia.* Retrieved from www.phrplus.org/Pubs/ess1.pdf.

Philips, R. (1964). "Water and electrolyte losses in cholera." *Federation Proceedings, 23*, 705–712.

Population Media Center. (2003). *Sabido Method.* Retrieved from www.populationmedia.org/programs/sabido.html.

Poznyak, V., et al. (2005). "Breaking the vicious circle of determinants and consequences of harmful alcohol use." *Bulletin of the World Health Organization, 83*, 803–805.

Primary Health Care Research and Information Service. (n.d.). Retrieved from www.phcris.org.au.

Resnikoff, S., et al. (2004). "Global data on visual impairment in the year 2002." *Bulletin of the World Health Organization, 82*, 844–851.

Rosen, G. (1993). *History of public health.* Baltimore: Johns Hopkins University Press.

Ruxin, J. (1994). "Magic bullet: The history of oral rehydration therapy." *Medical History, 38*, 363–397.

Sachs, J. (2005). *The end of poverty: Economic possibilities for our time.* New York: Penguin Press.

Sanders, D. (2004). *Twenty-five years of primary health care: Lessons learned and proposals for revitalization.* Retrieved from www.asksource.info/rtf/phc-sanders.RTF.

Seear, M. (2004). "History's lessons." *Canadian Medical Association Journal, 171*, 1487–1488.

Selander, P. (1950). "Carrot soup in the treatment of infantile diarrhea." *Journal of Pediatrics, 36*, 742–745.

Shattuck, L., Banks, N., & Abbot, J. (1850). *Report of a general plan for the promotion of public and personal health.* Boston: Massachusetts State Printers. Retrieved from www.deltaomega.org/shattuck.pdf.

Sidel, V. (1972). "The barefoot doctors of the People's Republic of China." *New England Journal of Medicine, 286*, 1292–1300.

Soucat, A., et al. (1997). "Local cost sharing in Bamako initiative systems in Benin and Guinea: Assessing the financial viability of primary health care." *The International Journal of Health Planning and Management, 12*, S109–S135.

Stein, D., & Gureje, O. (2004). "Depression and anxiety in the developing world: Is it time to medicalize the suffering?" *Lancet, 364*, 233–234.

Thompson, W. (1929). "Population." *American Journal of Sociology, 34*, 959–975.

Townson, M., et al. (2005). "Exploiting the potential of vector control for disease prevention." *Bulletin of the World Health Organization, 83*, 942–947.

UN Millennium Development Goals. (n.d.). Retrieved from www.un.org/millenniumgoals/.

UNICEF. (2006a). *Basic education.* Retrieved from www.childinfo.org/areas/education.

UNICEF. (2006b). *Child mortality.* Retrieved from www.childinfo.org/areas/childmortality.

UNICEF. (2006c). *Delivery care*. Retrieved from www.childinfo.org/areas/deliverycare.

UNICEF. (2006d). *Global and regional trends in immunization coverage*. Retrieved from www.childinfo.org/areas/immunization.

UNICEF. (2006e). *Overview of breastfeeding patterns*. Retrieved from www.childinfo.org/areas/breastfeeding/status.php.

UNICEF. (n.d.-a). *Baby-friendly hospital initiative*. Retrieved from www.unicef.org/programme/breastfeeding/baby.htm.

UNICEF. (n.d.-b). *Fertility and contraceptive use*. Retrieved from www.childinfo.org/eddb/fertility.

UNICEF. (n.d.-c). *Innocenti declaration*. Retrieved from www.unicef.org/programme/breastfeeding/innocenti.htm.

UN-Water. (2005). *Water for life 2005–2015*. Retrieved from www.un.org/waterforlifedecade.

Uzochukwu, B., & Onwujekwe, O. (2004). "Socio-economic differences and health-seeking behaviour for the diagnosis and treatment of malaria: A case study of four local government areas operating the Bamako initiative program in southeast Nigeria." *International Journal for Equity in Health, 3*, 6–12. Retrieved from www.equityhealthj.com/content/3/1/6.

Victoria, C., et al. (2000). "Reducing deaths from diarrhea through oral rehydration therapy." *Bulletin of the World Health Organization, 78*, 1246–1255.

Walsh, J., & Warren, K. (1979). "Selective primary health care: An interim strategy for disease control in developing countries." *New England Journal of Medicine, 301*, 967–974.

"Water with sugar and salt." (1978). *Lancet, 2*, 300–301.

Werner, D., et al. (1997). *Questioning the solution: The politics of primary health care*. Palo Alto: Health Wrights.

World Bank. (1993). *World development report 1993: Investing in health*. Retrieved from www.econ.worldbank.org/wdr.

World Bank. (n.d.) *The Flagship Program on Health Sector Reform and Sustainable Financing*. Retrieved from www.worldbank.org/wbi/healthflagship.

World Health Organization. (1981). *Global strategy for health for all by the year 2000*. Retrieved from whqlibdoc.who.int/publications/9241800038.pdf.

World Health Organization. (2000). *World health report 2000: Health systems: Improving performance*. Retrieved from www.who.int/whr/2000/en.

World Health Organization. (2003). *Global strategy for infant and young child feeding*. Retrieved from www.who.int/child-adolescent-health/NUTRITION/global_strategy.htm.

World Health Organization. (2005a). *Global immunization: Vision and strategy 2005–2015*. Retrieved from www.who.int/vaccines/GIVS.

World Health Organization. (2005b). *World health report 2005: Statistical annex*. Retrieved from www.who.int/whr/2005/annex/en/index.html.

World Health Organization. (n.d.-a). *The world health report*. Retrieved from www.who.int/whr.

World Health Organization. (n.d.-b). *Health and environment linkages initiative*. Retrieved from www.who.int/heli.

World Health Organization. (n.d.-c). *Immunization, vaccines, and biologicals*. Retrieved from www.who.int/immunization.

World Health Organization. (n.d.-d). *Water, sanitation, and health*. Retrieved from www.who.int/water_sanitation_health.

Recommended Reading

Campbell, C. (2003). *Letting them die: Why HIV/AIDS prevention programs fail*. Bloomington: Indiana University Press.

Elder, J. (2001). *Behavior change and public health in the developing world*. Thousand Oaks: SAGE Publications.

Rosen, G. (1993). *History of public health*. Baltimore: Johns Hopkins University Press.

Werner, D., et al. (1997). *Questioning the solution: The politics of primary health care*. Palo Alto: Health Wrights.

Wilson, P., et al. (2005). *Combating AIDS in the developing world*. London: Earthscan Publications.

Chapter 10

Basic Medical Care

> The desire to take medicine
> is perhaps the greatest feature which
> distinguishes men from animals.
> — William Osler

OBJECTIVES

After completing this chapter, you should be able to

- understand the medical treatments available for the major infectious diseases
- understand the theory and practice behind the Integrated Management of Childhood Illness (IMCI) initiative
- understand the minimum requirements for safe pregnancy-related health care and appreciate the urgent need for improved worldwide standards of care for pregnant women
- understand the developing world's need for improved access to safe, affordable, and effective drugs

---

Children do not turn up at a medical clinic complaining of poor maternal education or lack of sanitation; they arrive with urgent medical problems that demand immediate attention. It is easy to slip into the belief that treating those medical problems is the most important part of improving population health. Harsh experience with curative-based programs has shown clearly that long-term solutions must also be aimed at the underlying social problems. Once these are removed, measles, malnutrition, and dehydration slowly disappear (to be replaced by skateboard injuries). This does not, of course, mean that medical treatment has no value. Curative treatment is a vital part of the control of many diseases ranging from tuberculosis to gastroenteritis, but it is only a small part of a larger picture that has to include multiple interventions aimed at the underlying social inequities that produced those diseases in the first place. Treating a severely dehydrated child with oral rehydration solution can produce dramatic temporary improvement, but if the baby is sent back to squalid, overcrowded conditions with no access to clean water, it will not be long before that child returns. This chapter will examine the effective treatments available for the diseases that cause the great majority of adult and childhood deaths. It will also examine the subject of affordable access to the drugs needed to treat those diseases.

TREATING THE MAJOR INFECTIOUS KILLERS

Malaria

The belief is growing on me that the disease is communicated by the bite of the

mosquito…. She always injects a small quantity of fluid with her bite—what if the parasites get into the system in this manner?

—Ronald Ross

The Disease

Malaria has long infected humans (Centers for Disease Control and Prevention, 2004). Clear descriptions of the disease exist in the Hippocratic writings (5th century BC) and in the Yellow Emperor's Medical Classic (at least 1–2 centuries BC). The economic and social importance of the disease is reflected in the fact that three Nobel prizes have been awarded for research into malaria: Laveran for discovering the parasite, Ross for discovering the mode of transmission, and Müller for the introduction of DDT.

Malaria is caused by a single-cell protozoan from the genus Plasmodium. Four members of the family cause disease in humans: *P. falciparium*, *P. vivax*, *P. ovale*, and *P. malariae*. The most serious disease is caused by *P. falciparium*. Ancient names for the disease reflect its association with mosquito areas: "marsh fever" in English and *mal aria* (bad air) in Italian (Centers for Disease Control and Prevention, 2004). The parasite does not have an animal reservoir and is spread from human to human by the female anopheles mosquito (World Health Organization–Tropical Disease Research, 2004). After entering the body through mosquito saliva, it multiplies in liver cells for a few days before rupturing into the bloodstream and invading red cells. Waves of fever occur as merozoites subsequently break out of red cells on a regular basis. The Romans noted differences in this periodicity and distinguished between tertian and quartan fevers.

Table 10.1: A moment of Zen

Total number of children who died before their fifth birthday in 2003: 10,596,000	
Percentage that died in a developing country: 99.2 percent	
Number of seconds in a year: 60 x 60 x 24 x 365: 31,536,000	Time taken, by the average person, to order a decaffeinated, double grande, triple macchiato with half and half, plus extra foam:
One child dies of an avoidable cause every:	
2.97 seconds	**2.97 seconds**
Source: World Health Organization (2005b)	Source: Independent Research

---

Box 10.1: History notes

James Grant (1922–1995)

Grant was born in China as a Canadian citizen; his father was a medical missionary. He studied economics at the University of California and Harvard. He then became an American citizen after the war. He started at the UN Relief Rehabilitation Administration in China and worked up through several international agencies until founding and leading the Overseas Development Council. He became head of UNICEF in 1980. In this position, he introduced the concept of the Child Survival Revolution. As a result of targeted programs for immunization, oral rehydration, and breast-feeding, an unimaginable number of children (perhaps as many as 25 million) cheated early death. Many millions more grew up stronger and healthier than they might otherwise have done. He also instituted the annual Progress of Nations Report and the State of the World's Children Report. He worked 12-hour days, six days a week, helped by assistants who worked in shifts. He was still dictating letters on the day of his death. His greatest achievement was to organize the UN convention on the basic rights of the child in 1989. See the reference for further information (Bellamy et al., 2001).

Destruction of red cells leads to anemia, jaundice, and fever. Some patients progressively slide into shock, renal failure, lung failure, involvement of the brain blood vessels (cerebral malaria), and death (World Health Organization, 2000). Those with reduced immunity (children, travellers, and pregnant women) have a much higher mortality. Malaria kills roughly a million people each year, most of whom are children (850,000 in the most recent estimates, compared to 321,000 HIV deaths in children under

five years). Adults in endemic areas often have reasonable immunity. The estimated 350–500 million cases a year in these areas carry a low mortality, but they impose a huge disease burden that limits the performance of entire populations (Roll Back Malaria Partnership, 2005).

Treatment

Treatment relies on early use of effective anti-malarial drugs. This is a complex topic because of the extensive array of drugs (and drug combinations) and changing patterns of resistance (World Health Organization, 2006c). The earliest effective anti-malarial was Qinghao derived in China from *Artemesia annua* (sweet wormwood in Canada). Its use is described in the ancient manuscript, Fifty-Two Remedies, found in the 2,000-year-old Mawangdui Tomb. Artemesin drugs have been recently reintroduced as the "latest thing" in malaria treatment (World Health Organization, 2006a). Jesuit missionaries in South America introduced another early drug to Europe after they learned of an effective anti-malaria treatment derived from the bark of the quina quina tree (subsequently called cinchona tree after it was used to treat the countess of Cinchon). Quinine remained the mainstay of treatment until chloroquine was introduced in 1946. Apart from a few areas in the Middle East and Central America, chloroquine resistance is now so common that other drugs and regimes have had to be instituted. Chloroquine remains an effective drug against most strains of *P. vivax* and *P. malariae*. The topic is made more complex by the fact that two strains of malaria (*P. vivax* and *P. ovale*) have a persistent dormant form in the liver that must be

Table 10.2: Common anti-malarial drugs

Chemical Group	Example
Aryl amino alcohols	Quinine, mefloquine
Folate inhibitors	Sulphonamides, proguanil, pyrimethamine
4 aminoquinolines	Chloroquine, amodiaquine
8 aminoquinolines	Primaquine
Antibiotics	Doxycycline, tetracycline
Artemesin derivatives	Artemesin, artemether, arteether, artesunate
Naphthoquinones	Atovaquone

treated with a different set of drugs after the acute illness is over (World Health Organization, 2006c). Table 10.2 gives a list of some of the common anti-malarial drugs available.

The challenges of setting a rational drug policy are enormous. Variables include drug route (oral, rectal, intravenous), patient variability (children and pregnant women), choice of drug (resistance patterns), and the introduction of drug combinations (further unknown side effects and best-use practices). There is a growing trend to use combination therapy as standard treatment for malaria. Apart from combining the benefits of two individual therapies, it may also delay drug resistance (World Health Organization, 2006a). Early combinations such as sulphadoxine/pyrimethamine and atovaquone/proguanil are being replaced by Artemesin-based Combination Therapy (ACT). Numerous excellent reviews, guiding choice of anti-malarial treatment, are available (Ashley & White, 2005; World Health Organization, 2006a, 2006c).

Malaria Eradication

Unfortunately, the complexity of the malaria life cycle makes it very difficult to develop an effective vaccine (Targett, 2005). Several vaccines have been tested, but clinical efficacy has been low. In the early 1950s, the development of effective treatments (chloroquine) and effective long-lasting residual sprays (DDT) raised the hopes that malaria could be eradicated. The World Health Assembly proposed a worldwide eradication program in 1955 along the same line as the smallpox program. At the time, malaria had only just been eradicated from the United States and was still endemic in parts of Europe. The program was successful in many countries, but the emergence of drug resistance, insecticide resistance, wars, lack of funding, and poor involvement of affected communities ultimately led to abandonment of the project in 1969. Malaria control is complex and broadly based on a combination of the following interventions (World Bank, 2005):

- *Effective early treatment:* Patients should have access to treatment by active drugs within 24 hours of the onset of symptoms. Obviously this requires considerable medical and pharmaceutical organization (World Health Organization, 2006c). In some areas, prepackaged home treatment has been successful.
- *Prevention of infection:* On a large scale, this is achieved by insecticide spraying, which, again, requires extensive resources. Following the success of South Africa's Combined Malaria Program in Kwa-Zulu Natal, the use of household spraying

with DDT has been re-examined (Curtis & Lines, 2000). This has, of course, led to considerable controversy. At a personal level, insecticide-treated bed nets, when used regularly, have been shown to be an effective form of malaria control (Curtis & Minzava, 2000).

- *Harm reduction:* Treatment of high-risk groups such as pregnant women and children can be very cost effective. Treating women two or three times during their pregnancy reduces maternal anemia, reduces maternal mortality, and improves the health of their newborns (Shulman & Dorman, 2003). Intermittent treatment for children has also been shown to be beneficial and is now being given during immunization visits (Malaria intermittent preventive treatment ..., 2004).

- *International partnership:* Malaria control requires huge efforts in terms of education, access to effective drugs, vector control, and, of course, money. Lasting success is impossible without coordination of donors, government agencies, and close involvement with the target populations. The Roll Back Malaria Campaign, launched by WHO, UNICEF, and UNDP in 1998 (*Roll back malaria*, n.d.), is the biggest example. Their ambitious plan to halve the burden of disease by 2010 is not going as well as hoped, at least partly due to insufficient donor support. By mid-2004, global malaria deaths had actually risen ("Roll back malaria," 2004).

Tuberculosis

I saw pale kings and princes too,
Pale warriors, death pale were they all.
They cried — "La Belle Dame sans merci,
Hath thee in thrall."

—John Keats

Tuberculosis has been a scourge of humanity as long as malaria. Definite evidence of infection has been found in mummified pharaohs and Neanderthal skeletons (Dormandy, 2001). The disease was called "Phthisis" by Hippocrates; he also warned that the disease could be caught from infected patients. The name dates back to the 17th-century observation that infected lungs contain characteristic nodules (tubercles). Koch discovered the staining technique that allowed him to see the organism for the first time. Treatment relied upon nutrition and rest in sanitoria until the first tuberculosis drug (streptomycin) was developed in 1943. Waksman was awarded the Nobel Prize after searching for an active drug among 10,000 different soil microbes.

Tuberculosis is caused by a rod-shaped bacterium. Most disease is caused by Mycobacterium tuberculosis (Enarson et al., 2000). The principal source of infection is airborne droplets from infected patients, but intestinal infection still occurs in areas where milk from infected cattle is not pasteurized. After entering the lungs, the interaction between the organism and host depends on a number of factors, including the host's individual susceptibility, nutritional level, age, and associated diseases (particularly HIV/ AIDS).

Over 90 percent of well-nourished healthy people control the initial infection with no further disease spread outside the small focus of affected lung. A large percentage of the world's population is infected with TB that may remain latent for life or, under some circumstances, might reactivate years later. In susceptible patients, the bacterium spreads to other organs of the body, including the bones, kidneys, and brain. Overwhelming tuberculosis, often in children, leads to miliary tuberculosis. The World Health Organization (2006b) estimates there were 8 million new tuberculosis cases and nearly 2 million deaths in 2000, a mortality exceeded only by HIV/AIDs. Ninety-eight percent of all deaths occur in developing countries, particularly in Sub-Saharan Africa. Diagnosis is based on the clinical findings, chest X-ray, and stained infected material (usually sputum). A skin test (Mantoux test) is available, but interpretation is difficult, particularly in the presence of HIV/AIDS.

Treatment

> It was the fashion to suffer from the lungs; everybody was consumptive, poets especially; it was good form to spit blood after each emotion that was at all sensational, and to die before reaching the age of thirty.
>
> — Alexander Dumas

Patient compliance is an important factor in any form of drug treatment from hypertension to diabetes. Tuberculosis compliance is particularly important because open, untreated cases represent a threat to the greater population. Consequently, considerable effort has been put into ensuring that TB patients actually take their drugs. Whether in developed or developing countries, it has been shown that directly observed drug

Table 10.3: Common short-term tuberculosis treatment regimes

Two months of daily isoniazid, rifampicin, ethambutol, and pyrazinamide, followed by four months of isoniazid and rifampicin given two or three times weekly.
Two weeks of daily isoniazid, rifampicin, ethambutol, and pyrazinamide, followed by six weeks of twice-weekly isoniazid, rifampicin, ethambutol, and pyrazinamide, followed by four months of twice-weekly isoniazid and rifampicin.
Six months of three times-weekly isoniazid, rifampicin, and pyrazinamide.

therapy by a health worker or supervisor (DOT strategy) is a vital element in TB treatment (World Health Organization, 2004).

After the introduction of streptomycin, it soon became obvious that single drug treatment was associated with rapid development of drug resistance. Many variations of TB treatment courses exist, but all now rely on an initial period of three or four medications that are cut back to two drugs as time progresses (Blumberg et al., 2005). The Mycobacterium divides relatively slowly so intermittent treatment schedules can be used. Typical six-month programs are given inTable 10.3. Anti-TB drugs can have significant side effects so patients should be monitored carefully.

Disease Eradication

In 1991, the World Health Assembly recognized TB as a major threat to world health. The initial aims were to detect 70 percent of all new cases using sputum staining and successfully treat 85 percent of those cases. The DOTS strategy was widely introduced in 1994 and the Stop Tuberculosis Initiative was established in 1998 (*Stop Tuberculosis Partnership,* n.d.; World Health Organization, n.d.-b). By 2004, 20 million people had been treated, with a success rate of over 80 percent. Detection rates are now over 50 percent. Mortality rates have fallen everywhere except Sub-Saharan Africa and parts of Eastern Europe. Along with the Millennium Development Goals, long-term goals include halving the 1990 prevalence by 2015 and reducing incidence below one per million by 2050 (Figueroa-Munoz et al., 2006).

- *Vaccines:* The BCG vaccine (Bacillus Calmette-Guérin) was introduced in 1921 and has been shown to reduce mortality from tuberculosis in children. It appears to be less effective against reactivated pulmonary tuberculosis in adults. Several vaccines are under development around the world; it is hoped that a more effective vaccine will be available within a decade (Doherty & Rook, 2006).
- *Case detection:* New cases used to be detected by mobile population X-ray screening. Case detection now relies on sputum microscopy of symptomatic people seeking care (Figueroa-Munoz et al., 2006). This obviously requires investment in TB centres and trained technicians. Since HIV infection is closely related to an increased risk of tuberculosis, TB control centres should be closely linked with HIV/AIDS-control programs.
- *Drug treatment:* Treatment of tuberculosis is better regulated than the treatment of malaria. The accepted standard is Directly Observed Therapy using standardized Short course regimes (DOTS). Monitoring of treatment and definition of cure depend on accurate sputum microscopy. A clear protocol for managing drug-resistant TB must be in place (DOTS-Plus) (*Working group on DOTS-Plus*, n.d.). Drug treatment requires a supply of affordable and effective drugs, which, ideally, should be free of charge. Use of fixed drug combinations improves adherence to treatment. The Global Drug Facility (GDF) has recently been established to improve the global supply of effective anti-tuberculosis medication (*Global Drug Facility*, n.d.).

HIV/AIDS

I asked about the cabbages. I assumed it supplemented their diet? Yes, they chorused. And you sell the surplus at market? An energetic nodding of heads. And I take it you make a profit? Yes again. What do you do with the profit? And this time there was an almost quizzical response as if to say what kind of ridiculous question is that…. "We buy coffins of course; we never have enough coffins."

—Stephen Lewis

The first reports of a new acquired form of immune deficiency, predominantly among homosexual men, appeared in the Western medical literature in early 1981 (Gottlieb et al., 1981). Many initially believed that it was due to immune damage from recreational drug use, but epidemiological studies subsequently indicated an infectious etiology. By 1983, the Pasteur Institute had isolated what subsequently proved to be the causative virus. There was so much argument about the naming and discovery of the virus (and rights to the lucrative HIV test) between French and American laboratories (Gallo & Montagnier, 2003) that the presidents of both France and the US actually met to discuss the subject! The final agreed name was "human immunodeficiency virus" (HIV).

HIV is a single-strand RNA virus from the genus *Lentivirus*. Of the two forms, HIV1 is by far the most common; HIV2 is mostly found in West Africa. HIV is transmitted between humans by close contact with bodily fluids (blood, semen, breast milk), contaminated blood (needle exchange, transfusions), and mother-to-infant transmission (pregnancy, childbirth, breast-feeding). As Figure 10.1 shows, by 2004, roughly 40 million people worldwide were living with HIV infection (about 25 million of whom were in Africa)

Figure 10.1: Numbers of People Living with AIDS

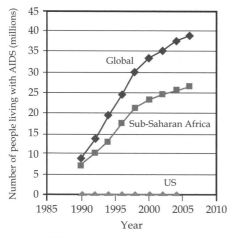

Source: UNAIDS (2004)

and over 20 million had died. Although the number of new cases has declined in developed countries, numbers living with the disease are slowly increasing because of improved survival.

The full clinical picture of HIV infection is enormous (Grant & De Cock, 2001), but its principal mechanism of action is to infect components of the immune system, particularly the CD4+ T cells. Cumulative damage to the cellular immune system leads to a growing risk of opportunistic infections (Pneumocystis pneumonia, tuberculosis, and cytomegalovirus) and also malignancies (Kaposis sarcoma, B-cell lymphomas, and cervical cancer in women). In late-stage disease, direct viral infection of other body organs such as the brain, kidneys, or liver can also cause significant disease.

Progression of the disease is very variable, ranging from months to years. The rate of progression is influenced by age of onset, nutrition, other infections, and effective viral treatment. During the early stages, the patient may be completely asymptomatic except for an initial fever and lymphadenopathy. As the disease progresses, weight loss and various skin infections such as Candida and herpes appear. Later stages are characterized by bacterial infections, tuberculosis, spread to the brain, and severe wasting.

The case fatality rate is ultimately very high. Roughly 5 percent of infected patients appear to remain stable over many years, but the majority slowly progress to fully expressed late-stage AIDS. Median interval from infection to severe immune deficiency is eight to nine years, but it is generally accepted to be shorter in most developing countries (Dorling et al., 2006). Survival time after onset of severe AIDS is also variable. In the absence of supportive care and anti-viral treatment, the progression from full-blown AIDS to death usually occurs in less than a year, but this can be dramatically altered by provision of effective anti-retroviral therapy.

Treatment

Before the introduction of Highly Active Anti-Retroviral Therapy (HAART), there were no treatments available other than supportive care, good nutrition, and treatment of common infections such as Candidiasis and pneumonia. At the time, feelings of frustration and resignation were a serious problem among developing world health workers (Marchal et al., 2005). The first anti-HIV drug (AZT, zidovudine) was introduced in 1987, followed by the steady introduction of many others in four different classes during the 1990s (Table 10.4). Their early use in combination therapy has dramatically changed the outlook for HIV-infected patients, but this comes with a significant number of side effects and a considerable drug bill (Reynolds et al., 2003). Drug treatment is not started until patients meet criteria based on CD4+ counts and measured viral

Table 10.4: The four common classes of anti-retroviral drugs

Protease Inhibitors (PI)

  • amprenavir, ritonavir, nelfinavir, saquinavir

Non-Nucleoside Reverse Transcriptase Inhibitors (nNRTI)

  • delavirdine, efavirenz, nevirapine

Nucleoside Reverse Transcriptase Inhibitors (NRTI)

  • zidovudine, lamivudine, abacavir, tenofovir

Entry Inhibitors (EI)

  • enfuvirtide

---

load. The fight by developed countries to obtain access to cheaper generic drugs is covered later in this chapter.

Mother-to-child transmission is the most important source of HIV infection in children. In developed countries, triple combination regimes used before and after delivery (both for the mother and child) can reduce transmission below 5 percent (from an untreated average of about 25 percent) (De Cock et al., 2000). This offers the promise of saving a generation of children in developing countries, but introduction has been shamefully slow. Even under poor resource conditions, short courses of effective drugs can reduce transmission significantly. Several regimes have been tested (Jackson et al., 2003; Taha et al., 2003), including zidovudine alone or in combination with lamivudine and nevirapine.

In 2003, an estimated 700,000 children were newly infected with HIV; about 90 percent of these occurred in Sub-Saharan Africa. In developing countries, the cumulative risk of transmission during pregnancy and delivery is estimated at 15–30 percent. Depending on duration and viral load, breast-feeding by an untreated mother increases the risk by a further 10–15 percent. There is no consensus on the correct management of an HIV-positive breast-feeding mother (Dadhich, 2005). Ideally, every child should be fed well-prepared formula, but, in large parts of the world, formula feeding is associated with significant diarrhea-associated risks of its own.

HIV Prevention

The growth of the fight against AIDS has been extraordinary. In 25 years, it has gone from a medical curiosity to a multibillion-dollar industry employing tens of thousands of people. Attempts to control the disease have been based on the following methods:

- *HIV vaccine:* When the viral cause of AIDS was discovered in the early 1980s, there was initial enthusiasm that a vaccine would soon be discovered; unfortunately, this hope has not been met. There are two problems confronting HIV vaccine research. Firstly, the virus expresses a surprisingly complex antigenic variation for such a seemingly simple organism (Peeters & Sharp, 2000). Secondly, the body's ability to respond to a vaccine is reduced by the fact that HIV infects some of the cells that mediate that response. Several vaccines have been tested, but, unfortunately, none has shown any significant results so far. Since a small percentage of people appear to have innate immunity to HIV and a few infected patients appear to live for many years with normal health, hopes still remain high that a vaccine will ultimately be found (*International AIDS Vaccine Initiative*, n.d.).
- *Routine testing:* After the initial discovery of HIV, there was considerable debate about universal testing, contact tracing, and even quarantine. The WHO took an early lead against the stigmatization of HIV-positive people. Cuba was the only country to carry this policy to its conclusion. Between 1988 and 1993, all Cubans who tested HIV positive were quarantined and allowed out only with a chaperone (Hansen & Grace, 2003). The country has subsequently adopted more enlightened policies; its provision of free anti-retroviral therapy now makes it a leader in HIV control among developing countries. In the single area of maternal to infant transmission, there is nearly universal support for routine prenatal testing because of the existence of highly effective treatment regimes that reduce the risk to the fetus (De Cock et al., 2000).
- *Behavioural change:* Changing human behaviour is not easy as the failure rates of weight-loss programs and anti-smoking programs easily show. The steps needed to alter behaviour must start with changing knowledge and beliefs about HIV. Building on this base leads to changes in attitude and, finally, personal practice. Education is not an easy or rapid process. Peer influence is an important factor in social change, whether dealing with teenage sexual practices or recreational drug use (Diaz et al., 2005). Unfortunately, the discussion of safe sex and provision of needles, syringes, and safe injection sites is opposed by some donor agencies and also by conservative governments.

In developed countries, education programs have caused significant changes in behaviour with measurable reductions in the incidence of HIV infections among heterosexuals, homosexuals, and drug users. Unfortunately, good-quality HIV control can become a victim of its own success. Improved survival produces a degree of complacency and high-risk behaviour starts to increase again (Ostrow et al., 2002). In the developing world, Uganda has shown a lead in HIV/AIDS interventions. High-level political support, backed by widespread community involvement, has produced real changes in the population's attitude toward safe sexual practices (Bunnell et al., 2006). Condom use is clearly beneficial, but its impact is limited by inconsistent use. Condoms should form only one part of a broad coordinated strategy (Hearst & Chen, 2004). Evidence would suggest that Uganda's approach has succeeded with a measurable decline in HIV prevalence from 15 percent in 1991 to 5 percent in 2001.

Treatment

Introduction of combination anti-retroviral drug therapy in the mid-1990s dramatically changed the picture of HIV in developed countries. Death rates fell and patients started to live longer and healthier lives. Apart from improving health, HAART regimes also reduce transmission risks because of the very low viral loads in many treated patients. The principal obstacle to widespread drug treatment in the developing world is obviously money. The topic of access to effective drugs will be covered later in this chapter, but the slow response to the provision of affordable AIDS drugs to badly affected countries does not reflect well on the industrialized world. Brazil was the first developing country to provide universal anti-retroviral therapy for infected patients. Brazil's AIDS program is estimated to have halved the country's predicted mortality and infection rates (Berkman et al., 2005). Success is due to a coordinated program that integrates prevention and treatment approaches.

Transferring this experience to other developing countries requires large amounts of funding. The global fund to fight AIDS, tuberculosis, and malaria (GFATM) has started with some successes, but its funding is well below the initial optimistic $10 billion a year; its emphasis is also on research rather than treatment. The US President's Emergency Plan for AIDS Relief (PEPFAR) has emerged as another new source of funds. It promises $15 billion over five years for care, prevention, and treatment programs in the most severely affected countries. More than half the total is committed for drug treatment.

On World AIDS Day in 2003, the WHO and UNAIDS announced a plan to have 3 million patients on anti-retroviral treatment by the end of 2005 (the "3 by 5 target") (World Health Organization, n.d.-a). At the time, WHO estimated that more than 4 million, of the 25 million people living with AIDS in Sub-Saharan Africa, needed anti-retroviral therapy, but only 315, 000 had access to it. By the end of 2005, it was estimated that 1.6 million were on treatment worldwide (500,000 of whom were in Africa). Although the initial estimates were optimistic, a huge amount of work has been achieved in training health workers and establishing affordable drug supply and delivery mechanisms.

Other Diseases

Visceral Leishmaniasis (Kala azar)

Different species of the protozoal parasite, Leishmania, can cause a spectrum of diseases ranging from superficial skin ulcers to invasive, slowly lethal multiorgan disease (Herwaldt, 1999). The organism is spread by the bite of a sand fly. In its most severe form (visceral Leishmaniasis or kala azar), the parasite causes invasive disease with fever, weight loss, and steady deterioration to death over a few months. Exact numbers are not known because asymptomatic infection is common. In endemic areas, the disease has become an increasingly common opportunistic infection associated with HIV infection. It is thought that 500,000 new cases occur each year, principally in Bangladesh, Brazil, and Sudan.

The most common form of treatment is a drug called pentavalent antimony, which has been available for over 50 years. It is a toxic drug with, in some cases, severe side effects, including death. Newer drug alternatives such as ambisome, miltefosine, and paromomycin have not been widely used in treatment because of the familiar story of expense and limited research targeted at developing world diseases. However, now that large numbers of "Western" soldiers are at risk of catching the parasite while serving in the Middle East, it is likely that research will soon be given greater priority (Zapar & Moran, 2005). So far, research in India has shown that miltefosine shows considerable promise as a safe oral alternative for invasive disease (Olliaro et al., 2005).

African Trypanosomiasis (Sleeping Sickness)

There are two closely related forms of sleeping sickness caused by different types of the protozoan parasite Trypanosoma brucei. The disease is spread by tsetse flies and is distributed widely throughout Central Africa. After infection, the first symptoms are relatively mild so that patients often remain undiagnosed. As the parasite spreads and invades the central nervous system, the patient's mental state undergoes a change that includes intense pain, confusion, somnolence, and ultimately death. The disease was well controlled in the 1960s by a combination of medical treatment and tsetse fly control. Unfortunately, war and social upheaval have interrupted control measures and the disease is returning. Disease surveillance is poor, but it is estimated there are 500,000 new cases each year. In some high-risk areas of Central Africa, sleeping sickness has become the most common cause of death, ahead of TB and AIDS.

Sleeping sickness is very difficult to treat (Jannin & Cattand, 2004). In its early stages, pentamidine and suramin are used for patients who have not progressed to the neurological stage. The drugs are expensive and associated with side effects. The treatment of late-stage, neurologically affected patients requires melarsoprol, which is toxic enough to kill about 5 percent of treated patients; drug resistance is also becoming increasingly common. Eflornithine is a safer and effective alternative for the West African disease, but it was withdrawn from manufacture in 1995. Political pressure persuaded the producer to restart production (Wickware, 2002). A new oral drug (so far only called DB 289) has entered clinical trials (Jannin & Cattand, 2004).

PREGNANCY-RELATED MEDICAL CARE

Complications of pregnancy and childbirth are the leading causes of death among women of reproductive age in most parts of the developing world. Each year, over half a million women die from pregnancy-related causes; 99 percent of them are in the developing world. A woman's lifetime risk of dying while pregnant ranges from one in 10,000 in some Scandinavian countries down to less than one in 20 in parts of Sub-Saharan Africa. The political will to do anything significant about this problem has been slow to develop (Hogberg, 2005). It was only 12 years ago that the UN finally considered it important enough to justify an international conference in Cairo (1994 International Conference on Population and Development, ICPD) (*United Nations International Conference on Population and Development*, n.d.). The result was an ambitious 20-year plan focusing on improving infant, child, and maternal mortality through improved reproductive health services.

There has been some progress, but the world's annual maternal mortality is still well over half a million women (Sheh et al., 1999). Reducing these numbers does not require exotic technology. Basic measures needed include access to trained midwives, drugs like magnesium sulphate for eclampsia, oxytocin for post-delivery bleeding, and communications to ask for assistance and transportation to an established emergency obstetric centre. The conference intended to fund one-third of the expenses from donors and the remainder from developing countries. Unfortunately, both sides have fallen below expectation so that no region in the developing world has met the goals of the ICPD program of action. The increasing AIDS epidemic has also diverted money away from specific child and maternal health projects.

Prior to the Cairo Conference in 1987, a partnership of donor governments, technical agencies, NGOs, and a range of women's health groups (the Inter-

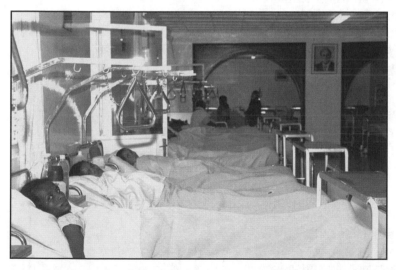

Figure 10.2: In 1959 two Australian obstetricians, Catherine and Reginald Hamlin, started working in Ethiopia. After years of effort they were able to open the Addis Ababa Fistula Hospital in 1974. A post-operative ward is shown in this photograph. Apart from helping thousands of socially ostracized women regain their health, the hospital also acts as a centre for research and training in the care of pregnancy-related complications, particularly the terrible complications of obstetric fistulas. (Photographer Pierre Virot; courtesy the WHO Mediacentre.)

Agency Group, IAG) launched the global initiative for safe motherhood at a meeting in Nairobi (*Safe Motherhood Inter-Agency Group*, n.d.). The Safe Motherhood Initiative promotes diverse interventions aimed at improving the health of women and their children. The group is also a vigorous advocate for governments and donor agencies to make safe motherhood a major priority in their development plans. The following elements are a central part of safe pregnancy-related care.

Antenatal Care

Routine antenatal visits were introduced in Britain during the 1930s with the hope that maternal mortality could be reduced by early identification of high-risk women. Subsequent research showed that many of the traditional elements of antenatal care (height and weight monitoring, blood pressure measurements) were surprisingly poor at predicting severe problems at time of delivery. The emphasis of antenatal care then shifted away from prediction and more toward improving maternal health, with obvious benefits to the mother but also for the survival and health of the subsequent children.

The paper by Villar et al. (2001) summarizes the current WHO recommendations for antenatal care. These include a minimum of four visits, with emphasis based on the mother's health such as screening for HIV/syphilis, monitoring of sugar, blood pressure, urine protein, iron and folic acid supplementation, and at least two doses of tetanus toxoid in areas where neonatal tetanus is common. In endemic malaria areas, it has been shown that intermittent preventive treatment (IPT), with at least two doses of an effective anti-malarial (sulphadoxine-pyrimethamine is commonly used), significantly reduces

maternal anemia, maternal mortality, and low birth weight (Van Eijk et al., 2004). In addition, mothers should be provided with treated bed nets to reduce their chances of contracting malaria. Clinic visits are also valuable opportunities for health workers to educate women about how to stay healthy during pregnancy and prepare them for the care of their baby.

Obstetric emergencies are often unpredictable and can only be managed by providing trained attendants backed up by referral emergency services. The shift in focus toward improved delivery care involves much higher investments in staff, training, and equipment compared to routine antenatal care. Figure 10.3 shows that coverage for delivery care in many developing countries lags 10–20 percent behind the provision of antenatal care. However, the situation has improved over the last decade (Figure 10.4).

Figure 10.3: Provision of delivery care and antenatal care in 138 countries

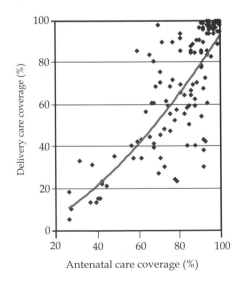

Source: UNICEF (n.d.-c)

Figure 10.4: Trends in provision of antenatal and delivery care in developing countries over the last decade

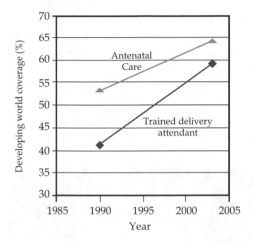

Source: UNICEF (n.d.-c)

Delivery Care

The single most important factor in reducing maternal mortality is the presence of a trained midwife (De Brouwere et al., 1998). Every labour and delivery should be supervised by a health worker with the skills needed to handle normal deliveries and the training to recognize when a woman has to be transferred. Clearly, this requires a regional centre with the capacity for Caesarean section and blood transfusion. A well-maintained ambulance, plus driver and communications, are also important to speed the process. In many parts of the developing world, delivery services are improving in the cities, but rural areas are still badly underserviced.

Post-delivery Care

The newborn baby should be dried, wrapped, and kept with the mother. Early baths are not necessary for the child. Early breast-feeding should be encouraged; colostrum should not be discarded. Hospital and clinic policies toward breast-feeding should be guided by the recommendations of the Baby-Friendly Initiative (UNICEF, n.d.-a). Minimum resuscitation equipment for a newborn should include clean umbilical cord care, tube and mask resuscitation (using air, not oxygen), and antibiotics for infants showing signs of sepsis.

Antenatal treatment and delivery care are not, of course, the end of pregnancy-related health care. A comprehensive maternal health service should also provide treatment for sexually transmitted diseases and a wide range of health education opportunities. This must all be backed up by a general societal approach that values women and understands the need to invest in maternal health.

It is particularly important that young mothers have access to family-planning services. Overall, roughly two-thirds of women in stable relationships use regular contraception throughout the developing world, but this ranges from 84 percent in East Asia to 23 percent in Sub-Saharan Africa. Women's ability to plan and space their children contributes greatly to their health and well-being. As the result of a number of factors (improved female education, improving child mortality rates, and the increasing availability of family-planning advice), fertility has fallen by one birth or more per lifetime in large parts of the developing world (Figure 10.5).

INTEGRATED MANAGEMENT OF CHILDHOOD ILLNESSES (IMCI)

In a perfect world, children everywhere should receive the same

Figure 10.5: Trends in contraception use and fertility in developing countries over the last decade

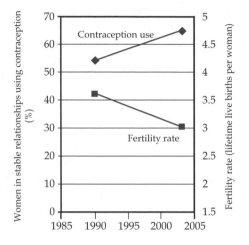

Source: UNICEF (n.d.-b)

level of comprehensive medical care. Unfortunately, budget restrictions in developing countries forced planners to concentrate on "packages" of cost-effective treatments. This was based on the observation that most of the major diseases have cheap and effective therapies that can be used in targeted eradication programs (Table 10.5). Following the adoption of selective primary health care in the 1980s, after the Alma Ata Declaration, the widespread implementation of vaccinations and immunizations certainly had a significant effect on child mortality. However, vertical programs with a narrow focus could never be a substitute for comprehensive pediatric care, but it was the best that could be achieved at the time (Oluwole et al., 1999).

UNICEF's enthusiasm for selective PHC led to their GOBI (Growth monitoring, Oral rehydration, Breast-feeding, and Immunization) child health initiative in the mid-1980s. With time, this basic

package was slowly expanded to include antibiotics for pneumonia and sepsis, specific drugs, insecticide-treated bed nets for malaria, plus vitamin A, iron, and food supplements for malnourished anemic children (Bryce et al., 2003). The more ambitious and comprehensive plan that grew out of this development was launched in the mid-1990s as the Integrated Management of Childhood Illnesses. This joint WHO/UNICEF initiative has been one of the most important new

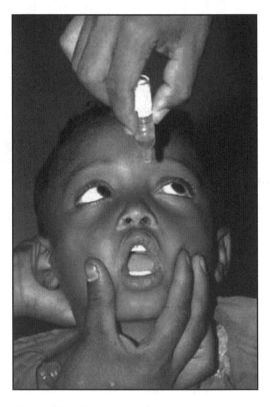

Figure 10.6: Young boy receiving oral polio immunization in a rural Ethiopian clinic. There were 350,000 cases of polio worldwide in 1988, the year that the WHO passed a resolution to eradicate polio. Over the last five years, there have been less than 2,000 cases a year. It is hoped that final eradication will occur within the next decade. (Photographer Pierre Virot; courtesy the WHO Mediacentre.)

Table 10.5: Cost and effectiveness of therapies used in targeted programs against the major infectious diseases of the developing world

Disease	Deaths in 2003	Treatment / Prevention Discovered	Management Program First Introduced	Cost of Treatment (US $)	Effectiveness (%)
Pneumonia	2.0 million children	1942: penicillin 1947: tetracycline 1952: erythromycin	Integrated Management of Childhood Illness (1995)	Five days of amoxicillin $0.27	90%
AIDS	3.0 million total (0.32 million children)	1980: latex condoms 1987: AZT 1992: HAART therapy	WHO Special Program on AIDS (1987)	Year's supply of condoms $14 WHO triple therapy $800–1,200/year	Condoms 99%
Diarrheal diseases	1.7 million children	1970s: Oral rehydration therapy	GOBI Strategy (1980s) (O for Oral rehydration)	Course of ORS crystals $0.33	90%
Tuberculosis	1.7 million total (0.25 million children)	1945: streptomycin 1952: isoniazid	Directly Observed Therapy Short Course (DOTS) (1980s)	Six-month TB course $20	95%
Malaria	1 million total (0.85 million children)	1942: DDT 1946: chloroquine 1951: pyrimethamine	WHO's first Malaria Eradication Program (1995)	WHO Artemesin combination therapy $2.40/course	95%
Measles	0.4 million children	1943: measles vaccine	Expanded Program on Immunization (EPI) (1970s)	Single-dose measles vaccine $0.26	98%

developments in the provision of health care to children in the developing world (El Arifeen et al., 2004).

Even the most inclusive treatment package is still only a superficial approach to medical problems that have their roots in poor living conditions, poverty, and lack of education. The IMCI recognizes this by also placing emphasis on education for parents and advocacy for improved standards of local health services. The introduction of oral rehydration therapy first put the health care worker in the position of educator since many affected children could be managed at home after suitable teaching. The IMCI process has taken this further by acknowledging that parents can play an important role in improving the health status of their children once they have access to accurate health counselling advice. Overall, there are three broad aspects to the IMCI strategy; specifics will vary from country to country:

- The IMCI clinical guidelines are principally tailored to the major diseases of young children (pneumonia, diarrheal diseases, measles, malaria, and malnutrition). Based on the initial assessment by the health care worker, a child is classified under three colour codes: pink (urgent referral after initial treatment), yellow (treatment in the clinic), green (treatment at home). The guidelines do not attempt to address the full range of childhood illnesses, but are pragmatically limited to the most common killers of small children. They do not describe management of trauma or other acute emergencies such as burns and poisonings.
- Emphasis is on health care workers counselling caretakers. Topics include home management of specific illnesses (how to take antibiotics or ORS), nutrition practices, fluids, and when to return to the clinic. If health care workers are given training to improve their communication and education skills, there are measurable improvements in parents' child care at home (Pelto et al., 2004). IMCI is planned with an understanding that the health system has a responsibility to help parents meet their child care responsibilities during periods of illness.

- The IMCI program also takes a broader approach to the improvement of local health care services. These vary in different countries, but they include the efficient supply of essential drugs, attention to referral services such as roads and ambulances, and provision of accessory health care workers who are needed to expand patient services. These range from organizing transport and arranging care for other children to home care visits and counselling. An excellent example of an ancillary service is the large Lady Health Worker Program, which reaches 30 million people in rural Pakistan (Douthwaite & Ward, 2005).

ACCESS TO ESSENTIAL DRUGS

I firmly believe that if the whole material medica could be sent to the bottom of the sea, it would be all the better for mankind and all the worse for the fishes.
—Oliver Wendell Holmes

The quote above is largely but not completely true. Of all the tens of thousands of prescription and non-prescription drugs listed in the pharmacies of developed countries, only a surprisingly small number are of any real value. When the World Health Organization first brought out its suggested essential drug list in 1977, it was possible to run a regional hospital with not much more than 100 drugs that included intravenous fluids and vaccines. Obviously, there is a need for a few new drugs—treatments for malaria, TB, HIV/

AIDS, and common bacterial and parasitic diseases are all good examples — but even the most recent list contains not many more than 300 drugs (World Health Organization, 2005a).

Easy access to effective drugs is an important part of health care in the developing world, but it has received attention only fairly recently (Department for International Development, 2004). There are two main problems affecting the supply of effective drugs: affordability and availability. Even a short course of cheap antibiotics can be prohibitively expensive for a poor rural family. This has always been a problem, but has been a particular issue over the last decade because of the cost of anti-retroviral therapy. The second problem is that research and development into effective developing world drugs is not likely to produce large profits for drug companies. The drug eflornithine was an effective, much less toxic alternative for the treatment of West African Trypanosomiasis, yet its only manufacturer stopped production. This decision was reversed in response to political pressure, but also because the drug proved to have a market as a hair remover (Wickware, 2002).

Drug Affordability

The World Health Organization and Médecins Sans Frontières (n.d.) have been leading advocates for access to affordable medicines. Since 1999, MSF has led a campaign to lower drug costs through increased use of generic alternatives, voluntary discounts by drug manufacturers, and local production in some countries. They also emphasize the need for increased research into "unprofitable" tropical diseases such as tuberculosis, malaria, sleeping sickness, and Leishmaniasis.

The subject came to a head in 2001 when South Africa decided to import generic anti-viral drugs for use in its fight against their HIV epidemic. At the time, triple therapy cost $10,000 per patient per year. An Indian generic company offered the same regime for $300 per person per year. South Africa intended to use the generic drugs only for its own patients, but 39 of the world's largest pharmaceutical companies took the South African government to court to stop the country from using cheap alternatives (Sidley, 2001). Basically, a trillion-dollar industry was suing a bunch of poor people with AIDS! There was widespread criticism of the drug companies' action, including a resolution from the European Union Parliament calling for them to drop their case. After it became obvious that they would have to publish their profits and justify their pricing, they abandoned the case.

Unfortunately, the subject becomes very complicated because patent restrictions on essential medicines are only one small part of ongoing debates surrounding world trade. Most developing countries signed on for a set of trade rules that included pharmaceutical patents in 1995. However, there is some flexibility in the Trade-Related Aspects of Intellectual Property Rights (TRIPS) agreements. The World Trade Organization's 2001 Doha Declaration specifically states that, "the TRIPS Agreement does not and should not prevent members from taking measures to protect public health." South Africa obviously argued that their overwhelming AIDS epidemic represented a very real public health need.

The problem is by no means solved. The Doha Declaration loophole applies to countries with domestic pharmaceutical manufacturing capacity. There is no general agreement on how developing countries, without their own manufacturing capacity, can obtain licences to import from manufacturing countries such as Brazil and India (Dionisio et al., 2006). Small countries lacking money and political influence are currently relying on first-generation anti-retrovirals. As time passes and resistance increases, the issue will be raised again as the price of newer drugs becomes an issue. It is not likely that the current drug patent laws will be scrapped so developing country governments, drug manufacturers, and various advocacy agencies, such as the Clinton Foundation, need to apply pressure to keep the price of essential drugs at a manageable level.

Drug Availability

Public health services in many developing countries are often in poor condition, particularly in rural areas. An overall lack of basic services and supplies can exacerbate local people's inability to receive adequate drug treatment for their illnesses. Numerous studies have shown that drugs in developing world markets are often repackaged expired drugs or, in some cases, have no pharmacological activity at all (Dondorp et al., 2004). In poorer districts where power is in short supply, drugs that require refrigeration (such as vaccines) may degrade rapidly in warm temperatures.

While local laws may stipulate that only hospital clinics and pharmacists can dispense medication, there is often little control over drug distribution. Informal dispensers usually lack sufficient knowledge about correct drug use and dosage; they may also be involved in straightforward deception in order to peddle worthless medications. Poor consumers, who cannot pay for a visit to a doctor or clinic, end up relying on anecdotal evidence supplied by dispensers; as a result, scarce money is spent on useless medicine. Due to the influx of Western pharmaceuticals and lack of government control, people are often able to purchase Western medicines without having to queue in crowded clinics. Instead, medications are bought and administered without a prescription, often on the advice of a shopkeeper or friend.

The cumulative effect of poor manufacturing standards, poor storage, repackaging of expired drugs, and straightforward counterfeiting is significant. The WHO estimates that counterfeit drugs alone make up 10 percent of worldwide supplies with much of the fake drugs ending in developing countries. The WHO held the first conference on the subject at Rome in 2006 (Zarocostas, 2006).

■ SUMMARY

One of the defining features of developing countries is that all measures of population health are significantly worse than those found in richer industrialized countries; infectious diseases are particularly overrepresented. Understandably, the first response of many is to try and deal with this problem using Western-style medical care. This was in fact the initial response of the developing aid industry in the years following World War II. Unfortunately, curative care on its own in the form of newly exported referral hospitals or top-down imposed eradications programs proved ineffective against the enormous reservoir of ill health. Through epidemiological research (and the hard lessons learned from practical experience), it is now clear that although medical therapy is an essential part of the control of disease, no sustainable progress is possible unless simultaneous efforts are also made to improve the living conditions of the target population. These initiatives must include improvements in water, sanitation, housing standards, and improved human rights.

Specific extra measures will be required for certain diseases. For example, drug treatment of HIV/AIDS must be supplemented with a concerted education campaign at a national level. Similarly, tuberculosis drug treatment must be augmented with contact tracing, testing of high-risk populations, and a similar emphasis upon disease education. Finally, malaria treatment must be accompanied by vector control through regular spraying and transmission interruption with treated bed nets. The only major disease for which social changes have little effect is maternal mortality. Pregnancy-related emergencies occur suddenly and unpredictably; the only way to improve maternal health statistics is to provide all pregnant women with easy access to good-quality obstetric care. Unfortunately, women's health has been given a shamefully low priority and it is only very recently that significant worldwide efforts have been made to improve pregnancy outcome for women in developing countries.

Finally, medical treatment requires effective medications and this brings two new problems. Firstly, modern drugs are often prohibitively expensive for poor populations, particularly the newer anti-retro viral medications. Once again, the rich drug manufacturing countries have been very slow to ensure that developing world populations have access to affordable drugs, although the situation is improving. Secondly, those drugs must be of high quality. Dispensed medications may be substandard for many reasons, including decomposition during storage, repackaging of time-expired drugs, adulteration with inactive or even toxic substances, and criminal drug counterfeiting. Sophisticated drug counterfeiting is likely to become a growing problem over the next few years, particularly where expensive drugs are concerned.

RESOURCES

References

Ashley, E., & White, N. (2005). "Artemesin-based combinations." *Current Opinion in Infectious Diseases, 18,* 531–536.

Bellamy, G., et al. (2001). *Jim Grant: UNICEF visionary.* Florence: UNICEF Innocenti Research Centre.

Berkman, A., et al. (2005). "A critical analysis of the Brazilian response to HIV/AIDS: Lessons learned for controlling and initiating the epidemic in developing countries." *American Journal of Public Health, 95,* 1162–1172.

Blumberg, H., et al. (2005). "Update on the treatment of tuberculosis and latent tuberculosis infection." *Journal of the American Medical Association, 293,* 2776–2784.

Bryce, J., et al. (2003). "Reducing child mortality: Can public health deliver?" *Lancet, 362,* 159–164.

Bunnell, R., et al. (2006). "Changes in sexual behaviour and risk of HIV transmission after antiretroviral therapy and prevention interventions in rural Uganda." *AIDS, 20,* 85–92.

Centers for Disease Control and Prevention. (2004). *The history of malaria, an ancient disease.* Retrieved from www.cdc.gov/malaria/history/index.htm.

Curtis, C., & Lines, J. (2000). "Should DDT be banned by international treaty?" *Parasitology Today, 16,* 119–121.

Curtis, C., & Minzava, A. (2000). "Comparison of house spraying and insecticide treated nets for malaria control." *Bulletin of the World Health Organization, 78,* 1389–1400.

Dadhich, J. (2005). "Exclusive breastfeeding and postnatal transmission of HIV." *Bulletin of the World Health Organization, 83,* 418–426.

De Brouwere, V., et al. (1998). "Strategies for reducing maternal mortality in developing countries: What can we learn from the history of the industrialized West?" *Tropical Medicine and International Health, 3,* 771–782.

De Cock, K., et al. (2000). "Prevention of mother-to-child HIV transmission in resource-poor countries: Translating research into policy and practice." *Journal of the American Medical Association, 283,* 1175–1182.

Department for International Development. (2004). *Access to medicines in under-served markets.* Retrieved from www.dfid.gov.uk/pubs/files/dfidsynthesispaper.pdf.

Diaz, S., et al. (2005). "Preventing HIV transmission in adolescents: An analysis of the Portuguese data from the health behaviour of school-aged children study and focus groups." *European Journal of Public Health, 15,* 300–304.

Dionisio, D., et al. (2006). "Affordable antiretroviral drugs for the under-served markets: How to expand equitable access against the backdrop of challenging scenarios?" *Current HIV Research, 4,* 30–20.

Doherty, T., & Rook, G. (2006). "Progress and hindrances in tuberculosis vaccine development." *Lancet, 367,* 947–949.

Dondorp, A., et al. (2004). "Fake antimalarials in Southeast Asia are a major impediment to malaria control: Multinational cross-sectional survey on the prevalence of fake antimalarials." *Tropical Medicine and International Health, 9,* 1241–1246.

Dorling, D., et al. (2006). "Global inequality of life expectancy due to AIDS." *British Medical Journal, 332,* 662–664.

Dormandy, T. (2001). *The white death: A history of tuberculosis.* London: Hambledon.

Douthwaite, M., & Ward, P. (2005). "Increasing contraceptive use in rural Pakistan: An evaluation of the Lady Health Worker Program." *Health Policy and Planning, 2,* 20–25.

El Arifeen, et al. (2004). "Integrated Management of Childhood Illness (IMCI) in Bangladesh: Early findings from a cluster-randomized study." *Lancet, 364,* 1595–1602.

Enarson, D., et al. (2000). *Management of tuberculosis: A guide for low-income countries.* Retrieved from www.iuatld.org/pdf/en/guides_publications/management_of_tb.pdf.

Figueroa-Munoz, J., et al. (2006). *The stop TB strategy: Building on and enhancing DOTS to meet the TB-related MDGs.* Geneva: World Health Organization. Retrieved from www.stoptb.org.

Gallo, R., & Montagnier, L. (2003). "The discovery of HIV as the cause of AIDS." *New England Journal of Medicine, 349,* 2287–2285.

Global Drug Facility. (n.d.). Retrieved from www.stoptb.org/gdf.

Gottlieb, M., et al. (1981). "Pneumocystic carinii pneumonia and mucosal candidiasis in previously healthy homosexual men: Evidence of a new acquired cellular immunodeficiency." *New England Journal of Medicine, 305,* 1425–1431.

Grant, A., & De Cock, K. (2001). "ABC of AIDS: HIV infection and AIDS in the developing world." *British Medical Journal, 322,* 1475–1478.

Hansen, H., & Grace, N. (2003). "Human immunodeficiency virus and quarantine in Cuba." *Journal of the American Medical Association, 290,* 2875–2878.

Hearst, N., & Chen, S. (2004). "Condom promotion for AIDS prevention in the developing world: Is it working?" *Studies in Family Planning, 35,* 39–44.

Herwaldt, B. (1999). "Leishmaniasis." *Lancet, 354,* 1191–1199.

"HIV and AIDS: United States 1981–2000." (2000). *Morbidity and Mortality Weekly Review, 50,* 430–434.

Hogberg, U. (2005). "The World Health Report 2005: 'Make every mother and child count' — including Africans." *Scandinavian Journal of Public Health, 33,* 409–411.

International AIDS Vaccine Initiative. (n.d.). Retrieved from www.iavi.org.

Jackson, J., et al. (2003). "Intrapartum and neonatal single dose nevirapine compared with zidorudine for prevention of mother to child transmission of HIV-1 in Kampala, Uganda: 18 month follow-up of the HIVNET 012 randomized trial." *Lancet, 362,* 859–868.

Jannin, J., & Cattand, P. (2004). "Treatment and control of human African trypanosomiasis." *Current Opinion in Infectious Diseases, 17,* 565–571.

"Malaria intermittent preventive treatment in infants, chemoprophylaxis, and childhood vaccinations." (2004). *Lancet, 363,* 2000–2001.

Marchal, B., et al. (2005). "Viewpoint: HIV/AIDS and the health work force crisis: What are the next steps?" *Tropical Medicine and International Health, 10,* 300–304.

Médecins Sans Frontières. (n.d.). *Campaign for access to essential medicines.* Retrieved from www.accessmed-msf.org.

Olliaro, P., et al. (2005). "Treatment options for visceral Leishmaniasis: A systematic review of clinical studies done in India, 1980–2004." *Lancet Infectious Diseases, 5,* 763–774.

Oluwole, D., et al. (1999). "Management of childhood illness in Africa." *British Medical Journal, 320,* 594–595.

Ostrow, D., et al. (2002). "Attitudes towards highly active anti-retroviral therapy are associated with sexual risk taking among HIV-infected and uninfected homosexual men." *AIDS, 16,* 775–780.

Peeters, M., & Sharp, P. (2000). "Genetic diversity of HIV-1: The moving target." *AIDS, 14,* 5139–5140.

Pelto, G., et al. (2004). "Nutrition counseling training changes physician behaviour and improves caregiver knowledge acquisition." *Journal of Nutrition, 134,* 357–362.

Reynolds, S, et al. (2003). "Antiretroviral therapy where resources are limited." *New England Journal of Medicine, 348,* 1806–1809.

Roll back malaria. (n.d.). Retrieved from www.rollbackmalaria.org.

"Roll back malaria: A failing global health campaign." (2004). *British Medical Journal, 328,* 1086–1087.

Roll Back Malaria Partnership. (2005). *World malaria report.* Geneva: UNICEF/WHO. Retrieved from www.rbm.who.int/wmr2005.

Safe Motherhood Inter-Agency Group. (n.d.). Retrieved from www.safemotherhood.org.

Sheh, D., et al. (1999). "Reproductive and sexual health and safe motherhood in the developing world." *European Journal of Contraceptive and Reproductive Health Care, 4,* 217–228.

Shulman, C., & Dorman, E. (2003). "Importance and prevention of malaria in pregnancy." *Transactions of the Royal Society of Tropical Medicine and Hygiene, 97,* 30–35.

Sidley, P. (2001). "Drug companies sue South African government over genesis." *British Medical Journal, 322,* 447–450.

Stop Tuberculosis Partnership. (n.d.). Retrieved from www.stoptb.org.

Taha, T., et al. (2003). "Short post-exposure prophylaxis in newborn babies to reduce mother-to-child transmission of HIV-1: NVAZ randomized clinical trial." *Lancet, 362,* 1171–1177.

Targett, G. (2005). "Malaria vaccines 1985–2005: A full circle?" *Trends in Parasitology, 21,* 499–503.

UNAIDS. (2004). *Report on the global AIDS epidemic.* Retrieved from www.unaids.org/bangkok2004/report.html.

UNICEF. (n.d.-a). *Baby-friendly hospital initiative.* Retrieved from www.unicef.org/programme/breastfeeding/baby.htm.

UNICEF. (n.d.-b). *Fertility and contraceptive use.* Retrieved from www.childinfo.org/eddb/fertility/index.htm.

UNICEF. (n.d.-c). *Maternal health.* Retrieved from www.childinfo.org/eddb/maternal.htm.

United Nations International Conference on Population and Development. (n.d.). Retrieved from www.iisd.ca/cairo.html.

Van Eijk, A., et al. (2004). "Effectiveness of intermittent preventive treatment with sulphadoxine-pyrimethamine for control of malaria in pregnancy in western Kenya: A hospital-based study." *Tropical Medicine and International Health, 9,* 351–360.

Villar, J., et al. (2001). "WHO antenatal care randomized trial for the evaluation of a new model of routine antenatal care." *Lancet, 357,* 1551–1564.

Wickware, P. (2002). "Resurrecting the resurrection drug." *Nature Medicine, 8,* 908–909.

Working group on DOTS-Plus for multiply resistant TB. (n.d.). Retrieved from www.stoptb.org/wg/dots_plus.

World Bank. (2005). *Rolling back malaria: The World Bank global strategy and booster program.* Retrieved from www.rollbackmalaria.org.

World Health Organization. (2000). *Management of severe malaria: A practical handbook.* Retrieved from www.who.int/malaria/docs/hbsm_toc.htm.

World Health Organization. (2004). *Treatment of tuberculosis: Guidelines for national programs.* Retrieved from www.who.int/tb.

World Health Organization. (2005a). *Essential medicines* (14th ed.). Retrieved from www.who.int/medicines/publications/essentialmedicines.

World Health Organization. (2005b). *World health report 2005: Statistical annex.* Retrieved from www.who.int/whr/2005/annex/en/index.html.

World Health Organization. (2006a). *Facts on ACTS: Artemesin-based combination therapies.* Retrieved from www.who.int/malaria/diagnosisandtreatment.html.

World Health Organization. (2006b). *Global tuberculosis control: Surveillance, planning, financing.* Retrieved from www.who.int/tb/publications/2006.

World Health Organization. (2006c). *Guidelines for the treatment of malaria.* Retrieved from www.who.int/malaria/docs/TreatmentGuidelines2006.pdf.

World Health Organization. (n.d.-a). *The 3 by 5 initiative.* Retrieved from www.who.int/3by5.

World Health Organization. (n.d.-b). *Global DOTS expansion plan.* Retrieved from www.who.int/tb/dots/expansion.

World Health Organization–Tropical Disease Research. (2004). *Life cycle of plasmodium.* Retrieved from www.who.int/tdr/diseases/malaria/lifecycle.htm.

Zapar, M., & Moran, K. (2005). "Infectious diseases during war time." *Current Opinion in Infectious Diseases, 18,* 395–399.

Zarocostas, J. (2006). "WHO to set up international task force on counterfeit drugs." *British Medical Journal, 332,* 444–447.

Recommended Reading

Gandy, M., & Zumla, A. (Eds). (2003). *The return of the white plague: Global poverty and the new tuberculosis.* London: Verso.

Ghosh, J., et al. (Eds.). (2003). *HIV and AIDS in Africa: Beyond epidemiology.* Malden: Blackwell Publications.

Leach, B., Palluzi, J., & Munderi, P. (2005). *Prescription for healthy development: Increasing access to medicines.* London: Earthscan Publications.

Seear, M. (2000). *Manual of tropical pediatrics.* Cambridge: Cambridge University Press.

Teklehaumanot, A., et al. (2005). "Coming to grips with malaria in the new millennium." London: Earthscan.

Chapter 11

Poverty Alleviation and Debt Relief

Money is like muck, not good
unless it be spread about.
— Sir Francis Bacon,
Essays, 1625

OBJECTIVES

After completing this chapter, you should be able to

- understand the benefits resulting from successful poverty alleviation and debt-relief initiatives
- understand the major methods used to combat poverty
- understand the history of debt relief initiatives over the last 25 years, up to the Gleneagles meeting in 2005

In Chapter 4, we looked at the origins, magnitude, and adverse health effects of general poverty and also the development of the vast debt accumulated by many developing countries. In this current chapter, we'll examine the practical side of these issues. What can be done to help? Poverty alleviation and, to a lesser extent, debt relief have attracted decades of research, analysis, and commentary, but it is only surprisingly recently that significant and measurable progress has been made with either. Making significant gains against endemic poverty is a slow process and, like any economic topic, there is no shortage of arguments about the best method to use. However, a few things are certain — poverty relief must be based on clear plans sustained over many years and should be combined, when possible, with improvements in human rights. Significant attempts to reduce the developing world's debt have been painfully slow to develop and have been influenced more by ideology than serious outcome analysis. The extraordinary level of worldwide popular support for the topic of debt relief helped to influence rich G8 countries to make significant debt concessions at the 2005 Gleneagles G8 meeting, but there is still a long way to go!

■ POVERTY ALLEVIATION

> To give aid to every poor man is far beyond the reach and power of every man. Care of the poor is incumbent on society as a whole.
>
> —Spinoza, 1677

Although poverty is an inevitable common denominator contributing to the ill health of developing world populations, this is not by any means the full story. As mentioned before, the origins of that poverty usually lie within some form of social injustice. The causes vary depending on the country, but whenever there is widespread poverty, there is usually obvious oppression or discrimination just below the surface (Feachem, 2000). Clearly, long-term sustainable solutions are very difficult unless there are accompanying improvements in any underlying social inequity.

Unfortunately, large-scale shifts in society occur slowly. However, while the social wheels are turning, there are approaches that can be used to make the burden of poverty more bearable. This section will examine some of the major means of reducing poverty. Whatever initiative is used, planners must always remember that benefits are measured in years; quick fixes do not exist. Effective programs must be based on careful research relevant to the specific country and backed by long-term commitments of money and skilled assistance (Sachs, 2005).

The first three graphs show some of the health and educational benefits that slowly accumulate after prolonged and consistent pro-poor economic growth—in this case, measured in the Chinese population. It is important to note that the timeline is measured in decades. After implementing sustainable projects aimed at access to health and education for the poor, plus an emphasis on economic growth, it later becomes difficult to tell which developments are "cause" and which are "effect." Better-educated and healthier parents have better-educated and healthier children. The process grinds on,

Figure 11.2: Infant mortality rate in China over the last 50 years

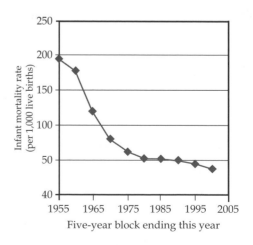

Source: United Nations Statistics Division (n.d.)

Figure 11.1: Literacy rates in China over the last 25 years

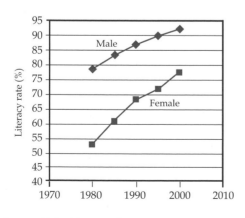

Source: United Nations Statistics Division (n.d.)

Figure 11.3: Life expectancy in China over the last 50 years

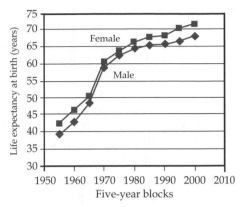

Source: United Nations Statistics Division (n.d.)

slowly gathering speed until, many years later, a generation of healthy children is reached that can barely believe the deprivations that their grandparents and great-grandparents suffered through. The results of development work take a long time to bear fruit—one of many reasons why short-term projects are of value only to the participants.

It should always be remembered that all the current wealthy countries have been through a period when their standards of health and living conditions were no different from those of any of today's developing countries. That is all the more reason why they should be keen to help poor countries climb out of poverty—not through the obligation of charity, but out of a sense of shared human experience. The following initiatives all include increased prosperity as a major end point:

Pro-poor economic development

In a state that is desirous of being saved from the greatest of all plague, there should exist among the citizens neither extreme poverty nor again excessive wealth.

—Plato, Laws, 5th century BC

Buckle up before driving through this topic; the literature is extensive, technical, and very contentious (Eastwood & Lipton, 2000). This section addresses the simple question, "Is economic growth automatically good for the poorest section of that country's society or does increased prosperity simply increase inequality, i.e., the rich get richer and the poor stay the same?" (Fuentes, 2005). This debate is a common one, particularly among those who study the broader effects of global markets. Remember that this is not the same as the question addressed in Chapter 9, which was, "Does financial aid produce measurable benefits for the poor?" That is a different problem altogether and, if possible, is even more contentious.

It is generally accepted that all developing countries that have achieved sustained economic growth over the last two or three decades have also reduced their absolute poverty levels (Pro-Poor Growth Research Program, 2005). Measures of economic disparity within a country, such as the Gini index, remain relatively stable over long periods, showing that economic growth is distributed throughout all segments of a population—not always equally, but at least some of that prosperity eventually trickles down to the poorest (Dollar & Kraay, 2002).

The arguments begin once the types of economic growth are analyzed. For many years, the emphasis of the major international financial institutes was upon pure economic growth—often at the expense of the poor. The topic of Structural Adjustment Policies will be covered fully later in this chapter, but briefly, starting around 1980, the increasing failure of poor countries to meet their international debt repayments gave the IMF and World Bank an unusual degree of influence over the internal economic policies of many developing countries. Both institutions increasingly tied their loans to a range of interventions that came to be called structural adjustment policies (SAPs) (Ismi, 2004).

Unfortunately, SAPs often included belt-tightening policies such as reduced food subsidies and cuts in education and health budgets. The poor, of course, bore the brunt of these economic interventions. The biggest criticism of the "adjustment" years is that there is little or no evidence to suggest that these interventions were beneficial and plenty to suggest they were measurably harmful (Easterly, 2001). Criticism of the process slowly grew; some of the most vocal critics were staff of the World Bank. The book by William Easterly (2002), senior World Bank economist, is a good example. The prefaces to different editions of his book give some idea of the results!

> My employer ... the World Bank, encourages gadflies like me to exercise intellectual freedom. (Easterly, 2001, World Bank economist), preface to his book, critical of World Bank development policies)

> My employer ... the World Bank, encourages gadflies like me to find another job. (Easterly, 2002, ex-World Bank economist, preface to the paperback edition one year later)

Even the chief economist of the World Bank, Joseph Stiglitz (2002), criticized the policy of imposed economic restructuring and said that the policy had failed.

The increasingly broad view of poverty that developed principally from the work of Sen and others gradually helped to soften these harsh growth policies. Economic growth moves a country's bell-shaped economic distribution curve to the right, but there are still a percentage of people who fall below a minimum measure of acceptable life. It seems logical and reasonable to redirect some of that country's increased wealth toward the poorest segment in an active as well as a passive attack upon poverty (Bourguignon, 2003).

The topic of inequality has now recently entered the debate (Beck et al., 2004). Directly targeting the poor involves redistributing wealth. This concept has proved rather too socialist for some tastes. The subject was certainly not openly discussed during the years of the Cold War; perhaps that is why the euphemism "pro-poor growth" is applied to the concept rather than economic redistribution (Pro-Poor Growth Research Program, 2005).

In response to internal and external criticisms of its policies (SAP Review International Network, 2004), the World Bank is slowly changing. Under the Enhanced Heavily Indebted Poor Countries initiative (EHIPC; see later in the chapter), the adjustment policies have been replaced by poverty-reduction strategy papers (PRSPs). Using this fairly new approach, the poor are actually included in a country's long-term economic restructuring plan. Is the World Bank turning into a soft and cuddly organization staffed by aging hippies? Perhaps not, but the current chief economist, François Bourguignon (Bourguignon, 2003), has published extensively on the need for reduction of inequality through redistribution of profits (Bourguignon, 2003).

It is important to remember that the health effects of economic policy changes are enormously complex and, of course, adverse effects will inevitably fall upon the poorest of that country's poor. Relationships between trade legalization, tax reform, privatization of public utilities, cost-recovery strategies, and their ultimate effects upon poverty are endlessly and infinitely complex. We do not know how to stop our own developed countries from swinging in and out of recession so our attempts to meddle with other countries should be tempered by some degree of humility and care. An investigation by an independent organization (Overseas Development Institute) has been cautiously optimistic about the process of poverty restructuring strategies in developing countries (Booth & Lucas, 2002). A series of extensive reviews of the PRSP process is also available at the World Bank Web site.

Microfinancing (Armendariz de Aghion & Morduch, 2005)

When it comes to financial services such as access to credit, savings accounts, money transfers, and insurance, the needs of the poor are no different to those of the rich — they just have less money to place into these services. Without these facilities, small savings have to be converted into livestock or jewellery. Houses and possessions cannot be insured and remittances from overseas are reduced by high service charges. In the absence of credit facilities, the poor can obtain money only through moneylenders, who usually charge high rates or from pawnshops. In fact, the oldest financial institution in

North or South America is a pawnshop on Mexico City Central Square, established in 1775 by the Spanish Crown ("The hidden wealth of the poor," 2005, November 3).

After small starts in the early 1970s, so-called microfinance or microcredit schemes have gained in popularity to the point that they are now considered a major means of helping the poorest to escape their poverty. The first on the scene was probably Opportunity International, a non-profit NGO that began lending small amounts in 1971 to the poor of Colombia. ACCION International made its first loans in Brazil, followed by the Grameen Bank in 1976 in Bangladesh. The Grameen is the best known of these early organizations, probably because of its emphasis on lending money to groups of women. Yunus's 2003 book about the founding of the Grameen, *Banker to the Poor*, is essential reading. The early model was often based on forming the lenders into groups, which had to meet at regular intervals. Hard collateral was replaced by the social pressures from within a group. Clearly, this was not a flexible model for individuals. As time passed, services such as savings, financial transfers, and insurance have grown. Banking services more recently resemble a conventional commercial bank except that they exist for the poor. Banco Sol in Bolivia is one example in Latin America.

Using small loans, families can begin projects like drying fish or selling kerosene. Large loans up to $200 can be used to start a small store, buy fertilizers and seed, or a bull for breeding. Once a small lender establishes a loan repayment history, then larger loans become available.

Types of lending institutions are so broad that there are no accurate statistics for their numbers. They are certainly

Table 11.1: A moment of Zen

	Country	Overseas Aid 2003 (US $Billion)
	Australia	1.219
	Austria	0.505
	Belgium	1.853
	Denmark	1.748
	Finland	0.558
US dog food sales 2003: $8.3 billion	Greece	0.362
	Italy	2.433
	Luxembourg	0.194
	New Zealand	0.165
US cat food sales 2003: $4.25 billion	Portugal	0.320
	Spain	1.961
	Switzerland	1.299
Total US dog and cat food sales in 2003: **US $12.6 billion**	Total aid from 12 developed countries in 2003: **US $12.6 billion**	
Source: Pet Food Institute (n.d.)	Source: Organisation for Economic Co-operation and Development (n.d.)	

measured in the tens of thousands; obviously some are good and, equally, some bad. One sign of the increasing importance of banking to the poor is the emergence of rating agencies that provide relatively objective measures of different banks. Microfinancing is now profitable enough that it has even attracted large commercial banks over the last few years (United States Agency for International Development, 2005).

Education for All

Lack of education is not the only factor that keeps poor people poor and unhealthy, but it is certainly a major contributor. From numerous perspectives, educating children (and removing gender disparity in education) has endless measurable advantages. Education raises economic productivity, lowers infant mortality, improves nutritional status and health of adults and children, reduces poverty, and helps control the spread of HIV/AIDS and other diseases. Lack of education is particularly harmful for girls. Along with immunization, education initiatives produce the best "bang" for a development "buck."

Not surprisingly, the Millennium Development Goals include two separate

Figure 11.4: Young girls going to school in post-Taliban Afghanistan. Shortage of space has forced the community to use a disused theatre in Kabul. (Copyright Lana Slezic; Global Aware Photo Library.)

educational targets within their eight development goals:

- *Target two:* Universal primary education for all by 2015.
- *Target three:* Reduce gender disparity in primary and secondary education by 2005 and reduce gender disparity in tertiary education by 2015.

Unfortunately, the first part of target three is already behind schedule (UNICEF, 2005). On the positive side, the number of children missing from school is below 100 million for the first time since records were kept. In 81 developing countries, participation in education will rise to 86 percent during 2005 as opposed to 82 percent in 2001. There are numerous explanations for this slow progress, but they should not disguise the fact that well-intentioned countries can make huge improvements in the face of very difficult circumstances. Uganda and Afghanistan have both greatly increased their enrolment and reduced gender disparity despite considerable obstacles.

Good-quality education is expensive and the benefits take years to appear, but it is worth the wait. India's first Nobel laureate, Rabindranath Tagore, came from a rich family, but was an enlightened man. He wrote extensively on the subjects of poverty and education. In 1901, he established a school (Santiniketan). Many years later, a young child called Amartya Sen received his first basic schooling there. He went on to make significant contributions to the field of poverty research for which he was also awarded a Nobel Prize.

The problems of providing education to poor people are identical to those found in providing adequate health care. The only approach that appears to work is to decentralize education and place management, administration, and at least a bulk of the funding in the hands of local people. Several models exist around the world. In Bangladesh, the Bangladesh Rural Advancement Committee (BRAC) runs a non-formal primary education program that has now grown to several thousand centres serving the children of poor rural families (*Bangladesh Rural Advancement Committee,* n.d.). Administration is provided by village management committees and parent-teachers' associations. Most teachers are women and at least half of the people are girls. Accommodation is usually modest with earth floors and basic teaching materials.

In the Philippines, a mobile teaching program for poor families in the remote northern areas is designed to address the same problems. In Brazil, voucher systems have been introduced aimed at allowing poor children to attend schools that have extra capacity (Denes, 2003). In some areas, this has been part of a larger scheme to reduce the number of children who have to work to support their families (called Bolsa Escola). The family is paid as long as the child stays in school. Although there are many ways to expose poor children to education, they all share a basic understanding—equitable education is the fundamental foundation upon which all other poverty-alleviation programs must be based.

Agricultural Improvement

During the 1960s and 1970s, the introduction of high-yield seeds pioneered by Dr. Norman Borlaug, combined with modern farming methods, produced a revolution in food production throughout India and Southern Asia—now widely called "the green revolution." Since that time, annual food production has continued to outpace population growth even though the total area under cultivation has declined (Davies, 2003) (Figure 11.5). For many reasons, particularly the shortage of irrigation, these advances could not be adopted in Sub-Saharan Africa. Advances in agricultural techniques, particularly in dry land farming and the development of new seeds, now means that those advances can be applied to areas of the world with less reliable water supplies such as Sub-Saharan Africa and Central Asia (Djurfeldt et al., 2005).

Figure 11.5: World coarse-grain production and area harvested over the last 45 years

Source: Food and Agriculture Organization (n.d.)

Until recently, agricultural improvement has received less emphasis than it deserves. In Africa, agriculture provides employment for 60–70 percent of the population. It produces half of the exports and an equally significant proportion of the gross national income. Clearly, any improvement in agricultural output will benefit the poor, both rural and urban. It has been shown that a 1 percent increase in agricultural yield can reduce severe poverty by between 0.6 and 1.2 percent (Irz et al., 2001).

Although the Millennium Development Goals do include a target of reducing by half the numbers suffering from hunger, there is still no direct mention of the agricultural improvement needed to feed those people. This is not to say that agricultural improvement is a panacea. The history of such projects is spotty. For every success (Kenyan farmers are now among the world leaders in cut-flower production), there are many other examples of projects that ended with abandoned irrigation machinery and rusting tractors.

Box 11.1: History notes

Norman Borlaug (1914–)

Although Borlaug was one of the major scientists of the 20th century, his name is not well known. He was awarded the Nobel Peace Prize in 1970 for his central role in the agricultural advances that, collectively, are called the Green Revolution.
After training as a plant pathologist and geneticist, he helped establish a wheat research program in Mexico with Rockefeller Foundation support. The improved yields and resistance of crops developed in the centre (mainly wheat, maize, and rice) have spread better nutrition and prosperity across large parts of the developing world, particularly India and other Asian countries. Due to these advances, from 1950 onwards, Malthaus was proved wrong—annual increase in food production exceeded population growth without increasing the area planted. Follow the reference (*Norman Borlaug Heritage Foundation*, n.d.) for more information, including recent criticism of the Green Revolution.

Repeating the Green Revolution in Africa and Central Asia is a complex and difficult task. Some of the many obstacles include access for the poor to land and water, investment for rural road upgrades, storage and distribution facilities, plus irrigation and farm machinery. The problems are further complicated by adverse national agricultural policies, international trade barriers, and low commodity prices. Taken together, agricultural improvement can hardly be viewed as an instant solution. However, it is a vital step and these problems are individually manageable. International aid agencies such as the British Department of International Development are already showing a renewed interest in investment in agriculture (Department for International Development, 2003). There is also a growing international emphasis on the need to liberalize agricultural trade, particularly in the European Union and North America. None of these tasks is easy, but if sustained investment can be assured, then it is possible that the Green Revolution, with all of its extended benefits, could be reproduced in some of the poorest parts of the world.

Trade Liberalization

The problem (with aggressive trade liberalization) is that the human development potential inherent in trade is diminished by a combination of unfair rules and structural inequalities within and between countries. (UNDP, Human Development Report, 2005)

As many as 90 percent of the world's poor obtain their small income from agriculture. The bulk of the remainder work in labour-intensive sweatshops in one form or another. Output from these industries must confront an indescribably complex set of national and international tariffs and trade barriers that affect every single exported item (World Bank, 2002).

A much-quoted example is the effect of enforced trade liberalization upon rice farmers. During the structural adjustment policy era, the IMF and World Bank often attached conditions to developing countries asking for loans. In 1995, for example, the IMF forced Haiti to cut its import rice tariff from 35 percent to 3 percent with the result that rice imports increased greatly over the next decade. Although urban Haitian consumers obtained a small benefit from the drop in imported rice cost, the indigenous Haitian rice growers suffered greatly through loss of a market. The only winners were the major rice exporters in the United States (Oxfam, 2005).

Although the worst examples of unfair trade have improved over the last few years, the international trade playing field can hardly be described as level. For example, the Common Agricultural Policy (CAP) is a system of subsidies for Europe's farmers. Agricultural subsidies currently run at about $350 billion per year in Europe alone. The result is an artificial reduction in the true cost of producing foods such as sugar, milk, soya beans, maize, poultry, and cattle. Unrealistically cheap surpluses can then be dumped on any country that does not have tariff restrictions to protect its own farmers.

Unfortunately, obtaining concensus only gets steadily more complex (Aisbett, 2005). Trying to obtain an agreement that covers all the trade barriers on all the imported and exported goods in all of the countries of the world seems a rather optimistic task. On the one hand, a group led by the United States, European Union, and Japan argues strongly that a reduction in world trade barriers would accelerate growth and ultimately lead to poverty reduction around the world (the so-called "Trade not Aid" school of thought). In the other corner are those who equate trade liberalization with the poorly defined term "globalization." Their response is that simple monetary improvement is not the main end point. When the full effects of globalization are calculated for all aspects of the lives of the poor, then they are ultimately losers.

Large-scale mathematical models by a variety of economic sources tend to show that trade liberalization over the last years has reached such a point that the overall result of completely free world trade would be relatively modest. These cumulative advances in trade have made the argument much less relevant than it might have been 10 years ago (Weisbrot & Baker, 2002). As with any economic debate, opinions differ.

Another problem with the debate on trade liberalization is that it undoubtedly will produce losers as well as winners. Some poor countries are already offered a range of trade quotas that allow them to sell a fixed amount of export merchandise at a price above the market rate. Removal of these quotas would not necessarily be an advantage to them. Some poor countries with less reliance on agriculture also benefit from access to cheap subsidized agricultural exports from richer countries. Again, removal of subsidies would not necessarily be an advantage (Weisbrot & Baker, 2002).

In 2001, the World Trade Organization weighed into this mess with the optimistic hope of sorting out everything, including subsidies on agriculture; Non-Agricultural

Market Access (NAMA includes everything from gem production up to industrial goods); access to services like electric power, health care, education; and Trade-Related Intellectual Poverty Rights (TRIPS).

The first round of talks was held in Doha Qatar in 2001. The subsequent negotiations are called the Doha Development Agenda (DDA). The first talks in Doha, unfortunately, reached no agreement and produced considerable friction. After two years, another attempt was made with a meeting in Cancun. The outcome in Cancun was even worse—talks collapsed after a few days. Europe (particularly led by France), Japan, and the United States pressed for trade liberalization while increasingly influential developing countries insisted upon protection for their young industries.

The WTO looked for a while as if it would collapse into smaller interest groups such as the so-called G20 (large developing countries led by China, India, Brazil, and South Africa), the G90 (a group of the least developed countries), the Africa-Caribbean and Pacific Group (ACP), and the African group. Up to this point, almost nothing had been achieved except for one small agreement under the TRIPS heading that allowed developing countries to import cheap generic versions of anti-HIV drugs.

After smaller preparatory meetings in Geneva and Paris, the most recent ministers' meeting was held in Hong Kong in December 2005. To the surprise of many, some important deadlines were agreed upon, particularly concerning reduction of agricultural subsidies and increased market access for developing countries. Future developments will be very interesting to follow (Hufbauer & Schott, 2006).

Human Rights Legislation

Where, after all, do universal human rights begin? In small places close to home. Such as the places where every man, woman and child seeks equal justice, equal opportunity, equal dignity, without discrimination.

— Eleanor Roosevelt

Over the last two decades, research has increasingly shown that poor people are not just short of money, they are short of everything that even remotely resembles the basic needs for a restful life. Quite apart from hunger and ill health, poverty carries with it feelings of helplessness and constant fear. At first glance, human rights legislation might not seem to be closely related to poverty alleviation, but it is, in fact, an absolutely necessary foundation. No agricultural interventions are possible until the poor have guaranteed access to land and water rights. Similarly, fair employment initiatives require protective labour laws. A community cannot take full part in any large-scale initiative until

everyone feels free in terms of religious observance and has access to fair legal process, effective property laws, and protection from corrupt state officials. Women and children are particularly at risk of abuse and require specific human rights legislation tailored to their unique needs (Donnelly, 2002).

This is an area where legislation acts as a catalyst speeding up changes and improves the general sense of safety that the poor experience. Numerous historical examples exist demonstrating the value of human rights legislation in the gradual improvement in health for populations of currently developed countries. In the United Kingdom, infant mortality in 1900 was as bad as it is in any developing country today. Infant mortality has fallen steadily in the subsequent century for many reasons, but at least part of the solution was the consistent series of legislation aimed at improving access to health for the poor (Figure 11.7). These included the Midwives Act in 1902, National Insurance Act in 1911, the Poor Law in 1927, the Family Allowance Act

Figure 11.6: Eleanor Roosevelt photographed in 1949 holding a copy of the newly ratified Universal Declaration of Human Rights. She was influential in its development and was also the first person to hold the chair of the UN Human Rights Commission. (Printed with permission of the United Nations Photographic Library.)

Figure 11.7: Historical relationship between infant mortality rate and social legislation in the United Kingdom

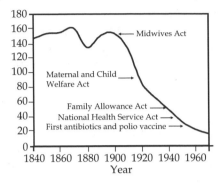

Source: Mckeown (1980)

in 1945, and the National Health Service Act in 1946.

The vital importance of legislated human rights is exemplified by the United Nations. Human rights were emphasized in that organization's founding charter shortly after World War II and its first major international success was the adoption of the Universal Declaration of Human Rights in 1948. This was later followed up by two further covenants on human rights adopted in 1966. Together, these now comprise the international bill of rights, which has had a profound effect upon the constitutions and laws of many countries around the world. Other major achievements of the human rights commission have been the agreement on the basic rights of all children in 1990 and the formal establishment of an international criminal court in 2002. Of course, lip service to legislation is of no use without the will to enforce that legislation. For example, the new South African constitution is an enlightened document that enshrines the rights of women yet, on a daily basis, women are exposed to

abuse, violence, and rape throughout that country's informal settlements.

Unfortunately, the Human Rights Commission has come under considerable recent criticism for being both ineffectual and excessively bureaucratic. Inclusion within the 53-member states of such countries as Zimbabwe, Sudan, and Syria has further reduced the commission's reputation. As recently as March 2005, the head of the United Nations actually called for the abolition of the Human Rights Commission and the establishment of a smaller Human Rights Council with membership restricted to countries whose governments understand the concept of human rights (*UN Human Rights Council*, n.d.).

Legislated protection for the poor and the weakest members of society is an essential foundation on which peace and prosperity can be built. The topic is important; the whole of Chapter 13 is devoted to the subject of human rights.

∎ HISTORY OF DEBT RELIEF EFFORTS

Like some physicians, we were too busy — and too sure of ourselves — to listen to patients with their own ideas. Too busy, sometimes, even to look at the individual countries and their circumstances. The economists and development experts of the Third World, many of them brilliant and highly educated, were sometimes treated like children. Our bedside manner was dreadful; and, as one patient after another couldn't help noticing, the medicine we dispensed abroad was, in important aspects, not really the same stuff we drank at home. (Stiglitz, 2004)

Before looking at the history of debt relief, it is important to get some of the terms sorted out as they can become confusing. Firstly, debt is held by three groups:

- *Multilateral debt:* This is lending by international financial institutions (IFIs). These are large banks, supported by various numbers of international governments. The best known are the International Monetary Fund and World Bank. There are many others, including the Islamic Development Bank, the Nordic Development Bank, and African Development Fund. These institutions are backed by government guarantees so are considered preferred creditors; that is, they are paid out first before other creditors. Without multilateral approval, particularly IMF approval, a country is unlikely to be given a credit by any other source. In particular, the country cannot apply for bilateral debt relief from Paris Club credit countries. Private banks and governments are able to write off debts, but the IMF and World Bank have, until recently, insisted that their rules do not allow them to cancel debt.
- *Bilateral aid:* This is money given by governments to governments. It includes bank debt that is insured by governmental institutions such as the export credit guarantees given by Britain, Frank, Sweden, and others.
- *Private aid:* Private sector banks that loan money without government guarantee.

1982: Start of the Debt Crisis

> During the long macroeconomic crisis that started at the end of the 1970s, poverty considerations were set aside. The neoliberal stream that dominated the 1980s downplayed distribution and poverty and insisted on re-establishing market mechanisms to promote growth.
> —James Wolfenson, 2004, then president of the World Bank (Wolfenson & Bourguignon, 2004:3)

In the mid-1970s, it was clear to a few commentators that the economies of several developing countries were in serious danger of collapse. The first sign of trouble was a steadily rising oil price. In succession, the Yom Kippur War, Arab oil embargo, Iranian Revolution, and the Iran-Iraq War all contrived to drive the price steadily higher. These profits (called "petrodollars") were recklessly invested in developing countries with little or no bank regulation and controls (Perkins, 2005). The rising oil price also triggered a recession in the West, leading to a drop in the commodity prices that supported many developing economies. At a time when developing countries were saddled with increasing debts, their ability to pay was reduced by a drop in commodity prices and a rise in interest rates. The market did not listen to these warnings and, as was the case in 1929, the final collapse of this financial house of cards seemed to come as a great surprise (Eichengreen & Lindert, 1992). Greater detail about the history behind the developing world debt is given in Chapter 4.

The crisis is often dated to August 1982 when Mexico's minister of Finance announced Mexico would be unable to meet its debt repayment. This was only the tip of the iceberg. By October 1983, 26 more countries, owing a total of $239 billion, were in a similar position. As a result, several of the world's largest banks faced the real prospect of major defaults and subsequent bank failures.

During the first phase of response, from 1982 to 1985, rich countries reacted to the possibility of default by simply providing new loans. Private lenders wanted to reduce their exposure since the commercial banks were already in enough trouble. However, the largest creditors represented by the Paris Club, IMF, and other multilateral development banks stepped in with more loans. They initially viewed the crisis as being due to an acute shortage of cash that would be solved by pouring in more money. It was claimed that this would allow poor countries to "grow" out of their debt.

By 1985, it was obvious that developing countries were not "growing" out of their debt but were clearly sinking below the weight of new short-term loans. It slowly became obvious that the problem was not liquidity but simply a case of excessive debt; clearly, a new approach was necessary. Without some form of debt relief, many countries would never be able to emerge from their crisis.

Debt forgiveness was not thought up by Tony Blair and George Bush in 2005 at Gleneagles; the concept had been around for more than 20 years (Daseking & Powell, 1999). Debt relief, in various forms, has been attached to a variety of concessions and interventions during this period. It has been a bumpy road between Mexico's default in 1982 and Gleneagles in 2005. The major twists and turns are outlined below.

1985: Baker and Brady Plans, Paris Club Terms, and SAPs

The mid-1980s was a confusing period as the various creditors tried new ways to help countries deal with their debts and repayments. The American government came up with the Baker and then the Brady plans. The IMF went further and further with its structural adjustment policies while the Paris Club countries tried a variety of rescheduling terms that changed with each annual meeting. It should be stressed that no matter what approach was used, the aim of those various initiatives was always to help the country become a better debt payer. The emphasis was always on repayment of debt; the poor came in a distant second. The concepts of forgiving debt and actually planning initiatives to help improve the health of the poorest of those countries were slow to develop.

- *Baker and Brady plans (Vasquez, 1996):* Suggested in 1985 by the current US Treasury secretary. Besides increased lending, the topic of conditionality was introduced. Interventions such as tax reduction, privatization of state-owned enterprises, and reduction of trade barriers were attempted. By 1988, it was apparent that this was not working so the next secretary (Brady) brought in a revised plan. This was one of the earliest attempts to provide real debt relief. New loans could be obtained below market interest rates and some commercial debts were written off. Various loan options were available to enable countries to extend their payback period. By 1994, 18 countries had agreed to Brady deals for a total debt forgiveness estimated at $60 billion spread over countries that were predominantly from Latin America.

- *Paris Club approach (Powell, 2000):* In 1987, the United Kingdom argued that Paris Club commercial loans to poor countries should be rescheduled at below market interest rates. Over the following years, at a variety of meetings, the rescheduling terms and amount of debt relief were slowly increased (Toronto terms, London terms, Naples terms, and, most recently, Lyon terms).

- *IMF approach:* As early as 1980, the IMF had tested various structural adjustment programs in the Philippines, Turkey, and Costa Rica. Over the next two decades, structural adjustment programs were extended to most of the developing world, which gave the IMF extraordinary (almost colonial) power to influence and remodel the economies of sovereign states.

The general approach taken in SAPs was straightforward: earn more and spend less. Interventions used in different countries were surprisingly similar — in fact, this "cookie-cutter" approach was one of the major criticisms of the SAP approach. In general, interventions included currency devaluation, cutbacks in government expenditure, elimination of subsidies and price controls, drop in wages, opening up markets for foreign competition, an emphasis on export-oriented industry, and privatization of government industries. Essential reading for this topic includes the following two books: *Globalization and Its Discontents* by Joseph Stiglitz (2002) and *The Chastening* by Paul Blustein (2003).

Poor countries had little option when confronted with these changes to their economies. Without the approval of the IMF, they would not be able to obtain credit from any other source. Although the IMF is made up of 184 countries, their voting structure is skewed toward the richest nations (Table 11.2). Voting percentage is proportional to the money a country pledges to the IMF. Consequently, the poorest countries have very little influence over IMF policy.

Table 11.2: Population and voting power at the IMF

Country	Population (millions)	Voting Percentage
United States	283	17.08%
India	1,009	1.92%
France	59	4.95%

Source: International Monetary Fund (n.d.-a)

The universality of the debt crisis meant that the IMF gained extraordinary power to control the economic organization of many of the world's poorest countries. The whole program was criticized as a form of recolonization: basically restructuring the world's economy on an IMF (and consequently an American) model. This might have been justified if SAPs were shown to work, but, unfortunately, evidence of any benefit is almost non-existent. The final result has been a worsening of life for the world's poor. SAPs have been criticized on many grounds, but the principal one is the inability to find any country in which the economic adjustments have clearly led to improved economic performance. The SAP review international network (SAPRIN) has published a detailed review of the problems associated with this period of IMF and World Bank policies (SAP Review International Network, 2004). These include the following:

- One size fits all—economic "shock tactics" designed in Washington and exported to indebted countries with little attempt to fit those policies to individual variations between different countries.
- The SAPs are designed by the IMF without consulting local people. There is no "ownership" by the developing country.
- The small macroeconomic gains of SAPs are more than countered by the profound adverse social effects of the interventions. These include sudden unemployment from rapid privatization, a reduction of service spending on healthy education and schooling, reduction of subsidies on vital food staples, and reduction of wages. All have deep effects on a country's poor.
- Developed countries took many decades to shift from protectionism toward a more open economy. Rapidly dropping import barriers allows richer exporting countries to flood local markets with cheap imports to the detriment of local manufacturing. Those exporting countries usually still enforce import restrictions on the poor country!

- Currency devaluation designed to make exports more attractive did not work as well as predicted because of the protective nature of many of the richest countries' markets. Tariffs applied to exports by developing countries mean that price reductions only had a limited effect on their ability to increase exports.
- Emphasis on exports at any cost increases activity such as logging and mining. In countries with limited regulations, such as Brazil, this leads to extensive deforestation and mining-associated pollution, all of which ultimately degrades life for the country's population.

Criticisms of SAPs grew steadily, but it was not until 1998 that the IMF commissioned external and internal reviews of its programs. Both were critical and revealed that the debt burden of countries implementing SAPs actually doubled between 1985 and 1995. Targets were not reached on reducing budget deficits or on raising government revenue. Although it was clear that many developing countries needed some kind of economic reform, the root of the SAPs has been deeply flawed, particularly from the perspective of the poorest. They played absolutely no part in the economic plan—even their governments had little say in what have been called "off the shelf austerity measures flown in directly from Washington." The perceived arrogance and inflexibility of the IMF ultimately led to calls for reductions in its power. The chastened IMF that finally emerged is probably little consolation to the millions upon millions of people whose lives have been adversely affected by its policies.

1996: Heavily Indebted Poor Countries Initiative (HIPC) (World Bank, n.d.)

The Bank's philosophy has changed, moving toward country specific and flexible analysis and away from the twin dogmas of pervasive state control (1960s–1970s) and unregulated markets (1980s–early 1990s…. Even the understanding of poverty has broadened from a narrow focus on income and consumption to a multidimensional notion of education, health, social and political participation, personal security and freedom, environmental quality and so forth.

— James Wolfenson, 2004, then president of the World Bank (Wolfenson & Bourguignon, 2004: 5)

Despite all these efforts, it was clear by mid-1990s that debt was still increasing at an unsustainable rate. In response, the World Bank and IMF established the HIPC initiative in October 1996 that was designed to provide a "robust exit from the burden of unsustainable debt." Although it was introduced as a major new response to the poorest countries, with its inclusion of debt relief, this was not entirely accurate. The main aim of the program was still to reduce debt only to the level where a country would become able to continue paying back interest.

The reputation of the World Bank and IMF had been badly damaged by the widely accepted failure of the structural adjustment era. Not surprisingly, there was plenty of cynicism about this new and improved approach to debt management. It should be said that the provision of a comprehensive debt framework did offer some apparent improvements. Poor countries no longer had to deal with separate creditors in lengthy, expensive, and uncoordinated attempts to reduce their debts. In addition, the World Bank and IMF agreed to drop their preferred creditor status and actually considered writing off some debts (under strict conditions, but it was a start).

Countries must first qualify for HIPC consideration by meeting a variety of criteria designed to ensure that they have unsustainable debts and are "worthy of assistance." This is not as cynical as it sounds. Both Nigeria and Zimbabwe meet the HIPC criteria, but are excluded from the process for reasons that are not clearly defined. Eligibility criteria include:

- Extreme poverty, poor social development and health indicators. Exports dependent on a few primary commodities and heavy reliance on financial aid.
- The country must have a track record of implementing IMF and World Bank economic reforms. Countries are still required to follow these interventions in order to qualify for debt relief. Although Nicaragua is a very poor country, it had trouble qualifying for HIPC because it was considered to have had a poor track record in implementing earlier imposed reforms.
- The country should have an unsustainable debt burden (usually defined as total debt to export ratio above 150 percent) and should also have been given maximal relief by other routes, particularly the Paris Club group of creditors.

Using these criteria, 42 countries have, to date, been declared eligible for HIPC assistance.

Under the HIPC criteria, the eligible country now entered a two-stage process. In the first three-year period, it had to establish a record of economic reform (simply SAPs by another name). If this was achieved to IMF/WB satisfaction, then a 67 percent relief of eligible debt was granted by Paris Club creditors. All other creditors (non-OECD bilateral creditors and commercial banks) were supposed to give comparable reductions. This was called the decision point.

If this did not produce a sustainable debt, the country moved into a second three-year period, during which time support was given from International Financial Institutes for further reforms and debt reduction. At the end of this period (the completion point), the country became eligible for 80 percent reduction in Paris Club debt. Criticism of the first HIPC was widespread and included the following (Gautam, 2003):

- Entry criteria not clearly established for all countries.
- Exit criteria ("cured" country) were arbitrary and still too high. Sustainability was defined in economic terms, not by measures of human and social development. The HIPC initiative reduced Burkina Faso's debt/exports below 150 percent, but the country still had half its population living below the poverty line and a life expectancy of 46 years—hardly a significant cure.
- HIPC was simply the same set of interventions that failed under the name SAP. Canada's prime

minister, Paul Martin, raised this point in a speech to the IMF in 2000: "…the requirement that developing countries undertake these adjustments at an unprecedented speed—a process that developed countries never had to undertake. The burdening of countries with a huge quantity of conditions to fulfill before receiving debt relief; the delay in countries reaching artificial completion points also delays debt relief plus the unrealistic growth expectations by creditors…." Even the chief economist of the World Bank, Joseph Stiglitz, criticized the project. When he stepped down from his job in 1999, he said that the process was not open and transparent enough and that the policy of imposing conditions on countries seeking economic aid had failed.

- The process made no mention of the fundamental illegality of much of the debt so played down the moral necessity for debt cancellation.
- The whole process remained imposed rather than collaborative with little or no input (ownership is the current term) by the indebted country.

In the first three years of the program, developing world debt climbed from US $2.2 trillion up to US $2.6 trillion while economic output fell slightly. The World Bank bowed to pressure and commissioned internal and external reviews—both of which were critical. The response was the Enhanced HIPC Program announced in 1999.

1999: Enhanced HIPC, PRSPs

This newest approach is still only a few years old so it is difficult to say whether these are true changes or simply another name for SAPs. The biggest change under EHIPC has been the introduction of Poverty Reduction Strategy Papers (International Monetary Fund, n.d.-b). During the first three-year period, a broad range of groups (including the poor) are gathered together to plan the country's future economic course. This is, of course, intended to include the provision of pro-poor choices. The PRSP is intended to act as the blueprint for progress through the second third-year period. Completion of a PRSP is one of the provisions that must be met by the decision point.

Time will tell if this is just lip service or whether there will be real measurable changes for the poor. There is some optimism in the literature (Driscoll & Evans, 2005) in support of EHIPC, particularly when countries have had time to get experience with the new rules (Booth, 2005).

2000: Pressure for Debt Cancellation

Although the HIPC initiative does provide debt relief, it still provides only enough relief to make a country's debt repayment sustainable. Open public discussion about true cancellation of all debts has been a very late development. Oddly enough, President George W. Bush was one of the first people to ask for large-scale debt cancellation. In his case, it was to obtain billions of debt relief for post-war Iraq. Much of the credit for this increase in popular support has to be given to various pressure groups, particularly Jubilee 2000, Make Poverty History, and the Live 8 concerts.

Only about five years ago, G8 meetings hardly made the news, but by 2000, these annual meetings attracted huge levels of protest and popular debate—much of it aimed at debt relief. It is difficult to know whether debt relief became a major G8 topic because of altruism of world leaders or whether these elected officials were simply responding to the popular opinion of the voting public. It is also possible that the devastation caused by the Boxing Day 2004 Tsunami had a significant effect on the debate. Discussion of debt cancellation for affected countries increased general interest in the topic. No matter what the reason was, substantive discussion of debt relief is finally a reality; relieving the developing world's debt burden was at the top of the agenda at the 2005 G8 summit meeting in Britain.

2005: Gleneagles Meeting and the Future

The 2005 Gleneagles G8 meeting resulted in the first serious attempt to write off debts of the poorest countries. A total of $40 billion of debt was written off for 18 of the poorest countries in the world that had already completed HIPC programs. In total, it is estimated they will save $1.5 billion a year in debt repayments. Nine more HIPC countries will qualify within another 18 months, which will take the total of debt relief to $55 billion. In addition, a doubling of aid to Africa from $25 billion to $50 billion was also announced.

The success of the initial G8 debt relief proposal led to its extension, under the Multilateral Debt Relief Initiative (MDRI) (World Bank, n.d.), to include relief of HIPC debts held by three institutions—the World Bank, the IMF, and the African Development Fund. Another significant step was the establishment in early 2005 of the Debt Sustainability Framework for low-income countries. This joint WB-IMF initiative is intended to monitor a country's debt and assess its ability to service further loans so that future unsustainable debt can hopefully be avoided.

■ SUMMARY

Lack of money and a huge debt burden are major contributors to the misery and ill health that afflict populations throughout the developing world. A good knowledge of both is central to an understanding of international health. Although the statistics concerning the extent of absolute poverty and the size of the developing world debt, discussed in Chapter 4, are quite overwhelming, solutions are available. However, they must be based on careful research specific to that country and the subsequent plans need to be supported over periods of years. Above all, the poor themselves must be given a voice in the solutions to their own problems. This might seem obvious, but it is only within the last 10−15 years that the poor have been given a central place in the debate.

History will likely be unkind in its assessment of the aid industry's approaches to poverty and debt management between the time of Mexico's payment default in 1982 and the Gleneagles meeting in 2005. Ideologically driven economic interventions were enforced long after it was clear they were a failure. During much of this period, the poor were largely ignored as economic belt tightening was recommended by short-term consultants. The adverse effects of budget cuts for health, education, or reduced food subsidies fell hardest upon the poor and their children. How many suffered directly or indirectly as a result of these policies over 20 years? No one knows, but it must be measured in many millions.

Over the past decade, particularly with the establishment of the Millenium Development Goals and the Enhanced Heavily Indebted Poor Countries initiative, there has been a growing understanding that improving the lives of the poor must be the primary aim of any long-term economic plan. The poor are important—aid must be targeted toward them and the planning of that aid must include their input at every level. It must be hoped that we are at a new beginning in our approach to the poorest people on this shared planet.

RESOURCES

References

Aisbett, E. (2005). *Why are the critics so convinced that globalization is bad for the poor?* (National Bureau of Economic Research working paper no. 11066). Retrieved from www.nber.org/papers/W11066.

Armendariz de Aghion, B., & Morduch, J. (2005). *The economics of microfinance.* Cambridge: MIT Press.

Bangladesh Rural Advancement Committee. (n.d.). Retrieved from www.brac.net.

Beck, T., et al. (2004). *Finance, inequality and poverty: Cross country evidence* (World Bank research paper 3338). Retrieved from www.worldbank.org.

Blustein, P. (2003). *The chastening: Inside the crisis that rocked the global financial system and humbled the IMF.* New York: Public Affairs.

Booth, D. (2005). *Missing links in the politics of development: Learning from the PRSP experiment* (Overseas Development Institute working paper 256). Retrieved from www.odi.org.uk/publications/working_papers/wp256.pdf.

Booth, D., & Lucas, H. (2002). *Good practice in the development of PRSP indicators and monitoring systems* (Overseas Development Institute, paper 172). Retrieved from www.odi.org.uk/publications/wp172.pdf.

Bourguignon, F. (2003). *The poverty-growth-inequality triangle.* Retrieved from www.worldbank.org.

Daseking, C., & Powell, R. (1999). *From Toronto terms to the HIPC initiative: A brief history of debt relief for low-income countries* (IMF working paper no. 142). Retrieved from www.imf.org/external/pubs/ft/wp/1999/wp99142.pdf.

Davies, W. (2003). "An historical perspective from the Green Revolution to the gene revolution." *Nutrition Reviews, 61,* 124–134.

Denes, C. (2003). "Bolsa Escola: Redefining poverty and development in Brazil. *International Education Journal, 4,* 137–146.

Department for International Development. (2003). *Agriculture and poverty reduction: Unlocking the potential.* Retrieved from www.dfid.gov.uk/pubs/files/agri-poverty-reduction.pdf.

Djurfeldt, G., et al. (2005). *The African food crisis: Lessons from the Asian green revolution.* Wallingford: CABI Publishing.

Dollar, K., & Kraay, A. (2002). "Growth is good for the poor." *Journal of Economic Growth, 7,* 195–225. Retrieved from www.undp.org/povertycentre/publications/economics/Growth_is_Good_for_Poor-Dollar-Sept02.pdf.

Donnelly, J. (2002). *Universal human rights in theory and practice.* Ithaca: Cornell University Press.

Driscoll, R., & Evans, A. (2005). "Second-generation poverty reduction strategies: New opportunities and emerging issues." *Development Policy Review, 23,* 5–25.

Easterly, W. (2001). *The effect of IMF and World Bank programmes on poverty* (United Nations University discussion paper no. 102). Retrieved from www.wider.unu.edu/publications/dps/dp2001-102.pdf.

Easterly, W. (2002). *The elusive quest for growth.* Cambridge: MIT Press.

Eastwood, R., & Lipton, M. (2000). "Pro-poor growth and pro-growth poverty reduction: Meaning, evidence, and policy implications." *Asian Development Review, 18, no. 2.* Retrieved from www.adb.org/Poverty/Forum/pdf/Lipton.pdf.

Eichengreen, B., & Lindert, P. (Eds.). (1992). *The international debt crisis in historical perspective.* Cambridge: MIT Press.

Feachem, R. (2000). "Poverty and inequity: A proper focus for the new century." *Bulletin of the World Health Organization, 78,* 3–18.

Food and Agriculture Organization. (n.d.). *FAOSTAT.* Retrieved from faostat.fao.org.

Fuentes, R. (2005). "Poverty, pro-poor growth, and simulated inequality reduction." *Human Development Report.* Retrieved from hdr.undp.org.

Gautam, M. (2003). *Debt relief for the poorest: An OED review of the HIPC initiative.* Washington: World Bank.

"The hidden wealth of the poor: A survey of microfinance." (2005, November 3). *The Economist.*

Hufbauer, G., & Schott, J. (2006). *The Doha round after Hong Kong.* Retrieved from www.iie.com/publications/pb/pb06-2.pdf.

International Monetary Fund. (n.d.-a). *IMF quotas.* Retrieved from www.imf.org/external/np/exr/facts/quotas.htm.

International Monetary Fund. (n.d.-b). *Poverty reduction strategy papers.* Retrieved from www.imf.org/external/np/prsp/prsp.asp.

Irz, X., et al. (2001). "Agricultural productivity growth and poverty alleviation." *Development Policy Review, 19,* 449–466.

Ismi, A. (2004). *Impoverishing a continent: The World Bank and the IMF in Africa*. Halifax: Canadian Centre for Policy Alternatives. Retrieved from www.policyalternatives.ca.

Mckeown, T. 1980. *The role of medicine: Dream, mirage, or nemesis?* Princeton: Princeton University Press.

Norman Borlaug Heritage Foundation. (n.d.). Retrieved from www.normanborlaug.org.

Organisation for Economic Co-operation and Development. (n.d.). *Official development assistance figures*. Retrieved from www.oecd.org/doc/stats.

Oxfam. (2005). *Kicking down the door: How upcoming WTO talks threaten farmers in poor countries* (Oxfam briefing paper 72). Retrieved from www.oxfam.org.uk.

Perkins, J. (2005). *Confessions of an economic hit man*. San Francisco: Berrett-Koehler.

Pet Food Institute. (n.d.). *US cat and dog populations*. Retrieved from www.petfoodinstitute.org/reference_pet_data.cfm.

Powell, R. (2000). "Debt relief for poor countries." *Finance and Development, 37, no. 4*. Retrieved from www.imf.org/external/pubs/ft/fandd/2000/12/powell.htm.

Pro-Poor Growth Research Program. (2005). *Pro-poor growth in the 1990s: Lessons and insights from 14 countries*. Retrieved from www.worldbank.org.

Sachs, J. (2005). *The end of poverty: Economic possibilities for our time*. New York: Penguin Press.

SAP Review International Network. (2004). *Structural adjustment: The SAPRI report. The policy roots of economic crisis, poverty, and inequality*. London: Zed Books.

Stiglitz, J. (2004). *The Roaring Nineties: A New History of the World's Most Prosperous Decade*. New York: W.W. Norton.

UN Human Rights Council. (n.d.). Retrieved from www.ohchr.org/english/bodies/hrcouncil.

UNICEF. (2005). *Gender achievements and prospects in education: The GAP report (part 1)*. Retrieved from www.ungei.org/gap.

United Nations Statistics Division. (n.d.). *Country profiles*. Retrieved from unstats.un.org/unsd/cdb.

United States Agency for International Development. (2005). *Banking at the base of the pyramid: A microfinance primer for commercial banks*. Retrieved from pdf.dec.org/pdf_docs/PNADD677.pdf.

Vasquez, I. (1996). "The Brady plan and market-based solutions to debt crises." *The Cato Journal, 16, no. 2*. Retrieved from www.cato.org/pubs/journal/cj16n2/cj16n2-4.pdf.

Weisbrot, M., & Baker, D. (2002). *The relative impact of trade liberalization on developing countries*. Retrieved from www.cepr.net/publications/trade_2002_06_12.htm.

Wolfenson, J., & Bourguignon, F. (2004). *Development and poverty reduction: Looking back, looking ahead*. Retrieved from www.worldbank.org.

World Bank. (2002). *Global economic prospects and the developing countries: Making trade work for the world's poor*. Washington: Author.

World Bank. (n.d.). *Economic policy and debt*. Retrieved from www.worldbank.org/hipc/.

Yunus, M. (2003). *Banker to the poor: Micro-lending and the battle against world poverty*. New York: Public Affairs.

Recommended Reading

Bellamy, C. (2004). *The state of the world's children, 2004: Girls, education, and development*. Darby: DIANE Publishing Company.

Donnelly, J. (2002). *Universal human rights in theory and practice*. Ithaca: Cornell University Press.

Federico, G. (2005). *Feeding the world: An economic history of world agriculture, 1800–2000*. Princeton: Princeton University Press.

Fogel, R. (2004). *The escape from hunger and premature death, 1700–2100: Europe, America, and the Third World*. Cambridge: Cambridge University Press.

Hertel, T., & Winters, L. (2005). *Poverty and the WTO: Impacts of the Doha Development Agenda.* Washington: World Bank.

Shiva, V. (2000). *Stolen harvest: The hijacking of the global food supply.* Cambridge: South End Press.

Stiglitz, J. (2004). *The roaring nineties: A new history of the world's most prosperous decade.* New York: W.W. Norton and Company.

Yunus, M. (2003). *Banker to the poor micro-lending and the battle against world poverty.* New York: Public Affairs.

Chapter 12

Human Rights Interventions

Acts of injustice done,
Between the setting and the rising sun,
In history lie like bones,
Each one.
— W.H. Auden, "The Ascent of F6"

OBJECTIVES
After completing this chapter, you should be able to

- appreciate the broad concept of human rights
- understand the slow development of human rights legislation both for adults and children
- understand the need for improvements in human rights as a basis for any lasting development intervention
- understand the details of some of the common human rights abuses

While it is true to say that the poor health of people living in adverse social conditions is largely due to the complicated end results of poverty, this is not the full story. It is certainly a lot better than the practice of earlier times when the poor were blamed for their situation but, for a full understanding of the problem, it is necessary to ask one more question: Why are these people poor in the first place? Unfortunately, the answer is invariably some form of social or political injustice. Lasting improvements in population health are not just based on a combination of medical treatments and social change. The third essential ingredient must be an improvement in that population's human rights. Rights are not a luxury given only to rich people; they are an indispensable component of any national development effort. A lot of lip service is paid to human rights improvements, but this is not always the fault of the aid agencies. Making lasting changes requires more political will and leverage than most donor organizations possess. Although huge advances have been made in the field of human rights, the subject is not yet viewed as a central part of any sustainable population health initiative. It is important to appreciate that human rights improvements are just as important as poverty alleviation; they are a central feature of sustainable development work (Annan, 2005). This chapter will examine the history and development of human rights (both for adults and children) and will also examine some of the more pressing human rights dilemmas.

WHAT ARE HUMAN RIGHTS?

Freedom, from which men are said to be free, is the natural power of doing what each please, unless prevented by force or law.

—Justinian Codex, AD 529

Human rights are discussed and analyzed in such detail by so many special interest groups that it is easy to lose sight of the big picture. Even those two simple words "human" and "rights" are debated endlessly. What does it mean to be a "human"? Do human rights apply to unborn children, those with mental disabilities, or prisoners? What about "rights"? Are they different from needs or obligations? Who imposes them, who monitors them, and how are violations to be punished? Are all human rights equal or are some more important than others?

As an example of the complex debate needed to establish widespread agreement on these issues, it took 1,400 rounds of voting on practically every word in every clause before the General Assembly adopted the Universal Declaration of Human Rights on December 10, 1948 in Paris (United Nations, 1998). Such legal and philosophical debates are necessary when setting international conventions and laws but, in practice, it is not that difficult to tell when rights have been trampled. There are endless and unambiguous examples of human rights abuses: state-sanctioned torture and murder, imprisonment without trial, sexual exploitation of children, trafficking of humans, slavery, female genital mutilation, child labour, and many more. Whenever there is poverty and powerlessness, there will inevitably be discrimination or inequity very close behind.

Human rights should be differentiated from the social and legal obligations that any citizen has to follow in a civil society. Human rights are rather more abstract entities. They are independent of culture, race, class, age, or any other human subset; they consist of a set of rights one has simply through being a human

Table 12.1: A moment of Zen

	Average number of passengers carried in a Boeing 747: 480
Total number of developing world women who died during pregnancy in 2000: **527,000**	Total number of deaths if three fully loaded 747s crashed every day for a year: 3 x 480 x 365: ~**527,000**
Source: UNICEF (2006)	Source: Boeing (n.d.)

(Australian Human Rights Commission, 2001). There is, of course, a debate about what constitutes the most basic rights, but most would agree that the steady growth of international legislation promoted by the UN over the last 50 years has shown that it is possible to establish a universally accepted set of basic human rights that are applicable to all countries and cultures in the world.

There are many ways to categorize human rights (Donnelly, 2003). The simplest is to divide them into negative and positive rights. These are not judgmental terms; they simply describe the degree of government involvement. The concept of negative human rights emerges from the English (and subsequently American) historical tradition of opposing government involvement in private life. Negative rights require nothing from government except that it should keep out of the way. These rights include freedom of speech, freedom of religion, and freedom of assembly (and freedom to carry arms in some countries). Positive rights trace their roots to the European (particularly French) tradition of expecting the government to do something useful. These include the rights to an education, rights to a livelihood, and the legal protection of equality for all citizens.

Another common form of categorization was derived by Karel Vasak, a former head of the International Institute of Human Rights. He proposed three generations of human rights based loosely on the concepts of the French Revolution (liberty, equality, and fraternity). The first generation, based on liberty, consists of civil and political rights and is mostly negative (right to life, liberty, free speech, movement, political and religious practice, fair trial, privacy, and voting). The second generation, based on equality, consists of social, economic, and cultural rights; they are mostly positive (rights to education, employment, and equality among citizens. The final group, based on fraternity, is less widely accepted and includes collective rights (right to a clean environment, respect for cultural traditions, and the right to peace).

Other specific categories of human rights exist, including humanitarian rights (protection for those affected by armed conflict) and special rights claimed by particular groups (rights of workers, women, children, minority groups, refugees, indigenous peoples, people with disabilities, etc.). Vasak's first- and second-generation rights can be seen in the two UN International Covenants adopted in 1966 (Covenant on Civil and Political Rights and the Covenant on Social, Economic, and Cultural Rights). These became legally binding obligations for all signatories in 1976. Third-generation rights have not been codified by an international agreement.

Whatever classification is used, rights are interdependent so attempting to place them into neat categories is, to some extent, artificial. For example, the rights to education and health cannot be entirely separated from the rights to life and liberty. The right to security may well conflict with the right to privacy (a good example is the current debate surrounding the Patriot Act). With all this complexity, it is easy to predict that some rights will conflict. The right to respect for cultural traditions, such as female circumcision, certainly conflicts with the right to self-determination and health. The right to a fair trial may conflict with the right to privacy and the right to work may conflict with the right to a healthy environment.

These should be viewed as challenges to be met by compromise; they are certainly not an excuse to abandon human rights.

Box 12.1: History notes

Nelson Rolihlahla Mandela (1918–)

Many leaders in history have paid a high price for their open support of human rights: Dr. Martin Luther King and Aung San Suu Kyi are good examples. Perhaps the most iconic is Nelson Mandela of South Africa. Mandela was born in the Transkei in 1918. After mission school, he enrolled in college, but was suspended for joining a student protest. He studied law by correspondence and served his clerkship in Johannesburg. He first entered politics by joining the African National Congress in 1942. Along with Sisulu, Tambo and others, he began to change the ANC to a far more radical organization. The organization launched its Campaign for the Defiance of Unjust Laws in 1952. Its only weapons were boycotts, strikes, and civil disobedience.

Arrested for his part in the campaign, Mandela was given a suspended sentence. He opened a law practice with Oliver Tambo to represent the poorest people. Mandela was constantly harassed during the 1950s, including being banned from the Law Society, arrested, and imprisoned. After the Sharpeville massacre in 1960 where 69 protesters were shot dead, the ANC was outlawed. Mandela had to go underground, but was arrested in 1962. He was initially sentenced to five years, but when retried for other charges, he was sentenced to life in prison. He was finally released in 1990. He consistently refused earlier release, in exchange for approval of apartheid, arguing, "Prisoners cannot enter into contracts. Only free men can negotiate." He was awarded the Nobel Peace Prize in 1993 and served as the first democratically elected president of South Africa from 1994 until he retired in 1999. Follow the reference for more information (African National Congress, n.d.).

Numerous controversies exist concerning human rights, but the most difficult is the challenge of setting universal human rights in a culturally diverse world (Ayton-Shenker, 1995). The imposition of universal rules was initially viewed as a form of cultural imperialism by which powerful countries dictated those rights they considered most important. With time, as more and more developing world countries sign on to international human rights treaties, this argument has weakened. While the argument is not over, it is increasingly accepted that there is a fundamental set of universal rules that can be applied to all countries and cultures.

■ ADULT HUMAN RIGHTS

> Man's inhumanity to man makes countless thousands mourn.
> —Robert Burns, 1786

There seems no end to the abuses that cruel or greedy people can impose upon weak and powerless populations. The full range of those abuses of human rights is enormous; a complete review would fill a library. Many of these situations are virtually unknown to the general public. Some affect only a few thousand unfortunate people, so are too small to attract much attention. Examples include the abuse of child camel-racing jockeys in the Middle East (Caine & Caine, 2005) or the practice of child temple prostitution in Southern India and Nepal (Mukhopadhyay, 1995). Others might affect millions and yet still be relatively unknown. For example, the rising price of gold has led to an enormous global gold rush. It is estimated that there are 15 million gold miners, working in 50 countries, mining under terrible working conditions (Spiegel, 2005); this includes 4 million women and 1 million children. The human and environmental costs are enormous. In this section, we will examine a few of the most obvious and topical human rights abuses, including slavery, human trafficking, and violence against women.

History of Human Rights Legislation

> I announce that everyone is free to choose a religion. People are free to live in all regions and take up a job provided they never violate the rights of others.
> —Cyrus the Great's First Charter of Human Rights, 539 BC

The idea that human beings have rights, simply because they are humans, is largely a 20th-century concept (United Nations, 1998). However, if history is examined closely, there have been brief flashes of enlightened law-making before this period. The quote at the start of this section is from a small baked clay cylinder uncovered in the 19th century at the site of Babylon. It is a document describing the treatment of Babylonians after their conquest by Cyrus the Great. It is considered the earliest human rights manifesto; a replica is kept at the United Nations headquarters. The great 3rd-century BC Indian ruler, Ashoka the Cruel, later became Ashoka the Early Hippie after embracing Buddhism. Numerous inscribed rocks and pillars around his large kingdom can still be read and lay out enlightened rules, including religious tolerance and the abolition of slavery.

The great religions of the world all make extensive commentary on human nature, but the emphasis is usually on the duties and obligations of humans rather than their rights. This is typified by the ancient philosophical principle, often called the "golden rule" ("Do unto others as you would have them do unto you") (Wattles, 1996). This concept can be found throughout literature ranging from the major religious texts to the popular character Mrs. Doasyouwouldbedoneby in *The Water Babies*. In the secular world, many ancient lawmakers collected lists of obligations and duties, but there was still very little emphasis on rights. The Code of Hammurabi from 1750 BC and the 6th-century Justinian Codex are good examples.

Throughout the Middle Ages, society was based on a hierarchical system, broadly separated into those who made war, those who prayed, and those who laboured (Bellatores, Oratores, et Laboratores). Very little time was wasted worrying about the rights of those at the bottom of the pile. The Magna Carta, signed by King John in 1215, is often thought to be the first crack in the structure of absolute power,

---

Box 12.2: The slow march toward human rights

539 BC	The Cyrus Cylinder
250 BC	Ashok's Edicts
529	Justinian Codex
1100	King Henry I, Charter of Liberties
1215	King John I, Magna Carta
1689	English Bill of Rights
1776	US Declaration of Independence
1789	French Declaration of the Rights of Man
1791	US Bill of Rights
1893	Women's Vote, New Zealand
1919	League of Nations formed
1994	Women's Vote, South Africa (Black)
2005	Women's Vote, Kuwait

but King Henry had already signed a charter of liberties limiting some of his powers 100 years earlier in 1100. By the 15th century, a small flicker of light had started to illuminate those dark European ages. Although various arbitrary names are given to the subsequent growth of humanism in Europe (Reformation, Enlightenment, Age of Reason), the rights we enjoy today can be traced back to the intellectual movement that started in Renaissance Italy (Rayner, 2006).

The Scottish philosopher, John Locke (1632–1704), reflected the feeling of the times with his writing on human rights ("Every man has a property in his own person. This, nobody has a right to, but himself."). Cromwell's revolution in 1640 did not do much for the rights of King Charles I, but the subsequent "Glorious Revolution" 40 years later, when the English swapped kings, led to the first European Bill of Rights in 1689. The desire for rights and freedom developed in the 17th and 18th centuries; ultimately it led to the Declaration of Independence by the American colonies in 1776. In common with many other attempts at human rights legislation, the words of the document ("We hold these Truths to be self-evident, that all Men are created equal") were more impressive than the subsequent deeds. Similarly, in 1789, the French Declaration of the Rights of Man and of the Citizen described human rights with equally impressive terms ("Men are born and remain free and equal in rights"), but that did not stop thousands of people from losing their heads during the subsequent reign of terror. Box 12.2 lists some of the main steps on the road to universal human rights.

The horrors of World War I and World War II managed to shock Western nations into realizing that human rights were not just an abstract debating point. In 1946, the newly formed United Nations established the Commission on Human Rights as the principal policy-making body for human rights legislation. Under the chairmanship of Eleanor Roosevelt, the commission started the difficult job of defining basic rights and freedoms. After an exhaustive process, the General Assembly adopted the Universal Declaration of Human Rights on December 10, 1948 in Paris (United Nations, n.d.-b).

The declaration did not have the legal force of a treaty, but widespread acceptance made it a cornerstone of the universal human rights movement. In 1966, the UN negotiated the International Covenant on Civil and Political Rights and another on Economic, Social, and Cultural Rights. Both came into force in 1976. Since they are legally binding, signatories are open to monitoring of their human rights practices. The two covenants plus the universal declaration are referred to as the International Bill of Rights (United Nations, n.d.-a); most modern countries are parties to both covenants. Six UN committees monitor compliance with various international treaties, including the Committee on the Rights of the Child, the Committee against Torture, and the Human Rights Committee. Box 12.3 summarizes the major human rights advances since World War II.

More recently, the UN has had mixed success with human rights. A major advance was the General Assembly's creation of the International Criminal Court (*International Criminal Court*, n.d.). This developed from a variety of smaller, short-term courts established in the 1990s to trial war crimes in Rwanda and Yugoslavia. On the other hand, the UN Human Rights Commission was heavily

Box 12.3: Human rights legislation in the 20th century

1945   United Nations formed
1946   UN Commission on Human Rights
1948   Universal Declaration of Human
         Rights
1951   Convention on Prevention and
         Punishment of Genocide
1961   Convention on the Status of
         Refugees
1966   International Covenants on Civil/
         Political and Economic/Social/
         Cultural Rights
1979   Convention on Elimination of
         Discrimination against Women
1984   Convention against Torture and
         Inhumane Treatment
1989   Convention on the Rights of the
         Child
1990   International Convention on Rights
         of Migrant Workers and Families
2002   Rome Statute on the International
         Criminal Court
2006   New Human Rights Council

criticized for allowing membership to countries with dreadful human rights records such as Zimbabwe and Sudan. In fact, in a report in 2005, the UN secretary general actually called for the abolition of the commission (Annan, 2005) and the establishment of a smaller council, which would meet throughout the year and restrict its membership to countries that meet accepted human rights standards. Despite opposition from the US, the new 47-member Human Rights Council held its first meeting in early 2006.

Slavery

> Whenever I hear anyone arguing for slavery, I feel a strong impulse to see it tried on him personally.
> — Abraham Lincoln

Human nature being what it is, there have probably been slaves as long as there has been organized society — certainly as long as there has been war. Ancient Egyptian and Assyrian wall reliefs clearly show military captives. It seems unlikely that they would have wasted such a cheap source of labour. The Vikings traded and raided deep into Russia and Eastern Europe; the term "slave" is derived from their word for Slavic captive. Although

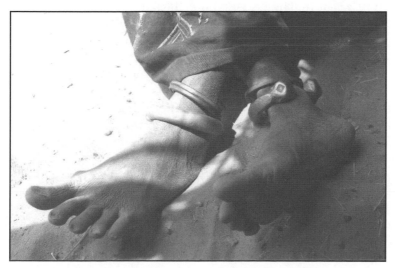

Figure 12.1: Shackles may have gone, but slavery persists in Niger. These metal anklets serve as a symbolic reminder that the wearer is part of the slave class. (Photographer G. Cranston; courtesy IRIN news.)

```
┌─────────────────────────────────────────────┐
│  Box 12.4: Anti-slavery legislation          │
│                                               │
│  1787        Freed European slaves            │
│              establish colony at              │
│              Freetown, Sierra Leone           │
│  1794        France abolishes slavery         │
│  1804        Haiti, first republic of ex-     │
│              slaves                           │
│  1807        British abolish slave trading    │
│  1822        First Black American settlers    │
│              land in Liberia (declared        │
│              independent in 1847)             │
│  1833        Abolition of slavery in British  │
│              colonies                         │
│  1861–1865   American Civil War               │
│  1865        Emancipation of US slaves        │
│  1926        Slavery banned globally by       │
│              League of Nations                │
│  1948        Universal Declaration of         │
│              Human Rights banned              │
│              slavery                          │
│  1956        UN Convention on the             │
│              Abolition of Slavery             │
│  1966        UN Covenant on Civil and         │
│              Political Rights, legally        │
│              binding agreement                │
│                                               │
└─────────────────────────────────────────────┘
```

to work in the various forms of slavery has become a separate but connected criminal activity. Box 12.4 summarizes the major advances in anti-slavery legislation. Once again, it is possible to lose sight of the larger picture by concentrating too much on the definitions of slavery. Although there are obvious differences between a bonded labourer on a Central American farm and a West African child sold into the European sex trade, they both share many common features that characterize the condition of slavery. These include the presence of force (mental or physical), physical restraint, absence of any individual power, and the ability to be sold or bought as a commodity. Modern examples of slavery include (Anti-Slavery International, n.d.):

- *Bonded labour:* This is probably the most common form of slavery worldwide. Poverty forces people to sell themselves or their children as workers to repay a loan. The pay will never cover the repayments so the debt never ends. The debt may also be passed on to the family's children.
- *Sex trade slavery:* This includes women and children forced into prostitution, pornography, or other forms of the sex trade. In some cases, debt or poverty is the motivation while others may be tricked into working in another country with offers of domestic work.
- *Forced labour:* This term covers people who are forcibly confined and made to work. Some are captured during war, as still happens in Sudan (Jok, 2001), while others are tricked into

all countries at least pay lip service to the concept of freedom, the widespread legal abolition of slavery has not brought the practice to an end. A recent review estimates there are 25–30 million people working as slaves today, probably more than there have ever been in history (Bales, 2004).

Slavery is common around the world, both in developed and developing countries. The Human Rights Center at the University of California, Berkeley, estimates there are 10,000 slaves within the United States working in agriculture, factories, restaurants, and hotels (Human Rights Center, 2004). There is no reason to suppose that other developed countries are any different. Now that slavery is universally illegal, the movement of people working and subsequently forced to endure harsh conditions with no pay through a variety of physical or mental threats.

The average person can do little about the organized crime aspect of trafficking and slavery, but consumers can bring pressure to bear on unethical manufacturers through their choice of purchases. The fair trade labelling concept developed initially around coffee and cocoa production, but it has spread to a wide range of other products (*Fairtrade Foundation*, n.d.). If manufacturers agree to introduce ethical codes of practice and follow international labour standards, their product is identified by a visible endorsement from one of a number of ethical trade organizations. As long as consumers subsequently buy those products, the ability to change practices is considerable.

Human Trafficking

The trafficking of humans, particularly women and children, is a rapidly growing global problem that is tied to international crime and slavery. The victim profiles given in the US Department of State's annual report on human trafficking (US Department of State, 2005) provide human faces to this inhumane practice. Like slavery, trafficking is a problem in all countries, developed (Kelly, 2002) and developing (Dottridge, 2002). Its illegal nature makes accurate numbers difficult to collect, but some estimates are available. The Department of State's report estimates that 600,000–800,000 men, women, and children are trafficked across international borders every year (US Department of State, 2005). Approximately 80 percent are women and up to 50 percent are minors.

The principal reason for trafficking is commercial sexual exploitation. These estimates include only people trafficked across international borders and do not include the larger numbers trafficked within their own countries (Laczko & Gozdziack, 2005). The International Labour Organization estimates that 200,000 women and children are internally trafficked in Southeast Asia alone (Derks, 2000) and that more than a million are moved globally every year. Reports from Bangladesh estimate that more than 13,000 children have been taken from the country over the past five years.

The US Federal Bureau of Investigation estimates that human trafficking generates $9.5 billion in annual revenue; it is closely connected with large-scale international criminal organizations (Vayrynen, 2003). Profits are so high that there is a shift away from trafficking arms and drugs toward the movement of human beings. Drugs can only be sold once, but humans can be sold over and over again, providing a profit on each transaction. Forced transportation of humans through abduction, fraud, or some form of deception should be differentiated from human smuggling in which the participants are more or less willing.

The roots of trafficking are complex, but they include poverty, organized crime, violence, and discrimination against women, war, and corruption. The most likely targets of traffickers are people from rural areas, children in large families, and ethnic minority groups (Omelaniuk, 2005). In some societies, there is a tradition of sending a young child to live with an extended family member in an urban centre. Traffickers can prey on such beliefs, promising the child's parents employment, training, or even marriage in town. In

Africa, there is a large pool of street children who are particularly vulnerable to trafficking. They are the product of armed conflict, rural migration, poverty, and loss of parents to HIV/AIDS.

Such a profitable endeavour will not be stopped easily; eradication requires a combined approach (UN High Commission for Human Rights, 2000). Improving educational and economical opportunities to vulnerable groups will give them better lives and reduce the likelihood that women and children will fall prey to human trafficking. Law enforcement has increasingly been helped by international treaties such as the United Nations Convention against Transnational Organized Crime and the Council of Europe's Convention on Action against Trafficking of Human Beings (Council of Europe, 2006). Reducing demand for the products of slave labour is also difficult. Ethical trade labelling can have an impact on a manufacturer's use of forced or slave labour, but the prosecution of those who travel to developing countries to use child prostitutes is still at a very early stage.

Violence against Women

The safest place for men is the home, the home is, by contrast, the least safe place for women.
— Susan Edwards, *Policing "Domestic" Violence*, 1989

Violence against women is a worldwide problem in developed and developing countries (Watts & Zimmerman, 2002). The United Nations defines violence against women as "any act of gender-based violence that will likely result in physical, sexual, or psychological harm." Within this broad definition, a wide range of abuses can be included. These range from the insanity of so-called "honour killings" (Pope, 2005) to domestic violence, rape, forced child marriage, female genital mutilation, sex-selected abortion, and infanticide.

Exact statistics are not kept, but hundreds of millions of women around the world are affected. Even the single issue of domestic violence has been shown to be far more common than was accepted in past years. A recent review of various countries revealed the following rates of physical assault by a partner: Switzerland (21 percent lifetime, 7 percent in previous 12 months), Egypt (34 percent lifetime, 16 percent in previous 12 months), India (40 percent lifetime, 14 percent in previous 12 months), New Zealand (35 percent lifetime, 21 percent in previous 12 months), Nicaragua (28 percent lifetime, 12 percent in previous 12 months), Canada (29 percent lifetime, 3 percent in previous 12 months) (Watts & Zimmerman, 2002). Research shows that almost all of the violence is perpetuated by men; women are at greatest risk from men they know, particularly male family members and intimate partners (Jeyaseelan et al., 2004). Physical abuse is usually also associated with long-standing psychological abuse. Experience has shown that social institutions have often blamed battered women or, at the very least, ignored them.

The cumulative results of such widespread abuse are enormous. The combination of early abortion of female fetuses and infanticide, in some areas of the world, has seriously disturbed the gender ratio. In India, it has been estimated that there are 0.5 million missing female births annually (Jha et al., 2006). The health consequences of violence obviously include adverse physical and mental effects. Apart from the risks of physical injuries and in some cases death, abused women are more likely to suffer from depression, anxiety, psychosomatic symptoms, eating problems, and sexual dysfunction.

Although the UN passed a Convention on the Elimination of All Forms of Discrimination against Women in 1979, it was not until 1993 that abuse was explicitly targeted by the Declaration on the Elimination of Violence against Women. The very existence of violent acts against women is a manifestation of an unequal relationship between men and women within a society (World Health Organization, 2003). Clearly, this has a long historical background. Apart from predisposing cultural attitudes toward women, some groups are at particular risk of abuse and violence. Examples include women in poverty, refugees, migrants, and minority groups.

As usual, the problem has to be dealt with at several levels. All countries should have strong laws prohibiting violent acts against women and, of course, those laws must be enforced. For example, the South African Constitution is a model of gender equality, yet violence against women in that country's informal settlements is a serious endemic problem. Slow changes in societal attitudes toward domestic violence do occur with time as economy and education improve, but the process can be speeded up (Penn & Nardos, 2003). Although it is a slow process, raising awareness of the issue of violence against women through educating boys and men is as important as passing laws protecting women's rights. It is also important to introduce education for the judicial

services, such as judges and police officers who enforce the rules.

In Brazil, specific police stations have been introduced that deal only with women's issues such as domestic violence; they are staffed by women. The cycle of abuse will be broken only by collaboration among educators, health care authorities, the judiciary, the police, and mass information services. The state should also provide shelters, legal aid, and medical services for girls and women who have suffered violence. Apart from enforcing appropriate punishment, there should also be a system of treatment and counselling for the perpetrators.

■ THE RIGHTS OF CHILDREN

Please, sir, I want some more.
— Charles Dickens, *Oliver Twist*

Prior to the 19th century, there were few supports for destitute children and little or no concept that a child might have rights. Abandoned children were collected by foundling hospitals, where they rapidly died. Children without homes either lived on the street or entered orphanages and workhouses. The idea of a long, happy childhood is a very recent development resulting from education and economic prosperity.

Development of Children's Rights

During the 19th century, there was a growing realization that children at least had the right to a roof over their heads. Dickens's work contributed to this sentiment. His books were accurate because he knew what he was writing about. By the age of 12, he had to work 10 hours a day, sticking labels on jars to support his family because his father was in debtors' prison. In the 1850s, it was estimated that 30,000 children were homeless in New York City alone. Charles Brace founded the Children's Aid Society in 1853 to help house these children. The approach of the day was to pick them off the streets and then send them west in trains to work on farms. This so-called "Orphan Train Movement" lasted into the 20th century and relocated over 120,000 children (Children's Aid Society, n.d.). A similar scheme was used in Britain. Between 1869 and the early 1930s, over 100,000 British "waifs and strays" were shipped off to Canada. Many suffered abuse and neglect while working as little more than bonded farm labourers (Snow, 2000).

The notion that children should be protected from the worst forms of child labour was reflected in the formation of the National Child Labor Committee in 1904 (*National Child Labor Committee*, n.d.). This organization still exists because there is still a need to protect children from exploitation in the workforce. The images of children working in early 20th-century America, captured by the society's photographer Lewis Hine, have become world famous (Freedman, 1998). The first humanitarian agency specifically aimed at children (Save the Children) was started in 1919 by the Jebb sisters in England. It was initially planned as a short-term organization designed to help feed children affected by World War I. Unfortunately, the need continued and it has now grown to become a large international agency (*International Save the Children Alliance*, n.d.).

Since World War II, all developed countries have established laws and societies aimed at protecting vulnerable children. However, until surprisingly recently, there was no international agreement specifically covering child rights. This was remedied in 1989 when a large meeting of world leaders accepted the Convention on the Rights of the Child (High Commission for Human Rights, 1989). One year later, it became the first legally binding international agreement establishing the basic rights of the world's children. It has been ratified and accepted by every country in the world except Somalia and the United States. The Committee on the Rights of Children monitors implementation of the basic convention and also the implementation of two optional protocols introduced in 2000 (Protocol on the Involvement of Children in Conflict and Protocol on the Sale of Children, Child Prostitution, and Child Pornography) (*Committee on the Rights of the Child*, n.d.). Other relevant legislation includes the Protocol to Prevent Trafficking in Persons (especially women and children), adopted in 2000, and the International Labour Organization's Convention on the Worst Forms of Child Labour, adopted in 1999. These "worst forms" include trafficking, sale of a child, sexual exploitation, debt bondage, pornography, or excessively hazardous work.

Child Labour

> But they answer, "Are your cowslips of
>   the meadows
> Like our weeds a near the mine?
> Leave us quiet in the dark of the coal
>   shadows
> From your pleasures fair and fine!"
>   —Elizabeth Barrett Browning,
>   "The Cry of the Children"

The above poem was written in 1843 at a time when British society was waking up to the fact that living conditions for the poor were truly appalling and certainly as bad as any developing country today. Although a bit sentimental for modern taste, it is impossible to read the poem without feeling a terrible sadness that such things were ever done to children (and are still done today). In 1833, the British Factory Commission Report revealed children were often employed from the age of six and made to work 14- to 16-hour days; they were kept awake by beating. The conditions in mines were even worse. The first legislation against child labour was passed in the same year that Barrett Browning wrote the above poem, but even then, it only raised the working age to nine years in factories and 10 years in the mines!

The concept that childhood is an age of innocence is a very recent development. When Daniel Defoe visited Halifax in 1727, he thought it admirable that no child above the age of four was idle (Defoe, 1727). The liberal philosopher, John Locke (1632–1704), recommended that poor children should be put to work at three years old, with a belly full of bread daily, supplemented, in cold weather, by a little warm gruel. In poor societies, children are viewed as small adults who have to work. Early in life, they are given jobs around the house and in the fields; this makes it very difficult to define acceptable and unacceptable forms of child labour.

Even the age limit of child labour is ambiguous. Most would agree that a six-year-old is too young to work, but where is the line to be drawn — 12 years, 14 years? Again, there is general agreement that the so-called "worst forms" of child labour (prostitution, forced labour, child soldiers, etc.) are all clearly unacceptable, but part-time work in the family shop or piecework picking fruit in a local farm are not nearly so clear-cut (International Labour Organization, 1999). The International Labour Organization (2002) keeps the best statistics on child labour. Table 12.2 gives the number of children around the world working in some form of economic activity. This

Figure 12.2: Young children working in dangerous and unhealthy conditions in a gravel quarry in Northern India. (Copyright Paul Jeffrey; GlobalAware. org.)

Table 12.2: Global estimates of economically active children in 2000

Age Group (years)	Total Population (1,000s)	Number at Work (1,000s)	Work Ratio (%)
5–9	600,200	73,100	12.2
10–14	599,200	137,700	23.0
15–17	332,100	140,900	42.4
Total	1,531,500	351,700	23.0

Source: International Labour Organization (2002)

includes unpaid and illegal work as well as work in the informal sector. In 2000, approximately 211 million children, five to 14 years of age, were working on a regular basis. Table 12.3 shows that the Asia and Pacific region has the greatest number of working children (particularly India), but Sub-Saharan Africa has the highest proportion of children working. In the developing world, roughly one of every

five children between five and 14 years works in some form on a regular basis. The gender ratio is equal until the age of 15.

A simple attitude of universal abolition is not sufficient to deal with the magnitude and complexity of child labour. Although pictures of children in the worst forms of forced labour are the ones that catch the most attention, this group is a relatively small part of the total. Of the 211 million five- to 14-year-olds working around the world, Table 12.4 shows that roughly 5 percent (8.4 million) are involved in work that is unarguably illegal. Obviously, every effort should be made to abolish all these practices, but what should be done about the remaining 95 percent? Working conditions for the less severe forms of labour vary from unacceptable (approximately 111 million children work in jobs defined as hazardous for age (Castro et al., 2005) to safe part-time employment. Boys outnumber girls in hazardous work across all age groups.

Table 12.3: Regional estimates of economically active children (five to 14 years) in 2000

Region	Number of Children Working (millions)	Work Ratio (%)
Developed countries	2.5	2
Transition economies	2.4	4
Asia and Pacific	127.3	19
Latin America and Caribbean	17.4	16
Sub-Saharan Africa	48.0	29
Middle East and North Africa	13.4	15
Total	211.0	18

Source: International Labour Organization (2002)

Table 12.4: Number of children in worst forms of child labour in 2000

Worst Form of Labour	Global Estimate (1,000s)
Trafficked children	1,200
Forced and bonded labour	5,700
Children in armed conflict	300
Child prostitution and pornography	1,800
Other illicit activities	600
Total	8,400*

Source: International Labour Organization (2002)

*Excludes trafficked children to avoid double counting

Children work for a variety of reasons, the most important of which is poverty (Admassie, 2002). Although children are not well paid, they still serve as major contributors to family income in very poor developing countries. In places where education is inaccessible or of low quality, many children work simply because there is nothing else to do. Parents may find no value in sending their children to school when they could be home learning a skill such as agriculture and supplementing the family income. Traditional practices are also important. There is still a pervasive notion, in some areas, that educated females will not get married or have children. Young girls may be raised solely to take care of the household duties in order to release the mother for paid labour. Such practices restrict the education of females and promote child employment. The acceptance of social class separation also perpetuates child labour. For example, people of India's lower castes are traditionally expected to perform manual labour; schooling may not even be considered.

There is a strong movement to abolish child labour in developing countries and require that children go to school (*International Programme on the Elimination of Child Labour*, 2002). This view is not as simple as it initially seems for a number of reasons. Although it is unfair that a young child should have to work every day, it is likely that many other factors in that child's life are also unfair. Simply banning work without putting in place other supportive social structures risks making a bad situation worse. This, of course, does not apply to the unconditional worst forms of child labour but, for the remainder, there are many grey areas to consider.

Children will not attend school without an economic change in their condition. Schools must make it worthwhile for children to attend in order to make up for lost earnings. One necessary provision is that these schools should be free. Another possibility is that schools serve food supplements. Parents might view this nutrition as valuable and so support school attendance. The quality of education should also be improved so that schooling is considered an important factor in the future success of a child. Only after the introduction of such substitutes will school attendance increase. Another problem with complete abolition of child labour is that education and employment for children are not mutually exclusive. Many children go to school and also work in their spare time. In fact, many children have to work, either to support their own tuition costs or those of their siblings.

Working children in developing countries may provide a significant income for their struggling family. Increasing economic prosperity, particularly increased family income, and education are probably the most reliable ways to reduce child labour (Hussain & Markus, 2003). During Britain's developing stage, children's contribution to family income paralleled those of present-day Peru and Paraguay. As a country develops, children start to consume more than they produce but, at certain levels of poverty, child labour may play an instrumental role in economic survival. Although the abolition of child labour is a worthwhile end, it is worth considering the situation carefully before making sweeping legislative changes (Basu & Tzannatos, 2003). From both theoretical and practical observations, it is clear that well-meaning but poorly designed policies can exacerbate the poverty in which these labouring children live. Removing their source of income without providing a substitute can lead to worsening poverty and may even force children into more undesirable forms of labour, such as prostitution.

Female Circumcision

Female circumcision (also known as "female genital cutting" or "female genital mutilation") is a term that covers a range of practices varying from a simple scratch of the clitoris to the partial or complete removal of the female genitalia. Box 12.5 gives the World Health Organization's classification system. It is widely practised in Central and Northern Africa and is almost universal in some countries such as Guinea, Egypt, Mali, and Eritrea (*Female genital cutting 1990–2004*, n.d.). It is also practised in parts of the Middle East and in small areas of Asia. Some immigrant populations have imported the practice to European countries and North America. The practice is not condoned by any major religion, but it is sometimes given religious significance. In Egypt and Sudan, female circumcision certainly predates both Christianity and Islam by many centuries.

Box 12.5: WHO Classification of FGM

Type I: Excision of prepuce and part or all of clitoris.
Type II: Excision of prepuce and clitoris together with partial or total excision of labia minora.
Type III: Infibulation: Excision of part or all of the external genitalia and stitching of the cut.
Type IV: Pricking, piercing, scraping, or other harming procedures to clitoris or labia. Introduction of herbs or corrosives into the vagina.

The justification for circumcision appears to be largely based on a belief that it will reduce sexual arousal in women (Kelly & Hillard, 2005), making them less likely to engage in premarital intercourse or adultery. There are many other justifications for the practice, including a belief that contact with the clitoris is harmful to the husband or newborn baby. In countries where circumcision is commonly performed, uncircumcised women may have difficulty finding a marriage partner. The side effects of the more mutilating procedures include hemorrhage, painful scars, and chronic urinary and pelvic infections. Later in life, it can cause sexual dysfunction, depression, and a wide range of gynecological and obstetric complications (Lovel et al., 2000).

The UN Convention on the Rights of the Child is ambiguous about female circumcision (High Commission for Human Rights, 1989). On one hand, Article 24 states that "parties shall take effective measures to abolish traditional practices prejudicial to the health of children," but Article 29 calls for "the development of respect for the child's parents and his/her own cultural identity and for the national values of the country in which the child is living." It is a question of personal rights, but whose rights? By making the eradication of female circumcision a human rights issue, it helps defuse accusations that this is just another example of cultural imperialism. Eradication of the worst forms of female circumcision is not aimed at cultures or religions; it is aimed at human rights.

The most mutilating forms of circumcision are found in areas of Northeast Africa. In other parts of the world, particularly in Indonesia and Malaysia, the procedure has largely evolved into a symbolic ceremony with limited injury to the genitalia. Many would argue this is now a cultural tradition that is no worse than the widely accepted circumcision of males. The WHO estimates that 100–140 million women currently live with the effects of the procedure and over a million are performed every year (Mohamud et al., 1999). Although it is important to pass laws making the practice illegal, legislation alone is not sufficient to reduce demand unless it is associated with interventions aimed at strategic points in society such as health professionals, health policy makers, and the mass media. Programs based on community advocacy by religious and community leaders, plus the substitution of an alternative rite that does not involve any cutting, have been shown to be successful in Kenya, Senegal, and Sudan (Almroth et al., 2001; Chege et al., 2001; Diop et al., 2004).

■ SUMMARY

Whether they are called natural rights, universal rights, or human rights, the concept that humans are entitled to a range of freedoms, simply because they are human, has taken a very long time to develop. Although there have been brief periods of enlightened rule in various countries, for much of human history average people have had little or no control over their own lives or over those who rule them. The theoretical ideas of human rights proposed by philosophers in the 17th and 18th centuries finally reached practical application during the late 18th century in the popular revolutions of America and France. It still took another 150 years and two world wars before the majority of the world's countries would come together in the mid-20th century to sign the first universal declaration of human rights.

It is easy to forget just how recently protocols against slavery, exploitation of children, and violence against women have been widely ratified. For example, universal agreement on the rights of children was not reached until the end of the 20th century. It is also easy to forget that the rights, privileges, and, perhaps above all, the freedom from daily fear enjoyed by much of the world is just a dream for those unfortunate enough to live under the world's most oppressive regimes. Arbitrary arrest, state-sanctioned torture, religious or political persecution and a host of other abuses are still daily realities for many of the world's population.

In a society where abuse and repression are the norm, it is difficult for donor agencies and the local people to escape the dead hand of their government and participate as full partners in aid projects. There has been a growing realization that the absence of human rights acts as a very real barrier to successful development work. Sustainable improvements in population health require more than medical treatment and economic initiatives. Long-lasting gains have to be based on a foundation of social change and improved rights and freedoms for that population. Such changes are becoming an increasingly important part of large-scale population health initiatives.

RESOURCES

References

Admassie, A. (2002). "Explaining the high incidence of child labour in Sub-Saharan Africa." *African Development Review, 14,* 251–275.

African National Congress. (n.d.). *The Mandela page.* Retrieved from www.anc.org.za/people/mandela.

Almroth, L., et al. (2001). "A community-based study on the change of practice of female genital mutilation in a Sudanese village." *International Journal of Gynecology and Obstetrics, 74,* 179–185.

Annan, K. (2005). *In large freedom: Towards development, security, and human rights for all.* Retrieved from www.un.org/largerfreedom/contents.htm.

Anti-Slavery International. (n.d.). *What is modern slavery?* Retrieved from www.antislavery.org/homepage/antislavery/modern.htm.

Australian Human Rights Commission. (2001). *What are human rights?* Retrieved from www.hreoc.gov.au/hr_explained/what.html.

Ayton-Shenker, D. (1995). *The challenge of human rights and cultural diversity.* Retrieved from www.un.org/rights/dpi1627e.htm.

Bales, K. (2004). *Disposable people: New slavery in the global economy.* Berkeley and Los Angeles: University of California Press.

Basu, K., & Tzannatos, Z. (2003). "The global child labour problem: What do we know and what can we do?" *The World Bank Review, 17,* 147–173.

Boeing. (n.d.). *747 family.* Retrieved from www.boeing.com/commercial/747family.

Caine, D., & Caine, C. (2005). "Child camel jockeys: A present-day tragedy involving children and sport." *Clinical Journal of Sports Medicine, 15,* 287–289.

Castro, C., et al. (2005). "The SIMPOC Philippine survey of children 2001: A data source for analyzing occupational injuries to children." *Public Health Report, 120,* 631–640.

Chege, J., et al. (2001). *An assessment of the alternative rites approach for encouraging abandonment of female genital mutilation in Kenya.* Retrieved from www.popcouncil.org/pdfs/frontiers/FR_FinalReports/Kenya_FGC.pdf.

Children's Aid Society. (n.d.). *The orphan train movement.* Retrieved from www.childrensaidsociety.org/about/train.

Committee on the Rights of the Child. (n.d.). Retrieved from www.ohchr.org/english/bodies/crc.

Council of Europe. (2006). *Action against trafficking in human beings.* Retrieved from www.coe.int/T/E/human_rights/trafficking.

Defoe, D. (1727). *A tour through the whole island of Great Britain.* London: Everyman's.

Derks, A. (2000). *Combating trafficking in South-East Asia.* Geneva: International Organization for Migration. Retrieved from www.iom.int/documents/publication/en/mrs_2_2000.pdf.

Diop, N., et al. (2004). *The TOSTAN program: Evaluation of a community-based education program in Senegal.* Retrieved from www.popcouncil.org/pdfs/frontiers/FR_FinalReports/Senegal_Tostan%20FGC.pdf.

Donnelly, J. (2003). *The universal declaration model in: Universal human rights.* Ithaca: Cornell University Press.

Dottridge, M. (2002). "Trafficking in children in West and Central Africa." *Gender and Development, 10,* 38–49.

Fairtrade Foundation. (n.d.). Retrieved from www.fairtrade.org.uk.

Female genital cutting 1990–2004. (n.d.). Retrieved from www.measuredhs.com/topics/gender/FGC-CD.

Freedman, R. (1998). *Kids at work: Lewis Hine and the crusade against child labour.* New York: Clarion Books.

High Commission for Human Rights. (1989). *Convention on the Rights of the Child*. Retrieved from www.unhchr.ch/html/menu3/b/k2crc.htm.

Human Rights Center, University of California, Berkeley. (2004). *Hidden slaves: Forced labour in the United States*. Retrieved from www.freetheslaves.net/files/Hidden_Slaves.pdf.

Hussain, M., & Markus, K. (2003). "Child labour use and economic growth: An econometric analysis." *World Economy, 26,* 993–1017.

International Criminal Court. (n.d.). Retrieved from www.icc-cpi.int.

International Labour Organization. (1999). *Convention C182, Worst Forms of Child Labour.* Retrieved from www.ilo.org/ilolex/cgi-lex/convde.pl?C182.

International Labour Organization. (2002). *Every child counts: New global estimates on child labour.* Retrieved from www.ilo.org/public/english/standards/ipec/simpoc/others/globalest. pdf.

International Programme on the Elimination of Child Labour. (n.d.). Retrieved from www.ilo.org/public/english/standards/ipec.

International Save the Children Alliance. (n.d.). Retrieved from www.savethechildren.net/alliance/index.html.

Jeyaseelan, L., et al. (2004). "World studies of abuse in the family environment: Risk factors for physical intimate partner violence." *Injury Control and Safety Promotion, 11,* 117–124.

Jha, P., et al. (2006). "Low male-to-female sex ratio of children born in India: National survey of 1.1 million households." *Lancet, 367,* 211–218.

Jok, J. (2001). *War and slavery in Sudan.* Philadelphia: University of Pennsylvania Press.

Kelly, E. (2002). *Journeys of jeopardy: A review of research on trafficking in women and children in Europe* (International Organization for Migration, Research Series, no. 11). Retrieved from www.un.org/depts/dhl/slavery.

Kelly, E., & Hillard, P. (2005). "Female genital mutilation." *Current Opinion in Obstetrics and Gynecology, 17,* 490–494.

Laczko, F., & Gozdziack, E. (Eds.). (2005). *Data and research on human trafficking: A global survey.* Geneva: International Organization for Migration. Retrieved from www.iom.int/DOCUMENTS/PUBLICATION/EN/Data_and_Research_on_Human_Trafficking.pdf.

Lovel, H., et al. (2000). *A systematic review of the health complications of female genital mutilation.* Retrieved from www.who.int/reproductive-health/docs/fgm.html.

Mohamud, A., et al. (1999). *Female genital mutilation programs to date: What works and what doesn't.* Geneva: World Health Organization. Retrieved from www.who.int/reproductive-health/publications/fgm/fgm_programmesreview.html.

Mukhopadhyay, K. (1995). "Girl prostitution in India." *Social Change, 25,* 143–153.

National Child Labor Committee. (n.d.). Retrieved from www.kapow.org/nclc.htm.

Omelaniuk, I. (2005). *Trafficking in human beings.* Retrieved from www.un.org/esa/population/publications/ittmigdev2005/P15_IOmelaniuk.pdf.

Penn, M., & Nardos, R. (2003). *Overcoming violence against women and girls: The international campaign to eradicate a worldwide problem.* Lanham: Rowman and Littlefield.

Pope, N. (2005). *Honor killings.* London: Palgrave Macmillan.

Rayner, M. (2006). *History of universal human rights: Up to WW2.* Retrieved from www. universalrights.net/main/histof.htm.

Snow, P. (2000). *Neither waif nor stray: The search for a stolen identity.* Boca Raton: Universal Publishers.

Spiegel, S. (2005). "Reducing mercury and responding to the global gold rush." *Lancet, 366,* 2070–2072.

UN High Commission for Human Rights. (2000). *Protocol to prevent, suppress, and punish trafficking in persons, especially women and children.* Retrieved from www.ohchr.org/english/law/protocoltraffic.htm.

UNICEF. (2006) *Maternal mortality*. Retrieved from www.childinfo.org/areas/ maternalmortality.

United Nations. (1998). *Human rights today: A United Nations' priority*. Retrieved from www. un.org/rights/HRToday.

United Nations. (n.d.-a). *The International Bill of Human Rights*. Retrieved from www.unhchr. ch/html/menu6/2/fs2.htm.

United Nations. (n.d.-b). *Universal Declaration of Human Rights*. Retrieved from www.un.org/ Overview/rights.html.

US Department of State. (2005). *Trafficking in persons annual report*. Retrieved from www.state. gov/g/tip.

Vayrynen, R. (2003). *Illegal immigration, human trafficking, and organized crime* (World Institute for Development Economics Research, discussion paper 2003/72). Retrieved from www.wider. unu.edu.

Wattles, J. (1996). *The golden rule*. Oxford: Oxford University Press.

Watts, C., & Zimmerman, C. (2002). "Violence against women: Global scope and magnitude." *Lancet, 359*, 1232–1237.

World Health Organization. (2003). *Multi-country study on women's health and domestic violence against women*. Retrieved from www.who.int/gender/violence/who_multicountry_study/ en/index.html.

Recommended Reading

Bales, K. (2004). *Disposable people: New slavery in the global economy*. Berkeley and Los Angeles: University of California Press.

Gruenbaum, E. (2000). *The female circumcision controversy: An anthropological perspective*. Baltimore: Johns Hopkins University Press.

Hochschild, A. (2006). *Bury the chains: Prophets and rebels in the fight to free an Empire's slaves*. Boston: Mariner Books.

Ishay, M. (2004). *The history of human rights: From ancient times to the globalization era*. Berkeley and Los Angeles: University of California Press.

Jok, J. (2001). *War and slavery in Sudan*. Philadelphia: University of Pennsylvania Press.

Kyle, D., & Koslowski, R. (2001). *Global human smuggling: Comparative perspectives*. Baltimore: Johns Hopkins University Press.

Meltzer, M. (1993). *Slavery: A world history*. New York: Da Capo Press.

Schmitz, C., et al. (Eds.). (2004). *Child labor: A global view*. Westport: Greenwood Press.

Weston, B. (2005). *Child labour and human rights: Making children matter*. Boulder: Lynne Rienner Publishers.

PART V

OTHER ASPECTS OF INTERNATIONAL HEALTH

Chapter 13
Natural and Humanitarian Disasters and Displaced Populations

Chapter 14
Health of Indigenous Populations

Natural and Humanitarian Disasters and Displaced Populations

"God's work," he would say
When the rain pelted down
And the floods rushed in the rivers
And storms lashed the tree-tops
"God's work!"
God should play more.
—Ian McDonald, "God's Work"

OBJECTIVES

After completing this chapter, you should be able to

- appreciate the human and financial costs associated with wars and natural disasters
- understand the differences between refugees, migrants, and other types of displaced populations
- understand the harsh realities of life as a refugee and develop a list of priorities aimed at keeping a refugee population as healthy as possible
- understand the general organizational framework needed to manage a complex human emergency

---

Wars and natural disasters (plus the forced migrant populations they produce) are constants in human history. On a global scale, the most common disaster facing a large number of developing countries is caring for displaced refugees. For the individual working in an unstable region, the most likely disaster scenario is a large influx of refugees secondary to local war. The human and financial costs of disasters are enormous. Their effects are felt worldwide so disasters should be part of any study of international health. As the recent Asian tsunami and Pakistan earthquake show, these events are not rare. Since their burden falls disproportionately upon countries with limited resources, anyone working in a developing country should have a good idea of the health problems confronting a displaced population. This module looks at the causes behind large-scale population migrations (particularly natural and humanitarian disasters) and also the international structures that have been developed to deal with these enormously complex problems. We will also look at the essential requirements needed to reduce mortality among a refugee population.

■ NATURAL DISASTERS

We had scarce sat down, when darkness overspread us, not like a moonless or cloudy night, but of a room when it is shut up and the lamp put out. You could hear the shrieks of women, the crying of children and the shouts of men.

> —Pliny the Younger, eyewitness account of the destruction of Pompeii, AD 79

The American College of Emergency Physicians defines a disaster as occurring when the effects of natural or manmade forces overwhelm the ability of a particular region to meet the demand for health care.

The Center for Research on Epidemiology of Disasters (CRED) was established in 1973 in Belgium. The organization collects data on all emergencies that have a significant human impact, including natural disasters such as hurricanes and earthquakes and also complex humanitarian emergencies such as famine and armed conflict (Center for Research on the Epidemiology of Disasters, n.d.-a, n.d.-b). As Figure 13.1 shows, disasters kill a significant number of people each year but, when expressed as a rate, the chance of being killed in a disaster is very small—no higher than 10 per million per decade (Figure 13.2). However, the total death rate is not the best indicator of the final human and economic cost of disasters.

In the decade starting 1994, Guha-Sapir et al. (2004) estimate that more than 255 million people (range 68–618 million) were affected by natural disasters every year and the average annual mortality was 58,000 people (range 10,000–133,000). In the same time period, the damage caused by disasters cost $67 billion per year (range $28–230 billion). This cost has increased

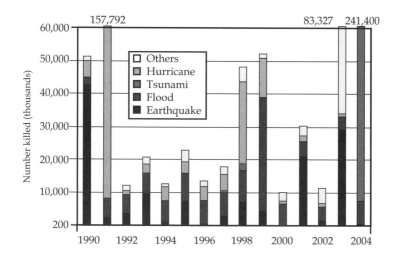

Figure 13.1: Annual deaths from disasters and the major types of disaster (1990–2004)

Source: Guha-Sapir et al. (2004)

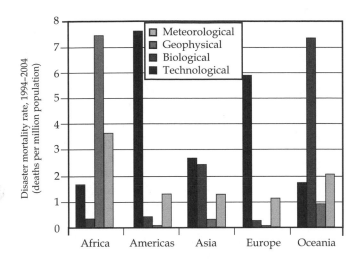

Figure 13.2: Average population death rates from disasters (1994–2004)

Meteorological: Floods, storms, avalanches, heat waves, drought
Geophysical: Earthquakes, tsunamis, volcanoes
Biological: Epidemics, insect infestations
Technological: Industrial accidents, transport accidents

Source: International Strategy for Disaster Reduction (n.d.)

14-fold since the 1950s. When the figures are averaged out, disasters cause roughly $1 billion of damage, kill 1,000 people and, in some way, adversely affect 5 million people every single week. During 2003, one in 25 people worldwide was affected by a natural disaster.

Major disasters are surprisingly common. As the population grows, more people live in areas at high risk of recurring events such as floods, hurricanes, and earthquakes. Consequently, the total number of disasters affecting humans rises steadily each decade (Figure 13.3). For each person that dies, many times that number are injured or economically affected. Despite the chaos surrounding the recent hurricane Katrina response, developed countries generally have the resources to minimize the adverse effects of natural disasters, but this comes with an impressive bill. The last few years have witnessed the most costly disasters in history, both in terms of lives and money. Hurricane Andrew cost $35 billion in 1992 and the 1995 Kobe earthquake caused $100 billion of property damage plus $50 billion

in reduced economic output. Hurricane Katrina caused $100 billion damage in New Orleans alone; the final bill will probably reach $200 billion (Schiermeier, 2006).

There is nothing new about disasters. The Minoan civilization was destroyed by the vast eruption and probable tsunami following the eruption of Santorini in 1600 BC. The early walls of Troy were toppled by earthquakes and the first eyewitness account of a disaster was written by Pliny the Younger, who described the eruption of Vesuvius in AD 79 that buried Pompeii. His uncle died in the disaster while trying to save a family friend. Some disasters attract considerable attention, while others are soon forgotten. Most people remember hurricane Mitch in 1998 as it killed over 10,000 people during its course through Central America. However, major earthquakes in Northern Afghanistan (1998, over 5,000 dead), Gujarat, India (2001, 20,000 dead), or Bam, Iran (2003, over 25,000 dead) attracted little media attention even while they were happening.

Figure 13.3: Number and type of disasters per decade for the last 50 years

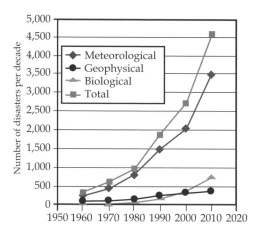

Meteorological: Floods, storms, avalanches, droughts, heat waves
Geophysical: Earthquakes, tsunamis, volcanoes
Biological: Epidemics, insect infestations
2010 predictions based on 2005 figures

Source: International Strategy for Disaster Reduction (n.d.)

As hurricane Katrina and the recent Pakistan earthquake have shown, the global effects of disasters are becoming increasingly important. Although death rates are small compared to the major infectious killers, the total numbers of people affected through property damage and economic disruption are significant. Anyone working overseas in a developing country should have a good practical knowledge of the care necessary for displaced populations. Table 13.1 lists some of the major disasters of recent times under various categories.

Disaster Management

Eritrea received seven truckloads of expired aspirin tablets that took six months to burn; a container full of unsolicited cardiovascular drugs with two months to expiry; and 30,000 bottles of expired amino acid infusion that could not be disposed of anywhere near the settlement because of the smell. Hogerzeil, et al. (1997)

Apart from immediate injury and loss of life, the property damage associated with a disaster can lead to deteriorating sanitation and environmental health with increased risk of communicable diseases. The desire of people to help others under these circumstances is quite understandable, but the enthusiasm of some responders greatly exceeds their competence. Health care is a serious undertaking at the best of times. Under suboptimal conditions of war and disaster where teams may face very real physical danger, high levels of training, coordination, and continuous assessment are vital. The need for international standards governing the coordination and management of disaster response teams is an urgent priority. Until quite recently, disasters have been viewed as unavoidable acts of God. Money and research were predominantly devoted to the emergency response effort. However, over the last few years, the concept of mitigating disasters through risk assessment and management has gained increased attention.

International Framework for Disaster Management

The United Nations Agency responsible for coordinating emergency relief is the Office for the Coordination of Humanitarian Affairs (OCHA). This was formed in 1998 from the earlier UN Disaster Relief Coordinator. A separate department of OCHA called the Integrated Regional Information Network (IRIN)

Table 13.1: Major disasters by type in recent times

Type of Disaster	Year	Results
Hurricanes:		
Katrina, US	2005	1,400 dead, as much as $200 billion damage.
Bay of Bengal	1970	Probably the biggest ever natural disaster. Bhola cyclone hit low-lying land. Estimated 500,000 deaths from drowning.
Tsunamis:		
Indian Ocean	2004	Enormous tsunami triggered by 9.1 earthquake. Over 200,000 people killed in India, Sri Lanka, Indonesia. Millions more left homeless and destitute.
Papua New Guinea	1998	Earthquake/tsunami, north coast of PNG, over 2000 dead.
Earthquakes:		
Kashmir	2005	Exact impact not known, but more than 80,000 deaths in remote regions. Millions left homeless in winter conditions.
Tangshan, China	1976	Official death toll 250,000, but probably much higher. Huge social impact; precipitated the end of the Cultural Revolution.
Volcanoes:		
Colombia	1985	Eruption of Nevado del Ruiz destroyed local town under a mudslide, killing 25,000 people.
Montserrat	1995	Recurrent eruptions since 1995. Death toll low, but much of the island has been destroyed. Population forced to emigrate.
Industrial:		
Bhopal, India	1984	Methyl isocyanate release; 4,000 dead instantly, thousands more over the few next years.
Chernobyl, Ukraine	1986	Reactor explosion; 30 dead instantly, thousands claimed dead over the next few years. Widespread radioactive contamination.
Biological:		
SARS epidemic	2002–2003	Worldwide infection (probably corona virus); 8,000 cases, 10 percent mortality. Enormous social and economic disruption.
Influenza epidemic	1968–1969	Most recent influenza epidemic (H3N2 strain). Approximately 1 million died worldwide.
Heat wave:		
Europe	2003	Widespread heat wave, total of 40,000 people died, 10,000 in France, 15,000 in Italy.
Southern US	1980	Heat wave caused estimated 1,500 deaths. Simultaneous drought caused US $4 billion (1980 dollars) agriculture losses.

acts as a specialized news agency that provides a broad range of radio, film, and news services concerning disasters. The Emergency Relief Coordinator (ERC) in charge of OCHA has access to immediate funds for humanitarian disasters through the Central Emergency Response Fund (CERF). It currently contains $450 million. In 2004, the WHO agency responsible for coordinating emergency responses (Health Action in Crises) started a three-year project with the aim of improving the efficiency and coordination of the world's disaster response efforts (*Integrated Regional Information Network*, n.d.; *United Nations Office for the Coordination of Humanitarian Affairs*, n.d.; World Health Organization, n.d.-a).

In general, once a disaster reaches the world's headlines, people are surprisingly generous; there is feeling that something must be done and done quickly. This can lead to considerable inappropriate effort such as airlifts of shoes, discarded clothing, and high-technology field hospitals, which simply add to the chaos. Disaster management attracts a lot of research attention and is emerging as a specific medical subspecialty with at least two medical journals devoted to the topic. There are also several field handbooks guiding management priorities during a disaster. The handbooks published by Médecins Sans Frontières and UNICEF both provide reliable guidelines for management priorities (Médecins Sans Frontières, 1997; UNICEF, 2005). The Sphere Project, started in 1997 by a group of NGOs, including the Red Cross and Red Crescent societies, has developed a useful handbook on the management of key disasters, but has also broken new ground by establishing standards of good practice and accountability (Sphere Project, 2004).

Common Problems with Disaster Responses

Emergency medical aid is not for amateurs.

— *Lancet* editorial

Apart from cases of acute trauma during the initial emergency, there is nothing medically unique about disasters, except the numbers involved. The sudden compression of large numbers of people into small areas, with poor sanitation and shelter, will inevitably lead to the usual diseases of poverty and overcrowding. As long as security can be assured, these problems are manageable using the basic principles of primary health care. This relief work should be done by agencies that are coordinated and, above all, are staffed by people who know what they are doing. The basic essentials of management will be covered later in the chapter, but some general comments about the problems associated with emergency responses are necessary at this stage.

Disasters are chaotic situations and large-scale emergency response efforts are still a relatively new development. Under these circumstances, it should be no surprise to learn that those efforts

Table 13.2: A moment of Zen

Average prevalence of childhood obesity (Body Mass Index > 95 percent for age) in US:	Average prevalence of severe underweight among children (< 3 standard deviations below median weight for age) in least developed countries:
10 percent	**10 percent**
Source: Dehghan et al. (2005)	Source: UNICEF (2006)

are frequently poorly coordinated and ineffective. This is not to say that the correct approach is a mystery. There is plenty of literature concerning best practice in humanitarian disasters. (Active Learning Network for Accountability and Performance in Humanitarian Action (n.d.) holds 500 reports in its accessible database.) Well-established recommendations concerning staff selection and training, team coordination, outcome assessment, and management have been established (Adinolfi et al., 2005). The problem concerns the application of those recommendations.

Although the extraordinary worldwide humanitarian response to the Indian Ocean tsunami mounted in early 2005 did have some positive end results, the process was far from perfect. It was so far from perfect, in fact, that the WHO organized a conference on the lessons to be learned from the international response as early as May 2005. The UN held a similar review process in August. The final reports (McGarry et al., 2005) from these two meetings contain many suggestions for improvements, the most significant of which are:

- *Coordination:* Several coordinating bodies exist, including the Interagency Standing Committee (WHO), the Disaster Emergency Committee (UK), and Alliance 2015 (various international NGOs). Unfortunately, there is room for improved coordination among these various groups. Complicating matters further are groups fired with religious or political certainties that feel no need (and are under no obligation) to talk to anyone. During the recent tsunami, over 300 agencies were registered with district health authorities in Ampara, Eastern Sri Lanka; many more remained unregistered. This can lead to the absurd situation of different groups actually fighting over patients. Clearly, there is a need for a unified international disaster coordination system (*Disasters Emergency Committee,* n.d.; World Health Organization, n.d.-b).

- *Competence:* The *Lancet* editorial quoted above should be noted. Emergencies are not places for untrained amateurs, and enthusiasm is no substitute for competence ("Emergency medical aid is not for amateurs," 1996). The UN recommends not only that there should be far fewer disaster response agencies, but also that their quality (in terms of personnel training and internal management) should be much higher. India solved the problem by refusing to accept any foreign aid after the tsunami. The Sphere Project (2004) has made a good start by establishing minimum standards of training required by emergency responders, but recommendations are of no use without monitoring and implementation.

- *Needs assessment:* Many agencies start by performing an initial needs assessment. Unfortunately, these assessments are usually neither standardized nor shared. Multiple assessments not only waste time, but also subject stressed populations to repeated questioning by different groups.

There is clearly a need for a unified disaster assessment system that identifies initial needs but also includes long-term surveillance and outcome measurements; there are signs of improvement. The UN Disaster Assessment and Coordination Team (UNDAC) consists of disaster management experts who can be rapidly deployed, within hours, to carry out an initial assessment of priority needs. The Field Assessment and Coordination Team (FACT) performs the same function for the International Federation of Red Cross and Red Crescent societies. Their assessment and coordination systems are compatible with UNDAC.

- *Forensics:* Most developing countries do not have the capacity to handle large numbers of casualties. The great majority of deaths in the Asian tsunami went unrecorded. In the rush to bury or cremate victims, adequate forensic information was not collected. There was also no standardization in forensic identification, which varied from Polaroid photos to DNA testing. The UN recommended that a pool of forensic pathologists should work to establish international standards for disaster victim identification and also for the safe storage of mass victims (Tun et al., 2005).

- *Women:* Gender imbalances, present worldwide, are exacerbated by acute disasters. Families headed by female survivors are particularly vulnerable to poverty and ill health during the disaster recovery phase. The reproductive health and safety issues unique to women should be given particular priority following a disaster (Chunkath et al., 2005). This will include feeding supplementation for pregnant women and also an emphasis on security.

- *Psychological trauma:* There also needs to be a wider understanding of the psychological trauma and chronic mental illness associated with the survivors of major disasters. Whole communities

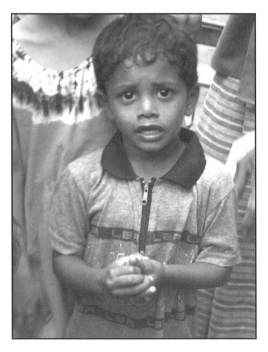

Figure 13.4: A young Sri Lankan boy photographed in a refugee camp three weeks after the Asian tsunami destroyed his coastal fishing village. Although he was physically unharmed, the psychological scars are clearly visible in his face and posture.

can be devastated by the psychological effects of a disaster. Support and counselling can be established within the community, particularly within the schools, but expert assistance is required to plan the necessary programs. "Counselling" is a term that has suffered from common use. Helping the child shown in Figure 13.4 to recover from psychological trauma requires long-term commitment and the assistance of professionally qualified staff. Properly planned, long-term counselling initiatives (given in the local language by trained local staff) are an important part of the recovery process. However, sessions given by well-meaning but untrained short-term visitors may well do more harm than good. Once schools restarted in Sri Lanka following the tsunami, self-appointed "counsellors" became so disruptive that the education authority had to ban all foreigners from the schools. This complicated matters for legitimate professional teams.

Disaster Mitigation

During the last two years, the world has witnessed some of the worst disasters in history, including the Asian tsunami, drought in Africa, hurricanes in the Gulf Coast and Central America, and the Pakistan earthquake. The world's biggest disaster insurance company, Munich Re Group (2004), estimates that disasters in the 1990s cost $608 billion—greater than total losses over the previous four decades combined. The concept that disasters can be mitigated by good planning is a surprisingly recent development. Given the expected increase in weather-related disasters, secondary to global warming, it is a timely development. The United Nations Agency responsible for disaster reduction planning is the UN International Strategy for Disaster Reduction (UNISDR).

Interest in the subject of disaster mitigation is growing. The annual *World Disasters Report*, published by the International Federation of Red Cross and Red Crescent Societies (2005), focused on disaster risk reduction in its 2002 edition. Increasing numbers of reports and recommendations are now available on the subject, and a recent world conference to discuss disaster mitigation was held in Kobe, Japan (Wisner & Walker, 2005). The topic has also earned its own acronym— Disaster Mitigation and Preparedness (DMP).

An exhaustive 2005 World Bank report on natural disaster hot spots revealed that over half of the world's population is exposed to one or more major natural hazards. It points out that between 1980 and 2003, the World Bank provided $14.4 billion in emergency lending to 20 developing world countries suffering from disasters (Dilley et al., 2005). The adverse economic effects of a large disaster add huge debts to a country, which slow its subsequent recovery and future development. Disasters should not be viewed as rare occurrences that affect only a few thousand people. In many parts of the world, they are relatively common and they can affect the lives of millions of people—even whole countries. The planning and management needed to reduce disaster damage should now be an integral part of development aid programs. Disasters are no longer "just" a humanitarian issue.

Disaster risk reduction is an enormous subject; it can be covered only briefly in this space, but there are several excellent sources for further research (Department for International Development, 2005). In summary, disaster mitigation consists of three broad elements:

- *Risk analysis:* Risk management must be based on the identification of risk based on the best available science (Dilley et al., 2005). The principal hazards facing a country depend on the vulnerability of populations in high-risk areas, the availability of disaster response teams, building standards, and the country's previous history of meteorological and geological disasters. Based on this complex analysis, it is possible to arrive at estimates of degree of risk and the expected impact of the most likely natural disasters.

- *Disaster mitigation:* A comprehensive mitigation program requires coordinated initiatives established at many levels of society (Kreimer & Arnold, 2000). Depending on the risk a country faces, mitigation might include land use regulations such as limiting building within 100 metres of the seashore, as was discussed in Sri Lanka; changes in building codes so that at least hospitals and schools meet earthquake requirements; and population warning systems such as sirens, radio broadcasts, and the currently discussed Pacific tsunami early warning system. Clearly, these must be backed up by enforcement and widespread population education. For example, education about earthquake response is a routine part of schooling in Japan and California. Every country should have a formal national disaster strategy based on their own estimate of risk and, of course, their available resources. The need for coordinated civil defence responses (and the use of army detachments) emphasizes the fact that efficient disaster preparedness can be achieved only with a national effort. The development and testing of emergency evacuation plans should be a continuing and routine process.

- *Disaster risk insurance:* In order to stop countries from entering a spiral of economic depression, from which it may take decades to recover, there are early moves to shift some of the financial burden onto disaster risk insurers (Kreimer, 1999). Regional insurance markets have been proposed that make the market size more attractive to the insurance industry and also lower the cost to individual countries. Another option, still in its infancy, is the issue of disaster bonds.

▌HUMANITARIAN DISASTERS

This is the excellent foppery of the world, that, when we are sick in fortune, often the surfeits of our own behaviour, we make guilty of our disasters, the sun, the moon, and the stars.

—Shakespeare, *King Lear*

The expression "complex humanitarian disaster" (also "complex emergency") was first used in the early 1990s by the United Nations to describe the increasing number of humanitarian crises typified by the chronic war and social disruption in Somalia and Sudan (Munslow & Brown, 1999). A complex humanitarian emergency may be defined as a situation where:

1. Political authority and public services deteriorate or collapse completely as a result of internal ethnic, tribal, or religious conflicts.
2. Widespread violence against civilians and mass starvation due to lack of food supply result in enormous population displacements.
3. Inadequate public health emergencies cause epidemics of communicable disease.
4. The chaos leads to macroeconomic collapse with general unemployment and destruction of the currency.

It is commonly claimed that complex emergencies are largely the result of the political changes caused by the end of the Cold War. While it is true that the abrupt loss of external influence caused enormous changes in many countries, the results were not always negative. Some countries (such as Germany, Poland, South Africa, and Czechoslovakia) navigated these new political waters without disaster, while others (such as the former Yugoslavia, Afghanistan, and the former Zaire) did not. Complex disasters did not begin with the fall of the Berlin Wall in 1989; they have been around for centuries. The name might have changed, but there is nothing new about revolution and human brutality.

The chaos of the Russian Revolution, the years of war following the French Revolution, and the more recent Chinese Cultural Revolution are all examples of lethal combinations of continuous unrest, economic collapse, widespread starvation, and disintegrating political authority that are currently called complex emergencies. The loss of superpower support for various tyrants and puppet governments acted as a catalyst, in some countries, for long simmering tensions to erupt into war. When complicated by economic collapse, drought, and crop failure, some degenerated into intractable chronic emergencies; African states have been particularly badly affected. Examples include Burundi, Sierra Leone, Rwanda, the former Zaire, Liberia, and Guinea-Bissau (Lautze et al., 2004). Somalia's war has been so destructive that the state has actually failed. In the absence of an effective national government, the country has been divided up between warlords.

Wars have changed over the last century. Conflicts fought between countries, such as the Iraq–Iran War of 20 years ago, are now uncommon. Civilians were certainly killed in "old-fashioned" wars, but they were usually not directly targeted. The mass indiscriminate bombings of cities in World War II started to change that attitude. Most modern conflicts now occur within countries and are often associated with deliberate targeting of civilians (including humanitarian workers). The very darkest side of human nature is reflected in brutal abuses of human rights, including mass murder, mutilations, sexual violence, and forced displacement of huge numbers of people (Fennell, 1998).

Internal destruction of the usual economic and social structures necessary for a functioning state contributes to a permanent state of insecurity, where a small, powerful elite rules the subjugated majority. In the colonial past, revolutions have been justified in the name of freedom from oppression, but there are no heroes or noble sentiments behind these current wars (Collier & Hoeffler, 2001). Modern conflicts are motivated by greed rather than grievance — greed for natural resources such as oil (Angola, Sudan) and diamonds (Sierra Leone, Democratic Republic of Congo) or for power and control over historical opponents (Rwanda).

Apart from death and disabilities caused by fighting, the health effects of chronic violence are enormous. Family disruption, forced displacement, economic and agricultural collapse, and a range of other factors (including unplotted land mines and environmental destruction) all contribute to lives of absolute misery and ill health for the powerless majority. Long-term solutions can be achieved only through political and increasingly military alternatives. Humanitarian interventions, based on models developed for natural

disasters, can only scratch the surface of these problems by providing some support for starving displaced populations. There has been considerable criticism that humanitarian interventions might even make complex disasters worse (Macrae & Leader, 2001). The legal status afforded to refugee populations inadvertently protects combatants who are illegally mixed among those refugees; the value of food and donated goods acts as a further source of trouble.

Complex emergencies pose enormous ethical dilemmas for humanitarian agencies; the Rwandan genocide of 1994 was a good example. Once the Rwandan Patriotic Front, under Paul Kagame, started to regain control of the country, those responsible for the genocide fled with their families into neighbouring countries (particularly what was then eastern Zaire). It is estimated that there were 2 million refugees, a proportion of whom had been guilty of appalling crimes. A huge humanitarian effort was mounted to support these refugees under very

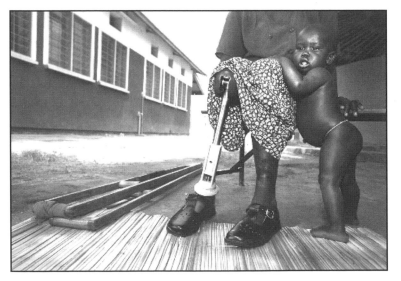

Figure 13.5: A Ugandan woman recently fitted with a prosthesis. She had lost her leg six years earlier due to a land mine. (Photographer Sven Torfinn; courtesy IRIN news.)

difficult circumstances. Over the next two years, camps became militarized and were used as bases to launch attacks against the new Rwandan government (Terry, 2002). The international community failed to disarm the camps and simply reacted by withdrawing their support, leaving the United Nations High Commissioner for Refugees (UNHCR) to do the best it could (Chaulia, 2002). The situation steadily worsened until, in 1996, combined attacks on the camps by Zairean rebels and Rwandan military killed many tens of thousands of people (Banatrala et al., 1998). The entire area was destabilized and descended into chronic war that still drags on today.

The Great Lakes refugee crisis was a watershed for many large agencies; there was a definite loss of innocence where complex emergencies were concerned (Rieff, 2002). Did the humanitarian response actually contribute to the Congo wars or was it simply a small part of an endlessly complex situation? The accusation that UNHCR was knowingly feeding murderers was answered by Sadako Ogata (the UN high commissioner at the time), who said, "There were also innocent refugees in the camps; more than half were women and children. Should we have said, 'You are related to murderers, so you are guilty too?'" Apart from the moral dilemmas, 26 UNHCR field personnel were killed or missing.

The Evolution of Responses to Complex Emergencies (Lautze et al., 2004)

The beginning of the modern response to complex emergencies is probably dated to the intervention in the Biafran War at the end of the 1960s. The inadequacy of the international response prompted a group of French doctors working in Biafra to start a new group, Médecins Sans Frontières (MSF), which would concentrate on the victims rather than worrying about political implications. These apolitical intentions were tested severely during the response to the Cambodian genocide in the late 1970s. Many NGOs, including MSF, had to start dealing with the ethical dilemmas caused by balancing impartiality against a desire to witness atrocities. One of the founders of MSF, Bernard Kouchner,

---

Box 13.1: History notes

Bernard Kouchner (1939–)

Kouchner was born in France and trained as a doctor and gastroenterologist. While working with the Red Cross during the Biafran War, he and a few colleagues became so disillusioned with the poor humanitarian responses of the day that they formed a new organization called Médecins Sans Frontières in 1971. This has grown to become a highly successful NGO that provides emergency support for refugees in many countries. MSF has subsequently broadened its scope and is also an influential advocate for affordable drug access. The organization was awarded the Nobel Peace Prize in 1999. Kouchner fell out with the leadership of MSF over the subject of whether aid agencies should comment on humanitarian abuses. In 1979 he organized a highly publicized "floating ambulance" for the aid of Vietnamese refugees (L'Île de Lumière). His understanding of the importance of public opinion is shown by his inclusion, on the boat, of journalists and photographers along with doctors and nurses. He built on the success of that initiative by forming a separate group called Médecins du Monde (Doctors of the World). Apart from his humanitarian work, he has also been a successful politician. He has been the French secretary for Health and a member of the European Parliament.

split with the leadership of MSF over this very subject and started a separate group (Médecins du Monde).

During the 1970s and 1980s, humanitarian agencies operated under the assumption that warring parties would follow the usual standards of international humanitarian law and would leave them alone to do their job. For a while, it looked as if this approach might even work. The signing of Operational Lifeline Sudan in March 1980 allowed international agencies to provide basic medical care and food to remote populations affected by the fighting (Taylor-Robinson, 2002). Similar negotiations with other belligerent or obstructive governments were also successful, at least for short periods, in other conflicts such as Angola and Sri Lanka. These "days of tranquility" sometimes lasted long enough to organize a mass immunization program or deliver a new crop to market.

Unfortunately, in the 1990s it became quite obvious, in the chaos of Somalia and Rwanda, that it would take more than the Geneva Convention to provide protection for civilians and humanitarians in war zones. The first attempt to support humanitarian action with military backing was tried in Somalia when a large multinational force landed in 1993 with the aims of restoring peace, establishing a working government, and helping agencies to deal with the country's famine victims (Clarke & Herbst, 1997). Unfortunately, after 24 Pakistani peacekeepers were killed by Somali militia, the force's impartiality was lost during the subsequent hunt for their leader. After the battle of Mogadishu, international forces were withdrawn and the country settled into anarchy. Deaths among the multinational force had a significant effect on subsequent intervention decision making.

The early 1990s also saw the start of an emphasis on greater professionalism among agency staff with the establishment of various standards of conduct, including the Sphere Project (Walker, 2005). The UN formed the Department of Humanitarian Affairs in 1992 with the aim of imposing some form of coordination on agencies responding to emergencies; in 1998, this became the Office for the Coordination of Humanitarian Affairs (OCHA). The ethical and practical dilemmas posed by governments that purposely wage war on their own populations have not been solved. Denying relief workers access to affected populations remains a major current concern in Sudan, which Operation Lifeline Sudan only partly addresses. A strong World Court to settle international disputes, backed by an effective and permanent UN army, is a real possibility for the future, but a military presence is still no guarantee of success (Shawcross, 2001). There were UN troops in Rwanda during the genocide, but they were forbidden to get involved and the declaration of a UN "safe haven" did not stop the massacre at Srebrenica.

There is also a subjective element in the definition of an emergency that depends, to some extent, on media access and public interest. For example, why send troops to Somalia in 1993 rather than Sudan, or to Sierra Leone in 1999 rather than a much earlier intervention in East Timor? There is an obvious reluctance to invade a sovereign state but, at some stage, intervention becomes a humanitarian necessity. Earlier intervention, with a credible force, would probably have saved tens of thousands of lives in Rwanda or East Timor. Unfortunately, such interventions carry a risk of casualties. For example, the deaths of Canadian troops in Afghanistan raise inevitable questions. Who wants their children to fight and die for a humanitarian ideal in a distant country and, more pragmatically, who pays for it? It is hoped that the recently established International Criminal Court will serve to make some tyrants pause before committing atrocities that might one day put them in a dock shared by Milosevic and the recently arrested Charles Taylor.

■ DISPLACED POPULATIONS

The Size of the World's Refugee Population

The last 20 years has seen some of the biggest migrations of refugee populations in history. An estimated 1 million Kurds

Table 13.3: Terminology of displaced populations

Refugee	Someone forced out of his or her own country due to persecution as defined in the 1951 Geneva Convention
Refugee Claimant	Someone claiming refugee status under the 1951 Convention
Internally Displaced Person (IDP)	Someone forced to move due to persecution but who remains within the original country
Migrant	Voluntary movement to another country
Internal Migrant	Voluntary movement within own country
Forced Migrant	Involuntary movement but usually because of a natural disaster and not due to persecution

left Iraq in 1991 and, in the space of a few weeks during the Rwandan genocide, neighbouring countries were flooded with an estimated 2 million refugees. In the late 1990s, hundreds of thousands more refugees were displaced by wars in Sudan, Sierra Leone, Liberia, and Indonesia. Refugees are defined as people who have left their country of origin because of well-founded fears of persecution due to race, religion, nationality, or political opinion. Table 13.3 gives definitions for the various types of displaced populations. People fleeing a natural disaster are not defined as refugees under the Geneva Convention. By far, the most common cause underlying refugee problems is escape from violence (*United Nations High Commissioner for Refugees*, n.d.).

Keeping track of refugee statistics is not easy. Those people who cross an international boundary may try to avoid attention, but reasonable estimates of numbers are available for these groups. However, probably at least equal numbers are displaced but remain within their country of origin. These people are termed "internally displaced persons" (IDP) and are much harder to count. They are also much harder to help because they still remain in their original country. External assistance is affected by sovereignty issues so they may remain at increased risk of continuing abuse. Other types of displaced people are identified, including economic migrants who cross to another country simply in search of a more prosperous life. Examples include Hispanic migrants (both legal and illegal) entering the United States and a large illegal immigrant population in Europe. Finally, the UN also uses the term "persons of concern" to describe populations at high risk of flight, usually due to war. The numbers of these various

Table 13.4: Numbers of refugees by type and geographic region (2004)

Region (UN major area)	Refugees	Asylum-Seekers	Others of Concern				Total Population of Concern
			Returned Refugees	IDPs	Returned IDPs	Various	
Africa	3,022,600	208,100	329,700	1,198,900	35,000	67,100	4,861,400
Asia	3,471,300	56,200	1,145,900	1,327,500	61,500	837,200	6,899,600
Europe	2,067,900	269,800	18,800	899,700	51,400	1,122,300	4,429,900
Latin America and the Caribbean	36,200	8,100	100	2,000,000	–	26,400	2,070,800
Northern America	562,300	291,000	–	–	–	–	853,300
Oceania	76,300	6,000	–	–	–	100	82,400
Total	9,236,600	839,200	1,494,500	5,426,100	147,900	2,053,100	19,197,400

Source: United Nations High Commissioner for Refugees (2004)

categories, in different world regions, are given in Table 13.4.

The UN agency responsible for refugees is the UN High Commissioner for Refugees (UNHCR). The UNHCR was established in 1950 and the first convention relating to the status of refugees was passed in 1951. Its initial focus was on European refugees escaping the fighting of World War II, but its scope was expanded to a global mandate by a 1967 Protocol. Since its formation, the UNHCR has helped an estimated 50 million people over its five decades of existence. The organization has been awarded the Nobel Peace Prize twice, most recently in 1981. Figure 13.6 shows how refugee populations have changed over the last 25 years. The recent return of hundreds of thousands of Afghanistan refugees has continued the recent downward trend. The UNHCR also provides care for other categories of displaced people, including internally displaced people, returning refugees, and asylum seekers.

Figure 13.6: Trend in global refugee population over 25 years

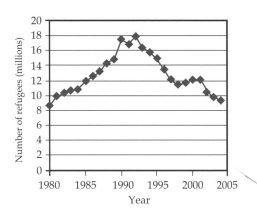

Source: United Nations High Commissioner for Refugees (2004)

The Care and Management of Displaced Populations

The first days and weeks of a disaster are chaotic times, which is all the more reason that aid agencies and their staff should be professional and well trained. It is convenient to divide the emergency into two broad groups (early and late) based on the crude mortality rate (CMR) (Burkholder & Toole, 1995). The CMR can be expressed as deaths per 1,000 per month (usually one to two in an average developing country) or as deaths per 10,000 population per day (usually less than 0.5). Depending on the baseline health of the affected population, the degree of violence they have faced, and the distance they have travelled, the early stage is marked by crude mortality rates as high as 20–40 times greater than normal. During this phase, management should be based on the well-established principles of primary health care such as shelter, water, and food.

Once mortality rates fall to the usual background level, refugee camps slowly turn into organized towns. Table 13.5 gives some of the UNHCR minimum recommendations for camp construction. Acute infectious diseases remain important, but other problems now need attention, particularly tuberculosis, HIV, and sexually transmitted diseases, mental

Table 13.5: UNHCR standards for refugee camps

Land	30–45 m²/person
Shelter	3.5 m²/person
Water	15–20 L/person/day
Food	2,100 kcal/person/day
Latrine	one per family (5–10 people)
Water tap	one per community (80–100 people)
Health centre	one per camp (20,000 people)
Hospital	one per 200,000 people
School	one per 5,000 people

Source: United Nations High Commissioner for Refugees (n.d.)

illness, and violence. It is important to provide basic public health programs (such as family planning, basic maternal and child health care) and to establish means of employment (such as providing seeds and fertilizer for small holdings).

As mentioned above, there is nothing medically unique about the care of displaced populations. Although each situation will have its unique complexities, the basics of shelter, security, water, food, and essential health care remain as constants (Tode & Waldman, 1990). The main management priorities are as follows.

Rapid Epidemiological Assessment

At least nine of the major relief organizations produce a disaster response manual (Médecins Sans Frontières, 1997; Sphere Project, 2004; UNICEF, 2005), each of which has its own version of an initial assessment protocol. There have been repeated calls for greater uniformity, but the collection and distribution of standardized information during the early stage of a disaster has not yet been achieved (Bradt & Drummond, 2002). Careful information gathering (within the limitations imposed by the situation) is an essential first step in planning and managing a displaced population. Although there is little standardization, there is no shortage of literature. The WHO alone has produced a steady stream of reports, ranging from rapid evaluation techniques developed during the smallpox program, to a more recent handbook (World Health Organization, 1999). The following information should be collected:

- *Social/political situation:*
  Information needed includes the

reasons behind the population displacement; the security situation in the original country and host country; traditional relations between the host and the original country; and whether the refugees are accepted, tolerated, or actively disliked by the host government.

- *The refugee population:* Basic demographic information should include an estimate of the total population and rough distribution by age and gender, particularly the numbers of vulnerable groups such as unaccompanied children, the elderly, and pregnant women. Is the refugee population homogeneous or does it include warring parties within the camp? Are there remnants of previous health workers, police, or administrative personnel?
- *The camp:* Information needed includes the total area available, the climate of the region, a map of the site and local countryside, and the state of the roads. Information on the camp facilities should include type of shelters, latrines, local water sources, and available power.
- *Population health:* Using information from health care workers and measurements of samples of children, the following health information should be available: crude mortality rate, frequency of the most common and expected diseases (such as measles, diarrheal diseases, pneumonia, and malaria), degree of malnutrition, information about the population's past health

(common diseases, degree of vaccination coverage).

- *Resources available:* Is health and social support available in the region and what is the degree of willingness of the host population to support the refugees? What is the number of trained medical and support staff within the refugee population? What material is available to the refugees (pots, pans, food, clothing, water container, wood or paraffin stoves)?

The initial assessment should be completed rapidly in a few days to allow agencies to make the first decision about whether they can, or even should, intervene. Once the aid effort is underway, some degree of continuous monitoring is essential and should be the sole task of one particular group to allow adjustments to be made in the recovery program.

Water and Sanitation
- *Water:* The provision of water is a major problem facing refugee camps (Roberts et al., 2001). If tankers are required, then the monthly cost is significant. The bare minimum needed for some degree of hygiene and hydration is 5 litres of water per person per day. A minimal supply of clean water will reduce the risk of diarrheal diseases, but will do nothing to limit hygiene-related diseases such as trachoma and scabies. In order to clean clothes, dishes, and maintain personal hygiene, it is necessary to provide 15–20 litres per person per day. Water sources include wells,

boreholes, and surface water. Failing this, water will have to be transported using trucks and stored in large bladders. Turbid water can be treated by settlement with flocculation additives and subsequent chlorination. This procedure requires specially trained staff.

- *Sanitation (Harvey, 2005):* Until the camp is organized, limited control of contamination can be obtained using a defecation field. With tape and stakes, a large field can be divided into strips. Starting with the strip furthest from the camp, a different area can be used for defecation every day. Unless some means of covering the field with soil can be found, this is only a very temporary approach. Until it is possible to provide each family with their own latrine, the best interim approach is to dig communal latrines, which are relatively quick and cheap to construct. One trench latrine should be available for 50 people.

The trench should be about 2 metres deep and spanned by pairs of wooden boards. Each day, the contents should be covered by a layer of soil to reduce smell and flies. When the trench is full, a new trench is dug at another site. Although a trench is a simple structure, it requires daily cleaning and supervision or the population will not use it. Safe sanitation can be achieved only with the full co-operation of the community. It is important that the community is involved in the management of the waste disposal and the water

storage systems. The routine care of the water and sanitation should be handed over to camp occupants as soon as suitable people can be trained.

Household waste should be collected regularly and is best handled by a landfill system. Again, this is a task that should be handed over to the refugee population as soon as possible. Contaminated waste from health posts and clinics should be burned or buried deeply. A cemetery area should be available. Soap should be provided as part of the routine public health education for the camp. The basic need is one bar per person per month. If attention is not paid to waste disposal, then problems of flies, rats, and other vectors can become uncontrollable.

Nutrition (World Food Programme, 2002)

In the past, malnutrition has been a major problem in refugee camps due to underestimation of the basic requirements of the population and also lack of funds to buy sufficient food. Bare survival is obtained with 1,500–1,800 kilocalories per person per day, but the target should be 2,100 kilocalories per person per day. Once intake reaches 2,400 kilocalories, the need for supplementary feeding is much reduced. Although there have been great improvements in the feeding of displaced populations, current reports of the presence of scurvy and pellagra show that micronutrient deficiencies are still present (Young et al., 2004).

The UNHCR and the World Food Programme's practice is to include fortified blended cereal in the food rations of all food aid-dependent populations.

However, the best approach is to include a more diversified diet with provision of fresh vegetables and fruit. In situations where the population has access to local markets, they have been encouraged to sell or bargain a portion of their ration for fresh produce. With time, the development of family garden plots improves the food sufficiency of camp households. Selective feeding programs for high-risk groups, such as undernourished children and pregnant women, will also be necessary.

Young children are the most vulnerable section of the camp in terms of malnutrition, so nutritional surveys of the under-five-year-olds will provide a reasonable indication of the nutrition of the camp as a whole. As discussed in Chapter 5, the nutritional status of children is best measured by weight for height expressed as a z-score. If more than 5 percent of sampled children have a weight for height score below minus 2 z, this should act as a warning that the camp's nutrition is inadequate. A rising crude mortality rate may also be another indicator that nutrition is poor.

Shelter

For reasons of culture and social acceptance, it has been shown that refugees do best if they can build their own housing, as long as the necessary material and organization is provided. In the short term, plastic sheeting stretched across rough wooden supports is the usual shelter that each family is able to construct. In cold climates, the wide daily swings in temperature, and lack of adequate shelter and clothing will soon have a major adverse affect on health. In addition to basic shelter, there should be provision of blankets and clothing. Once again, it is important that refugees should help build their own housing. This reduces costs and ensures that it better meets their needs.

Tents may be necessary in the short term if local materials are not available. The lifespan of a well-constructed tent is one to two years; adequate supplies of repair materials should be available. Ideally, the tent should provide enough height to allow occupants to stand upright and should have an outer flysheet to protect the tent underneath. Tents are difficult and expensive to heat and the risk of fire is significant. They are not ideal as cold-climate shelters, but there may be no options, as the current Pakistan earthquake has shown. Shelters for Sri Lankan tsunami refugees were predominantly made of UV-resistant, heavy-duty plastic sheeting. The large blue UNHCR tarpaulins were a common sight throughout the camps. Wooden support frames can be easily constructed using locally produced framing material. When designing the camp, there is a need to ensure that protection principles are taken into account from the start. Water sources, latrines, and communal areas should be well lit to reduce the risk of violence against women and children.

Environmental Issues

The question of the impact of refugee camps on the local environment is increasingly being examined. The use of firewood for cooking by a large number of refugees may have a significant impact on the ability of the local population to access firewood themselves for cooking. Environmental degradation is one of the major sources of potential conflict between refugees and the local population and if such conflict occurs, it can have a major effect on the ability of aid agencies to conduct their work.

Basic Health Care

Apart from the effects of violence, the majority of mortality in the refugee camps is caused by a very limited number of diseases, particularly diarrheal diseases, pneumonia, measles, and malaria. As with any developing world population, malnutrition acts as an aggravating factor in all of these conditions. The most basic health services will consist of two components: peripheral health posts and community outreach services delivered by community health workers (Hafeez et al., 2004). With time, traditional birth attendants and others with training as health workers will probably be found within the population of the camp. With further training and supervision, they can play a valuable role by providing basic health education, identifying those who need treatment, and collecting health-monitoring data such as the number of deaths and their causes. Once trained, suitable ratios are one health care worker per 1,000 population and one traditional birth attendant per 3,000.

The basic health post needs to be a simple, clean building with the ability to treat common diseases. It should, at the very least, have supplies of effective malaria medication, oral rehydration solution, oral antibiotics, and storage facilities for measles vaccine. In populations with poor vaccination coverage, measles epidemics are a major health risk for children. During the early stages of the camp, measles vaccine and vitamin A should be given to all children below the age of 15 even if measles is not yet evident. Ideally, there should be one health post per 5,000 people.

As services become available, a larger health centre should be available for up to 20,000 people. The centre should be able to treat most cases except those requiring general anaesthetic and major obstetric emergencies. These can hopefully be managed through referral to existing local hospital services after suitable negotiations. Ideally, the health facility should be open 24 hours a day with eight-hour shifts. There will also need to be 24-hour security arrangements. The facility should be able to care for uncomplicated deliveries, minor surgery, short-term pediatric hospitalization, and basic wound dressing. A well-run unit will also act as a centre for epidemiological surveillance and health education initiatives.

■ SUMMARY

Taken together, humanitarian and natural disasters are surprisingly common. The last few years has witnessed some of the most severe and certainly some of the most expensive disasters in history. Apart from the immediate death and injury caused by a disaster, the subsequent economic and social chaos (plus the effects of displaced populations) can be enormous. Poor building standards, lack of civil defence organizations, concentrations of population in high-risk areas and lack of money are some of the reasons why developing countries can be so badly affected by disasters.

There is a very understandable human desire to help the survivors of a disaster. However, as experience with the recent Asian tsunami has shown, the sudden influx of hundreds of uncoordinated groups is not the most efficient way to respond. The initial emergency aid for survivors, followed by the reconstruction of their shattered society, is an overwhelming job. Apart from money and materials, there is a need for well-trained experts in subjects ranging from nutrition and sanitation to construction and public planning. While the international disaster response agencies have achieved valuable work under very difficult conditions, it is widely accepted that there is room for improvement in the areas of coordination, professionalism, and standardization.

Until recently, the response to disasters has principally concentrated on the emergency response, but this emphasis is changing. Although earthquakes, storms, and volcanic eruptions cannot be avoided, their effects can, to some extent, be predicted and effective plans made to reduce their adverse effects. Disaster mitigation is still a relatively new subject. It is based on specific risk analysis, local response strategies, and, most recently, on disaster insurance. It is hoped that improvements in the international disaster response, plus more widespread mitigation planning, will greatly reduce the burden of major disasters.

RESOURCES

References

Active Learning Network for Accountability and Performance in Humanitarian Action. (n.d.). Retrieved from www.odi.org.uk/alnap.

Adinolfi, C., et al. (2005). *Humanitarian response review.* New York and Geneva: Office for the Coordination of Humanitarian Affairs. Retrieved from www.cfr.org/publication/8918/ humanitarian_response_review.html.

Banatrala, N., et al. (1998). "Mortality and morbidity among Rwandan refugees repatriated from Zaire, November 1996." *Prehospital Disaster Medicine, 13,* 17–21.

Bradt, D., & Drummond, C. (2002). "Rapid epidemiological assessment of health status in displaced populations: An evolution towards standardized minimum, essential data sets." *Prehospital Disaster Medicine, 17,* 178–185.

Burkholder, B., & Toole, M. (1995). "Evolution of complex disasters." *Lancet, 346,* 1012–1015.

Center for Research on the Epidemiology of Disasters. (n.d.-a). *CE-DAT: A database on the human impact of complex emergencies.* www.cred.be/cedat.

Center for Research on the Epidemiology of Disasters. (n.d.-b). *EM-DAT: The international disaster database.* www.em-dat.net.

Chaulia, S. (2002). "UNHCR's relief, rehabilitation, and repatriation of Rwandan refugees in Zaire (1994–1997)." *The Journal of Humanitarian Assistance.* Retrieved from www.jha.ac/articles/a086. htm.

Chunkath, S., et al. (2005). "Gender dimensions and human rights aspects to responses and recovery." *Prehospital Disaster Medicine, 20,* 404–407.

Clarke, W., & Herbst, J. (Eds.). (1997). *Learning from Somalia: The lessons of armed humanitarian intervention.* Boulder: Westview Press.

Collier, P., & Hoeffler, A. (2001). *Greed and grievance in civil war.* Retrieved from www.worldbank. org/research/conflict/papers/greedgrievance_23oct.pdf.

Dehghan, M., et al. (2005). "Childhood obesity, prevalence, and prevention." *Nutrition Journal, 4,* 24–32.

Department for International Development. (2005). *Natural disaster and disaster risk reduction measures.* Retrieved from www.unisdr.org/news/DFID-Economics-Study-for-DfID.pdf.

Dilley, M., et al. (2005). *Natural disaster hotspots: A global risk analysis.* Washington: World Bank. Retrieved from www.ldeo.columbia.edu/chrr/research/hotspots.

Disasters Emergency Committee. (n.d.). Retrieved from www.dec.org.uk.

"Emergency medical aid is not for amateurs." (1996). *Lancet, 348,* 1393–1394.

Fennell, J. (1998). "Hope suspended: Morality, politics, and war in Central Africa." *Disasters, 22,* 96–108.

Guha-Sapir, D., et al. (2004). *Thirty years of natural disasters, 1974–2003: The numbers.* Louvain-la-Neuve: Presses Universitaires de Louvain. Retrieved from www.em-dat.net/documents/Publication/publication_2004_emdat.pdf.

Hafeez, A., et al. (2004). "Integrating health care for mothers and children in refugee camps and at district level." *British Medical Journal, 328,* 834–836.

Harvey, P. (Ed.). (2005). *Excreta disposal in emergencies: A field manual.* Oxford: Oxfam.

Hogerzeil, H., et al. (1997). "Guidelines for drug donations." *British Medical Journal, 314,* 737–738.

Integrated Regional Information Network. (n.d.). Retrieved from www.irinnews.org.

International Federation of Red Cross and Red Crescent Societies. (2005). *World disasters report.* Dordrecht: Martinus Nijhoff.

International Strategy for Disaster Reduction. (n.d.). *Disaster statistics 1991–2005.* Retrieved from www.unisdr.org/disaster-statistics/introduction.htm.

Kreimer, A. (1999). *Managing disaster risk in Mexico: Market incentives for mitigation investment.* Washington: World Bank.

Kreimer, A., & Arnold, M. (Eds.). (2000). *Managing disaster risk in emerging economies.* Washington: World Bank. Retrieved from www.proventionconsortium.org/?pageid=37&publicationid=12.

Lautze, S., et al. (2004). "Assistance, protection, and governance networks in complex emergencies." *Lancet, 364,* 2134–2141.

Macrae, J., & Leader, N. (2001). "Apples, pears, and porridge: The origins and impact of the search for 'coherence' between humanitarian and political responses to chronic political emergencies." *Disasters, 25,* 290–307.

McGarry, N., et al. (2005). "Health aspects of the tsunami disaster in Asia." *Prehospital Disaster Medicine, 20,* 368–377.

Médecins Sans Frontières. (1997). *Refugee health: An approach to emergency situations.* London: Macmillan.

Munich Re Group. (2004). *Annual review: Natural catastrophes.* Retrieved from www.munichre.com/publications/302-04321_en.pdf.

Munslow, B., & Brown, C. (1999). "Complex emergencies: The institutional impasse." *Third World Quarterly, 20,* 207–221.

Rieff, D. (2002). *A bed for the night: Humanitarianism in crisis.* New York: Simon and Schuster.

Roberts, L., et al. (2001). "Keeping water clean in a Malawi refugee camp: A randomized intervention trial." *Bulletin of the World Health Organization, 79,* 280–287.

Schiermeier, Q. (2006). "The costs of global warming." *Nature, 439,* 374–375.

Shawcross, W. (2001). *Deliver us from evil: Warlords and peacekeepers in a world of endless conflict.* London: Bloomsbury Publishing.

Sphere Project. (2004). *Sphere handbook.* Retrieved from www.sphereproject.org.

Taylor-Robinson, S. (2002). "Operation Lifeline Sudan." *Journal of Medical Ethics, 28,* 49–51.

Terry, F. (2002). *Condemned to repeat? The paradox of humanitarian action.* Ithaca: Cornell University Press.

Tode, M., & Waldman, R. (1990). "Prevention of excess mortality among refugee and displaced populations in developing countries." *Journal of the American Medical Association, 263,* 3296–3302.

Tun, K., et al. (2005). "Forensic aspects of disaster fatality management." *Prehospital Disaster Management, 20,* 455–458.

UNICEF. (2005). *Emergency field handbook: A guide for UNICEF staff.* Retrieved from www.unicef.org/publications/files/UNICEF_EFH_2005.pdf.

UNICEF. (2006). *Malnutrition*. Retrieved from www.childinfo.org/areas/malnutrition/underweight.php.

United Nations High Commissioner for Refugees. (2004). *Statistical year book*. Retrieved from www.unhcr.org/cgi-bin/texis/vtx/statistics.

United Nations High Commissioner for Refugees. (n.d.). Retrieved from www.unhcr.org.

United Nations Office for the Coordination of Humanitarian Affairs. (n.d.). Retrieved from ochaonline.un.org.

Walker, P. (2005). "Cracking the code: The genesis, use, and future of the code of conduct." *Disasters, 29*, 323–336.

Wisner, B., & Walker, P. (2005). *Beyond Kobe: A proactive look at the world conference on disaster reduction*. Medford: Feinstein International Famine Center. Retrieved from www.undp.org.

World Food Programme. (2002). *Emergency field operations pocketbook*. Rome: Author. Retrieved from www.unicef.org/emerg/files/WFP_manual.pdf.

World Health Organization. (1999). *Rapid health assessment protocols for emergencies*. Geneva: Author.

World Health Organization. (n.d.-a). *Health action in crises*. Retrieved from www.who.int/hac.

World Health Organization. (n.d.-b). *Inter-Agency Standing Committee*. Retrieved from www.who.int/hac/network/interagency/backgroundIASC.

Young, H., et al. (2004). "Public nutrition in complex emergencies." *Lancet, 364*, 1899–1909.

Recommended Reading

Briggs, S., & Brinsfield, K. (2003). *Advanced disaster medical response*. Boston: Harvard Medical International Trauma & Disaster Institute.

Ciottone, G. (2006). *Disaster medicine*. Philadelphia: Mosby Elsevier.

Dilley, M., et al. (2005). *Natural disaster hotspots: A global risk analysis*. Washington: World Bank.

Macrae, J. (2001). *Aiding recovery: The crisis of aid in chronic political emergencies*. London: Zed Books.

Médecins Sans Frontières. (1996). *World in crisis: The politics of survival at the end of the 20th century*. London: Routledge.

Médecins Sans Frontières. (1997). *Refugee health: An approach to emergency situations*. London: MacMillan.

Terry, F. (2002). *Condemned to repeat? The paradox of humanitarian action*. Ithaca: Cornell University.

Chapter 14

Health of
Indigenous Populations

It is often easier to become outraged
by injustice half a world away
than oppression and discrimination
half a block from home.
—Carl T. Rowan,
African-American journalist, 1925–2000

OBJECTIVES

After completing this chapter, you should be able to

- appreciate the extent and diversity of the world's indigenous populations
- understand the historical features that lie behind the current poor health of many indigenous populations
- understand the common health problems found among many indigenous populations
- understand the approaches needed to improve the health of indigenous populations

---

Indigenous or Aboriginal peoples are usually defined as those who inhabited a country or region prior to the arrival of later cultural or ethnic immigrants; such groups inhabit every corner of the earth, from the Arctic to the South Pacific. Accurate data is a constant problem, but common estimates of their numbers range from 300–350 million (roughly 5 percent of the world's population) (International Work Group for Indigenous Affairs, n.d.).

Examples include the large Maya groups of Central America, Inuit and Aleutian islanders of the circumpolar region, the Saami of Northern Scandinavia, Australian Aboriginal groups, and the Maori (and broader Polynesian groups) of New Zealand and other Pacific islands. Many indigenous peoples have managed to retain their unique cultural and linguistic traditions despite depressingly similar colonial histories of discrimination and oppression. Although the situation for Aboriginal peoples has certainly improved with time, the size of the world's indigenous population, combined with its high rate of significant health problems, makes this topic an important part of international health.

AN INTRODUCTION TO INDIGENOUS PEOPLES

Indigenous Peoples never did the Europeans any harm whatever; on the contrary, they believed them to have descended from the heavens, at least until they or their fellow citizens have tasted, at the hands of these oppressors, a diet of robbery, murder, violence, and all other manner of trials and tribulations.
—Bartolome de las Casas, Spanish missionary, early proponent of Native rights and author of "A Short Account of the Destruction of the Indies," 1552

There is no unambiguous definition of indigenous peoples that clearly distinguishes between ethnic minorities and original inhabitants, but the outline given by Alderete (1999) provides a good starting point for discussion. Indigenous groups have the following characteristics:

• They are descendants of people who were in the territory of the country long before other groups of different cultures or ethnic origin arrived.
• Because of isolation from the dominant segment of the country's population, they have preserved customs and ancestral traditions, religion, dress, livelihood, and lifestyles that characterize them as

being indigenous.
• They often live within a state structure that incorporates social and cultural characteristics alien to their own traditions.

Estimates of their numbers vary between widely (International Work Group for Indigenous Affairs, n.d.; World Bank, n.d.). The most commonly quoted figure is 300 million people, composed of 5,000–6,000 different groups spread over 70 countries. Collectively, their contributions to the world have been extensive and usually underappreciated. Apart from lessons to be learned from their attitudes to the stewardship of the environment, many groups have accumulated a knowledge of the pharmaceutical properties of plants that is of great contemporary value—so valuable that efforts are being made to protect and pay for the use of that knowledge (Brush & Stabinsky, 1996).

Indigenous populations show extraordinary variation in their lifestyles, traditions, and cultures. They range from small communities, measured in tens of thousands (such as the San Bushmen of Southern Africa), to populations in the millions (such as the diverse descendants of the Mayan peoples in Mexico and Central America). Unfortunately, during the long colonial history of the European powers, the collision of cultures between the new immigrants and existing populations was rarely a happy one (Coates, 2004). Many Aboriginal peoples share a common history of conquest, land appropriation, and depopulation until they became minorities in their own land. At best, they subsequently suffered from discrimination and, at worst, some groups lived through periods of terrible deprivation.

Despite the growing influence of indigenous movements over the last 25 years, Aboriginal peoples all over the world still face the loss of their lands and ways of life. For example, the Ainu of Japan are struggling to preserve their culture in the midst of a modern technological society and the Saami of Northern Europe are seeking self-rule over traditional lands included within the borders of Sweden, Finland, Norway, and Russia. In the very recent past, indigenous peoples in El Salvador and Guatemala have also been the targets of severe political violence that included widespread torture and murder.

In spite of the extraordinary cultural and ethnic diversity of indigenous peoples around the world, there are often striking similarities between their social grievances and common health problems. With time, indigenous organizations have developed a voice for their people and the situation for many groups has improved. However, despite enlightened government policies and a great deal of financial investment, the health indices of Native populations in countries such as Canada, Australia, New Zealand, and the United States lag far behind national averages. It is still possible to find developing world conditions affecting Aboriginal communities in the reserves, settlements, and downtown cores of all these countries.

With time, the voices of Native populations are slowly being heard. Some of the highlights from the last 30 years are given in Table 14.1, but there

Table 14.1: Major milestones in establishing rights for indigenous peoples

1840	New Zealand's Native Land Treaty signed at Waitangi.
1920s	Native American and Mayan leaders both petitioned the early League of Nations on behalf of indigenous peoples, but they were denied access to the forum.
1975	New Zealand's government grants limited legal recognition of Waitangi treaty; extended recognition granted in 1985.
1979	Denmark grants home rule to the largely Inuit Greenland.
1982	The first working group on indigenous populations (WGIP) was formed as a subcommittee of the UN Economic and Social Council.
1985	The WGIP began work on the draft of a Declaration on the Rights of Indigenous Peoples. The draft was completed in 1993, and by 1995 the Commission on Human Rights had set up its own working group to review the draft and make recommendations.
1989	International Labour Organization adopts Convention no. 169 Concerning Indigenous and Tribal Peoples in Independent Countries. The convention reversed the ILO's earlier integrationist approach by emphasizing the rights of indigenous groups to determine their own future.
1994	The UN General Assembly launched the International Decade of the World's Indigenous Peoples from 1995–2004. Its achievements included the finalization of the Draft Declaration on Indigenous Rights and also the first move toward a permanent United Nations forum on indigenous issues.
1999	Canada forms self-governing territory of Nunavut, with a largely Inuit population.
2000	The UN Permanent Forum on Indigenous Issues (UNPFII) was formally established. It meets annually and makes its recommendations to the UN Economic and Social Council.
2005	The first decade was generally considered a success so the UN proposed a second decade from 2005–2010 with the theme of "partnership for action and dignity." A voluntary trust fund has been established to support the projects associated with this decade.
2006	UNHCR passes the non-binding Declaration on Indigenous Rights, but without full consensus.

is still a long way to go. Indigenous issues are now given some degree of attention by large international agencies (Table 14.2); the most significant of these developments has been the establishment of the UN Permanent Forum on Indigenous Issues (UNPFII). The impressively titled "Declaration of Indigenous Rights" that was much discussed during the first Decade of the World's Indigenous Peoples has recently been accepted in non-binding form. Universal consensus has not been reached because of unresolved issues, such as autonomy, self-governance, and control of natural resources.

When Denmark granted independent rule to Greenland in 1979, it marked a major step in self-determination for largely indigenous communities. The establishment of a new territory in Northern Canada (Nunavut, 1999) has continued that trend. Other countries, including Norway and New Zealand, have also shown enlightened policies toward autonomy for their indigenous population. It is hoped that the recently announced second decade for indigenous

Table 14.2: Indigenous representation within international organizations

UN High Commission for Human Rights	Indigenous peoples' Web site (www.unhchr.ch/ indigenous/main.html)
International Labour Organization	Newsletter and Web site (www.ilo.org/public/english/ indigenous)
United Nations	Permanent Forum on Indigenous Issues (UNPFII) (www.un.org/esa/socdev/ unpfii/index.html)
World Bank	Indigenous Web site (Search "indigenous peoples" at www.worldbank.org)

peoples will produce rather more tangible results in the area of self-rule than the first.

North American Native Peoples

There is a large (and growing) Aboriginal population in North America. In Canada alone, there are more than a million indigenous peoples divided into three groups, spread throughout the country: First Nations, Métis, and Inuit. The most recent US census review estimates there are 2.8 million Aboriginal peoples, ranging from Inuit and Aleut groups in Alaska to the wide diversity of Native groups that still exist across the American mainland (US Census Bureau, 2005). Based on a variety of archaeological sites (particularly Clovis, New Mexico), it was assumed, until fairly recently, that modern Native Americans crossed over from Siberia roughly 13,000–14,000 years ago. However, recent findings at Topper and other sites have moved that estimate back by thousands of years. The route of migration has also been challenged by theories that include transatlantic and transpacific alternatives.

The collision of cultures caused by the westward migration of largely European colonists produced a very sad history whose effects are still apparent today. Collectively, these various raids, skirmishes, and battles are known as the Indian wars. They began with early fights between English settlers and local Native tribes, starting from the earliest days of the Jamestown settlement around 1610. They ended with what is generally considered the final large engagement (probably better termed a "massacre") at Wounded Knee in 1890. In total, there were probably many thousands of separate incidents over this period; the best known is the

Table 14.3: A moment of Zen

| Canada Health expenditure (US $/capita/year): US $1,783

Infant mortality rate: | Burundi Infant mortality rate (infant deaths/1,000 newborns): 114

Per capita health expenditure: |
|---|---|
| **Six** | **Six** |

Sources: UNICEF (2006); World Health Organization (2000)

destruction of Custer's forces at Little Big Horn. Although the death rate was low compared to the mortality from disease and forced relocation, many of the engagements were noted for their brutality. An extensive bibliography of the subject is available (Osborn, 2001).

In Canada, the history was much less violent, but was still far from ideal. Misguided policies of forced assimilation, through compulsory schooling, have left deep scars on Aboriginal society. Between 1880 and the 1970s, Indian children were removed from their homes and sent to residential schools where their language and culture were suppressed. Excessive corporal punishment and even sexual predation resulted in an entire generation of Native peoples who lost their identity. The resulting pattern of substance abuse, family violence, suicide, and social disruption are common legacies of that policy; all may be found in First Nations' communities across Canada (Adelson, 2005).

Australia's Aboriginal Population

The indigenous peoples of Australia are commonly called "Aboriginals"; they arrived in the country tens of thousands of years before the European settlers. They are a diverse group spread throughout Australia and some offshore regions such as the Torres Strait Islands and Tasmania. Estimates of the pre-European population vary between 500,000 and 1 million, but this dropped sharply after the arrival of the Europeans. At one point, it was widely accepted that the Aboriginal population would die out but, since the mid-1960s, their numbers have increased (Australian Bureau of Statistics, n.d.). The most recent estimate is roughly 470,000 for 2006. The Aboriginals are ancient people who crossed a land bridge to Australia from Southeast Asia. Australian archaeological sites have provided the oldest human remains outside of Africa. A skeleton found at Mungo Lake is widely believed to be 40,000 years old and the first settlers may have arrived 10,000 years earlier than that.

The first British settlements were founded in 1788. After losing the American War of Independence, the British had to find somewhere else to ship their convicts; they chose the newly discovered southeast coast of Australia. Inevitably, there were conflicts as the new settlers slowly took over the fertile parts of the country (Hughes, 1996). Aboriginals had no military tradition and no modern weapons so these fights were little more than massacres. In Tasmania, the original population of several thousand people was reduced to a few hundred in a matter of years. The last surviving Tasmanian Aboriginal died in the late 19th century.

The combination of newly introduced diseases, loss of traditional land, and oppressive treatment caused a steep population decline well into the 20th century before it started to rebound. Unfortunately, the government also followed a policy of forced assimilation similar to the Canadian practice. Until as late as 1972, large numbers of Aboriginal children were forcibly removed from their parents and either fostered into a White family or put in residential care. The social results of this so-called "stolen generation" are exactly the same as those suffered by the North American indigenous population—high rates of suicide, substance abuse, family violence, and ill health (Ring & Brown, 2002).

Maori and Polynesian Islanders

Despite the voyage of the *Kon-Tiki* and Thor Heyerdahl's early theory about the South American origin of Polynesian peoples, it is now widely accepted that the Polynesian settlers of Tonga, Samoa, Tahiti, Hawaii, the Marquesas, and New Zealand had their origins in Southeast Asia, probably around Taiwan. Slow eastward migration across the Pacific reached New Zealand (Aotearoa) by AD 800–1000. New Zealand's isolation meant that the first European colonists did not arrive until the early 19th century. Unfortunately, the introduction of firearms to the warlike Maori culture led to a series of murderous intertribal wars. In order to control the situation, the British government intervened in 1839. By 1840, Britain claimed the country as a colony at the Treaty of Waitangi; the agreement has subsequently been the source of a great deal of political controversy. More recently, the New Zealand government has been a pioneer in honouring early treaties by basing subsequent settlements on that early document.

The peace imposed by colonial treaty initially seemed beneficial for all, but it did not last. Inevitable conflicts over land erupted into war by 1845. The Maoris were no pushover and soundly beat elite British troops on several occasions. Fighting lasted over 30 years before a final peace was agreed. The Maori population in 1840 was estimated at 115,000, but the gradual loss of land and traditional practices led to a steady decline in these numbers. In keeping with the Australian experience, it was believed that Maori

---

Box 14.1: History notes

Rigoberta Menchú (1959–)

Rigoberta Menchú is a controversial character. Since her widely read autobiography was published in 1982 and her subsequent Nobel Peace Prize in 1992, she has become a symbol of the discrimination and violence suffered by indigenous peoples. Later research cast doubts on the accuracy of her book and led to a "battle of books" between opposing intellectual factions. Although some of her claims were exaggerated, her family certainly suffered severely from the murderous Guatemalan army during the country's 35-year-long civil war. The true story contains more than enough evil without the need for elaboration. Her brother was not burned alive, as claimed; he was "only" shot to death. She also lost her mother, father, brothers, and other relatives through murder and torture.

Menchú was born in Guatemala. She is a member of the Quiché branch of the much broader Mayan population. After basic schooling, she became increasingly involved in protest movements against the oppression of peasants in Guatemala. By the time her oral autobiography was widely published in 1983, she had been forced to flee her country and live in Mexico. After the end of the war in 1996, Menchú continued her activism on behalf of Native peoples. In 2004, Guatemala's president invited Menchú to join his government as a monitor of the country's adherence to the negotiated peace treaty (Arias, 2001).

culture would cease to exist. Fortunately, indigenous culture again proved more resilient than expected. Although health indicators such as obesity, diabetes, and family violence are higher than national averages (Bramley et al., 2006), the Maori people are largely well adapted in modern New Zealand society. Currently, over half a million people are classified as Maori; they make up roughly 15 percent of the population.

Circumpolar Yupik

Indigenous groups previously referred to as Eskimos (now more commonly called "Inuit" in Canada or "Yupik" in Russia and Alaska) are people who inhabit the high Arctic above the treeline. Related groups can be found in the Aleutians, Northern Canada, Greenland, and Northeastern Russia. The Inuit arrived in North America long after the Native American Indians and retained a distinctly different culture. The Inuit are derived from the Thule people, who had populated Alaska by AD 500 and arrived in Canada by AD 1000, where they displaced the existing Dorset people.

Their adaptation to a harsh environment allowed them to avoid European contact until the 18th century when whalers and later fur traders moved north. Inuit had little contact with the rest of Canada until the Canadian government began to establish a presence in the North during the 1940s. Communities have now abandoned their traditional seasonal camps and moved into permanent settlements, which are supported with medical care, social services, and a police presence. Some communities have had significant problems with substance abuse (particularly alcohol and glue sniffing), combined with a high rate of

tuberculosis and other diseases associated with poverty (Bjerregaard et al., 2004). The current community of Inuit in Canada is 55,000; over half live in the new territory of Nunavut.

Inuit organizations have been very successful in lobbying for indigenous rights. The Nunavut land claims agreement reached in 1993 ultimately led to the establishment of the territory of Nunavut in 1999, where Inuit form much of the population. In 1977, the Inuit Circumpolar Conference (ICC) was created to represent the interests of Inuit groups in Canada, Greenland, Russia, and Alaska (*Inuit Circumpolar Conference*, n.d.). The ICC promotes Inuit rights and interests at an international level.

Maya and Central American Indigenous Groups

> We are not myths of the past, ruins in a jungle or zoos. We are people and we want to be respected, not to be victims of intolerance and racism.
>
> —Rigoberta Menchu

Central and Southern America has seen great Amerindian civilizations rise and fall. The current theory is that indigenous groups migrated down through North America, but other theories (including a transpacific route) have also been proposed. Some of those early peoples—such as the Olmec, Maya, and Aztec—developed civilizations with sophisticated knowledge of mathematics and astronomy. In some parts of Mexico, Belize, and Guatemala, Native American indigenous groups form up to 50 percent of the population, although they certainly do not share 50 percent of the available wealth.

Figure 14.1: Indigenous Ecuadorian Quechua girl, with a llama, on the long daily walk for water. (Copyright Clive Shirley; GlobalAware.org.)

The arrival of three small ships, led by Columbus in 1492, forever altered the existing indigenous culture. The subsequent story of murder, slavery, and introduced diseases is a dark chapter in human history (Stannard, 2002). Despite everything, the Mayan culture has proved resilient. Today, approximately 6 million Maya are spread principally through Mexico, Guatemala, Belize, and Honduras. The Maya are predominantly agricultural and still suffer varying degrees of discrimination. During the 30-year war in Guatemala, many thousands of Mayans were killed in the fighting.

CANADA'S INDIGENOUS PEOPLES

It is not too much to say, that the intercourse of Europeans in general, without any exception in favour of the subjects of Great Britain, has been a source of many calamities to uncivilized nations. Too often, their territory has been usurped; their property seized; their numbers diminished … they have been familiarized with the use of our most potent instruments for the subtle or the violent destruction of human life, viz. brandy and gunpowder.
—House of Commons Select Committee Report on Aborigines, 1837

Early legislation passed by the British Crown, such as the 1763 Proclamation on Aboriginal land title and the 1876 Indian Act, principally referred to Canadian First Nations, but it is important to appreciate that the Aboriginal population of Canada does not fit into one neat category. Based on the 2001 Aboriginal Peoples' Survey (APS) (Statistics Canada, 2004), there are more than 1 million people of Aboriginal descent in Canada. They are represented throughout the country, ranging from 1 percent of the population in Ontario up to 85 percent of the population in Nunavut. The population is also young and growing. The 2001 census showed that half of the Aboriginal population was under the age of 25 (32 percent below 25 in the non-Aboriginal population) and

Figure 14.2: A young Canadian First Nations boy photographed at a fishing camp in northern British Columbia.

the birth rate was up to twice the national average. Average age of first pregnancy is also significantly lower than the Canadian average.

Indigenous Canadians are split into three main groups: First Nations (65 percent), Métis (30 percent), and Inuit (5 percent). Aboriginal peoples registered as "Indian" under the Indian Act are more commonly referred to as "First Nations" and have certain rights and benefits protected by law. They are represented by the Assembly of First Nations. Those Aboriginal peoples not registered are referred to as "non-status" and are represented by the Congress of Aboriginal Peoples. The Métis are Aboriginal peoples

with mixed ancestry; they are represented by the Métis National Council. The Inuit primarily live in Northern Canada and are represented by the Inuit Tapiriit Kanatami (ITK) (*Assembly of First Nations*, n.d.; *Congress of Aboriginal Peoples*, n.d.; *Inuit Tapiriit Kanatami*, n.d.; *Métis National Council*, n.d.).

It is not necessary to travel outside Canada to see the results of poverty and poor access to health care. The Canadian health care system is one of the best and most progressive in the world, but jurisdictional disputes, cultural barriers, and geographic isolation have impeded many Aboriginal peoples' access to adequate housing and health care. Those Canadians interested in studying the health of developing world populations should start with a good understanding of the socio-economic and health standards of indigenous peoples living within their own borders.

Socio-economic Status of Indigenous Canadians

We have survived Canada's assault on our identity and our rights.... Our survival is a testament to our determination and will to survive as people. We are prepared to participate in Canada's future—but only on the terms that we believe to be our rightful heritage.

—Wallace Labillois, Council of Elders, Royal Commission on Aboriginal Peoples (1996)

Although the general health of Canada's Aboriginal population is much better than that of many other indigenous populations around the world, indigenous health indices still lag behind those of non-Aboriginal Canadians (Canadian

Table 14.4: Health indices for indigenous Canadians

	Non-Aboriginal	First Nations	Inuit	Métis
Female life expectancy (years)	82	77	70	n.d.
Male life expectancy (years)	76	69	68	n.d.
Infant mortality rate (per 1,000 live births)	5.3	8.0	15	n.d.
Suicide rate (deaths/100,000)	13	28	79	n.d.
Self-rated health status (%):				
Excellent	61	40	56	58
Poor	12	27	12	17

Source: Canadian Institute for Health Information (2004)
n.d.: No data available

Institute for Health Information, 2004). As Table 14.4 shows, broad health indicators such as life expectancy, suicide rate, infant mortality, and self-reported health status are all significantly worse among indigenous populations. There is no single cause for the poorer health of Aboriginal peoples; it is the end result of a range of inequities—both historic and contemporary. Identifying and quantifying every variable would be difficult, but lower socio-economic standards, lack of self-determination, and the legacy of the residential school system are just a few of the factors that have had significant adverse health effects. Figure 14.3 shows that the socio-economic status of Aboriginal peoples (represented by educational attainment, unemployment rate, and average income) are all significantly lower than national averages.

Some of the principal variables influencing the health of indigenous Canadians are as follows.

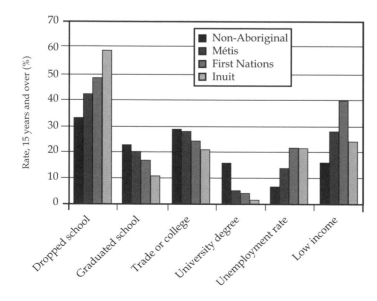

Figure 14.3: Education and employment rates for indigenous Canadians

Source: Canadian Institute for Health Information (2004)

Education

With increasing awareness of the importance of higher education and the establishment of various organizations such as the First Nations Education Council, all three Aboriginal groups have made slow but steady progress in school completion rates. Statistics Canada figures for 2001 (Figure 14.3) show that 48 percent of First Nations, 59 percent of Inuit, and 42 percent of Métis children drop out of school. Boys reported that the most common obstacles to completion of schooling were boredom and a desire to work. Among girls, the most common reasons were either pregnancy or the need to care for children. Reasons for not completing post-secondary studies were family responsibilities among women and lack of money for men (O'Donnell & Tait, 2001). There is clearly a need for more Aboriginal teachers and aides in the classroom to help make the educational experience more culturally relevant and interesting for Aboriginal students.

Effects of Residential Schooling

> While it is not uncommon to hear some former students speak about their positive experiences in these institutions, their stories are overshadowed by disclosures of abuse, criminal convictions of perpetrators and the findings of various studies such as the Royal Commission on Aboriginal Peoples, which tell of the tragic legacy that the residential school system has left with many former students. (Indian and Northern Affairs Canada, 2004a)

The residential school system officially began in 1892; most were closed by the 1970s. Schools were funded by the federal government and usually operated by the churches (Indian and Northern Affairs Canada, 2004a). Children were forbidden to speak their own language and practise their own traditions and beliefs. The subsequent loss of culture and language weakened the collective identity of indigenous peoples. Apart from numerous lawsuits and class actions stemming from abuse, the federal government also acknowledged this injustice with an apology in 1998.

The schooling experiment harmed many of the estimated 93,000 former residential students who are still alive today (Canadian Institute for Health Information, 2004). Specific harmful effects of residential schooling are difficult to disentangle from other socio-economic variables affecting indigenous populations, but it is widely accepted that it was a significant contributor to current high levels of suicide, substance abuse, and family violence (Smith et al., 2005). These effects also subsequently harm succeeding generations. Residential schooling still runs like a rip through the fabric of indigenous society.

Housing Standards

Adequate standards of housing and water quality are essential foundations for good health—both these basic necessities are of poorer quality in indigenous communities (Indian and Northern Affairs, 2005). The most recent data shows that of the more than 90,000 houses in First Nations' communities, 12 percent are overcrowded (more than one person per room), 21.9 percent need major repairs, and 5.7 percent need to be replaced (Canadian Institute for Health Information, 2004). In addition, the growing Aboriginal population means that a steady supply of new houses is also needed. Housing is a particular problem in the north, where 53 percent of Inuit live in crowded conditions. Crowding is a particular risk for the transmission of tuberculosis. Not surprisingly, tuberculosis is many times more common among the Inuit than the rest of Canada.

Clean Water and the Environment

Water contamination resulting from inadequate and poorly managed treatment plants can lead to numerous health problems; it is a common problem on First Nations' reserves (Rosenberg et al., 1997). In 2005, over 1,000 people were evacuated from Kashechewan reserve because of chronic health problems from chronically contaminated water. This has prompted urgent government action (Eggertson, 2006). In 2006, roughly one in six Native reserves had a "boil water" advisory in place; the North is particularly badly affected.

Over the last 40 years, there has been a significant rise in the temperature in Canada's north varying from 0.5–1.5°C. This is predicted to continue during the near future and threatens to alter traditional Inuit hunting areas. More immediately, the Inuit are also threatened by environmental contaminants that have accumulated in Arctic wildlife. Studies have shown that human exposure to mercury and organic toxins exceeds daily levels set by Health Canada, in some cases, by an order of magnitude (Butler-Walker et al., 2006). The Inuit continue to consume traditional hunted food, partly because of the expense of imported food and because of the place of traditional hunting within the Inuit social structure.

Aboriginal Language

Language is an essential part of cultural identity. Partly due to the residential schooling legacy, many indigenous languages are at risk. The percentage of indigenous peoples who can speak an Aboriginal language fell from 20 percent in 1996 to 16 percent in 2001 (O'Donnell & Tait, 2001). The Métis are the least likely to know an Aboriginal language and the Inuit are the most likely to have retained a language skill. The Aboriginal Head Start Approach (HSA) is an early childhood development program for indigenous children and their families. There are currently well over a 100 HSA programs throughout Canada (*Aboriginal Head Start Association of British Columbia*, n.d.). These and other educational initiatives include Native languages as part of their program. The HSA Program began in the US with the aim of supporting early child development for Aboriginal peoples. The Canadian federal government adopted the Head Start Approach in 1985.

Addressing the Determinants of Native Ill Health

> Lack of control over important dimensions of living, in itself contributes to ill health. Aboriginal people want to exercise their own judgment and understanding about what makes people healthy, their own skills in solving health and social problems. (Royal Commission on Aboriginal Peoples, 1996)

The influential 1996 Royal Commission on Aboriginal Peoples (RCAP) included hundreds of recommendations concerning solutions for indigenous health and social problems. The government's response to the commission was to release

Gathering Strength: Canada's Aboriginal Action Plan, which has led to many new policy developments since its release. One obvious shift in policy has been a move to give Aboriginal peoples greater control over their own affairs. One part of this involves the slow process of land claims and treaty negotiations. The second occurs at a local level and involves a move toward indigenous control over their own services, particularly health, education, police, and fire services. In a British Columbia study (Chandler & Lalonde, 1998), it was found that the suicide rate was 138 per 100,000 population in communities with no control over local services, but there was a steady drop in suicide rate as the number of Native-controlled facilities increased. In communities with complete control over their own services, the suicide rate was almost zero.

Several national institutes have also been created, including the National Aboriginal Health Organization (advocates for the health and well-being of Aboriginal peoples), the Research Institute of Aboriginal Peoples Health (supports indigenous health research), the Aboriginal Healing Foundation (supports healing initiatives aimed at reducing the impact of residential schooling), and the much needed First Nations Statistical Institute (regular collection of indigenous health and social data). In addition, greater investment has been made in the Head Start Program and a housing renovation fund intended to provide water, sewage, and housing upgrades on reserves (*Institute of Aboriginal Peoples' Health*; n.d.; *National Aboriginal Health Organization*, n.d.).

Health Status of Indigenous Canadians

Canadian Aboriginal peoples die earlier than their fellow Canadians and, on average, sustain a disproportionate burden of chronic physical and mental illness (Health Canada, 2006) (Table 14.5).

Table 14.5: Rates of chronic diseases for indigenous Canadians

	Non-Aboriginal	First Nations	Inuit	Métis
Obesity (%)	14	24	22	23
Diabetes (%)	4	11 (M); 17 (F)	2	6
Arthritis (%)	16	18 (M); 25 (F)	9	20
Heart disease (%)	4	12	5	7
Hypertension (%)	8 (M); 11 (F)	22 (M); 26 (F)	8	13
Smoking (%)	22	38	61	37
Tuberculosis (per 100,000)	1.3	30	92	5.6
Chlamydia (per 100,000)	82 (M); 194 (F)	532 (M); 1,366 (F)	1,410 (M); 2,918 (F)	no data

Source: Canadian Institute for Health Information (2004)

Although exact causes are not known in detail, the relatively poor status of Native health is clearly associated with the unfavourable economic and social conditions discussed in the previous section. On the bright side, there have been significant improvements over the last two or three decades. Life expectancy at birth is steadily increasing (Figure 14.4) and, most dramatically, the infant mortality rate for Aboriginal populations has fallen rapidly; it is now only slightly higher than the national average (Figure 14.5). The following conditions are of particular importance among Canada's indigenous groups.

Diseases of Lifestyle (Obesity, Diabetes, Cardiovascular Diseases)

It is widely accepted that the principal risk factors for diabetes, heart attacks, strokes, and high cholesterol are the so-called lifestyle factors (poor nutrition, lack of exercise, and smoking). These are not the

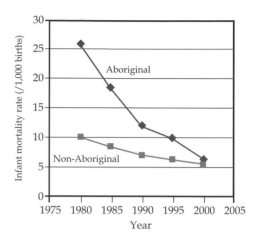

Figure 14.5: Infant mortality rates for Aboriginal and non-Aboriginal Canadian children

Sources: Health Canada (2005); Public Health Agency of Canada (n.d.)

only causes of vascular disease, but they are the main ones over which people have some control. Unfortunately, indigenous peoples have high levels of all these risk factors. Smoking rates are two to three times the national average and obesity has become a major health problem facing First Nations' communities, including the children (Caballeros et al., 2003).

Compared to Canadian averages, strokes and heart attacks are more common among Aboriginal peoples and have become the leading causes of death in indigenous adults over 45 years (Figure 14.6). Type 2 diabetes has now reached epidemic levels, particularly in First Nations communities, where almost one in five now has diabetes (Young et al., 2000). Type 2 diabetes is also increasingly diagnosed among Aboriginal children. The government has responded with the Aboriginal Diabetes Initiative, which is a collaborative venture between the government and representatives of indigenous groups.

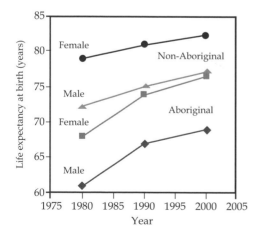

Figure 14.4: Canadian life expectancy at birth by gender and ethnicity

Source: Health Canada (2005)

Infectious Diseases (Tuberculosis, HIV/AIDS)

The most important infectious diseases affecting indigenous peoples are tuberculosis and HIV/AIDS. Tuberculosis is over five times more common among Aboriginal peoples (Clarke & Riben, 1999). This is only an average; in some communities, rates are even higher. Wherever there is poverty and poor housing, tuberculosis will not be far behind. Clearly, socio-economic factors are the cause of the high rate of tuberculosis in the indigenous communities. Although rates are much lower than they were during epidemics in early 20th-century Canada (the peak rate was 700 per 100,000), significant improvements in the current rate will require extensive investment in First Nations housing standards.

In 1992, indigenous peoples formed 1.7 percent of the total HIV/AIDS cases in Canada. By 2001, this had risen to 7.2 percent (Health Canada, 2005). Ethnicity is not reliably reported on notification forms so this is certainly an underestimate. Aboriginal communities make up 3.3 percent of the Canadian population. The most common means of transmission was IV drug use (Craib et al., 2003). The HIV epidemic has had a significant effect on indigenous women. The Canadian national rate of HIV infection among pregnant women is 3.4 per 10,000 population; among indigenous women, it is 33.3 per 10,000 (Health Canada, 2005).

Other infectious risks for indigenous communities include a higher rate of water-borne diseases such as hepatitis A and shigellosis, reflecting the poorer water standards in Native communities (Rosenberg et al., 1997). There is also evidence that Native children are at higher risk of chest infection compared to the Canadian average (Seear & Wensley, 1997).

Trauma (Injuries, Family Violence, Suicide)

Among indigenous peoples, the potential years of life lost to injury is greater than all other causes of death combined and is also three to four times higher than the average Canadian rate (Health Canada, 2001). Injuries and poisoning combined were the most common causes of death for First Nations peoples one to 44 years. Suicide and self-injury made up a significant part of this total. Aboriginal peoples are at greater risk of death and injury from a range of sources, including motor accidents, drowning, fire, family violence, and suicide.

Deaths and injuries due to motor vehicle accidents are much higher than national averages (Health Canada, 2001). Contributing factors include high rates of alcohol use, poorer-quality rural roads, and greater use of higher-risk vehicles such as snowmobiles and all-terrain vehicles.

Figure 14.6: Comparative Rates for Four Common Diseases

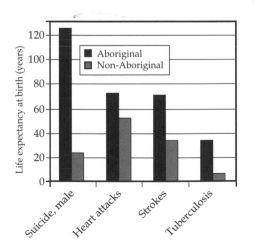

Source: Health Canada (2005)

The location of Indian communities near rivers and lakes also increases the risk of drowning. One study showed that only 6 percent of Aboriginal drowning victims had worn a flotation device and two-thirds of drowning victims over 15 years old had an alcohol level above the legal limit (compared to 27 percent for non-Aboriginal drowning) (Chochinov, 1998). The greatest risk for children was falling into open water. Higher smoking rates, wood-frame housing, lower building standards (particularly lack of smoke detectors), and poorly equipped rural fire services all combine to produce a much greater risk of serious fires on Aboriginal reserves. Almost one-third of all fire deaths in Aboriginal population are between the age of one and 14, compared to an average of 16 percent in the total Canadian population.

The high suicide rate noted in many Aboriginal communities tends to be associated with predictable adverse social characteristics (Mignone & O'Neil, 2005). These include a high number of occupants per household, more single-parent families, fewer elders, lower average income, and lower average education. The Canadian government and First Nations' groups have taken the problem seriously with advisory groups and various reports, but there are no easy solutions for such a complex problem. How are phrases, such as "creating strategies for building youth identity, resilience and culture" (Suicide Prevention Advisory Group, 2001), actually translated into action for young indigenous youths on rural reserves across a country as big as Canada? The association between suicide rates and community self-determination, mentioned earlier, offers some hope for interventions that have measurable results (Chandler & Lalonde, 1998).

High rates of family violence have been reported in indigenous communities, but the problem is greatly underreported. A review of earlier studies by Health Canada quotes abuse rates as high as 80 percent against women and 40 percent against children (Health Canada National Clearinghouse on Family Violence, 1996). It is suspected that elder abuse is increasing, but no accurate figures exist. Apart from the absence of reliable survey data, two recent reviews of Aboriginal health do not even mention the subject (Canadian Institute for Health Information, 2004; O'Donnell & Tait, 2001)! Family violence is viewed by many First Nations peoples as a social ill that has evolved due to the results of historical injustices and cultural assaults experienced over centuries of colonization; it is clearly a problem with deep roots. A 1991 study by the Aboriginal Nurses Association found that the three most common factors behind family violence were poverty, substance abuse, and a history of intergenerational abuse (Kiyoshk, 2001).

The federal government became involved in the 1970s once the scope of the problem became obvious. Programs included the Family Violence Initiative, Child Sexual Abuse Initiative, and the construction of federally funded women's shelters on reserves across Canada. Involvement of the justice system and child protection agencies is clearly necessary, but prevention through education and community initiatives offers the only long-term solution to this problem (Indian and Northern Affairs Canada, 2004b).

Substance Abuse

Substance abuse, including drug and alcohol abuse, is a common problem and a major issue concerning Canada's

Native peoples. Research suggests that Fetal Alcohol Syndrome (FAS) may be more common among Native children, but there is insufficient evidence about the prevalence of fetal alcohol syndrome among the non-Native population to be able to draw firm conclusions. The inhalation of volatile substances such as glue, gasoline, paint, and dry-cleaning fluids is also a growing problem among some indigenous children (Weir, 2001). There is no accurate information, but the problem is common in remote Canadian reserves. It has been reported in children as young as four years old.

The issue came to national attention in 2000 when leaders of the Innu community of Davis Inlet on the Labrador coast asked for assistance to deal with an uncontrollable epidemic of glue sniffing and alcoholism among its children and the highest rate of suicide anywhere in Canada. Children were taken south to detox centers and did well, but ultimately had to be returned to a community that was little better than it had been when they left. No long-term solutions to these terrible social dilemmas can be achieved unless there is widespread improvement in the socio-economic status of remote rural communities.

THE HEALTH OF OTHER MAJOR INDIGENOUS POPULATIONS

We were all part of a world community of Indigenous Peoples spanning the planet, experiencing the same problems and struggling against the same alienation, marginalization and sense of powerlessness. We had gathered there united by our shared frustration with the dominant systems in our own countries and their consistent failure to deliver justice. We were all looking for, and demanding, justice from a higher authority.

—Michael Dodson, Australian Aboriginal representative to UN Working Group on Indigenous Health

Within the approximately 300–350 million indigenous peoples, there are thousands of separate tribal groupings. Despite this enormous social and cultural diversity, these communities face surprisingly similar health challenges. The unifying factor common to most indigenous peoples is a history of conflict and mistreatment during the period of European expansion, spreading over the last five centuries. Whole tribes, entire cultures, and unknown numbers of lives were lost forever due to violent oppression, slavery, and introduced diseases such as smallpox, measles, and tuberculosis (Coates, 2004).

While sipping coffee in Vancouver, Brisbane, or Auckland, it is easy to imagine that this is all ancient history—certainly sad, but nothing to do with the modern enlightened world. Nothing could be further from the truth. As recently as the mid-20th century, it was accepted that Aboriginal Australians and New Zealand Maoris would die out as separate races (Kunitz, 2000). Although their numbers are now increasing, general standards of health still lag far behind the averages in these prosperous countries. Guatemala's Supreme Court of Justice calculated that between 100,000 and 200,000 Indigenous Mayan children lost one or both parents from military violence during their civil war (Melville & Lykes, 1992). The war ended in 1996.

The infectious diseases and violence that indigenous peoples suffered in the past have now largely been replaced by behavioural and psychiatric problems resulting from the common history of discrimination and inequity that many still suffer in their own countries. High rates of suicide can be found from Torres Strait islanders to Brazilian Amerindians (Loenaars, 2006). Depression, family violence, and alcoholism are all common from the northernmost indigenous communities of Russia down to remote Aboriginal reserves in Australia (Fardahl & Poelzer, 1997; Ring & Brown, 2002). In every case where figures are available, the life expectancy of indigenous populations is always several years below their own country's national average (Figure 14.7).

This point brings up the topical issue of statistical data. One problem confronting the concept of global indigenous health is the absence of reliable and easily available health information. In 2002, Australia, Canada, and New Zealand rose to this challenge. All three countries have large indigenous populations whose health outcomes are significantly poorer than those of the general population. In 2002, all three countries agreed to share their research expertise in indigenous health and to develop collaborative research projects (Cunningham et al., 2003). There are very few comparative studies of indigenous health in different countries (Bramley et al., 2004, 2006; Paradies & Cunningham, 2002). The available work strongly suggests that there are very obvious similarities between otherwise widely different indigenous groups. The broad range of common diseases can be grouped under three broad headings:

- *Diseases due to non-traditional lifestyles:* Cardiovascular disease, heart attacks, strokes, obesity, and diabetes.
- *Diseases due to poverty and poor living conditions:* Tuberculosis, exposure to environmental toxins, injuries, and diseases of contaminated water (shigellosis, hepatitis A).
- *Diseases resulting from past injustice and social exclusion:* Substance abuse, family violence, suicide.

Figure 14.7: Comparative life expectancies at birth for indigenous populations around the world

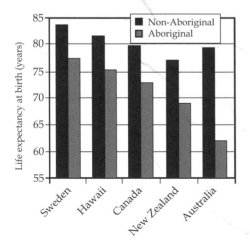

Sources: Australian Bureau of Statistics (n.d.); Bramley et al. (2004, 2006); Braun et al. (1996); Hausler et al. (2005); Statistics Canada (2004)

■ SUMMARY

No matter what definition is used, there are probably well over 300 million people around the world whose culture and language distinguish them as descendants of pre-colonial inhabitants. The diverse languages and cultures accumulated by traditional indigenous populations make their own countries and the world in general a more interesting place to live. In addition, the enormous scientific (particularly pharmaceutical) value of some of their botanical knowledge has only recently been appreciated. A common history of invasion, colonization, and subsequent oppression means that the international community bears some responsibility for the current poor state of health of many indigenous groups around the world. It is hoped that they recognize this responsibility and help to redress old wrongs by placing more emphasis on the health of indigenous peoples in the future.

Current evidence suggests that the health status of many indigenous groups is actually improving, but there is a long way to go. Improvements in global communications will hopefully make it harder to exploit indigenous groups without the rest of the world finding out. Communication advances also make it easier for small indigenous groups to be heard (Kunitz, 2000). As Durie (2003) has pointed out, maintaining those long-term improvements in health will require active interventions that include economic revival, specific indigenous health research, increased funding and resources for indigenous peoples, and constitutional and legislative changes to improve their degree of self-determination.

RESOURCES

References

Aboriginal Head Start Association of British Columbia. (n.d.). Retrieved from www.ahsabc.com.

Adelson, N. (2005). "The embodiment of inequity: Health disparities in Aboriginal Canada." *Canadian Journal of Public Health, 96* (Supp. 2), S45–S561.

Alderete, E. (1999). *The health of indigenous peoples*. Retrieved from www.who.int/hhr/activities/indigenous/en.

Arias, A. (2001). *The Rigoberta Menchu controversy*. Minneapolis: University of Minnesota Press.

Assembly of First Nations. (n.d.). Retrieved from www.afn.ca.

Australian Bureau of Statistics. (n.d.). Retrieved from www.abs.gov.au by searching "Aboriginal population."

Bjerregaard, P., et al. (2004). "Indigenous health in the Arctic: An overview of the circumpolar Inuit population." *Scandinavian Journal of Public Health, 32*, 390–395.

Bramley, D., et al. (2004). "Indigenous disparities in disease specific mortality, a cross-country comparison: New Zealand, Australia, Canada, and the United States." *New Zealand Medical Journal, 117*, 1215–1223.

Bramley, D., et al. (2006). "Disparities in indigenous health: A cross-country comparison between New Zealand and the United States." *American Journal of Public Health, 95*, 844–850.

Braun, K., et al. (1996). "Life and death in Hawaii: Ethnic variations in life expectancy and mortality, 1980 and 1990." *Hawaii Medical Journal, 55*, 278–283.

Brush, S., & Stabinsky, D. (Eds.). (1996). *Valuing local knowledge: Indigenous people and intellectual property rights*. Washington: Island Press.

Butler-Walker, J., et al. (2006). "Maternal and umbilical cord blood levels of mercury, lead, cadmium, and essential trace elements in Arctic Canada." *Environmental Research, 100*, 295–318.

Caballeros, B., et al. (2003). "Body composition and overweight prevalence in 1,704 school children from seven American Indian communities." *American Journal of Clinical Nutrition, 78*, 308–312.

Canadian Institute for Health Information. (2004). "Aboriginal peoples' health." In *Improving the health of Canadians*. Retrieved from www.cihi.ca by searching "Improving the health of Canadians."

Chandler, M., & Lalonde, C. (1998). "Cultural continuity as a hedge against suicide in Canada's First Nations." *Transcultural Psychiatry, 35,* 191–219.

Chochinov, A. (1998). "Alcohol 'on board,' man overboard – boating fatalities in Canada." *Canadian Medical Association Journal, 159,* 259–260.

Clarke, M., & Riben, P. (1999). *Tuberculosis in First Nations communities.* Ottawa: Health Canada. Retrieved from www.dsp-psd.communication.gc.ca/Collection/H35-4-7-1999E.pdf.

Coates, K. (2004). *A global history of indigenous peoples: Struggle and survival.* New York: Palgrave MacMillan.

Congress of Aboriginal Peoples. (n.d.). Retrieved from www.ab-peoples.org.

Craib, K., et al. (2003). "Risk factors for elevated HIV incidence among Aboriginal injection drug users in Vancouver." *Canadian Medical Association Journal, 168,* 19–24.

Cunningham, C., et al. (2003). "Health research and indigenous health." *British Medical Journal, 327,* 445–447.

Dodson, M. (1998). "Linking international standards with contemporary concerns of Aboriginal and Torres Strait islander peoples." In Pritchard, S. (Ed.), *Indigenous peoples, the United Nations, and human rights.* Leichhardt: The Federation Press.

Durie, M. (2003). "The health of indigenous peoples: Depends on genetics, politics, and socio-economic factors." *British Medical Journal, 326,* 510–511.

Eggertson, L. (2006). "Safe drinking water standards for First Nations' communities." *Canadian Medical Association Journal, 174,* 1248.

Fardahl, G., & Poelzer, G. (1997). "Indigenous peoples of the Russian north." *Cultural Survival Quarterly, 21,* 30–33.

Hausler, S., et al. (2005). "Causes of death in the Sami population of Sweden, 1961–2000." *International Journal of Epidemiology, 34,* 623–629.

Health Canada. (2001). *Unintentional and intentional injury profile for Aboriginal people in Canada.* Retrieved from www.hc-sc.gc.ca/fnih-spni/pubs/injury-bless/2001_trauma/index_e.html.

Health Canada. (2005). *First Nations comparable health indicators.* Retrieved from www.hc-sc.gc.ca/fnih-spni/pubs/gen/2005-01_health-sante_indicat/index_e.html.

Health Canada. (2006). *First Nations and Inuit health.* Retrieved from www.hc-sc.gc.ca/fnih-spni/index_e.html.

Health Canada National Clearinghouse on Family Violence. (1996). *Family violence in Aboriginal communities: An Aboriginal perspective.* Ottawa: Health Canada. Retrieved from www.phac-aspc.gc.ca/ncfv-cnivf/familyviolence/html/fvabor_e.html.

Hughes, R. (1996). *The fatal shore.* London: Harvill Press.

Indian and Northern Affairs Canada. (2004a). *Backgrounder: The residential school system.* Retrieved from www.ainc-inac.gc.ca/gs/schl_e.html.

Indian and Northern Affairs Canada. (2004b). *Family violence prevention program: National manual.* Ottawa: INAC. Retrieved from www.ainc-inac.gc.ca/ps/mnl/fvp/fvp_e.pdf.

Indian and Northern Affairs Canada. (2005). *First Nations' housing.* Retrieved from www.ainc-inac.gc.ca/pr/info/info104_e.html.

Institute of Aboriginal Peoples' Health. (n.d.). Retrieved from www.cihr-irsc.gc.ca/e/8668.html.

International and Labour Organization. (n.d.). *Indigenous and tribal peoples.* Retrieved from www.ilo.org/public/english/indigenous.

International Work Group for Indigenous Affairs. (n.d.). *Indigenous issues.* Retrieved from www.iwgia.org/sw155.asp.

Inuit Circumpolar Conference. (n.d.). Retrieved from www.inuitcircumpolar.com.

Inuit Tapiriit Kanatami. (n.d.). Retrieved from www.itk.ca.

Kiyoshk, R. (2001). *Family violence in Aboriginal communities: A review*. Ottawa: Aboriginal Nurses Association of Canada.

Kunitz, S. (2000). "Globalization, states, and the health of indigenous peoples." *American Journal of Public Health, 90*, 1531–1539.

Loenaars, A. (2006). "Suicide among indigenous peoples: Introduction and call to action." *Archives of Suicide Research, 10*, 103–115.

Melville, M., & Lykes, M. (1992). "Guatemalan Indian children and the sociocultural effects of government-sponsored terrorism." *Social Science and Medicine, 34*, 533–548.

Métis National Council. (n.d.). Retrieved from www.metisnation.ca.

Mignone, J., & O'Neil, J. (2005). "Social capital and youth suicide risk factors in First Nations' communities." *Canadian Journal of Public Health, 96*, S51–S54.

National Aboriginal Health Organization. (n.d.). Retrieved from www.naho.ca/english.

O'Donnell, V., & Tait, H. (2001). *Aboriginal Peoples Survey 2001 – initial findings: Well-being of the non-reserve Aboriginal population*. Ottawa: Statistics Canada. Retrieved from www.statcan.ca/Daily/English/030924/d030924b.htm.

Osborn, W. (2001). *The wild frontier: Atrocities during the American Indian War from Jamestown colony to Wounded Knee*. New York: Random House.

Paradies, Y., & Cunningham, J. (2002). "Placing Aboriginal and Torres Strait islander mortality in an international context." *Australia New Zealand Journal of Public Health, 26*, 11–16.

Public Health Agency of Canada. (n.d.). *Perinatal surveillance system*. Retrieved from www.phac-aspc.gc.ca/rhs-ssg/factshts/mort_e.html.

Ring, I., & Brown, N. (2002). "Indigenous health: Chronically inadequate responses to damning statistics." *Medical Journal of Australia, 177*, 629–631.

Rosenberg, T., et al. (1997). "Shigellosis on Indian reserves in Manitoba, Canada: Its relationship to crowded housing, lack of running water, and inadequate sewage disposal." *American Journal of Public Health, 87*, 1547–1551.

Royal Commission on Aboriginal Peoples. (1996). *Report of the Royal Commission on Aboriginal Peoples*. Retrieved from www.ainc-inac.gc.ca/ch/rcap/index_e.html.

Seear, M., & Wensley, D. (1997). "Chronic cough and wheeze: Do they all have asthma?" *European Respiratory Journal, 10*, 342–345.

Smith, D., et al. (2005). "Turning around the intergenerational impact of residential schools on Aboriginal people: Implications for health policy and practice." *Canadian Journal of Nursing Research, 37*, 38–60.

Stannard, D. (1992). *American holocaust: Columbus and the conquest of the New World*. New York: Oxford University Press.

Statistics Canada. (2004). *2001 Aboriginal Peoples survey community profiles*. Retrieved from www12.statcan.ca/english/profil01aps/home.cfm.

Suicide Prevention Advisory Group. (2001). *Acting on what we know: Preventing youth suicide in First Nations*. Ottawa: Health Canada. Retrieved from www.hc-sc.gc.ca/fnih-spni/pubs/suicide/prev_youth-jeunes/index_e.html.

UNICEF. (2006). *Child mortality*. Retrieved from www.childinfo.org/areas/childmortality.

United Nations High Commission for Human Rights. (n.d.). *Indigenous peoples*. Retrieved from www.unhchr.ch/indigenous/main.html.

United Nations Permanent Forum on Indigenous Issues. (n.d.). Retrieved from www.un.org/esa/socdev/unpfii/index.html.

US Census Bureau. (2005). *Annual estimates of the population by race alone and Hispanic or Latino origin*. Retrieved from www.census.gov/popest/states/asrh/SC-EST2005-04.html.

Weir, E. (2001). "Inhalant use and addiction in Canada." *Canadian Medical Association Journal, 164*, 397–400.

World Bank. (n.d.). Retrieved from www.worldbank.org by searching "indigenous people."

World Health Organization. (2000). "Selected national health accounts indicators for all Member

States, estimates for 1997." In *World health report 2000: Health systems — improving performance*. Retrieved from www.who.int/whr/2000/en/annex08_en.pdf.

Young, T., et al. (2000). "Type 2 diabetes mellitus in Canada's First Nations: Status of an epidemic in progress." *Canadian Medical Association Journal, 163*, 561–566.

Recommended Reading

Arias, A. (2001). *The Rigoberta Menchu controversy*. Minneapolis: University of Minnesota Press.

Brody, H. (2002). *The other side of Eden: Hunters, farmers, and the shaping of the world*. New York: North Point Press.

Cardinal, H. (2000). *The unjust society*. Seattle: University of Washington Press.

Coates, K. (2005). *A global history of indigenous peoples: Struggle and survival*. New York: Palgrave Macmillan.

Dean, B., Levi, J. (Eds.). (2003). *At the Risk of Being Heard: Identity, Indigenous Rights and Postcolonial States*. Michigan: University of Michigan Press.

Keal, P. (2003). *European Conquest and the Rights of Indigenous Peoples: The Moral Backwardness of International Society*. Cambridge: Cambridge University Press.

Maybury-Lewis, D. (2001). *Indigenous peoples, ethnic groups, and the state*. Boston: Allyn and Bacon.

Waldram, J., & Herring, D. 2006. *Aboriginal health in Canada: Historical, cultural, and epidemiological perspectives*. Toronto: University of Toronto Press.

PART VI

WORKING SAFELY
AND EFFECTIVELY IN A
DEVELOPING COUNTRY

Chapter 15
**Planning and Preparing
for Safe, Effective
Development Work**

Chapter 16
**Managing a Sustainable
Aid Partnership**

Planning and Preparing for Safe, Effective Development Work

*He was wearing his favorite T-shirt, which featured
a multiple-choice questionnaire for relief workers:
(a) Missionary? (b) Mercenary? (c) Misfit? (d) Broken Heart?
Henry had ticked (b), which was a joke since his family
owned half of northeast England. Me? I was a (c)/(d) hybrid.*
—Helen Fielding, *Cause Celeb*

OBJECTIVES

After completing this chapter, you should be able to

- prepare and plan for an overseas development project
- appreciate the ethical problems associated with aid projects
- know how to stay healthy working in a developing country
- understand how to work effectively and co-operatively in a new culture

Apart from the hundreds of thousands of people who work full-time in the aid industry, there are probably 10 times that number who volunteer or spend large amounts of their time and money on short-term aid projects in developing countries. As the interest in the recent debt-relief talks showed, there are many millions more people around the world who have a deep interest in the plight of developing world populations even if they are not actively involved in a project. Surely, this evidence of the good side of human nature should be celebrated and remain beyond criticism?

For a long time, this has been the prevailing attitude in news articles about aid projects. However, when you get a message that your expensive slit lamp has been broken at the airport, while you are in the middle of a jet-lagged screaming match with a team member who will not stop making a sucking noise with his teeth, you will realize that heartwarming fairy tales of successful, problem-free aid projects are not a good way to prepare for reality.

This does not mean that short-term projects are of no value; they can be of profound value (for the team members), but it is best to go into them with a proper appreciation of the seriousness of the task. Clearing away many of the misconceptions about aid will require some straight talk — not gratuitous criticism, but practical, unsentimental advice about development work in the real world. If you have ever asked any variant of the question, "I just want to get involved. How can I do something to help?" then please read the next two chapters carefully.

OVERSEAS DEVELOPMENT WORK

Two roads diverged in a wood, and I –
I took the one less traveled by,
And that has made all the difference.
    — Robert Frost, "The Road Not Taken,"
                                              1920

If you have decided to take Robert Frost's advice, that is great, but remember that the results of that decision do not just affect yourself. Perhaps you are going to do a clinical rotation in a hospital, help build houses, or work as a teacher. No matter what you hope to achieve, a poorly planned and performed project not only reflects badly on you (and, by extension, your country of origin), but also adversely affects the population you choose to work with (Maren, 2002). Quite apart from any problems you might suffer as a result of poor preparation, the effects on your hosts may range from unfairly raising their hopes, all the way to being involved in a medical disaster. Clearly, this is something to be taken very seriously.

In the spirit of frank discussion, we may as well start by diving straight into the deep end. The average person has limited access to information about life in very

Box 15.1: A moment of Zen

Number of women dying in labour per 100,000 births in Sub-Saharan Africa: 700	
In Canada: Five	
Sub-Saharan African woman's lifetime risk of dying while having a baby:	Average death rate for all climbers attempting K2 in the Himalayas 1954–1994:
One in 25	**One in 25**
Source: Safe Motherhood (n.d.)	Source: Huey & Eguskitza (2000)

poor countries. The general impression given by news reports of developing countries or by fundraising advertisements for aid agencies is one of hopeless grinding poverty. While such images help to raise money and are fair reflections of *life* in some parts of the world, they are not accurate representations of the *people*; this distinction must be appreciated.

People living in poverty are not helpless; they are unlucky. They do not respond to hardship by huddling in huts, waiting desperately for the next planeload of aid workers to arrive. In essence, their lives are the same as ours. They do the best they can, work hard under terribly difficult circumstances, care for their children, and somehow manage to retain their humanity and dignity under circumstances that would reduce most of us to tears. They do not need or want religious conversion, pity, or free handouts.

What they do want is equal partnerships with hard-working, committed individuals working in well-planned, sustainable assistance projects with clearly defined goals and measured results. Working this way with people who live in poverty will give you insights into your own life that you might never have gained by staying at home. Under these circumstances, aid projects can truly be life-altering experiences, but you must enter the process understanding that you are the learner and not the teacher.

A small example might help to give a different perspective. Imagine you are sitting with a beer and pizza watching "Hockey Night in Canada." You answer a knock on the door and find two Ethiopian students who tell you they are part of a North African charity called "Buckets of Tears for Canada." They start giving you advice about eating fresh vegetables, exercising, and not watching so much television. What would your opinion be and what would you do? What if they then decided to hand out some advice about your sexual practices or tried to change your political and religious beliefs? By this point, you would probably be fairly irate, so why should people in developing countries be any different when you arrive at their door?

In a more realistic scenario, the students would not have prepared for their trip so would not know your language or have organized an interpreter. Neither side would have understood the other. They would then leave saying, "He didn't seem to understand a word we were saying," while you would have been left wondering "What was that all about?" — not a bad analogy for the average aid project (Hancock, 1992).

The success rate of large aid projects is, to say the least, a subject of debate (Huetter, 2003). There is no reason that short-term aid projects should fare any better. Although literature does exist

---

Box 15.1: History notes

Rudolph Virchow (1821–1902)

It is difficult to imagine how Virchow managed to fit so much work into one life. Apart from being one of the greatest medical researchers of the 19th century, he was also a politician, archaeologist (he excavated Troy with Schliemann), and writer. He started a journal (Virchow's Archives) after other journals would not publish his work; it is still published today. After studying a typhus outbreak in what is now Poland, he became an active social reformer. His report condemned the government for not providing adequate living conditions. He stressed that disease was the result of socio-economic conditions and lost his government job as a result. He never believed in the germ theory, but realized that social change could improve health. He was the first to claim that health was a constitutional right. He annoyed the government so much that Bismarck challenged him to a duel; he declined. Follow the reference for more information (Hajdu, 2005).

---

showing that short-term projects can lead to measurable benefits (Clemens et al. 2004), that paper's definition of "short term" was four years. Very specialized surgical teams or large-scale immunization campaigns can certainly achieve substantial work in a matter of weeks, but the timeline for most aid projects (education, nutrition, or poverty relief) will be measured in many months and more often in years.

Short-term projects also face other problems. Anyone familiar with foreign travel will be aware of the numerous practical difficulties encountered when travelling or working in a developing country. When a project has only a few weeks to work with, even small delays and obstructions will become significant. Apart from the disinclination of most humans to be told what to do, human nature will also provide you with other obstacles in the form of personal team dynamics. If you find yourself saying, "He'll behave better when he has some work to do" or "We'll sort this out when we get there," you are probably in for big disappointments.

Given the large number of people who are interested in development work, there is surprisingly little material to meet this educational demand. Degree courses in international health are given by large centres, but for the average student, access to university-level courses in international health is surprisingly limited. Handbooks and Web sites are available, but they are usually written with medical student electives in mind (Heck & Wedemeyer, 2000; Hope et al., 2004). Unfortunately, this means that many members of short-term projects will have little or no experience of the history and framework of the aid industry in which they will be working. Apart from making sure the specific skills you need for your project are up-to-date, it is also important to put a great deal of research into the language, culture, and history of your host country. In order to get the best out of a project, it is necessary to start planning and studying at least a year before you decide to leave.

I'll Be Fine. What Could Possibly Go Wrong?

Tens of millions of North Americans of all ages travel overseas each year and only about 5,000 of this number die during travel — most from pre-existing medical conditions (Baker et al., 1992; Hagarten et al., 1991). From a statistical point of view, your chances of dying during a trip are very small (Klein, 1995). However, a study of Peace Corps workers revealed that non-lethal but still significant health problems are quite common (Table 15.2) (Bernard et al., 1989). Overall, the most common cause of a ruined trip is intestinal infection while the most common cause of mortality or severe injury is traumatic injury (cars, motorbikes, horses, boats, etc.). Despite all the emphasis placed on immunizations and malaria prophylaxis, the dangers of road traffic accidents greatly exceed the mortality from malaria and other infectious diseases (Odero et al., 1997).

Table 15.2: Common health problems reported by Peace Corps volunteers

Diarrhea	48%
Amebiasis	24%
Injuries	20%
Skin infections	19%
Giardiasis	17%
Hepatitis Schistosomiasis Malaria Filariasis Dengue	< 1%

Source: Bernard et al. (1989)

The biggest danger facing anyone who travels away from the beaten path is ignorance. At best, poor preparation will result in you wasting limited resources of time and money. At worst, you will be exposed to significant risks that, in most cases, could have been avoided and predicted with adequate pre-trip research. In preparation for this chapter, friends and colleagues with extensive experience in international projects were asked to send in their most memorable examples of what can go wrong. All the extracts given below are true and unedited.

Drugs and Alcohol

Afterwards, some of the team members told me that the only reason she had come on the project was because of the cheap and easy supply of drugs in that part of the world. I wish they had told me before we left. She would not listen to advice and fell into increasingly bad company. It came to a head when she was admitted to the local psychiatric ward after a bad experience with unknown drugs. We finally managed to get her home by medical evacuation. The expense and worry were considerable.

The dumbest thing I ever did in my life was to accept a friend's teenage son onto a project. I got little work done because I was constantly searching for this boy downtown after dark. At the end of the first week, he was brought back to the hospital by two local police, who basically said "Put him on the plane tomorrow or he'll be cracking rocks in jail for the next 10 years." The boy's parting words at the airport were, "You should have called their bluff; they aren't allowed to arrest US citizens."

It is not worth the risk to carry drugs or to use them when travelling overseas. It is important to remember that several countries (including Thailand, Singapore, Indonesia, Malaysia, and Vietnam) have severe penalties for drug offences that include life imprisonment and even the death penalty. Little distinction is made between soft and hard drugs. Travellers in a foreign country are subject to that country's laws. The local consular office has the right to visit you, but cannot override local laws and certainly cannot get you out of jail simply because you are

a nice person on an aid project (Foreign Affairs and International Trade Canada, 2004).

Apart from staying away from drugs altogether, the usual common-sense precautions apply: Ensure that any prescription medications you take are not considered illegal, and never leave your bags with a stranger or carry packages for another person. Each year, 2,500 Americans are arrested overseas; one-third on drug-related charges (US Department of State, n.d.-a).

Infectious Diseases

It was years ago, during my first trip as a student. Once I got back, I found I had amebiasis and it had spread to my liver. I did not realize how much weight I had lost until my mother burst into tears when she met me at the airport.

I found afterwards that she had not had any of her childhood immunizations. She caught measles from a kid in the clinic that turned into pneumonia a couple of days later. She ended up in the local hospital for several days and took weeks to recover fully, all for an avoidable disease.

Way back when I was a medical student, a group of us went to work in a big hospital outside of Johannesburg. Two of us tested strongly positive for tuberculosis when we got back to Canada and ended up taking isoniazid for six months. It was a disaster—no beer for six months.

Whatever else you might leave out before travelling, it is a very good idea to organize traveller's health insurance. Good-quality medical care can be found in

Figure 15.1: I'm sure the brochure said "comfortable shared cooking facilities." Perhaps I should do some planning next time!

most countries as long as you have money. Charges for hospital admission may exceed $2,000 per day. If surgeons and anaesthetists are involved in your care, those prices will rise rapidly. Repatriation using international medical air ambulance will cost tens of thousands of dollars.

Those people directly involved with sick patients will face a variety of risks if they do not take adequate barrier precautions, not least of which is tuberculosis (Kain et al., 1997). However, for the average aid worker, almost all the significant infectious risks will either be carried by mosquitoes (malaria, dengue, yellow fever, filariasis) or contaminated water (gastroenteritis, amebiasis, and giardiasis) (Travel Doctor, 2005a, 2005b). If the average traveller takes appropriate precautions to avoid

mosquito bites, is careful about food and water sources, and follows pre-travel advice about basic immunizations and malaria prophylaxis, then the chances of significant illness will be greatly reduced and more time can be spent worrying about traffic accidents. We will cover this topic later in the chapter.

Sex

We were working so hard in the chaos after the tsunami; social rules were the last things we were thinking of. One of the team members started meeting a married nurse from the ward. In such a small community, this was soon discovered and led to a great deal of trouble. We served out our time, but our relationship with the community was never the same afterwards. The nurse was never seen on the ward again. I don't know what happened to her.

The adventure of exotic travel can make people do things they would never dream of doing at home, particularly if alcohol is added to the mix (Moore et al., 1995). Sexually transmitted diseases, including HIV, are found everywhere, but are particularly common in some developing countries. Hepatitis B is the only STD for which there is a vaccine; past infection and treatment for any of the others does not confer immunity. Although several STDs can be treated with antibiotics, widespread resistance to antibiotics is a growing problem (World Health Organization, 2001). Sexual relations between project workers and the target population are ethically highly questionable. The impression of coercion or undue influence will, at the very least, harm relations between the project team and their host. At worst, it can lead to social results that affect people's entire lives. Common sense should guide your actions. It is very unwise to have sex with strangers, casual contacts, or commercial sex workers. If you are going to have sex, follow safe sexual practices and use good-quality latex condoms (Hamlyn & Dayan, 2003).

Traumatic Injury

One night, four of us crammed into a three-wheeler, heading off for yet another meeting. Halfway round a curve, we met a truck with no lights coming in the other direction. We finished upside down in a drainage ditch—one broken arm and a lot of scratches. With a tiny difference in

the roll of the dice and we would all have been dead.

He was actually unharmed in the crash between his rented motorbike and the ox cart, but required medical treatment for the injuries he received in the fight after the accident when the farmer demanded payment.

The United Nations estimates that 1.17 million people are killed each year in road traffic accidents, 70 percent occur in developing countries. Fifteen times that number are crippled or injured (World Health Organization, 2004). It is also important to note that the majority of victims are not occupants of a motor vehicle but are pedestrians, motorcyclists, or cyclists. Traumatic injury, particularly due to a motor-vehicle accident, is the most common cause of serious injury or death during overseas trips. The US Department of State estimates that over 200 American tourists are killed each year in road traffic accidents (US Department of State, n.d.-b). There are, of course, many other potential sources of trauma ranging from bungee jumping to horseback riding. It is important to be aware of this problem and to use common sense, particularly when travelling by road.

Psychological Risks

It was my first time on a project, teaching at a village school. I had no training about what to expect and no support when I was there. I was homesick, crying and unhappy for a couple of weeks. Thought there was something wrong with me because I hated everything about the place. After six months there, it was almost as bad when I got home again.

Electric lights, running water, and the supermarket just seemed so excessive. No one understood what I was talking about.

Attention has only very recently been paid to the psychological dangers of aid work. Depression, severe culture shock, chronic fatigue, and post-traumatic stress disorder are now well-recognized risks of aid work (McFarlane, 2004). All are minimized with adequate preparation and in-country support from experienced managers.

Bad Decisions and Odd Behaviour

A group of teachers had come out to work at a local missionary school when I was a government health officer in that area. For unknown reasons, one of these guys decided he wanted to shoot an elephant before going home. As you know, they are as common as rabbits down there — it is about as difficult as shooting a slow-moving bus. His first shot bounced off the elephant's head without killing it. Unfortunately, the missionary could run faster than his wife. When the elephant charged them, his wife was badly injured. The poor woman was brought into me later that day with fractures of her pelvis and both legs. I don't understand how she wasn't killed.

A Scandinavian teacher, who had worked in the area when he was a student, brought out a bunch of his schoolchildren to work on a project in a Batonga village in the middle of nowhere. Don't forget that this was during an active guerilla war! Several children ended up on the ward with dehydration and gastroenteritis, but two of them caught falciparum malaria.

I have often wondered if the parents had any clue about the risks this guy was taking with their kids' lives.

I couldn't even begin to describe some of the odd characters that turned up on the east coast of Sri Lanka shortly after the tsunami. Survivors in those early chaotic camps had enough problems without having to deal with scientologists and bands of religious teenagers from all over the world. How do they get there on such short notice? The oddest group I met was a bunch of religious veterinarians who wouldn't treat your animal until you had been purified by a religious lecture first. Strange times and some very strange people.

Female Travellers

In the local culture, women who travelled alone without observing dress and behaviour conventions were viewed as either crazy or promiscuous. A single female colleague of mine, who prided herself on her general independence, was in the habit of walking alone at night. Two men molested her one night, claiming later they believed she wanted their attentions. It was only the intervention of some other local men that prevented this from progressing into a severe assault.

In general, women display greater caution than men in new surroundings, which tends to keep them out of trouble. Statistics support this since mortality and morbidity from all causes are both lower for female travellers compared to males.

Unfortunately, in many countries, female travellers are more affected by local religious and cultural beliefs than men. In order to work and travel safely, women may be expected to change the way they dress and behave, particularly in their interactions with men. Women who have grown up in North America or Europe are, quite understandably, unused to accepting imposed limitations on their personal freedoms. Unfortunately, this is a fact of life in many countries and it is not going to change overnight. It is very important for women to research the social and cultural expectations of any country they will be visiting so that decisions about work and personal freedom can be made calmly, long before travelling. The best source of information is women from the local area. This will be much more reliable than any information put out by the country's government. Web sites and books, specifically aimed at female travellers, are also available (Foreign Affairs Canada, 2004; *Journeywoman*, n.d.).

ETHICAL CONSIDERATIONS IN DEVELOPMENT WORK

Hell is paved with good intentions, not bad ones. All men mean well.

— G.B. Shaw

For no clear reason, the ethical implications of working in developing countries are rarely discussed. Codes of conduct established by the Sphere Project (2004) or the Australian Council for International Development (2006) provide guidance for large agencies, but there is little or no material governing personal behaviour. The topic is given little research attention even though almost all overseas workers will face some form of moral ambiguity at some point in their visit (Baratrala & Doyal, 1998).

Although there is a vast literature concerning the ethics of health care in developed countries, ethical analysis of health projects (particularly medical research) in developing countries has only recently gained attention. For example, the first large trials of oral contraceptives were carried out in Puerto Rico because US state laws controlling contraception did not allow the drug to be tested in America. Complaints of side effects among the women in the study group (and also three deaths) attracted little attention at the time (Bernard, 1995).

More recently, attitudes toward the ethics of medical research in developing countries have changed significantly. The testing of anti-HIV drugs in developing countries has raised numerous ethical dilemmas that have attracted attention in the medical press. For example, research into drug treatments that might reduce HIV transmission from mother to child has been carried out in several African countries. Study designs often involved treatment of one group with a known active anti-HIV drug while the other group received only an inactive placebo. Numerous commentators felt that this was a highly unethical study approach (Lurie & Wolfe, 1997).

The subsequent debate became very heated. Some commentators went so far as to compare this practice to the Tuskegee study of African-American men with syphilis who were observed, but not treated, long after penicillin was available. At the time, it was stated that they probably would not have been treated anyway. Others argued that when working in a country where the standard of care is basically no treatment at all, then the use of an inactive placebo is warranted on the grounds of pragmatism (Halsey et al., 1997).

The current opinion is that research ethics should not be modified by local circumstances; all populations should have access to the same levels of ethical research standards wherever they are (Eaton, 2005). Pragmatism comes into play when the results of that research are applied to a community. Even if you are not involved in a multicentre trial, there are still plenty of ethical problems to consider. Some practical examples will illustrate this point:

- Imagine you are a Canadian obstetric resident who wants to gain experience in surgery by working in a rural African hospital. Local shortages mean that women are often inadequately anaesthetized during Caesarean section and some of their newborns die because of lack of resuscitation equipment. Do you continue to work, arguing that inadequate care is better than no care, or do you leave knowing that practising this way could get you sued at home?
- You are an anthropology student staying with a family in a remote part of Indonesia. You are invited to a large family party, but halfway through you realize that this is actually a circumcision ceremony for their youngest daughter. Do you risk offending the whole family by walking out or do you continue to attend knowing that such a practice carries a jail sentence at home?

- You are a recent teaching graduate working at a small school in rural Pakistan. Local elders will not allow the girls to go to school. Do you continue to teach the boys, hoping that the elders will eventually relent or do you try to make a point by flatly refusing? You decide to remain in the village and just teach the boys. After a few months, half of the village insists that their daughters must also attend. The other half is outraged by such an idea. Your excellent intentions have led to threats of violence within the local community. What will you do now?
- After working as a doctor in Sudan for a year, you have gained the trust of local people. One day, senior women come to ask you how to perform female circumcision without causing infection and bleeding. They will not listen to your request that they stop doing the procedure altogether. Do you provide clean instruments and teach them to help reduce side effects or do you refuse to teach them, knowing they will still continue to do circumcisions without your advice?

There are no clear answers to such questions. The "correct" answer is the one with which you are most comfortable. Whether your problem is personal (accepting significant limitations on dress and behaviour), scientific (use of a placebo control), or social (introducing major reforms such as female education), there are no rules that will help you to reach the best solution. The only advice that can be given is to ensure that ethical topics are confronted openly and thoroughly long before you leave home.

PLANNING AND PREPARING TO TRAVEL

Everyone thinks of changing the world but no one thinks of changing himself.
— Leo Tolstoy

Before going on a project, it is very important to ask yourself why you wish to put yourself through the expense and hard work of an overseas project. Please examine your motives honestly. The following list of reasons why someone should not go on an aid project will hopefully help this process:

- Aid projects are not an opportunity to solve personal problems, particularly if those problems include drug and alcohol abuse.
- The aid industry is not an exotic travel agency designed to provide free trips to interesting places.
- Aid projects are not an opportunity to practise surgical procedures, drug treatments, or medical research that you are not allowed or qualified to perform at home.
- A foreign aid project is not a dating agency.
- Aid projects are not intended to provide a captive audience for religious or political opinions.

If your motives stand up to close scrutiny, then it is time to start planning your trip. To a large extent, the safety and success of your time overseas will depend on the effort you put into the planning stage. Fortunately, there are many helpful sources of information available. Examples include Web sites for travellers produced by the Australian and Canadian governments, the Centers for Disease Control and Prevention, and the World Health Organization (Australian Department of Foreign Affairs and Trade, n.d.; Centers for Disease Control and Prevention, 2006; Public Health Agency of Canada, 2005; World Health Organization, 2005).

The list of things to take will depend on your individual situation, but remember that you do not have to bring the kitchen sink. Most of your list will be available in large towns even though they may be a bit more expensive (another reason to know your country before travelling). Whatever else you pack, do not bring jewellery, expensive watches, or anything that you cannot afford to lose. Taking a backpack, plus a smaller pack for daily use, is a convenient way to travel. If rougher accommodation is likely, you will need a tent, sleeping bag, air mattress, and even a portable stove.

Avoiding mosquitoes and obtaining clean water are both very important. An effective mosquito net needs to be large enough to tuck in under a mattress and should also be treated with long-acting insecticide (National Travel Health Network and Centre, n.d.). Good ones are bulky (particularly if they have a spreader), so it is often better to make this your first purchase when you arrive. The small nets sold in packets at the local camping shop are more of a fashion statement. If you do not have a ceiling hook, you will need some imagination and a ball of string.

Obtaining clean water also requires careful planning, depending on the circumstances you will be facing (British Columbia Ministry of Health, 2004). Larger organisms such as bacteria and protozoa (*Giardia, Cryptosporidium*) are effectively removed using 0.2 micron hand-pumped filters. Viruses such as hepatitis A and Norwalk can slip through such a filter so water will still need further purification (boiling, iodine tablets). Remember that neither procedure removes dissolved chemical pollutants. A wide range of filters and purifiers is available at any camping store.

Clothing will obviously depend on the climate and local custom. Whatever you take should be light and easy to wash. Personal items will depend on the remoteness of the location, but will include personal photographs, camera, flashlight, radio, electric adaptors, and books. Your toilet kit and medical kit will be governed by personal requirements such as asthma and local malaria recommendations. All should be planned before travel. It is a good idea for a group to carry a standard first aid kit among them.

Whatever corners you are forced to cut due to time or money, it is always worthwhile to obtain good-quality travel insurance that covers medical repatriation. It will provide you (and your parents) with some peace of mind. On arrival in the country, many aid workers do not bother to register at the local Canadian High Commission or embassy, but it is well worth taking the time to do this (Foreign Affairs and International Trade Canada, 2006). Embassy staff can help in an emergency and, to some extent, are responsible for you, but they have to know that you exist. People at home can also locate you through the High Commission.

A list of the main documents and forms to be taken is given in Box 15.2. Box 15.3 lists the papers required if you want to renew a lost passport rapidly. Keep these separate from your passport.

Box 15.2: Necessary documents and forms

- Passport
- Tickets
- Health insurance and flight insurance
- Immunization record
- Entry visas
- Licence and permit to work/study
- Money; check credit card expiry dates
- International driver's licence
- International student card for discounts
- Contact information for Canadian embassy or consulate
- Specific information about project site

Box 15.3: Passport emergency kit

- Photocopy of your passport identification page
- Photocopy of one other document supporting your identity
- Original birth certificate or citizenship certificate
- Two recent passport photographs
- Contact details of closest Canadian consulate or embassy

This is a suitable place to add a few comments about interpretation. When working overseas, language will be one of the most difficult barriers to overcome. An effective translator can resolve many of the cross-cultural dilemmas that you will initially face, but success depends on careful selection. When recruiting and hiring translators, you must ensure that they are readily available and are also unaffected by the numerous racial, ethnic, and economic hierarchies that exist within any culture.

In medical projects, avoid asking family members of a patient to translate, particularly if they are emotionally involved. Deception, omission, or just friendly misleading will be the result if you unknowingly place a translator in a socially difficult situation. You may require a female translator in order to talk to a woman and young interpreters may be very uncomfortable asking detailed personal questions of older people. You will have to rely on body language signals to determine if you have unwittingly placed participants in a socially unacceptable position.

Preparing Your Project

> Before anything else, preparation is the key to success.
> — Alexander Graham Bell

Each year, 100,000 people apply for the available 3,000 Peace Corps positions. When it comes to working overseas, there are a lot of people chasing a limited number of jobs. For those interested in long-term overseas work or who plan to make their career in international health, the large aid organizations have hiring mechanisms similar to any corporation. Contact them through their Web sites for information about employment or volunteer opportunities. Another source of information is the International Health Exchange, which also publishes a magazine every three months with job advertisements, articles, and information about training courses (*RedR-IHE*, n.d.).

For short-term projects, word of mouth is the best place to start. Ask faculty and students who have participated in previous courses for their advice and recommendations. Every developed country has a variety of international health organizations run by students, non-governmental, and governmental organizations. Their mandates differ, but most will offer help for those looking for short-term overseas employment opportunities. Box 15.4 lists some of the Canadian examples of such organizations and their Web sites.

Box 15.4: Canadian organizations offering help with overseas volunteer positions

---

- Canadian Cross Roads International (www.cciorg.ca)
- Canadian Society for International Health (www.csih.org)
- Canada World Youth (www.cwy-jcm.org)
- World University Service of Canada (www.wusc.ca)
- Canadian University Services Overseas (www.cuso.org)

Lastly, there are several books on the subject of working abroad. Jean Marc Hachey's book, *The Canadian Guide to Working and Living Overseas,* is very useful; it is regularly updated (Hachey, 2004). Similar books listed at the end of this chapter provide contact information for agencies and projects abroad and also offer useful travel and preparation advice.

Forming a Project Team

Although some students will find individual positions, many find it better to form a team so they can pool their resources of energy and talent. Most universities have a Student International Health Society. Clearly, this is the best place to start when looking for advice and support for your own team. Peace and harmony between humans does not occur by accident; it must be carefully managed from an early point in the team's formation (please read Chapter 16 carefully). It is very important that the team starts with regular meetings to develop common objectives and goals. Once jointly agreed-upon aims have been clearly established, they tend to act as a "constitution" for the project and will help to focus future plans and reduce arguments.

Conflicts cannot be avoided, but anticipating the major points of friction will help to keep the peace. Common sources of trouble are money, distribution of work, and failing to stick to the established goals. These and many other problems are best managed by regular meetings, clear communication, and team members who are prepared to be flexible and accommodating. Apart from the information given in the next chapter, there are also several books that give excellent advice on the subject of building and maintaining small teams (Harrington-Mackin, 1994).

Finances and Fundraising

The major cost facing most small projects will be air travel, but other factors will need to be considered such as health insurance, visa and licence fees, in-country travel, food, lodging, and project expenses (e.g., translators and local labour). Clearly, a budget is required, both for your own purposes and also to show potential funding sources how much money you need and what you propose to do with it. A well-prepared budget and timeline will show you have put serious thought into your project. Both are also necessary if you are making a grant application.

Careless money management can be the source of a great deal of trouble so it is important to choose a treasurer who is competent, responsible, and organized. If you register as a charity, you will have to deal with Canada Revenue Agency's tax laws and if you run lotteries, raffles, or bingo games, you will probably be governed by local gambling laws. If you accept significant donations from various people, you will also have to be prepared to answer the obvious question, "What did you do with that money I gave you?" In each case, an accurate record of income and expenditure will be essential.

Fundraising will depend on the ingenuity and energy of each group, but examples include lotteries and raffles, bingo nights, dances, charity runs, Christmas present wrapping at the local mall, snow clearing, and gardening. If your planned project gives you an opportunity to do some research, it is possible to apply for a research grant from funding agencies. Many universities also have travel grants or bursaries for students involved in overseas projects. Many go uncollected each year because they are not advertised; you will not know if they exist unless you ask.

Learning about the Country

Obviously, it is important that you have detailed knowledge about the country you will be working in and its customs. Again, the best place to start is to find people who have worked in that country. Other reliable sources include the CIA's *World Factbook* and the "Lonely Planet" Web sites (Central Intelligence Agency, 2006; *Lonely Planet*, n.d.). Both contain excellent information on just about any country in the world. The Department of Foreign Affairs (or equivalent) of every developed country publishes a Web site with up-to-date information for its travelling citizens. The Web site of Foreign Affairs Canada is a good example (Foreign Affairs and International Trade Canada, n.d.).

Find out as much as you can about local customs before you travel. Attitudes toward dress, behaviour, drugs, and even corruption may differ sharply from those at home. Your responses to those differences will be an important part of an enjoyable stay. Your efforts to accommodate yourself to local society will likely be noticed and appreciated, particularly if you spend time gaining a basic knowledge of the local language. If you are going to be studying or employed in a new country, it is important to understand very clearly what you are getting yourself into. You should clarify the hours you will be expected to work, your periods of time off, and any expected additional expenses long before you travel.

WORKING SAFELY AND EFFECTIVELY IN A NEW COUNTRY

When you travel, remember that a foreign country is not designed to make you comfortable. It is designed to make its own people comfortable.
— Clifton Fadiman

The normal physical and psychological responses that result when someone is suddenly immersed in very unfamiliar surroundings are collectively called "culture shock." The term has, to some extent, been trivialized by common usage, but that does not mean that the sensations

of culture shock are imaginary. Culture shock is a form of depression and can, for some people and in some circumstances, become disabling (Stewart & Leggat, 1998).

Attitudes and emotions change in a fairly predictable way as someone moves through the different phases of a project. During the rushed preparation stage before travel, the average person often swings between excitement and anxiety. After arriving in the country, emotions and energy levels may remain high for the first few days, but many people then go through a period of depression, confusion, or anger in response to very unfamiliar customs and practices. The timing and severity of the low phase depends on many variables, including individual variation, prior experience, and pre-departure preparation. Obviously, after a while, most people adapt to their circumstances. Finally, after lengthy visits, there is often a reverse culture shock during the reintegration process at home. Box 15.5 gives some of the common symptoms of culture shock.

Every traveller suffers culture shock to some extent. It is found under any stressful

Box 15.5: Symptoms of culture shock

- Irrational anger
- Extreme homesickness
- Intense feeling of loyalty to one's own culture
- Unexplained crying
- Loss of ability to work or study effectively
- Withdrawal from people who are different from you
- Symptomatic complaints such as headache and excessive tiredness

circumstance and is well reported in space crews making long flights (Kanas, 1998).

A study by the Canadian Foreign Service Institute found that the following characteristics were predictive of successful adaptation (Vulpe et al., 2001):

- respect and sensitivity for local social and cultural realities
- perseverance and confidence when dealing with frustrations
- skill at reading social interactions and flexibility when responding to difficulties

The full list is actually quite a bit longer and may give the impression that an impressive list of human qualities is necessary in order to work overseas. This is not, of course, the case. The absolute requirements are a flexible attitude combined with careful pre-trip preparation so that you will have a good idea of what to expect.

Culture shock is the body's response to profoundly unfamiliar surroundings. If that unfamiliarity is minimized by careful preparation, then you will feel more comfortable during the adaptation period. Pre-trip planning should give you a detailed understanding of the country. If you know how the buses, taxis, and shops work, plus you can make your basic needs understood in the local language, then unpleasant somatic responses to strange surroundings should be bearable.

Staying Healthy

There are so many excellent sources of information on travel health that the only problem is knowing which one to choose (Centers for Disease Control and Prevention, 2005; Rose & Keystone, 2005). Books, Web sites, and local specialized travel clinics are all valuable resources to help you plan for a healthy stay during your overseas trip. There are no absolute guarantees of safety, but if you avoid mosquitoes, drink clean water, wash your hands, and always behave as if your grandmother were watching, you should be as safe abroad as you are at home.

There is no widely accepted "standard" vaccination schedule so personal research is necessary, depending on your destination. Although public health authorities differ, most recommend that travellers get boosters for their childhood vaccines (polio, diphtheria, tetanus) plus a full course of hepatitis A and B (Martin, 2004). There is an ever-growing list of other vaccinations whose use will depend on individual variations and opinions. Examples include vaccines against yellow fever, pneumococcus, typhoid, influenza, Japanese encephalitis, rabies, and several others. Obviously, it is important to obtain careful, professional advice.

Only a few countries require vaccination records prior to entry. A record of yellow fever vaccination is necessary for travel in some African and South American countries. Meningococcal vaccine is necessary for entry to a few Middle Eastern countries during periods of pilgrimage. Obviously, it is important to check before you travel. Remember that your body responds to a vaccine by producing protective antibodies. This process takes time so make sure that you get any necessary shots early.

Apart from immunizations, it is important to determine the malaria risk in the region you will be visiting and also the extent of drug resistance (Butcher, 2004). If regular malaria prophylaxis is recommended, remember to start the drugs before you leave and to continue taking them for a time after you return. Time periods will depend on the medication so it is important to obtain specialist advice based on current conditions in the country you will be visiting. Drug quality can be unreliable in developing world pharmacies so ensure that you have a supply of drugs before you travel.

Apart from traumatic accidents, it is worth repeating that the principal risks to health for the average traveller are carried either by contaminated water or mosquitoes. It takes only one contaminated ice cube or a single mosquito bite to ruin your holiday. Just because you have lived in the country for six months does not mean that you are in any way immune. It is important to maintain a regular awareness of basic hygiene and common sense. Avoid mosquitoes by using a treated bed net plus appropriate repellents and clothing. Drink only treated or commercially bought bottled water and use common sense when eating. Finally, avoid swimming in fresh water in schistosomiasis areas, strongly resist the temptation to nurse

sick animals, and do not drink milk unless you are certain it has been pasteurized. If you become sick within a year of return, particularly if you have a high fever, seek urgent medical attention and remember to provide a detailed travel history.

■ SUMMARY

There is a large and apparently growing level of interest worldwide in the broad topic of international health. Many of those people are prepared to take their interest a bit further by investing time and energy working on overseas development projects. For several reasons (including a lack of training courses and underestimation of the seriousness of overseas work) the general levels of project planning and personal preparation are often less than ideal. Apart from showing a lack of respect toward the host population, poor planning will inevitably result in a waste of time and money. At worst, it exposes project participants to significant (and often largely avoidable) personal risks.

Figure 15.2: Detailed pre-trip planning is vital for anyone thinking of working in complex humanitarian situations such as this refugee camp in Northern Uganda. Inadequate preparation exposes team members to significant potential physical and also psychological risks. (Photographer Sven Torfinn; courtesy of IRIN news.)

It is vital that anyone preparing to join a development project is aware of the potential risks associated with overseas work. The magnitude of these physical and psychological risks should not be underestimated — they range from trauma and infectious diseases through to culture shock and post-traumatic stress. Risks cannot be entirely avoided, but they can certainly be minimized by careful pre-trip planning. Adequate preparation is time consuming; at least a year is required to do the job properly. The most important steps include preparing your project (choosing a team, including local people in the planning process, fundraising, and carefully considering the ethical problems associated with the project) and, of course, preparing yourself (studying the history and culture of the country, gaining a basic knowledge of the language, and keeping yourself healthy). It should always be remembered that road traffic accidents are a far greater risk to health than infectious diseases.

At some level, the basic aim of any aid project is to improve the lives of others. It doesn't matter if the target is a small family or a large city; this is a serious undertaking. The benefits of a well-run project can be significant for all concerned, but the adverse results of a badly organized project can be equally significant. Teams willing to take on that challenge should be congratulated, but they should understand that they are shouldering a major responsibility. The levels of planning and preparation should reflect the seriousness with which the project team takes that responsibility.

RESOURCES

References

Australian Council for International Development. (2006). *Code of conduct.* Retrieved from www.acfid.asn.au/code/code.htm.

Australian Department of Foreign Affairs and Trade. (n.d.). *Smarttraveller.* www.smartraveller.gov.au.

Baker, T., et al. (1992). "The uncounted dead: American civilians dying overseas." *Public Health Reports, 107,* 155–159.

Baratrala, N., & Doyal, L. (1998). "Knowing when to say 'no' on the student elective: Students going on electives abroad need clinical guidelines." *British Medical Journal, 316,* 1404–1405.

Bernard, A. (1995). *The pill: A biography of the drug that changed the world.* New York: Random House.

Bernard, K., et al. (1989). "Epidemiological surveillance in Peace Corps Volunteers: A model for monitoring health in temporary residents of developing countries." *International Journal of Epidemiology, 18,* 220–226.

British Columbia Ministry of Health. (2004). *Traveller's diarrhea.* Retrieved from www.bchealthguide.org by searching "traveller's diarrhea."

Butcher, C. (2004). "Malaria: A parasitic disease." *American Association of Occupational Health Nurses Journal, 52,* 302–309.

Centers for Disease Control and Prevention. (2005). *Health information for international travel, 2005–2006.* Philadelphia: Mosby Elsevier.

Centers for Disease Control and Prevention. (2006). *Travelers' health.* Retrieved from www.cdc.gov/travel.

Central Intelligence Agency. (2006). *The world factbook.* Retrieved from www.cia.gov/cia/publications/factbook.

Clemens, M., et al. (2004) *Counting chickens when they hatch: The short-term effect of aid on growth* (Center for Global Development, working paper no. 44). Retrieved from www.cgdev.org/files/2744_file_CountingChickensFINAL3.pdf.

Eaton, L. (2005). "Nuffield Council calls for ethical framework for developing world research." *British Medical Journal, 330*, 618.

Foreign Affairs and International Trade Canada. (2004). *Drugs and travel*. Retrieved from www.voyage.gc.ca/main/drugs_menu-en.asp.

Foreign Affairs and International Trade Canada. (2006). *Embassies and consulates*. Retrieved from www.dfait-maeci.gc.ca/world/embassies/menu-en.asp.

Foreign Affairs and International Trade Canada. (n.d.). *Consular Affairs: Information & assistance for Canadians abroad*. Retrieved from www.voyage.gc.ca.

Foreign Affairs Canada. (2004). *Her own way: Advice for the woman traveler*. Retrieved from www.voyage.gc.ca/main/pubs/PDF/her_own_way-en.pdf.

Hachey, J.-M. (2004). *The big guide to living and working overseas*. Toronto: Intercultural Systems/Systèmes interculturels.

Hagarten, S., et al. (1991). "Overseas fatalities of United States citizen travelers: An analysis of deaths related to international travel." *Annals of Emergency Medicine, 20*, 622–626.

Hajdu, S. (2005). "A note from history: Rudolph Virchow, pathologist, armed revolutionist, politician, and anthropologist." *Annals of Clinical and Laboratory Science, 35*, 203–205.

Halsey, N., et al. (1997). "Ethics and international research." *British Medical Journal, 315*, 965–966.

Hamlyn, E., & Dayan, L. (2003). "Sexual health for travelers." *Australian Family Physician, 32*, 981–984.

Hancock, G. (1992). *Lords of poverty: The power prestige and corruption of the international aid business*. New York: Atlantic Monthly Press.

Harrington-Mackin, D. (1994). *The team building tool kit: Tips, tactics, and rules for effective work place teams*. New York: American Management Association.

Heck, J., & Wedemeyer, D. (Eds.). (2000). *The international health medical education consortium guidebook*. Retrieved from www.globalhealth-ec.org.

Hope, R., et al. (2004). *The elective pack: The medical student's guide to essential international health and development*. Retrieved from www.ihmec.ucl.ac.uk.

Huetter, P. (2003). "Overseas aid: A leg-up to struggling states or corrosive dead weight?" *Australian Policy Online*.

Huey, R., & Eguskitza, X. (2000). "Supplemental oxygen and death rates on Everest and K2." *Journal of the American Medical Association, 284*, 181.

Journeywoman. (n.d.). Retrieved from www.journeywoman.com.

Kain, K., et al. (1997). "The risk and prevention of tuberculosis in travelers." *Canada Communicable Disease Report, 23*, 1–8.

Kanas, N. (1998). "Psychosocial issues affecting crews during long duration international space missions." *Acta Astronautica, 42*, 339–361.

Klein, M. (1995). "Deaths of Australian travelers overseas." *Medical Journal of Australia, 163*, 277–280.

Lonely Planet. (n.d.). Retrieved from www.lonelyplanet.com.

Lurie, P., & Wolfe, S. (1997). "Unethical trials of interventions to reduce perinatal transmission of the Human Immunodeficiency Virus in developing countries." *New England Journal of Medicine, 337*, 853–856.

Maren, M. (2002). *The road to hell: The ravaging effects of foreign aid and international charity*. New York: Free Press.

Martin, J. (2004). "Travel vaccination: an update." *Nursing Standard, 18*, 47–53.

McFarlane, C. (2004). "Risks associated with the psychological adjustment of humanitarian aid workers." *The Australian Journal of Disaster and Trauma Studies, 1.*

Moore, J., et al. (1995). "HIV risk behaviour among Peace Corps Volunteers." *Aids, 9,* 795–799.

National Travel Health Network and Centre. (n.d.). Retrieved from www.nathnac.org/travel/misc/travellers_mos.htm.

Odero, W., et al. (1997). "Road traffic injuries in developing countries: A comprehensive review of epidemiologic studies." *Tropical Medicine and International Health, 2,* 445–460.

Public Health Agency of Canada. (2005) *Travel Health.* Retrieved from www.phac-aspc.gc.ca/tmp-pmv/index.html.

RedR-IHE. (n.d.). Retrieved from www.redr.org/london/.

Rose, S., & Keystone, J. (2005). *International travel health guide.* Philadelphia: Mosby Elsevier.

Safe Motherhood. (n.d.). Retrieved from www.safemotherhood.org.

Sphere Project. (2004). *The humanitarian charter.* Retrieved from www.sphereproject.org/content/view/27/84.

Stewart, L., & Leggat, P. (1998). "Culture shock and travelers." *Journal of Travel Medicine, 5,* 84–88.

Travel Doctor. (2005a). *Insect-borne diseases.* Retrieved from www.traveldoctor.co.uk/insects.htm.

Travel Doctor. (2005b). *Travellers' Diarrhoea.* Retrieved from www.traveldoctor.co.uk/diarrhoea.htm.

US Department of State. (n.d.-a). *Drugs abroad.* Retrieved from www.travel.state.gov/travel/living/drugs/drugs_1237.html.

US Department of State. (n.d.-b). *Road safety overseas.* Retrieved from www.travel.state.gov/travel/tips/safety/safety_1179.html.

Vulpe, T., et al. (2001). *A profile of the interculturally effective person.* Ottawa: Foreign Affairs and International Trade Canada.

World Health Organization. (2001). *Global prevalence and incidence of selected curable sexually transmitted diseases: Overview and estimates.* Retrieved from www.who.int/hiv/pub/sti/who_hiv_aids_2001.02.pdf.

World Health Organization. (2004). *Road safety: A public health issue.* Retrieved from www.who.int/world-health-day/2004/.

World Health Organization. (2005). *International travel and health.* Retrieved from www.who.int/ith.

Recommended Reading

Ausenda, F., & Mcloskey, E. (Eds.). (2003). *Green volunteers: The world guide to voluntary work in nature.* New York: Universe.

Ausenda, F., & Mcloskey, E. (Eds.). (2003). *World volunteers: The world guide to humanitarian and development volunteering.* New York: Universe.

Backhurst, P. (Ed.). (2005). *Alternatives to the Peace Corps: A directory of global volunteer opportunities.* Oakland: Food First.

Centers for Disease Control and Prevention. (2005). *Health information for international travel, 2005–2006.* Philadelphia: Mosby Elsevier.

Collins, J., et al. (2001). *How to live your dream of volunteering overseas.* New York: Penguin.

Ehrenreich, J. (2005). *The humanitarian companion: A guide for international aid, development, and human rights workers.* Rugby, Warwickshire: ITDG Publishing.

Fadiman, A. (1998). *The spirit catches you and you fall down.* New York: Farrar, Straus, and Giroux.

Fielding, H. (2002). *Cause celeb.* New York: Penguin.

Hachey, J.-M. (2004). *The big guide to living and working overseas.* Toronto: Intercultural Systems/Systèmes interculturels.

Rose, S., & Keystone, J. (2005). *International travel health guide.* Philadelphia: Mosby Elsevier.

Wilson, M. (2004). *The medic's guide to work and electives around the world.* London: Hodder Arnold.

World Health Organization. (2005). *International travel and health.* Retrieved from www.who.int/ith.

Managing a
Sustainable Aid Partnership

Coming together is a beginning,
keeping together is progress,
working together is success.
— Henry Ford

OBJECTIVES
After completing this chapter, you should be able to

- appreciate the fundamental importance of true partnering as a basis for successful development projects
- understand the common pitfalls and problems confronting partnerships
- appreciate the organizational problems of aid workers in the field
- understand how to plan a supportive working framework for development partnerships

On first view, this material might seem a bit dry, but anyone who has completed a development project of any form will know that partnership planning and management are the most important factors determining the final outcome. Unfortunately, since each project is different, the partnership and management literature tends to deal in generalizations rather than specifics. This can be off-putting, particularly when management jargon is added. However,

it is worth persevering — behind the slick inspirational messages and sports analogies, there is a lot of solid common sense that will help you to get the best out of your own project.

It does not matter if you are a medical student planning an attachment to a clinic or a UNICEF official trying to coordinate dozens of agencies for an immunization program — sustainable success requires lots of characters to get along together. This does not happen by accident; it requires a great deal of preparatory work. This chapter offers a basic overview of management planning for those interested in getting the most out of their overseas projects; jargon and generalizations will be kept to a minimum! Whatever your team plans to do, this chapter will help you to do it more efficiently.

INTRODUCTION TO PROJECT MANAGEMENT

> All happy families resemble one another, each unhappy family is unhappy in its own way.
>
> —Leo Tolstoy, *Anna Karenina*

For the purposes of analysis and discussion, it is convenient to break a project down into three components: (1) the people who do the work; (2) the organizational framework within which they operate (which usually involves a partnership of some sort); and, finally, (3) the work they produce. Until now, this book has concentrated on the third component (the content of project work). However, this current chapter is concerned only with the first two: the basic mechanics of managing aid workers and their organizational support structure.

Tolstoy may have been right about families, but he was wrong about projects; unhappy ones are not all unhappy in different ways. No matter what other problems might have occurred, there is usually a common thread of inadequate planning and preparation running through them. From the very start, considerable effort must be devoted to predicting and managing the inevitable problems that occur when humans have to co-operate, particularly when they are working together under difficult circumstances.

No team works in isolation; the success of any project depends on the ability of the people involved to get along with each other. Even the smallest overseas initiative will require a fair amount of social interaction between the visitors and other people involved in the project (hosts, student groups, clinic staff, patients, etc.). In larger studies, the

Figure 16.1: Canadian students working in a rural Ugandan village. Partnership management is important for projects of all sizes.

involvement of government agencies, university departments, local population representatives (and a host of other professionals who accumulate once a project is planned) endlessly multiply the possibilities for disagreement. Once differences in culture, religion, politics, and language are added to the mix, it is easy to see why so many joint international projects fail to meet their initial objectives. The ability to form stable groups for mutual benefit is a basic human quality; we are not solitary animals. It could be argued that many of the dramas of history would have turned out very differently if the groups involved had used peaceful conflict-resolution methods rather than war to solve their differences. What would Alexander have been like if Aristotle had taught him the basics of peaceful partnership management?

Since all aid projects involve partnerships of one form or another, anyone interested in international development work must understand the basic requirements that make up a successful partnership. There is no shortage of literature in this area, ranging from philosophy to sociology with stops at psychology and anthropology along the way. The book by Dr. Melville Kerr (1996), listed in the "Resources" section, is a thoughtful review of partnering based on extensive overseas experience. It is essential reading for anyone involved in project planning. Two Web sites (www.partnerships.org. uk and www.ourpartnership.org.uk) both offer good advice for those forming a small partnership. The British Council supports partnerships between British schools and others overseas. Its Web site also offers useful advice about starting and running joint arrangements (British Council, n.d.).

A true example will help to illustrate some of the main points of project management:

Everything started with great enthusiasm. The funding agency would not give money for an initial meeting between the teams so all contact was maintained by telephone and e-mail, with an occasional video conference. Planning progressed reasonably well, although we were surprised by the slow turnaround time for any letters or decisions. The partners were members of two strong universities and the project certainly looked good on paper. It was awarded a large grant; the various teams set to work.

Unfortunately, there were faults on both sides right from the start. One of the members of the partner team was very unwilling to accept outside assistance and made no secret of these views. One of the joint writing teams failed to get along and could not agree on the emphasis or content of their material. In another team, there were concerns about the competence of one of the writers and worries that the final material was not good enough.

Another problem, which should have been foreseen, was the distribution of money. The partner team was understandably sensitive to any perception of unfairness in the distribution of funding. This was aggravated by the donor agency's unwillingness to support any salaries in the partner country. In addition, our university's financial department was going through a reorganization so there was considerable delay in the transfer of funds on two occasions.

Despite these problems, work progressed fitfully so that an acceptable postgraduate course was developed in the prescribed time. However, our contribution was now fairly small and limited to providing money for work performed — there was no longer any pretense that this was a joint undertaking. Amazingly enough, common sense finally prevailed; both teams included well-meaning, competent staff who organized a face-to-face confrontation that should have happened two or three years earlier.

During these very frank exchanges, it became obvious that members in the two countries interpreted even the most basic assumptions in very different ways. There was no common thread amongst participants' motivations (these included altruism, financial gain, career opportunities, religious convictions, and a desire to travel). It was necessary to go back to the absolute basic goals before unequivocal agreement about anything could be found. If we had started with a clearer understanding of the complexities of partnerships, we would all have saved ourselves two or three years of bad feeling and wasted work.

No matter how optimistic and excited everyone feels at the beginning of a project, remember, the honeymoon will end one day. One of the benefits of forming a group is to get different experiences and points of view, but this does have a drawback. Active debate strengthens the final plan, but it is not far from debate to argument. Group members will probably disagree about objectives and how to reach them. When that hurdle is passed, they will certainly disagree again when it comes to division of money and work.

People disagree; that is just their nature. Disagreement should be predicted and

managed with clear conflict guidelines, not suppressed because of a worry that the partnership is fragile. Every time you read the example above, you will probably find another mistake the teams made. There were problems with people and problems with the partnership structure. Much of that trouble could have been avoided with better planning and leadership at the very first meeting. The broad characteristics of

Box 16.1: Characteristics of successful partnerships

- Respect and trust between people involved
- Complete agreement that the partnership is necessary
- Competent leadership with support of all members
- Clearly agreed-upon goals
- Collaborative decision-making process
- Regular communications
- Clearly defined organizational structure
- Fully agreed-upon conflict-resolution procedure
- Fully agreed-upon budget

Box 16.2: Characteristics of unsuccessful partnerships

- Manipulative or dominating partner
- Lack of clear purpose
- Unrealistic goals
- Dishonesty, particularly hidden agendas
- Unequal balance of power and control
- Unresolvable differences in philosophy or ways of working
- Poor communication
- Poorly trained, unqualified team members
- Money and time commitments outweigh the potential benefits
- Poor money management

successful and unsuccessful partnerships are given in boxes 16.1 and 16.2. We'll look at the two aspects of people and process separately.

■ MANAGING THE PROCESS

Management is efficiency in climbing the ladder; leadership determines whether the ladder is leaning against the right wall.

— Stephen Covey

No matter how skilful a team might be, they will almost certainly need the help of others at some stage in their project. For example, a visiting surgical team may need hospital beds, operating facilities, and a range of other logistical support while a nutrition-assessment project might need the support and assistance of local teachers, elders, and parents. The simplest argument in favour of partnerships is that they are almost unavoidable. They are a convenient way to bring all the skills and logistic support needed for an initiative under one roof. A well-organized, broad-based partnership is also more attractive to granting agencies and is much more likely to attract project funding. Once they are established and running, the group also provides mutual support to maintain everyone's enthusiasm when facing inevitable obstacles.

Ensuring that you are committed to a true partnership is particularly important when working directly with a developing world community. Imposed solutions, based on a colonial mindset (no matter how well intentioned), usually lead to passivity and dependence among the targeted population. Active and equal involvement of local people helps to ensure a project's future because there will be committed local staff able to sustain it after the expatriate workers have returned home. The complex, often intangible, variables that exist within any society are also automatically included in the planning process if members of that community are enthusiastically welcomed as planning partners. Finally, partnerships lead to numerous unpredictable benefits that emerge as the project proceeds. Once a community's skills and enthusiasm are harnessed, it is extraordinary what can be achieved.

Types of Partnership

Good battle is healthy and brings to a marriage the principles of equal partnership.

— Ann Landers

In the past, a good deal of lip service has been paid to terms such as "partnership" and "grassroots" involvement. Unfortunately, reality does not always meet the high ideals mentioned in the grant proposal. Recipients of top-down projects may have been referred to as partners, but this is simply an indication of the difficulties of using language to express something as complex as human relationships. Careless choice of definitions can easily give offence in the area of international health. When one half of the team is referred to as the donor university or developed country university and the other half is referred to as the recipient, Third World, or developing university, linguistic battle lines have already been drawn.

The term "partnership" has also been used imprecisely to describe a spectrum of relationships ranging from a true partnership to short-term working arrangements. This does not, of course, mean that partnerships are always necessary. At one end of the spectrum are groups that just happen to be working together on the same project. Through mutual benefit, they might move closer by sharing logistics (transport or accommodation). Once they start sharing information or swapping staff, a closer union is formed until they end up together under a unified set of goals and management. Other arrangements include short-term consultancies or clearly defined subcontracts. While clearly defined rules of engagement will still be necessary for these various degrees of working together, they should not be called partnerships.

Whatever definition is chosen to describe a partnership, it should certainly be more than a sterile agreement between two or more groups working together to achieve common aims. Whatever the scale of the project, the key characteristics that make something a true partnership include a feeling of reciprocity where all members feel they are able to gain something from the relationship. There has to be a sense of mutual trust and respect and, of course, an attitude of openness and equality in all the shared dealings.

A good example of the changing nature of partnerships is given by the experience of the Onchocerciasis Control Program (OCP). In the late 1980s, an effective drug for control of onchocerciasis (ivermectin) was made available to the OCP (Collins, 2004). In addition to inhibiting the vector with insecticides, it became necessary to distribute this drug once or twice a year to large numbers of people living in a high-risk belt running from West Africa across to parts of Central and Southern America (Hopkins, 2005). Although the drug administration process was labelled "community-based," it became clear that it was, in reality, a top-down imposed process with little or no real community involvement.

Slow progress in onchocerciasis control led to a review of the program in 1994. Poor involvement of local communities was identified as a significant barrier to sustainable distribution so it was decided to change to a more inclusive partnership with target populations. Based on successful programs in Mali, where a community-based drug-delivery system had been practised for several years, communities in other countries were encouraged to take control of their own treatment. Community members collected drugs from supply points, treated eligible members in their community, and referred cases with severe adverse

---

Box 16.3: History notes

George Marshall (1880–1959)

Marshall was born in the United States and trained as a career soldier. He served in World War I and subsequently rose to become chief of staff in charge of all American troops throughout World War II. In 1947, he was appointed secretary of state under Truman. In this position, he devised the European Recovery Program (subsequently called the Marshall Plan), which played a major role in the reconstruction of Europe and is generally accepted as the start of modern large-scale aid projects. Despite this, he was criticized during the McCarthy era as being soft on communism and subsequently resigned in disillusion with politics. He received the Nobel Peace Prize for his humanitarian contribution in 1953. For further information, follow the reference (*George C. Marshall Foundation*, n.d.).

reactions (UNDP/World Bank/WHO, 1996).

By 1996, it was clear that this approach to partnership was working well. Within 10 years of the start of the program, onchocerciasis transmission had been almost eliminated in West Africa; in 2003 alone, 40 million people were treated with ivermectin. The community-directed therapy approach was so successful that it even attracted its own acronym (ComDT). The international eradication program against another disease called lymphatic filariasis also requires the periodic administration of an oral drug treatment. ComDT methodology was selected for this initiative after it was shown to be significantly more efficient than conventional approaches to drug distribution (Gyapong et al., 2001).

As a further example of the need for well-planned partnerships, there were initial worries that funds and resources put into the ComDT process would divert money and staff away from the existing health care systems of target countries. At an early planning stage, representatives from these countries were included as equal planning partners to ensure that ComDT was well integrated into their various health services. It should also be added that the Special Program for Tropical Disease Research, which developed the ComDT methodology, is itself co-sponsored and funded by another large partnership consisting of UNICEF, UNDP, the World Bank, and the World Health Organization (UNDP/World Bank/WHO, n.d.). You cannot avoid partnerships!

Getting Started

Partnering is a co-operative human endeavour, so inevitably there will be problems. Most people feel some apprehension when joining a new group; forming a partnership is no different. The fear of losing a separate identity, lack of trust, and confusion about the nature of involvement are all challenges that face a room full of strangers who decide they are going to work together. Rather than pretending such unworthy emotions do not exist, it is better to be realistic and open in the early discussion phase.

These early meetings, during which the various partners get to know each other, are an absolutely basic requirement for any successful partnership. A hurried process that does not allow the development of mutual respect and trust is unlikely to result in a sustainable working relationship. Some team members might want to leave seemingly boring details of organization and management until later and just jump straight to the action. Resist this temptation; forming a firm foundation for the partnership is essential and it takes time. It is also important not to swing too far the other way. Partnerships are important, but they are not an end in themselves. They should always be viewed as a means to an end.

Once the initial ice has been broken, it is time to start substantive discussions. No matter what you plan to do, there are a few common questions that need to be answered. It is very useful to have someone with experience in partnerships to guide these discussions. Try searching around for groups or partnership committees that seem similar to your own and ask if some of their members would be prepared to help guide you through the process of developing goals and organizing a practical management framework. Larger organizations might consider consulting a professional partnership facilitator.

There are many ways of getting a group of strangers to focus on a given question (Harrington-Mackin, 1994). One approach is to ask participants to write their ideas on a small card. You will need to ask a clear, unambiguous question such as, "What are your goals for this partnership?" After writing down their ideas, cards are pinned to a board and reviewed by all team members. Anyone who disagrees with a statement can move that card to another board. Substituting a new idea on another card is also allowed. After everyone has had a turn, those cards remaining represent the main goals that have support from every member of the group. Of course, if there are no cards left on the board, then you have major problems with this particular partnership.

Whether you come to agreement by open discussion with or without a facilitator, or by using various group activities like the one described above, there are a few essential questions that have to be answered in detail. The Alberta

Table 16.1: A moment of Zen

	Total population of African subcontinent in 2002: 839 million
Population of Canada in 2002: 31.9 million	Total energy consumption of African subcontinent, ranging from: Algeria: 1.331 x 1015 Btu to Zimbabwe: 0.189 x 1015 Btu
Total annual energy consumption by Canada: 13.4 x 1015 British thermal units	
13.4 quadrillion Btu	**13.4 quadrillion Btu**

Sources: US Census Bureau (2006); US Energy Information Administration (n.d)

Government Department of Community Development publishes a very useful short guide that helps small groups through these necessary partnership steps (Alberta Community Development, 2001). The major questions that must be answered include the following:

- *Do we need a partnership?* Before embarking on a complex group activity like a partnership program, it is a good idea to decide if you actually need to do it. Would a looser arrangement, such as a formal financial subcontract or information-sharing network, serve the group's goals equally well?

- *What are the goals of the partnership?* The goals or aims of the project should not be viewed as abstract entities that are simply needed to fill in a grant application form. Inevitable disagreements between various team members will be easier to manage if everyone involved is motivated and influenced by an agreed-upon set of objectives no matter how far in the future these achievements may lie.

- *How do you plan to reach those goals?* Once goals are established, it is time for serious discussions at a "nuts-and-bolts" level. This process should not be rushed since it is from these discussions that activities, timelines, costs, and an overall budget will emerge. It is always important to maintain a sense of pragmatism so that your plans (and budget) are grounded in practical, achievable reality. A project of any reasonable size will probably be broken into different tasks, with each requiring a separate subcommittee.

- *How will the project be managed?* During the partnership building process, plans and ideas will change with each meeting. Until a stable plan has been achieved, it is best to have an interim decision-making process in place. Decide on the final management structure after you have all clearly agreed upon what you want to do and how you plan to do it.

Running the Project

It has been said that democracy is the worst form of government, except all the others that have been tried.
— Winston Churchill

Children start saying, "You're not the boss of me" in kindergarten and that attitude strengthens as they get older. Humans do not like being told what to do, but they mostly realize that some form of leadership is often necessary. Given the problems of money, goals, deadlines, and personalities associated with partnership plans, an orderly decision-making process is essential. There is no ideal management structure; it can only be stressed that one will be needed. Each group will find its own solution based on their individual needs. The description of a typical project life cycle given by ourpartnership.org.uk (n.d.) is a very helpful overview of the process of organizing and managing a partnership. Various management alternatives include:

- *Election of a leader by the group:* Problems of equal representation

are multiplied in large partnerships. In order to keep meetings at a manageable size, it will probably be necessary to elect or appoint representatives from different interest groups onto a steering committee. Under these circumstances, it is important that the voting process is transparent and clearly agreed upon by everyone involved.

- *General group consensus:* This method mainly applies to small groups and is probably the most common one used by student groups. It can be argued that a limited management structure is a good way to select out plans that aren't likely to succeed. If the group cannot agree in the comfort of Vancouver, then they probably should not be working overseas together. Despite this, it is still a good idea to sort out what the group plans to do in the event of major disagreement.

- *Rotating leadership:* This is a rather awkward approach to the need for general equality between large vested interests. For example, regular rotation was used to select new members to the UN Commission on Human Rights. The unelected appearance of Sudan and Zimbabwe on the committee is probably the principal reason behind the collapse of that organization. The method lacks consistency and may bring round a leader that no one wants.

- *The biggest partner is the leader:* Control in a partnership is unavoidably influenced by the skills, resources, and money that individual partners bring to the group. For example, votes in the IMF are influenced by money contributed by member states, not their population. In the past, partnerships formed between large aid agencies and small developing world communities have certainly suffered from inequality in terms of planning and direction. These problems can be avoided only when the participants (particularly the ones with the money) enter the agreement in a spirit of true respect—not just lip service—but a real understanding that long-term success depends on giving everyone involved an equal voice.

Once the framework has been selected, it is important to maintain clear communication through regular meetings. It should be emphasized that there is no substitute for face-to-face meetings, even when the partners live in different countries. Video conferences, telephone calls, and e-mail are all valuable, but intangible team building benefits do result from meetings between the main people involved in the project, particularly in the early planning stages. Unfortunately, planning often occurs before grant money has been awarded so expensive travel might not be an option. A particular point should be made about money. Careful division of any available grants or donations will not be the only worry, but it will probably be the biggest and certainly the most predictable. Again, regular communication and a transparent allocation process are essential. It is

important to accept the divisive risks caused by money and plan accordingly.

Remember that no matter how close the team members are, there will be moments of disagreement as the project progresses. Serious disputes are destructive and they can also be very expensive once lawyers and mediators are involved. They can be minimized, but certainly not avoided altogether by including an agreed-upon conflict-resolution process early in the partnership process. Methods vary, but it can be useful to ask an uninvolved third party, acceptable to both teams, to act as an arbitrator. If the project is funded by a grant agency, then a senior member of that agency is often selected. The Center for Effective Dispute Resolution website, www.cedr.co.uk, is a good source of information and so is the handbook, *"You're Not Listening to Me!"*, published by the National Council of Voluntary Organizations (Laurence & Radford, 2003).

Evaluation

I know not any thing more pleasant, or more instructive, than to compare experience with expectation, or to register from time to time the difference between idea and reality. It is by this kind of observation that we grow daily less liable to be disappointed.

—Samuel Johnson

The aid industry has a long history of failing to evaluate its initiatives and then being surprised at the last moment by poor results. The approach often taken is to alter the original goals so it seems as if the original plan wasn't such a failure after all. The changes follow a progression as each target is missed:

- We will eradicate this disease in 10 years.
- We will halve the incidence in 10 years.
- We will halve the rate of increase of this disease in 10 years.
- Through the fault of a lot of other people, this disease cannot be controlled; we will practise harm reduction.

The IMF and World Bank imposed structural-adjustment policies on developing countries for many years before external evaluation finally persuaded them that they had done more harm than good (Structural Adjustment Participatory Review International Network, 2004). Western-style medicine was exported for 20 years before it was finally accepted at Alma Ata that other methods might be worth trying (Venedictov, 1998). In fact, it was not until the Millennium Development Goals in 2000 that a large project actually published clearly defined and measurable outcomes. They may not all be met by 2015, but at least it is a good start. Unfortunately, monitoring and evaluation are often viewed as obligations imposed by the granting agency rather than being an essential part of running an efficient project. If outcomes are not measured, then all sorts of fairytale endings can be dreamed up for the annual report. Increasingly, there is a sense that outcomes should be evaluated for the project's sake rather than to complete a quarterly grant report. Even the smallest project needs an evaluation process to ensure that it is achieving something useful.

The Canadian International Develop-ment Agency (2006) relies on the widely used Results-Based Monitoring and Evaluation system. This, like other evaluation techniques, has a jargon of its own. Once you have mastered the differences between goals and objectives, or impacts and outcomes, RBM is a convenient way to combine planning and evaluation in one package. From the earliest stages, measurable outcomes are included as part of the overall plan. Regular evaluation of each of these measured points gives everyone involved a realistic idea about progress (Kusek & Rist, 2004). Other agencies use similar approaches. The International Fund for Agricultural Development produces an excellent handbook on management and evaluation that is worth downloading (Lavizzari, 2001). The World Bank also produces a useful evaluation handbook (Baker, 2000). Its version is aimed more toward assessment in terms of poverty reduction, but still has lessons for the broad field of aid projects.

■ MANAGING THE PEOPLE

Selecting Project Staff

> Never hire someone who knows less than you do about what he's hired to do.
> — Malcolm Forbes

Staff selection is rarely considered for short-term projects. Most student groups seem to choose themselves based on no criteria other than having enough money for the air ticket and enough enthusiasm to attend committee meetings. Given the size of the average student loan and the pressures of course work, these criteria do at least show some degree of commitment, but they are far from perfect. The trouble produced by a badly behaved team member can be significant so some form of selection is worth considering. Unfortunately, this is easier said than done. In an egalitarian society like a university campus, any group that sets up a selection (and rejection) process for membership will be open to a range of criticism. The defence, of course, is that overseas work is a serious undertaking so it is necessary to choose people with appropriate skills, but the whole process remains a social minefield.

Less confrontational methods are available. Requiring regular attendance at committee meetings will help to select out the uncommitted or you might simply choose to approach people on an individual basis to see if they are interested in joining the project. Whatever approach you take to the selection dilemma, this is a nettle that should be grasped. If you do not like or trust someone in Vancouver, it is very unlikely that the relationship will blossom once you work together in a refugee camp.

Choosing staff for large projects, where they might be spending several years overseas, should be (but often is not) taken very seriously. In the business world, it was realized long ago that the financial costs associated with training, relocation, salary, and accommodation are significant. Early return of such a worker due to dissatisfaction or poor performance is a disaster. It jeopardizes the project and wastes large amounts of money; this is not a minor issue and has great relevance for the aid industry. It has been estimated that nearly 350,000 US nationals work on overseas assignments and the failure rate (measured by early return before job completion) is 25–40 percent (Ashamalla & Crocito, 1997). It has taken quite a while for that lesson to be learned by the aid industry, probably because volunteer workers are a lot cheaper.

Figure 16.2: Large projects present enormous management problems. The smallpox eradication program required the coordination of thousands of people working around the world over several years. This historic photograph, taken by Dr. Stan Foster in 1975, shows a young girl called Bilkisunnessa receiving her reward for reporting the last naturally occurring case of smallpox in the world. The patient, Rahima Banu, survived to marry and have her own children. (Courtesy CDC's Public health image library.)

This attitude is reflected in the very limited amount of research available on the subject of selecting and supporting overseas project staff, either for non-governmental organizations or large established agencies (McCall & Salama, 1999; Moresky et al., 2001). Both of these studies revealed a surprising lack of standardization. For example, selection techniques ranged from a single telephone call to a multistage process of interviews that last all day. Respondents expressed frustration at the lack of a validated interviewing technique or similar instrument that might improve the sensitivity of the selection process. Although there has been plenty of research into the ideal characteristics of an overseas worker (both among aid workers (Vulpe et al., 2001) and business personnel (Ioannou, 1995)), it is difficult to apply the results in practice. While it is useful to know that flexibility, communication, and adaptability are important qualities in an applicant, it is difficult to measure and assess these variables during an interview. In practice, selection remains based on ill-defined personal opinion.

Attempts have been made to make the assessment of intercultural effectiveness more of a science than an art. The International Personnel Assessment tool (iPAss), developed by the Center for Intercultural Learning at Foreign Affairs Canada (2006) and the work of Langdon and Morrelli (2002), are both good examples. However, there is an understandable reluctance to trust measurements of complex variables such as character and behaviour and to feel that one's own intuition about a candidate is superior to a questionnaire. For example, a study of the results of personality testing of astronaut applicants showed no correlation between test results and subsequent selection to the astronaut corps (Musson et al., 2004). It is difficult to tell if this was due to inaccuracy in the personality tests or skepticism of the admission committee but, whatever the reason, it seems likely that selection of aid workers will depend on nothing more than an interview for the foreseeable future.

Pre-trip Briefing and Training

If you do not know where you are going, any road will get you there.

—Lewis Carroll

It would seem fairly obvious that, after selecting staff for a complex overseas position, it would be a good idea to offer them pre-trip training and support once they start working. Unfortunately, this approach has been very slow to develop among large aid organizations. Sending poorly prepared staff overseas to fend for themselves does not toughen them up—it just leads to failure. Inadequately trained and unqualified overseas staff have a high early return rate and those who stay may suffer from high stress, poor achievement, and depression (Foyle et al., 1998).

Not surprisingly, McCall and Salama's 1999 study of relief agencies also showed that standards of pre-trip training for relief workers were much the same as those used for worker selection—highly variable and largely inadequate. Better standards of training were provided for leaders and managers, but the average worker was simply given a bundle of printed notes. Most organizations had no idea how useful the material was; in fact, they did not bother to ask if the new recruits even read the information. Moresky et al.'s 2001 study showed that NGOs were no better. Training manuals usually provided notes on the worker's job and physical health advice, but there was little or no mention of psychological stress management, conflict resolution, and working in different cultures.

Perhaps the basic problem is the easy availability of volunteers for overseas work. Early return due to dissatisfaction or stress is not taken seriously if there are many more people willing to fill that empty place. If staff records are not kept, it is hardly even noticed! If aid workers are cheap and easy to find, why bother to invest money training them? As the aid industry becomes more complex (and more dangerous in many places), the selection and training of project staff are both receiving more attention, but there is still a long way to go. The days of the "disposable" aid worker have not passed yet (Macnair, 1995).

Supporting Workers in the Field

Long-term personnel and their families require orientation, training, and regular support to help them adapt and be effective while living and working in unfamiliar countries. These steps all need to be based on a clear knowledge of the experiences of previous workers on the project. The basic requirement is an institutional attitude that values the people who are doing all the hard work. It does not matter if you are an international space crew on a long flight or an aid worker in an unfamiliar country. Research has clearly shown that regular support and management are vital to the success of your mission and your own mental health (Ahmad, 2002; Kealey, 2004; Morphew, 2001).

A recent Swedish study showed that the aid industry has been slow to learn these lessons (Bjerneld et al., 2004). Interviews of returning relief workers revealed high

levels of stress and frustration. The authors concluded that recruiting organizations could improve volunteer performance (and their job satisfaction) by accepting better-trained staff, providing specific preparatory training, and giving better support during the assignment. Similarly, a study of Canadian fieldworkers in Egypt found that many did not feel supported or trusted by managers outside the country whom they also felt were out of touch with the practical reality of work in the country (Kealey, 2004).

The feeling that aid workers are cheap and easy to find is reflected in the prevailing attitudes toward their mental health. Although it is well established that psychological stress is minimized by training and support, it has taken a long time before attention has been paid to the psychological risks associated with aid work, particularly in disasters and conflict zones. Much of this attention is very recent. The Centers for Disease Control did not publish its own study of depression among relief workers until 2005 (Cardozo et al., 2005). Other research has linked high-stress aid work with a range of disorders, including depression, chronic fatigue syndrome, and post-traumatic stress disorder (Eriksson et al., 2001; Lovell, 1999).

Most of the organizations studied by McCall and Salama (1999) admitted that worker-support mechanisms were underdeveloped. One agency asked workers to nominate a few selected people, who were then given extra training in counselling. Another organization provided in-country mental health support for teams working in high-risk areas, but the general approach was that workers were expected to recognize any problems themselves and then apply for help from senior staff. This system is not likely to work well. Apart from the fact that self-diagnosis of depressive illness is unreliable, many workers will avoid asking for help because of the stigma associated with psychological illness.

In the last few years, several new organizations have been formed in response to the need for better standards of support for expatriate aid workers. Examples include the Antares Foundation (currently involved with CDC in a longitudinal study of stress in aid workers) and the Center for Humanitarian Psychology (*Antares Foundation*, n.d.; Center for Humanitarian Psychology, n.d.). Both take the attitude that the best way to protect project staff from burnout and depression is to train them well and support them in the field with experienced managers who have had extra training in stress recognition and counselling.

Clearly, for many reasons, a development initiative's chances of success are greatly improved if careful attention is paid to the in-country support of that project's staff. Regular communication and assessment of information will improve staff performance and also allow early recognition and treatment of severe stress-related illness.

Post-trip Debriefing and Evaluation

> Errors using inadequate data are less than those using no data at all.
> — Charles Babbage

It is essential that project managers have access to regularly updated information about staff health, staff performance, conditions in the country, and the outcomes of project activities. Detailed, compulsory debriefing of returning health workers is an important part of that process. It is also important to maintain accurate staff records so that retention rates and health problems can be monitored. If there is no mechanism to receive feedback from staff, it is possible to live in a dream world where every worker is happy and every project successful.

It is necessary to be realistic about the potential inaccuracies of self-assessment during debriefing. In a study of Canadian technical advisers, 75 percent expressed high personal satisfaction with their performance although only 20 percent were rated as being highly effective by their colleagues or superiors (Kealey, 2001). The excitement and novelty of working overseas may give a sense of satisfaction that is out of proportion to the effectiveness of that work. Just because you are having a good time does not necessarily mean you are being effective. Important decisions are based on debrief reports so they should be based on as many information sources as possible.

■ SUMMARY

During the initial excitement and enthusiasm of a new project, it is easy to forget that development projects are the same as any other joint human endeavour — without careful planning, staff selection, and management, the aims are unlikely to be met. In order for an overseas aid initiative to stand the best chance of success, it is important to employ competent, stable, well-trained personnel chosen by a carefully established selection procedure. Potential workers should be briefed and trained adequately before leaving and then fully supported during their overseas assignment. The process should constantly be updated using information gained from regular communications plus the results of a detailed post-assignment debriefing.

Working overseas is a difficult and demanding job that, under some circumstances, involves considerable physical and psychological risks. People who are prepared to take on this challenge deserve the highest levels of preparation and support. Anything less will result in dissatisfaction, poor performance, avoidable ill health, and wasted aid money. There is an urgent need for practical research into the area of selecting and supporting aid workers.

RESOURCES

References

Ahmad, M. (2002). "Who cares? The personal and professional problems of NGO field workers in Bangladesh." *Development in Practice, 12,* 177–191.

Alberta Community Development. (2001). *Working in partnership: Recipes for success.* Retrieved from www.cd.gov.ab.ca/ by searching "working in partnership."

Antares Foundation. (n.d.). Retrieved from www.antaresfoundation.org.

Ashamalla, M., & Crocito, M. (1997). "Easing entry and beyond: Preparing expatriates and patriates for foreign assignment success." *International Journal of Commerce and Management, 7,* 106–114.

Baker, J. (2000). *Evaluating the impact of development projects on poverty: A handbook for practitioners.* Washington: World Bank Publications. Retrieved from www.worldbank.org by searching for title.

Bjerneld, M., et al. (2004). "Perception of work in humanitarian assistance: Interviews with returning Swedish health professionals." *Disaster Management Response, 2,* 101–108.

British Council. (n.d.). *Developing school partnerships.* Retrieved from www.britishcouncil.org/globalschools.

Canadian International Development Agency. (2006). *Results-based management.* Retrieved from www.acdi-cida.gc.ca/CIDAWEB/acdicida.nsf/En/NIC-31595014-KEF.

Cardozo, B., et al. (2005). "The mental health of expatriate and kosovar Albanian humanitarian aid workers." *Disasters, 2,* 152–170.

Center for Humanitarian Psychology. (n.d.). Retrieved from www.humanitarian-psy.org.

Collins, K. (2004). "Profitable gifts: A history of the Merck ivermectin donation program and its implications for international health." *Perspectives in Biology and Medicine, 47,* 100–109.

Eriksson, C., et al. (2001). "Trauma exposure and PTSD symptoms in international relief and development personnel." *Journal of Traumatic Stress, 14,* 205–212.

Foreign Affairs and International Trade Canada. (2006). *What is iPass?* Retrieved from www.international.gc.ca/cfsi-icse/cil-cai/what_is_ipass-en.asp.

Foyle, M., et al. (1998). "Expatriate mental health." *Acta Psychiatrica Scandinavica, 97,* 278–283.

George C. Marshall Foundation. (n.d.). Retrieved from www.marshallfoundation.org.

Gyapong, M., et al. (2001). "Community-directed treatment: The way forward to eliminating lymphatic filariasis as a public health problem in Ghana." *Annals of Tropical Medicine and Parasitology, 1,* 77–86.

Harrington-Mackin, D. (1994). *The team-building tool kit: Tips, tactics, and rules for effective workplace teams.* New York: American Management Association.

Hopkins, A. (2005). "Ivermectin and Onchocerciasis: Is it all solved?" *Eye, 19,* 1057–1066.

Ioannou, L. (1995). "Unnatural selection." *International Business, 83,* 95–99.

Kealey, D. (1996). *Interpersonal and cultural dimensions of Canadian development assistance in Egypt.* Ottawa: Canadian International Development Agency.

Kealey, D. (2001). *Cross-cultural effectiveness: A study of Canadian technical advisors overseas.* Ottawa: Government of Canada, Department of Foreign Affairs.

Kealey, D. (2004). "Research on intercultural effectiveness and its relevance to multicultural crews in space." *Aviation, Space, and Environmental Medicine, 75* (Suppl. 1), C58–C64.

Kerr, M. (1996). *Partnering and health development: The Kathmandu connection.* Calgary: University of Calgary Press.

Kusek, J., & Rist, R. (2004). *Ten steps to a result-based monitoring and evaluation system.* Washington: World Bank.

Langdon, D., & Morrelli, A. (2002). "A new model for systematic competency identification." *Performance Improvement, 41*, 16–23.

Laurence, L., & Radford, A. (2003). *You're not listening to me! Dealing with disputes: Mediation and its benefits for voluntary organizations.* London: National Council of Voluntary Organizations.

Lavizzari, L. (2001). *A guide for project management and evaluation: Managing for impact in rural development.* Retrieved from www.ifad.org/evaluation/guide/.

Lovell, D. (1999). "Chronic fatigue syndrome among overseas development workers: A qualitative study." *Journal of Travel Medicine, 6*, 16–23.

Macnair, R. (1995). *Room for improvement: The management and support of relief and development workers.* London: Overseas Development Institute.

McCall, M., & Salama, P. (1999). "Selection, training and support of relief workers: An occupational health issue." *British Medical Journal, 318*, 113–116.

Moresky, R., et al. (2001). "Preparing international relief workers for health care in the field: An evaluation of organizational practices." *Pre-hospital Disaster Medicine, 16*, 257–262.

Morphew, M. (2001). "Psychological and human factors in long duration space flight." *McGill Journal of Medicine, 6*, 74–80.

Musson, D., et al. (2004). "Personality characteristics and trait clusters in final stage astronaut selection." *Aviation, Space, and Environmental Medicine, 75*, 342–349.

Ourpartnership.org.uk. (n.d.) *The partnership lifecycle.* Retrieved from www.ourpartnership.org.uk/anncmnt/anlist.cfm?ANID=28.

Structural Assignment Participatory Review International Network. (2004). *Structural adjustment: The SAPRI report: The policy roots of economic crisis, poverty, and inequality.* London: Zed Books.

UNDP/World Bank/WHO Special Programme for Research and Training in Tropical Diseases. (1996). *Community-directed treatment with ivermectin: Report of a multi-country study.* Retrieved from www.who.int/tdr/publications/publications/comdti.htm.

UNDP/World Bank/WHO Special Programme for Research and Training in Tropical Diseases. (n.d.). Retrieved from www.who.int/tdr/.

US Census Bureau. (2006). *World population information.* Retrieved from www.census.gov/ipc/www/world.html.

US Energy Information Administration. (n.d.). *International energy data and analysis.* Retrieved from www.eia.doe.gov/emeu/international/contents.html.

Venedictov, D. (1998). "Alma Ata and after." *World Health Forum, 19*, 79–86.

Vulpe, T., et al. (2001). *A profile of the interculturally effective person.* Ottawa: Government of Canada, Department of Foreign Affairs.

Recommended Reading

Baker, J. (2000). *Evaluating the impact of development projects on poverty: A handbook for practitioners.* Washington: World Bank.

Chambers, R. (2002). *Participatory workshops: A source book of 21 sets of ideas and activities.* London: Earthscan Publications.

Danieli, Y., Rodley, N., & Weisaeth, L. (Eds.). (1995). *International responses to traumatic stress.* Amityville: Baywood Publishing.

Harrington-Mackin, D. (1994). *The team-building tool kit: Tips, tactics, and rules for effective workplace teams*. New York: American Management Association.

Kerr, M. (1996). *Partnering and health development: The Kathmandu connection*. Calgary: University of Calgary Press.

Kusek, J., & Rist, R. (2004). *Ten steps to a results-based monitoring and evaluation system*. Washington: World Bank.

Roche, C. (2000). *Impact assessment for development agencies: Learning to value change*. Oxford: Oxfam.

Rubin, F. (1995). *A basic guide to evaluation for development workers*. Oxford: Oxfam.

Wilson, A., & Charlton, K. (1997). *Making partnerships work: A practical guide for the public, private, voluntary, and community sectors*. York: Joseph Rowntree Foundation.

Copyright Acknowledgments

All of the tables and figures in this book, unless otherwise noted, were created by the author, based on the source material indicated.

Figures

Figure 4.10: "Principal types of Developing World External Dept Over the Last 35 Years," adapted from "Composition of Outstanding External Debt of Developing Countries, 1970-2003," in *Global Development Finance 2005: Mobilizing Finance and Managing Vulnerability*, (Washington: The World Bank, 2005): 74.

Photographs

Figure 1.4 by Stephanie Colvey, "New Delhi," #1157. Reprinted by permission of International Development Research Centre (IDRC) Photo Library.

Figure 1.5 by Integrated Regional Information Network. Reprinted by permission of Integrated Regional Information Network.

Figure 1.6 by Francois Goemans © European Commission Humanitarian Aid Office (ECHO), 2006. Reprinted by permission of ECHO.

Figure 1.7 by Pierre Virot. Reprinted by permission of World Health Organization (WHO) Media Centre.

Figure 1.8 by Brian Atkinson. Reprinted by permission of GlobalAware.org.

Figure 1.9 by Sven Torfinn. Reprinted by permission of Integrated Regional Information Network.

Figure 1.10 by Integrated Regional Information Network. Reprinted by permission of Integrated Regional Information Network.

Figure 1.11 by Claire McEvoy. Reprinted by permission of Integrated Regional Information Network.

Figure 2.1 by United Nations Photo Library. Reprinted by permission of United Nations Photo Library.

Figure 2.2 by U.S. National Library of Medicine. Reprinted by permission of U.S. National Library of Medicine.

Figure 3.1 by Pierre Virot. Reprinted by permission of World Health Organization (WHO) Media Centre.

Figure 3.3 by Andy Crump. Reprinted by permission of Tropical Research Programme Image Library.

Figure 4.3 by Dr. William Grut. Reprinted by permission of Rose Charities.

Figure 4.4 by Stephanie Colvey, "Dharavi slum in Bombay," #1110. Reprinted by permission of International Development Research Centre (IDRC) Photo Library.

Figure 5.4 by Hector Barrios, "Ipoti Village," #11099. Reprinted by permission of International Development Research Centre (IDRC) Photo Library.

Figure 5.6 by Francois Goemans © European Commission Humanitarian Aid Office (ECHO), 2006. Reprinted by permission of ECHO.

Figure 6.1 by Dr. S Foster. Reprinted by permission of Public Health Image Library (PHIL).

Figure 6.2 by Dr. William Grut. Reprinted by permission of Rose Charities.

Index

Aboriginal Head Start Approach (HSA), 294, 295
Aboriginal peoples. *See* indigenous peoples
Aboriginal Peoples, Royal Commission on (RCAP), 294–295
abortion, 136*t*, 180, 246
absolute poverty, 56
Addis Ababa Fistula Hospital, 8*f*, 201*f*
adult health, in developing world
    and aid project success stories, 153
    and budgetary concerns, 125–128
    and cost-effective interventions, 126–128, 128t, 138
    data on, 114–115
    and morbidity/burden of disease, 123–125
    and mortality, 114, 120–123
    and rise of global middle class, 121, 122
    and risk assessment, 126, 127t, 138
    and urban hospitals, 25, 125–126, 138, 146, 167, 208
adult human rights, 240–247
Afghanistan, 218*f*, 219, 269, 272–273, 274
Africa, Sub-Saharan, 5, 6*f*, 26, 133, 154, 199, 203, 220, 250
    birth and death statistics in, 105, 107, 120
    health service user fees in, 182
    HIV/AIDS in, 199
    maternal mortality in, 114, 134, 135, 308
    tuberculosis deaths in, 194, 195
African Development Fund, 225, 231
African trypanosomiasis, 200, 207
agencies, aid. *See* aid agencies
agricultural surpluses, donation of, 19, 90–92
agriculture
    Green Revolution in, 24, 28t, 90, 153, 219–220, 221
    improvements in, 219–221
    as neglected by aid industry, 89–90
    and trade liberalization, 221–222
aid, food, 90–92
aid, overseas, 143–144, 144*t*, 160–161
    see also aid projects
    dollar value of, 151, 151f, 161, 218t

future of, 157–160
to "good"/difficult countries, 155, 157
history of, 17–30, 145–146
and medical services, 24–26
milestones in, 27t, 28t
Monterrey conference on, 149, 157–158, 160
as percentage of GNI, 150, 150f
as percentage of GDP, 24, 28t, 149, 149t, 160
postwar, 20–21, 143, 149
as problematic, 150–151, 152
reasons for, 145–146
sources of income for, 147–149
success/failure of, 151–155
two main types of, 21, 145–146
aid agencies, 144–145, 159–160
    and competence/professionalism of workers, 265, 267, 272, 274, 279–280
    and disaster management, 262, 264–267, 275
    and disaster mitigation, 267–268
    employment/volunteer opportunities with, 319
    ethical issues for, in war, 269–271
    workers of, as targeted during war, 269, 271, 272
aid projects
    as ambitious but problematic, 23–26, 125–126, 138, 146, 152, 160–161
    reasons for failure of, 155–156
    short-term, 309–310
    student teams for, 319–320
    success stories of, 153–154
    technical assistance to, 151, 153, 159
aid projects, as partnerships, 329–331, 343–344
    and debriefing/evaluation of staff, 343
    evaluation of, 338–339
    and face-to-face meetings, 338
    and involvement of other groups, 333–335
    leadership of, 337–338
    and questions to ask, 336–337

running, 337–338
selecting staff for, 339–341
starting, 335–337
as successful/unsuccessful, 330–333
and support for staff, in field, 342–343
training staff for, 341–342
aid projects, working on, 156, 307–308, 323–324
see also aid workers
and culture shock, 314, 321–322
and ethical considerations, 315–317
financing/fundraising for, 320
and health of workers, 310–315, 322–323
and importance of preparation, 309, 330
information available on, 310
motivation for, 317
and research on countries, 320–321
and respect for poor, 308–309
and team dynamics, 310
and team formation, 319–320
travel preparations for, 317–321
aid workers
as "cheap"/easy to find, 340, 342
competence/professionalism of, 265, 267, 272, 274, 279–280
and consulate/embassy contact, 318
and culture shock, 314, 321–322
documents/forms needed by, 318
drug use by, 311
early return of, 340, 341
employment/volunteer opportunities for, 319
ethical considerations for, 315–317
health insurance for, 311–312, 318, 320
health problems/risks for, 310–315, 322–323
language issues for, 318–319, 320, 321, 322
and issues to be aware of, 156
post-trip debriefing/evaluation of, 343
pre-trip training of, 341–342
psychological risks for, 313–314, 342–343
and road traffic accidents, 310, 313
selection of, for projects, 339–341
support for, in field, 342–343
as targeted during war, 269, 271, 272
and translators, 318–319, 320
vaccination for, 322
women as, and issues for, 314–315
AIDS. See HIV/AIDS
alcohol, 126, 127t, 128t
abuse of, 124t, 125t, 289, 298
Aleutian Islands, indigenous peoples of, 283, 286, 289

Alma Ata conference, 25, 27t, 47, 125, 126, 132, 138, 146, 165–166, 168–170, 172, 174, 181, 204, 339
anemia, 76, 81, 93, 112t, 124t, 136
antibiotics, 22, 43
anti-retroviral drugs, 137, 197, 199, 205t, 207
Assembly of First Nations, 291
atherosclerosis, 43, 45, 122
Australia, Aboriginal peoples of, 287–288, 299
avian flu, 19, 102
AZT, 197, 205t

baby formula, 84–87, 88, 174
Baby-Friendly Hospital Initiative, 88, 174, 203
Bacillus Calmette-Guérin (BCG), 114, 195
bacteria, 36, 42–43, 176, 190, 193, 194
Baker, James, and plan to resolve debt crisis, 226
Balmis, Francisco Xavier de, 18, 27t
Bamako Initiative, on user fees, 182
Bandung conference, and non-aligned movement, 24, 28t
Bangladesh, 102f, 148, 153f, 217, 219, 245
Banker to the Poor (Yunus), 217
Bataan nuclear power station (Philippines), 64
Bauer, Peter, 146
Bengal, famine in, 89
Bhola cyclone, 263t
Bhopal, industrial disaster in, 263t
Biafra, war in, 271
bilateral aid, as type of debt, 66–67, 147, 225
Bill of Rights, International, 242
Bill of Rights, 1689 (English), 241, 242
"Bills of Mortality," 100–101, 102
biological disasters, 262t, 263t
influenza, 19, 102, 263t
SARS, 19, 27t, 102, 153, 263t
birth registration, 105, 129, 134, 167
Black Report, 43f, 43–44, 45f, 45
Blair, Tony, 3, 61, 226
blindness, and vitamin A deficiency, 80–81
Body Mass Index (BMI), 78, 82t, 83, 264t
Bono, 61
Borlaug, Norman, 219, 220
Bourguignon, François, 216–217
Brace, Charles, 248
Brady, Nicholas F., and plan to resolve debt crisis, 226–227
Brazil, 122, 199, 219, 228, 247
breast-feeding, 26, 76, 81, 87–88, 132, 137, 203
as element of Primary Health Care, 169, 170, 171, 174–175, 204

and HIV/AIDS transmission, 132, 196, 197, 198
Bretton Woods Institutions, 53, 66*t*
Buffett, Warren, 19*t*, 148
burden of disease, leading causes of, 111, 112*t*
burden of disease, measurement of, 108–109, 123
    global reports/studies on, 107, 109, 111, 112t, 114, 120, 137, 177–178
    and health gap, 108, 108f, 110–112
    and life expectancy, 108f, 108–109
    morbidity and, 123–125
    and mortality-morbidity measurement, 109
    and poor living conditions, 177–178
Bush, George W., 61, 226, 231

calcium, 75, 137
The Canadian Guide to Working and Living Overseas (Hachey), 319
Canadian International Development Agency (CIDA), 339
cancer, 121*t*, 122*t*
census taking, 100, 104
Center for Research on Epidemiology of Disasters (CRED), 260
Centers for Disease Control (CDC), 103, 342, 343
Central America, indigenous peoples of, 289–290
cerebrovascular disease, 122*t*, 123, 124*t*, 125*t*
Chadwick, Sir Edwin, 27*t*, 35, 36, 40–41, 45, 166
Charter of Liberties (English), 241, 242
The Chastening (Blustein), 227
Chernobyl, industrial disaster in, 263*t*
child health, in developing world
    and birth rate, 128–129, 179, 179f
    and cost-effective interventions, 26–27, 132
    data on, 112–114
    as element of Primary Health Care, 169
    and Integrated Management (IMCI) program, 27t, 171, 203–206
    and mortality, 120, 122, 124, 129–132
    in refugee camps, 275
child labour, 248–252
    and education, 251
    global/regional estimates of, 249–250
    history of, 248–249
    reasons for, 251–252
child mortality, in developing world, 120, 122, 124
    causes of, 113, 129–132

and contraception, 128–129, 129t
and malnutrition, 79f, 80
and measurement of grief, 131
and poverty, 54, 54f, 60, 60f
rates of, 112–113, 129t, 129–130, 171, 171f
statistics on, 112–113
Child Survival Revolution, 27*t*, 127, 132, 133
children
    birth registration of, 105, 129, 134
    education of, 113, 251
    health data on, 112–114
    human rights legislation, as crucial to, 223
    illnesses of, 7–8, 43, 76, 102
    medical therapies targeted at, 26–27
    and report on health needs of, 24
    in urban slums, 59f, 177–178
children, growth of, 78–79, 80, 113
    charts measuring, 82, 82t, 83–84
    monitoring of, under GOBI programs, 26, 132, 170, 204
children, human rights of, 247–253
    and child labour, 248–252
    convention on (UN), 248, 252
    development of, 247–248
    and female circumcision, 252–253
    and human trafficking, 245–246, 248, 250t
Children's Aid Society, founding of, 248
China, 80, 90, 93, 122, 190, 191
    "barefoot doctors" in, 25f, 168
    effects of poverty alleviation in, 214f, 214–215, 215f
    Primary Health Care in, 168, 172
cholera, 19, 27*t*, 37, 52, 102, 103, 175
chloroquine, 191, 192*t*, 205*t*
chronic obstructive lung disease, 121*t*, 122*t*, 123, 124*t*
CIA World Factbook (Web site), 115, 320
circumcision, female, 10, 114, 252–253
class, and population health, 44–47
clean water. *See* water, cleanliness of
colonialism, 20, 23–24, 62–63, 145
community-directed therapy (ComDT), 334–335
condoms, use of, 114, 199, 205*t*. *See also* contraception
Confessions of an Economic Hit Man (Perkins), 63
Congress of Aboriginal Peoples, 291
consumption analysis, 58–59
contraception, 76, 114, 128–129, 129*t*, 179, 180, 203, 204*f*, 315
Convention on the Rights of the Child, UN, 248, 252

counterfeit drugs, 208
crude mortality rate (CMR), of displaced
    persons, 275, 276, 278
Cuba, 166, 172, 172*t*, 198
culture shock, for aid workers, 314, 321–322
Cyrus the Great, human rights charter of, 241
cystic fibrosis, 104

Darfur, 10, 10*f*, 93. *See also* Sudan
Davis Inlet, substance abuse problems in, 299
death registration, 106–107, 134, 167
deaths, recording of, 100–101, 102
DDT, as used to combat malaria, 190, 192,
    193, 205*t*
debt, in developing world, 51–52, 61–70, 144*t*
    after disasters, 267
    and colonial legacy, 62–63, 68
    as compared to foreign aid, 67, 67*f*
    and defaulting nations, 26, 66, 146, 225–226
    forgiveness of. See debt relief
    and global recession, 66–67
    and indiscriminate lending, 63–65, 68
    magnitude of, 66–68
    as "odious," 62, 64–65, 68
    and rising interest rates, 65, 65*f*
    types of loans involved in, 66–67, 67*f*, 225
debt crisis, 26, 65–66, 225–226
    see also structural adjustment policies
    Baker and Brady plans for, 226–227
    Paris Club approach to, 227
    and world price of oil, 65, 65*f*, 225
debt relief, 3, 28*t*, 61–62, 68–69, 157, 213, 232
    and Gleneagles G8 meeting, 3, 28*t*, 69,
        213, 226, 231–232
    and Heavily Indebted Poor Countries
        Initiatives, 26, 28t, 57, 69, 146, 184, 216,
        229–231
Declaration of Independence (American),
    241, 242
Declaration of the Rights of Man and of the
    Citizen (French), 241, 242
Declaration on the Rights of Indigenous
    Peoples (UN), 285*t*, 286
depression, 112*t*, 123, 124*t*, 125*t*, 177–178, 247,
    252, 300, 314, 321, 342
developing world. *See* adult health, in
    developing world; child health, in
    developing world; debt, in developing
    world
Development Assistance Committee (DAC),
    24, 28*t*, 66*t*, 150–151, 157

diabetes, 295*t*, 296, 300
diarrhea/diarrheal diseases, 7–8, 80, 112*t*,
    113, 177, 206, 310*t*
    and morbidity, 124*t*, 125*t*
    and mortality, 121*t*, 122*t*, 131, 171, 171*f*,
        205*t*
    oral rehydration for, 131, 175–176, 205*t*
    in refugee camps, 276, 279
Dickens, Charles, 52, 247–248
diphtheria, 113, 173, 174, 322
Directly Observed Treatment Short-course
    (DOTS) therapy, for tuberculosis, 194–195,
    205*t*
disability, 111, 112*t*, 123
disability-adjusted life expectancy, 108–110,
    115–116
Disability-Adjusted Life Year (DALY), 110–
    112, 114, 116, 126
disaster management, 262, 264–267
    and competence/professionalism of aid
        workers, 265, 267, 272, 274, 279–280
    and coordination of groups, 265
    and forensics, 266
    handbooks on, 264, 275
    international framework for, 262, 264
    and multiple needs assessments, 265–266
    and psychological trauma of survivors,
        266–267
    and women, needs of, 266
disaster mitigation, 267–268, 280
disasters, 259–260, 279–280
    deaths and death rates from, 260f, 260–
        261, 261f
    increasing number of, 261, 262f
    insurance for, 267, 268, 280
    major, by type, 263t
    management of, 262–267
    mitigation of, 267–269, 280
disasters, humanitarian, 268–273
    see also war
    ethical issues of, for aid agencies, 269–271
    evolution of responses to, 271–273
    military intervention in, 272
disasters, natural, 9–10
    and aid to victims, 92, 153–154
    and displaced populations, 262
    costs of, 260–261, 267
    "hot spots" for, 267
    increasing number of, 261, 262f, 267
    poverty caused by, 56
disease, theories of, 101, 102

disease burden, leading causes of, 111, 112*t*
disease burden, measurement of, 108–109, 123
    global reports/studies on, 107, 109, 111,
      112t, 114, 120, 137, 177–178
    and health gap, 108, 108f, 110–112
    and life expectancy, 108f, 108–109
    morbidity and, 123–125
    and mortality-morbidity measurement, 109
    and poor living conditions, 177–178
disease control, as element of Primary Health
  Care, 169
disease eradication, 42–44, 102
    see also specific diseases
    postwar Western-style programs for,
      22–23, 27t, 29, 167, 208, 339
disease measurement
    definitions used in, 103–104
    errors in, 106–108
    health monitoring systems, 105–106
    vital statistics, 104–105
disease surveillance/monitoring, 102, 103
diseases, non-lethal, 112*t*, 116, 123, 132, 137
displaced populations, 152, 262, 269, 273–279
    see also refugees
    care and management of, 274–275. See
      also refugee camps
    crude mortality rate of, 275, 276, 278
    size of, 273–274, 274t
    terminology associated with, 273t
Doha round of trade talks (WTO), 24, 28*t*, 91,
  207, 222
"dollar a day" measurement of poverty, 56,
  57*t*, 58, 59, 69, 99
drug use, by aid workers, 311
drugs
    affordability of, 207–208
    availability of, 169, 208
    cost and effectiveness of, 205t
    counterfeit, 208
    essential, 206–208
    generic, 197, 207, 222
    for HIV/AIDS, 197, 198, 205t, 207, 222, 315
    for malaria, 22, 191–192, 192t, 205t
    patent restrictions on, 207–208
    testing of, 315–316
    for tuberculosis, 42f, 194t, 194–195, 205t
Dunant, Henri, 19

earthquakes, 260*f*, 261, 261*f*, 262*f*, 263*t*, 268
  in Pakistan, 9, 153, 259, 262, 267, 278
Easterly, William, 144, 157, 216

economic aid, 21, 28*t*
economic development, pro-poor. *See*
  poverty alleviation
economic poverty, 55
education, 113, 169, 268
    and child labour, 251
    of girls/women, 10, 76, 218, 219, 251, 293
    and health care, 205–206
    and poverty alleviation, 218–219
    and residential schools, 287, 292, 293, 294
Enhanced Heavily Indebted Poor Countries
  Initiative (EHIPC), 26, 28*t*, 57, 184, 216, 230,
  231
environmental issues, 178, 270, 278
    for Canadian indigenous peoples, 294, 300
essential drugs, 206–208
ethical considerations, for aid workers, 315–317
Ethiopia, 4, 8*f*, 39*f*, 42*f*, 204*f*
Europe
    agricultural subsidies to, 221
    postwar aid to, 20–21, 28*t*, 143, 149, 334
European Union, 92, 207, 221, 222
eye diseases/infections, 22, 80, 125*t*, 153, 177,
  334–335

family planning, 178–181, 203, 275
family violence, among indigenous peoples,
  287, 293, 297, 298, 300
famine, 4, 89
Farr, William, 101
female circumcision, 10, 114, 252–253
fertility rate
    and contraception use, 203, 204f
    and population, 179, 179f
fetal alcohol syndrome, 299
First Nations, of Canada, 286, 287, 291
    see also indigenous peoples, of Canada
    housing standards of, 293–294, 297
    obesity and diabetes among, 295t, 296
    residential schooling of, 287, 292, 293, 294
    water contamination, as problem for, 294
floods, 260*f*, 261*f*, 262*f*
food aid, 90–92
Food and Agriculture Organization (FAO),
  21, 28*t*, 90, 113
food fortification, 81
food security, 88–90
foreign aid. *See* aid, overseas
Foreign Direct Investment (FDI), 147–48, 149
formula, infant, 84–87, 88, 174

Gambia, infant/child mortality rates in, 171–172, 172*f*

gastroenteritis, 76, 81, 93, 174, 175

Gates, Bill and Melinda, foundation of, 106, 148, 174

GDP
    and gross national income, 149
    growth of, in relation to financial aid, 154–155
    and life expectancy, 39–40, 40f, 44
    per capita inflection point of, 40, 41
    percentage of, as recommended in aid, 24, 28t, 149, 149t, 160
    of poor nations, 19t
    and population health, 39–40

Geldof, Bob, 61

General Agreement on Tariffs and Trade (GATT), 21, 66*t*

generic drugs, 197, 207, 222

genetically modified crops, 91

Geneva Convention, 145, 272, 273, 274

genital mutilation, female, 10, 114, 252–253

Ghana Health Assessment Team, 109, 126, 138

Gini index/coefficient, as measurement of poverty, 57t, 60, 215

Gleneagles, G8 meeting at, 3, 28t, 69, 213, 226, 231–232

Global Alliance for Vaccines and Immunization, 27t, 174

Global Fund to fight AIDS, Tuberculosis and Malaria (GFATM), 27t, 159–160, 199

Globalization and its Discontents (Stiglitz), 227

GOBI and GOBI-FFF programs, 26–27, 132, 170–171, 204, 205*t*

Gomez system, for measuring malnutrition, 82, 82*t*, 84

Grameen Bank, 217

Grant, James, 26, 170, 191

Graunt, John, 100–101

Great Lakes refugee crisis (Rwanda), 270–271

Green Revolution, 24, 28t, 90, 153, 219–220, 221

Greenland, 285t, 286, 289

Gross Domestic Product. *See* GDP

Gross National Income (GNI), 149, 150, 150*f*

Group of Eight (G8), 3, 28t, 66t, 159
    debt forgiveness by, 61–62, 68–69, 213, 226, 231–232

Group of Twenty (G20), 28t, 222

growth, of children, 78–79, 80, 113
    charts measuring, 82, 82t, 83–84
    monitoring of, under GOBI programs, 26, 132, 170, 204

Haiti, 221

Hamlin, Catherine and Reginald, 8f, 201f

Hammurabi, Code of, 241

Haq, Mahbub ul, 56

Harrod, Roy, and Evsey Domar, economic theories of, 22, 146, 155

health. *See* population health

health care. *See* Primary Health Care

health care, costs of, 125–126
    and cost-effective interventions, 126–128, 128t, 138
    for drug treatments, 205t
    and risk assessment, 126, 127t, 138
    sources of funding for, 182–183
    and user fees, 182

health expectancy, 108–110. *See also* life expectancy

"Health for All by 2000" strategy, 25, 30, 146, 169–170, 172, 183–184

health insurance, 182
    for aid workers, 311–312, 318, 320

health gap, 108, 108f, 110–112

Health Metrics Network, 106

health planning/cost management, 103

heart disease, 43, 112t, 121t, 122t, 123, 124t, 125t

heat waves, 263t

Heavily Indebted Poor Countries Initiative (HIPC), 26, 28t, 69, 146, 216, 229–230, 231

Heavily Indebted Poor Countries Initiative, Enhanced (EHIPC), 26, 28t, 57, 184, 216, 230, 231

Henderson, Donald, 24

hepatitis A and B, 313, 322

hidden poverty, 56

Highly Active Anti-Retroviral Therapy (HAART), 197, 199, 205t

Hine, Lewis, 248

Hippocrates, 190, 193

HIV/AIDS, 22, 23, 26, 27t, 29, 43, 76, 102, 200, 218
    about the disease, 195–197
    and behavioural change, 23, 198–199
    among Canadian indigenous peoples, 297
    and contraception, 114
    drug testing for, 315
    generic drugs for, 207, 222
    and Global Fund to fight, 159–160, 199
    identification of, 103
    and life expectancy, 40, 40t
    and morbidity, 124t, 124–125, 125t
    and mortality, 121, 122, 122t, 131, 194, 196, 205t

mother-child transmission of, 132, 196,
    197, 198
and pregnancy, 132, 137, 202
prevention of, 128t, 197–199
in refugee camps, 275
in Sub-Saharan Africa, 133
treatment of, 137, 197, 199, 205t, 207
and tuberculosis, 76, 193, 195, 196
vaccine for, as not yet found, 198
hospitals, 7f, 8f, 42f, 201f
    urban, as exported to developing world,
        25, 125–126, 138, 146, 167, 208
housing
    as basic element of Primary Health Care,
        177–178
    of Canadian indigenous peoples, 293–
        294, 295, 297
Human Development Index, 56, 57t, 59
Human Poverty Index, 56, 57t, 59
human rights, 237–238, 253
    of adults, 240–247
    categories of, 239–240
    of children. See human rights of children
    definition of, 238–239
Human Rights, UN Commission on, 223, 224,
    242–243, 337
Human Rights, UN High Commissioner for
    (UNHCHR), 223, 224, 242–243, 286t
Human Rights, Universal Declaration of, 223,
    224, 238, 242, 243
human rights abuses, 10, 223, 238
    child labour, 248–252
    female circumcision, 10, 114, 252–253
    human trafficking, 245–246, 248, 250t
    slavery, 243–245, 250t
    violence against women, 246–247
    in war, 269
Human Rights Council, UN, 224, 243
human rights legislation, 223–224, 224f, 239,
    244
    history of, 241–243
human rights of children, 247–253
    and child labour, 248–252
    convention on (UN), 248, 252
    development of, 247–248
    and female circumcision, 10, 114, 252–253
    and human trafficking, 245–246, 248, 250t
human trafficking, 245–246, 248, 250t
humanitarian disasters, 268–273
    see also displaced populations; war
    as "complex," 269

ethical issues of, for aid agencies, 269–271
    evolution of responses to, 271–273
    military intervention in, 272
hurricanes, 260f, 261, 263t, 267
    Katrina, 9, 148, 261, 262, 263t
hygiene, personal, 36–37, 177, 276
hypothyroidism, 75, 93

immunization, 5, 26, 27, 81, 132, 146, 272
    see also vaccination
    as basic health intervention, 128t
    cost of, 173
    as element of Primary Health Care, 169,
        170–171, 171f, 173–174, 204
    Expanded Program on (EPI), 173–174, 205t
    statistics on, 113
income
    and child mortality, 54, 54f, 60, 60f
    and education, 53f, 54
    as measure of poverty, 57t, 57–58
income analysis, 58
India
    Bhopal industrial disaster in, 263t
    caste system in, 13, 251
    child labour in, 249f
    drug manufacturing in, 207, 208
    Institutes of Technology in, 153
    maternal mortality in, 135
    Primary Health Care in, 172, 172t
    and progress on malnutrition, 90, 93
    refusal of foreign tsunami aid by, 265
    sex-selected abortion in, 246
Indian Act (Canada), 290, 291
indigenous peoples, 8–9, 283–284, 300–301
    assimilation/oppression of, 284–285,
        287, 287–288, 299
    botanical/pharmaceutical knowledge of,
        284, 301
    characteristics of, 284
    conflicts of, with White settlers/
        explorers, 286–287, 287, 288, 290, 299
    health of, 299–300
    health statistics on, 300
    life expectancies of, 300, 300f
    numbers of, 284
    psychiatric problems/suicide among, 300
    representation of, in international
        organizations, 286t
    rights for, milestones in history of, 285t,
        285–286
    UN working group on, 285t

indigenous peoples, of Canada, 286, 287,
    290–291, 300–301
    see also First Nations; Inuit
    alcohol abuse among, 289, 298
    education of, 292t, 293
    employment rates for, 292t
    environmental problems for, 294, 300
    family violence among, 287, 293, 297,
        298, 300
    and fetal alcohol syndrome, 299
    health indices for, 291–292, 292t
    health organizations created for, 295
    health standards of, 295–296
    housing standards of, 293–294, 295, 297
    infant mortality rate of, 292t, 296, 296t
    infectious diseases among, 297
    and injuries/deaths from injuries, 297–
        298, 300
    language of, 294
    life expectancy of, 292t, 296, 296t
    lifestyle diseases among, 295t, 296, 300
    residential schooling of, 287, 292, 293, 294
    self-determination of, 295, 298
    suicide among, 9, 287, 292t, 293, 295, 297,
        297t, 298, 300
    substance abuse among, 9, 287, 289, 293,
        297, 298–299, 300
    water contamination, as problem for,
        294, 297, 300
indigenous peoples, global
    in Australia, 287–288
    in Canada, 286, 287, 290–291, 300–301
    in Central America, 289–290
    in circumpolar regions, 289
    in New Zealand and Polynesia, 288–289
    in North America, 286–287
Indonesia, 59, 62, 263t, 273
industrial/technological disasters, 261t, 263t
infant formula, 84–87, 88, 174
infant mortality
    and formula use, 86–87, 88
    global trends in, 5, 5f
    and maternal mortality, 130, 130t, 136
infant mortality rate (IMR), 112–113, 129, 129t
    of Canadian indigenous peoples, 292t,
        296, 296t
    in China, and poverty alleviation, 214f
    and maternal mortality rate, 130, 130t
    in United Kingdom, and social
        legislation, 223, 224f
infants, feeding of, 85. See also breast-feeding;
    infant formula

infectious diseases, 13t, 19, 52
    see also specific diseases
    cost/effectiveness of therapies against,
        204, 205t
    decline in, reasons for, 42–44
    and malnutrition, 76
    and mortality, 120–123
    and postwar eradication programs,
        22–23, 29, 167
    in refugee camps, 275
influenza, 19, 102, 263t
Innocenti Declaration on breastfeeding, 87, 174
insects
    control of, 22, 178, 190, 192–193, 205t
    diseases borne by, 176, 199–200. See also
        malaria
    infestations of, 9f
Integrated Management of Childhood
    Illnesses (IMCI), 27t, 171, 203–206
internally displaced persons (IDPs), 273, 273t,
    274t. See also displaced populations
International Conference on Population and
    Development (ICPD), 201
International Criminal Court, 224, 242, 273
International Federation of Red Cross and
    Red Crescent Societies, 266, 267
international financial institutions (IFIs), 66,
    225, 230
International Financing Facility (IFF)
    Proposal, 160
International Fund for Agricultural
    Development, 339
international health, 4–5
    agencies for, 19
    major events in, 27t
    problems in, 5–10
International Health Exchange, 319
International Institute of Human Rights, 239
International Labour Organization, 245, 248,
    249–250, 285t, 286t
International Monetary Fund (IMF), 21, 26,
    56, 225
    and Debt Sustainability Framework, 232
    and developing world debt, 64, 66–67,
        216, 226, 227–228
    and Heavily Indebted Poor Countries
        Initiatives, 26, 229–230, 231
    structural adjustment policies of, 26, 28t,
        66, 144, 146, 215–216, 227–228, 230,
        231, 339
    and trade liberalization, 221
    voting power at, 227, 227t, 338

International Strategy for Disaster Reduction (UN), 10, 267
international trade organizations, 66*t*
interventions, health, as cost-effective, 126–128, 128*t*, 138
Inuit, 283, 285*t*, 286, 291
    see also indigenous peoples, of Canada
    environmental problems for, 294
    language of, 294
    tuberculosis among, 289, 294, 295t
Inuit Circumpolar Conference (ICC), 289
Inuit Tapiriit Kanatami (ITK), 291
iodine, 75, 80, 81
iron, 75, 137, 204
iron-deficiency anemia, 81, 112*t*, 127*t*
ischemic heart disease, 112*t*, 121*t*, 122*t*, 123, 124*t*, 125*t*

Jubilee 2000 Coalition, 23, 68, 69
Justinian Codex, 238, 241

Kariba Dam, 152
Kashechewan reserve, 294
Kennedy, John F., 23
Keynes, J.M., 53
Kouchner, Bernard, 271
kwashiorkor, 79, 86

labour, bonded/forced, as forms of slavery, 244–245, 250*t*
Lalonde Report (Health Canada), 168
language issues, for aid workers, 318–319, 320, 321, 322
League of Nations, 19, 21, 27*t*, 241, 244, 285*t*
leishmaniasis, visceral, 199–200, 207
Lend-Lease Program, 20, 28*t*
leprosy, 22, 27*t*, 102, 153
Liebig, Justus von, 85
life expectancy
    at birth, as measurement, 104
    and burden of disease, 108–110
    in Canada, for Aboriginals/non-Aboriginals, 296, 296*t*
    in China, and poverty alleviation, 215f
    disability-adjusted, 108–110
    and GDP, 39–40, 40f, 44
    global trends in, 5, 5f
    and HIV/AIDS, 40, 40t
    improvements in, over time, 35–36
    of indigenous peoples, 9
    of malnourished children, 77–78

    of newborns, compared, 37t
    and socio-economic factors, 44–47
literacy rate
    in China, and poverty alleviation, 214f
    female, and teenage pregnancy, 180f, 180–181
Locke, John, 242, 249
lung disease, chronic obstructive, 121*t*, 122*t*, 123, 124*t*

macronutrients, 74, 75, 78–80
Magna Carta, 241
Mahler, Halfdan, 169, 184
malaria, 8, 80, 102, 112*t*, 152, 177, 206, 207
    about the disease, 190–191
    and bed nets, as used against, 202, 204, 323
    and eradication/eradication programs, 22, 27*t*, 192–193
    and Global Fund to fight, 159–160, 199
    and insecticide spraying (DDT), 22, 190, 192, 192–193, 205t
    and morbidity, 125t
    and mortality, 121*t*, 122*t*, 131, 191, 205t
    preventative treatment for, 310, 322–323
    in refugee camps, 276, 279
    Roll Back Malaria program, 27t, 29, 146, 193
    as spread by mosquitoes, 177, 190, 312, 323
    treatment of, 22, 191–192, 192t, 205t
malnutrition, 6, 7, 69, 73–75, 206, 276
    see also breast-feeding; infant formula
    and brain development, 79
    causes of, 75–77
    and children's growth, 78–79, 80
    and food aid, 90–92
    and food security, 88–90
    and immune system, 79–80, 93
    macronutrient, 75, 78–80
    Malthusian theory of, 92
    measurement of, 81–82, 82t, 83–84
    micronutrient, 80–81
    prevalence of, 77–78
    in refugee camps, 277–278, 279
    statistics on, 113
    trends in, 90, 90f
    types of, 75, 78–81
Malthus, Thomas, 92, 220
Mandela, Nelson, 62, 240
Maori, 283, 288–289
Marcos, Ferdinand, 20, 63, 64
Marshall, George, 21, 334

Marshall Plan, 20–21, 22, 23, 28*t*, 143, 149, 155, 334
Martin, Paul, 230
Maslow, Abraham, 38
maternal health, in developing world
    see also mothers; pregnancy
    conferences on, 133–134
    as element of Primary Health Care, 169
    and mortality, 134–136, 137
    need for investment in, 136–137
    in refugee camps, 275
maternal mortality
    see also mothers; pregnancy
    in developing world, 8, 134–136, 137
    and infant mortality, 130, 130t, 136
    and pregnancy, 8, 131, 134–136, 137, 200–201, 238t
    statistics on, 114, 134–135
    in Sub-Saharan Africa, 114, 134, 135, 308
    in United States, 137
    ways of reducing/preventing, 137
Mayan peoples, 8*f*, 283, 284, 285*t*, 288, 289, 290, 299
McNamara, Robert, 25, 28*t*, 170
measles, 76, 206, 299
    immunization against, 114, 173, 174, 205t, 279
    and morbidity, 112t, 124t
    and mortality, 8, 36, 93, 112t, 121t, 122t, 131, 132, 171, 171f, 173, 205t
    in refugee camps, 276, 279
    and vitamin A deficiency, 80–81
Médecins sans Frontières, 207, 264, 271–272
medical care
    as element of Primary Health Care, 169
    as industry, 42
    and overseas aid, 24–27
    and population health, 41–44
Medical Nemesis (Illich), 168
Menchú, Rigoberta, 288
mental illness. *See* psychiatric illness; *see also* depression
Métis, 286, 291, 294. *See also* indigenous peoples, of Canada
Mexico
    and debt repayments, 26, 62, 66, 146, 225–226
    indigenous peoples of, 289
microfinancing, 217–218
micronutrients, 75, 77, 80–81, 93, 126, 137
midwives/trained birthing attendants, 134*t*, 136–137, 171, 171*f*, 203, 223, 279

migrants, 273. *See also* displaced populations
military, and health care/hygiene, 36–37
Millennium Challenge Account, 158, 159
Millennium Development Goals (MDGs), 14, 24, 28*t*, 29–30, 58, 60, 102, 127–128, 146, 158, 161, 181, 184, 195, 339
    acceleration of funding for, 160
    agriculture, as not mentioned in, 220
    for clean water, 114–115, 176
    for contraception, 114
    for education, 113, 218–219
    and health measurement, 105–106, 119
    indicators for, 29, 113, 114
    for maternal mortality, 136
    for nutrition, 61, 84, 90, 93
    for poverty, 7, 29, 70
    for reducing under-five mortality, 132–133
Mobutu Sese Seko, 20, 63, 64
Monterrey conference on development financing, 149, 157–158, 159–160
morbidity
    and burden of disease, 123–125
    in developing world. See specific diseases
    and mortality, measurement of, 109
    and statistics on mothers, 114, 136
Morley, David, 82, 167
mortality, in developing world
    of adults, 120–123, 126, 127t
    of children, 129–132
    of mothers, 134–136, 137
    and rise of global middle class, 121, 122
mortality, maternal. *See* maternal mortality
mortality, neonatal
    of infants, 13t, 131, 131t
    of mothers, 134–137
mortality, premature, 111, 112*t*, 123
mortality rate
    see also child mortality; infant mortality; maternal mortality
    age-specific, as measurement, 104, 105t
    crude, of displaced persons, 275, 276, 278
    determining, from statistics, 104–105, 105t
    effect of health care on, 42–44
    errors in, 106–107
    and social class, 43f, 43–44, 45f, 45
    in Victorian London, 35, 40
mortality registration, 104–105
mortality statistics, 112–113, 114
mosquitoes, 176, 177, 190, 312, 323

mothers
see also maternal health; maternal
  mortality; pregnancy
and child nutrition, 76, 81
and disease monitoring, 102
and infant feeding, 26, 76, 81, 84–88, 132,
  137
mortality/morbidity statistics on, 114, 136
mortality of, 134–136
multilateral debt, 66–67, 225
Multilateral Debt Relief Initiative, 3, 14, 28*t*, 231

Nasser, Gamal Abdel, 24
National Center for Health Statistics, 83–84
National Child Labor Committee, 248
nationalism, of former colonies, 20, 23–24
Native peoples, of North America, 286–287.
  See also First Nations
natural disasters, 9–10
see also displaced populations
and aid to victims, 92, 153–154
and displaced populations, 262
costs of, 260–261, 267
"hot spots" for, 267
increasing number of, 261, 262f, 267
poverty caused by, 56
Nehru, Jawaharlal, 24
neonatal mortality
of infants, 13t, 131, 131t
of mothers, 134–137
Nestlé, Henri, 85
Netherlands, 62, 156
neuropsychiatric disorders, 123, 124. *See also*
  depression; psychiatric illness
New International Economic Order, 24, 28*t*, 30
New Partnership for Africa's Development
  (NEPAD), 160
"new poor," 56
New Zealand, 286
Maori of, 283, 285, 288–289, 299
and Waitangi treaty, 285t, 288
Nightingale, Florence, 36, 145, 166
Nobel Peace Prize, 24, 27*t*, 220, 240, 271, 288,
  334
non-aligned movement, 23–24, 28*t*
non-governmental organizations (NGOs), 23,
  28*t*, 145, 148
and disaster management, 264, 265
employment/volunteer opportunities
  with, 319
and issue of impartiality, 271–272

microfinancing by, 217
training of staff by, 341–342
non-lethal diseases, 112*t*, 116, 123, 132, 137
Nunavut, 285*t*, 286, 289, 290
nutrition, in refugee camps, 277–278. *See also*
  malnutrition

obesity, 6, 83, 126, 127*t*, 264*t*, 295*t*
Observations on the Bills of Mortality (Graunt),
  100–101
Office for the Coordination of Humanitarian
  Affairs (OCHA), 262, 264, 272
Office International d'Hygiène Publique, 19
Official Development Assistance (ODA), 147,
  148, 159
as percentage of GDP, 24, 28t, 149, 149t
oil, world price of, 65, 65f, 225
Olmsted, Frederick Law, 37
Onchocerciasis Control Program, 334–335
oral rehydration, of children, 26, 131, 132,
  205*t*, 279
as element of Primary Health Care, 170,
  171, 175–176, 204, 205, 205t
Organisation for Economic Co-operation and
  Development (OECD), 21, 23, 28*t*, 66*t*, 147*t*,
  149–150
Organisation for European Economic Co-
  operation (OEEC), 21, 28*t*, 149
overseas aid. *See* aid, overseas
overseas development work. *See* aid projects,
  working on
Oxfam, 23, 148

Pacini, Filippo, 37
Pakistan, earthquake in, 9, 153, 259, 262, 267,
  278
Pan American Health Organization, 19, 27*t*, 183
Papua New Guinea, 155, 263*t*
Paris Club, 66*t*, 225, 226, 227, 229–230
partnerships. *See* aid projects, as partnerships
pasteurization, 193, 323
patent restrictions, on essential drugs, 207–208
Peace Corps, 310, 310*t*, 319
Pearson Commission on Aid, 24, 28*t*
penicillin, 22
perinatal diseases, 8, 112*t*, 121*t*, 122*t*, 124*t*, 125*t*
Permanent Forum on Indigenous Issues, UN,
  285*t*, 286, 286*t*
personal hygiene, 36–37, 177
pertussis (whooping cough), 43, 76, 114, 173,
  174

plagues, 19, 100, 102
pneumonia, 93, 112*t*, 204, 206
    and morbidity, 124, 124t, 125t
    and mortality, 121t, 122t, 123, 131,205t
    in refugee camps, 276, 279
    treatment of, 105t
polio, 102, 113, 132, 153, 173, 174, 204*f*
Polynesia, indigenous peoples of, 288
Poor Laws, British, 53, 223
population, and fertility rate, 179, 179*f*
population count, 104
population health, 35–48
    and average income, 39–41
    basic requirements for, 36–39
    and medical care, 41–44
    and poverty, 53–54
    and social inequality, 44–47, 54
    surveillance of, 103
population health, measurement of, 99–100
    adult health data, 114–115
    child health data, 112–114
    history of, 100–101
    reasons for, 102–103
population statistics, 114, 115
poverty, 6–7, 52–54
    and child mortality, 54, 54f
    definitions of, 55–57
    and developing world debt, 51–52
    early initiatives on, 18–20
    and education, 53f, 54, 251
    and GDP, 19t, 39–40
    health risks of, 53–54
    in historical perspective, 52–53
    magnitude and trends of, 60–61
    measurement of, 56, 57t, 57–60, 69, 99
    progress in reduction of, 60–61, 61f
    severe, global trends in, 5, 6f, 7
    and social inequity, 54, 214
    in United States, 40, 52
    in Victorian London, 35, 40–41, 52
poverty alleviation, 213, 214–224
    and agricultural improvement, 219–221
and economic development, 215–217
and education, 218–219
effects of, in China, 214–215
and human rights legislation, 223–224
and microfinancing, 217–218
and redistribution of wealth, 216–217
and trade liberalization, 221–222
poverty indices
    consumption analysis, 58–59

    Human Development Index, 56, 57t, 59
    Human Poverty Index, 56, 57t, 59
    income analysis, 58
    relative poverty indicators, 60
    sense of well-being, 59–60
Poverty Reduction Strategy Papers, 158, 216,
    217, 231
pregnancy
    see also maternal health; maternal
        mortality; mothers
    complications of, 136
    deaths related to, 8, 131, 134–136, 137,
        200–201, 238t
    diseases related to, 8, 121t, 122t, 124t, 125t
    and HIV/AIDS, 132, 137, 196, 197, 198, 202
    and malnutrition, 76, 81
    teenage, and female literacy rate, 180f,
        180–181
    trained attendants/midwives for, 134t,
        136–137, 171, 171f, 203, 279
    and treatment of malaria, 193
pregnancy, and medical care, 8f, 137, 200–203
    antenatal care, 202f, 202–203, 203f
    delivery care, 202f, 203, 203f
    post-delivery care, 203
premature mortality, 111, 112*t*, 123
Primary Health Care (PHC), 26–27, 146
    Alma Ata conference on, 165–166, 168–
        170, 172, 174, 181
    comprehensive versus selective, 27,
        170–173, 181, 204
    as contrasted with Western curative
        model, 25, 125–126, 138, 146, 167
    decentralization of, as current trend, 183
    definition of, 165–166
    and evolution towards "business
        model," 181
    funding of, 182–183
    history of, 166–168
    and infant/child mortality rates, 172, 172f
    and provision of services, 181–182
Primary Health Care (PHC), basic elements
    of, 169, 171, 17*f*
    breast-feeding, 174–175
    family planning, 178–181
    immunization, 173–174
    oral rehydration therapy, 175–176
    water and sanitation, 176–178
private aid, as type of debt, 66–67, 225
projects, aid
    as ambitious but problematic, 23–26,
        125–126, 138, 146, 152, 160–161

reasons for failure of, 155–156
short-term, 309–310
student teams for, 319–320
success stories of, 153–154
technical assistance to, 151, 153, 159
pro-poor economic development. *See* poverty alleviation
protein-energy malnutrition, 75, 78–80
psychiatric illness, 112*t*, 116, 123, 124*t*, 125*t*
see also depression
in refugee camps, 275
and violence against women, 247, 252
and years lost to disability, 177–178
psychological risks, for aid workers, 313–314
psychological trauma, of disaster survivors, 266–267
public health, concept of, 18, 36–37, 121, 166–167. *See also* Primary Health Care; sanitation; water, cleanliness of
purchasing power parity (PPP) dollar, 58

Questioning the Solution (Werner et al.), 176
quinine, 191, 192*t*

Red Cross, International Committee of the, 19, 27*t*, 145, 264
Red Cross and Red Crescent Societies, International Federation of, 266, 267
refugee camps, 7*f*, 8*f*, 9*f*, 10*f*, 266*f*, 275–279, 323*f*
basic health care in, 279
environmental issues in, 278
information gathering/assessment in, 275–276
nutrition in, 277–278
shelter in, 278
standards for (UNHCR), 275t
violence in, 275, 278
water and sanitation in, 276–277
refugees, 22*f*
see also displaced populations
definition of, 273, 273t
Geneva Convention on, 273, 274
genocide perpetrators as, 270–271
numbers of, 273–274, 274t
UN High Commissioner for, 21, 28t, 271, 274
Vietnamese, 271
relative poverty indicators, 60
remittance income, as source of overseas aid, 148–149
Réseau Espérance de Vie en Santé (REVES), 109

residential schools, 287, 292, 293, 294
respiratory infections, 7, 113, 177
Results-Based Monitoring and Evaluation system, 339
rheumatic fever/heart disease, 43
rickets, 77
road to health charts, 82, 82*t*, 84
road traffic accidents, 112*t*, 121*t*, 122*t*, 124*t*, 125*t*, 297, 310, 313
Roll Back Malaria program, 27*t*, 29, 146, 193
Roman Empire, 18, 37, 100, 166, 190
Roosevelt, Eleanor, 223*f*, 242
Roosevelt, Franklin Delano, 21
Rowntree, Seebohm, 57
Royal Commission on Aboriginal Peoples (RCAP), 294–295
Rwanda, 4, 10, 242, 270–271, 272, 273

Saami, 283, 285
Sabido, Miguel, 180
Sachs, Jeffrey, 29, 126, 144, 157, 170
Sack, Alexander, 64
Safe Motherhood Initiative, 202
safe/unsafe sex, 27, 126, 127*t*, 128*t*, 181, 198, 199
sanitation, 114–115
see also water, cleanliness of
as basic element of Primary Health Care, 169, 171, 177–178
in Britain and Europe, 35, 36, 37, 40–41, 52, 166–167
in refugee camps, 277
in Roman Empire, 18, 37, 52, 166
in United States, 52, 167
SARS, 19, 27*t*, 102, 153, 263*t*
Save the Children, 248
schistosomiasis, 107*f*, 152, 323
scurvy, 75, 93, 103, 277
Semmelweis, Ignaz, 101
Sen, Amartya, 12, 38, 56, 88–89, 92, 216, 219
sexual human rights abuses
female contraception, 10, 114, 252–253
human trafficking, 245–246, 248, 250t
sex trade slavery, 244, 250t
violence against women, 246–247, 269
sexually transmitted diseases, 275, 313. *See also* HIV/AIDS
Shattuck, Lemuel, 167
Simon, Johann, 85
skin-fold thickness, for measuring malnutrition, 82*t*, 83
slavery, 243–245, 250*t*

sleeping sickness, 200, 207
slums, urban, 35, 36, 37, 40–41, 52, 59*f*, 177–178
smallpox, 18, 19, 102*f*, 153*f*, 299
    eradication of, 24, 27t, 74t, 102, 153, 167, 174, 340f
smoking/tobacco use, 46, 101, 123, 126, 127*t*, 295*t*, 298
Snow, John, 27*t*, 101, 103
soap operas, educational, 180
social inequality, and population health, 44–47, 54
Solomon Islands, 154–155
Somalia, 9, 269, 272
South Africa, 4, 62, 64, 67, 207, 224, 247
Soviet Union, 20, 65
Sphere Project, 264, 265, 272, 315
Sri Lanka, 55*f*, 92, 154*f*, 172, 267, 268, 272, 278
Stiglitz, Joseph, 216, 227, 230
streptomycin, 194, 205*t*
structural adjustment policies, 26, 28*t*, 66, 144, 215–216, 227–228, 230, 231, 339
    criticisms of, 216, 227–228
    and reductions in social spending, 26, 146, 216, 228
stunted growth, in children, 77, 77*f*, 78–79, 80, 83, 113, 132, 133*t*
Sub-Saharan Africa, 5, 6*f*, 26, 133, 154, 199, 203, 220, 250
    birth and death statistics in, 105, 107, 120
    health service user fees in, 182
    HIV/AIDS in, 199
    maternal mortality in, 114, 134, 135, 308
    tuberculosis deaths in, 194, 195
substance abuse, among Canadian indigenous peoples, 9, 287, 289, 293, 297, 298–299, 300
Sudan, 4, 9, 243, 244, 269, 270, 272, 273, 337
    Darfur region of, 10, 10f, 93
suicide, among Canadian indigenous peoples, 9, 287, 292*t*, 293, 295, 297, 297*t*, 298, 300

Tagore, Rabindranath, 219
technical assistance, to aid projects, 151, 153, 159
tetanus, 113, 131*t*, 132, 173, 174
Thompson, Warren, 128, 179
tied aid, 145, 150–151
Tito, Josip Broz, 24
tobacco, 46, 101, 123, 126, 127*t*, 128*t*

trachoma, 22, 177, 276
trade liberalization, 221–222
Trade-Related Aspects of Intellectual Property Rights (TRIPS) Agreements, 207, 222
trafficking, human, 245–246, 248, 250*t*
translators, 318–319, 320
tropical medicine, 19–20, 27*t*, 207, 335
Truman, Harry S., 20, 334
trypanosomiasis, African, 200, 207
tsunamis, 260*f*, 261, 261*f*, 262*f*, 263*t*
    in southeast Asia, 4, 9, 55f, 92, 148, 153, 154f, 231, 259, 263t, 265, 266–267, 278
tuberculosis, 22, 27*t*, 29, 52, 53, 76, 102, 167, 207, 295*t*, 299, 312
    about the disease, 193–194
    among Canadian indigenous peoples, 297, 297t, 300
    chemotherapy for, 128t
    decline in, 36, 42–43
    eradication of, 194–195
    and Global Fund to fight, 159–160, 199
    and HIV/AIDS, 76, 193, 195, 196
    among Inuit, 289, 294, 295t
    and morbidity, 112t, 124t, 125t
    and mortality, 112t, 121t, 122t, 123, 194, 195, 205t
    in refugee camps, 275
    treatment of, 42f, 194t, 194–195, 199, 205t
    vaccination against, 42, 114, 174, 195
typhoid, 52

Uganda, 7*f*, 9*f*, 199, 219, 270*f*, 330*f*
UN, 10, 20, 23, 243, 265
    and "decades of development," 23–28
    and conference on development financing (Monterrey), 149, 157–158
    health-related bodies of, 21, 22f
    statistics databases of, 115
UN Children's Fund. *See* UNICEF
UN Commission on Human Rights, 223, 224, 242–243, 337
UN Conference on Trade and Development (UNCTAD), 24, 28*t*
UN Covenant on Civil and Political Rights, 239, 242
UN Covenant on Social, Economic, and Cultural Rights, 239, 242
UN Convention on the Rights of the Child, 248, 252
UN Development Programme (UNDP), 28*t*, 29, 56, 157

UN Disaster Assessment and Coordination Team (UNDAC), 266

UN Educational, Scientific, and Cultural Organization (UNESCO), 113

UN High Commissioner for Human Rights (UNHCHR), 223, 224, 242–243, 286*t*

UN High Commissioner for Refugees (UNHCR), 21, 28*t*, 271, 274, 277

UN Human Rights Council, 224, 243

UN International Strategy for Disaster Reduction (UNISDR), 10, 267

UN Permanent Forum on Indigenous Issues (UNPFII), 285*t*, 286, 286*t*

UNAIDS, 102, 199

Under Five Mortality Rate (U5MR), 113, 128–129, 129*t*, 131*t*, 132–133, 171, 171*f*

underweight children, 29, 77, 78, 78*f*, 80, 83, 113, 126, 127*t*, 132, 132*t*, 133, 264*t*

UNICEF, 21, 26–27, 99
    see also WHO-UNICEF collaboration
    child health programs by, 127
    and child mortality rates/data, 113, 129–130
    disaster management handbook of, 264, 275
    disease surveillance/monitoring by, 102
    Nobel Peace Prize awarded to, 24, 27*t*
    and Primary Health Care, 167–168, 170–171

United Nations. *See* UN

United States
    agricultural surplus donations by, 19, 90–92
    debt forgiveness by, 68
    maternal mortality in, 137
    overseas aid by, 150, 150f, 151f
    postwar aid to Europe by, 20–21
    poverty in, 40
    and refusal of colonial debt, 62
    slavery, as still existing in, 244

Universal Declaration of Human Rights, 223, 224, 238, 242, 243

upper arm circumference, for measuring malnutrition, 82*t*, 83

vaccination, 8, 27, 114, 131–132, 173–174
    see also immunization
    for aid workers, 322
    funding initiatives for, 174
    hepatitis A and B, 313, 322
    measles, 114, 174, 205*t*, 279
    meningococcal, 322
    polio, 131, 174, 322
    smallpox, 18

tuberculosis, 42, 114, 174, 195
whooping cough, 43, 114, 174

Vasak, Karel, 239

vertical eradication programs, 22–23, 27*t*, 29, 167, 204

violence, against women, 246–247, 252–253, 269, 298

violence, family, 178, 181

Virchow, Rudolph, 102, 166, 309

visceral leishmaniasis, 199–200, 207

vitamin A, 80–81, 127*t*, 137, 204, 279

volcanoes, 261, 261*f*, 262*f*, 263*t*

Wald, Lillian, 121

Walkerton, Ontario, water contamination in, 44

war, 9, 76, 269–273
    as "complex humanitarian disaster," 269
    ethical issues of, for aid agencies, 269–271
    and human rights abuses, 269
    humanitarian interventions in, as problematic, 270
    military intervention in, 272
    as motivated by greed, 270
    and targeting of aid workers, 269, 271, 272
    and targeting of civilians, 269, 272

wasting, of children, 78–79, 83, 113

water, cleanliness of
    see also Primary Health Care; sanitation
    and access to, 114–115
    as basic element of Primary Health Care, 169, 171, 171f, 176–177
    as basic requirement of health, 36–39, 44
    and child nutrition, 76
    as necessity for aid workers, 312, 318, 323
    as problem for Canadian indigenous peoples, 294, 297
    in refugee camps, 276–277
    in Roman Empire, 18, 37, 166
    and water privatization, 177

water, sources of, as not easily accessible, 39*f*, 290*f*

water-borne disease, 52, 101, 176, 177, 297, 312. *See also* malaria

Waterlow system, for measuring malnutrition, 82*t*, 83, 84

well-being, 57*t*, 57–58, 59–60

Wellcome classification, for measuring malnutrition, 82*t*, 83, 84

Western curative health care model
    and eradication programs, 22–23, 27t, 29, 167, 189–190, 204, 208, 339

limitations of, 167, 189–190, 208–209
and urban hospitals, 25, 125–126, 138,
    146, 167, 208
Western lifestyle, diseases associated with, 6,
    121, 122–123, 126, 127t, 295t, 296
WHO, 19, 21, 24, 27, 29, 81, 99, 101, 110, 120
    and access to essential drugs, 206–208
    and child mortality rates, 113
    disease surveillance/monitoring by, 102
    and emergency response coordination,
        264, 265
    and female circumcision, 252–253
    and health budgets, 126
    and health/disease measurement, 106, 109
    and literature on managing displaced
        populations, 275
    and malnutrition measurement, 81–84
    and report on primary health care,
        167–168
    and smallpox eradication, 153
    and water sanitation/health, 115
WHO-UNICEF collaboration
    on campaign against baby formula,
        86–87, 88
    on Child Survival Revolution, 27t, 127,
        132, 133
    on immunization, 174
    on infant/young child feeding strategy,
        174–175
    on Integrated Management of Childhood
        Illnesses (IMCI), 27t, 171, 203–206
    on maternal mortality rates/data, 134–136
    and monitoring of underweight
        children, 29
    and report on Primary Health Care,
        167–168
    on Roll Back Malaria program, 193
    on water supply/sanitation, 177
whooping cough (pertussis), 43, 76, 114, 173,
    174
Williams, Cicely, 86
women
    see also mothers; pregnancy
    as aid workers, and issues for, 314–315
    education of, 251
    and family planning, 178–181, 203
    and female circumcision, 10, 114, 252–253
    GOBI programs for, 26–27, 132, 170–171,
        204

human rights abuses of, 10, 114, 244,
    245–247, 252–253
human rights legislation, as crucial to,
    223
and malnutrition, 76–77
needs of, following disasters, 266
as second-class citizens, 134, 247
violence against, 246–247, 252–253, 269
Working Group on Indigenous Populations
    (WGIP), 285t
World Bank, 21, 23, 25, 26, 28t, 29, 99, 101,
    110, 115, 148, 170, 174, 225, 286t
    and Debt Sustainability Framework, 232
    and decentralization of health care, 183
    and definition of poverty, 56–57, 58, 60
    and developing world debt, 63, 66–69,
        216, 339
    disaster funds lent by, 267
    and funding of Kariba Dam, 152
    and Heavily Indebted Poor Countries
        Initiatives, 26, 57, 69, 216, 229–230
    under McNamara, 25, 28t, 170
    project evaluation handbook of, 339
    and trade liberalization, 221
World Development Report, 27t, 181
World Food Programme, 92, 277
World Health Organization. See WHO
World Trade Organization (WTO), 21, 24, 28t,
    66t
    and Doha round of trade talks, 24, 28t,
        91, 207, 222

X-ray screening, for tuberculosis, 194, 195

yaws, 22, 27t, 167
years lost to disability (YLD), 111, 112t, 123
years lost to premature death (YLL), 111,
    112t, 123
yellow fever, 19, 102, 177, 322
Yugoslavia, 10, 13, 63, 242, 269, 272
Yunus, Muhammad, 217
Yupik, 289

z-score, for measuring malnutrition, 81, 82t,
    83, 84, 84t, 278
Zaire, 269, 270
Zambia, 91, 152
Zimbabwe, 243, 337